RESHAPING OF CYPRUS:
A TWO-STATE SOLUTION

RESHAPING OF CYPRUS:
A TWO-STATE SOLUTION

HALIL IBRAHIM SALIH

To order additional copies of this book, contact:
Xlibris Corporation
1-888-795-4274
www.Xlibris.com
Orders@Xlibris.com
127410

To my parents and my brothers Hasan and Behzat

TABLE OF CONTENTS

PREFACE

To accomplish great things, we must not only act
but also dream, not only plan but also believe.
—Anatole France

This book was written by a political scientist who was born in Girne (Kyrenia), Cyprus, a Turkish Cypriot who is now an American citizen. I have tried to provide the reader with an evolving picture of the Cyprus crisis since 1963, and the on-and-off inter-communal negotiations for the reunification of the island. I have traveled to Cyprus many times to visit family and friends. During these travels, I received the opportunity to converse with the political leaders, professionals, educators, and laymen from both communities. I have traveled on both sides of the divided island and was fortunate to have informative discussion as to the Cyprus problem.

My understanding of the Cyprus problem has been enriched by sources dealing with books and articles on Cyprus, mediation and resolution of disputes, nationalism, and international law. Over the years, I had opportunities to interview the political leaders of both communities, including the foreign diplomats. As a result of my ethnicity, I tend to sympathize more with the Turkish Cypriot cause, but I am also influenced by family members and friends who are still living in Northern Cyprus and are affected by the political events. Many years have been devoted to studying and writing about the Cyprus political quagmire, and I developed the book's argument due to the unwillingness of either community leaders to compromise to reach an amicable settlement. The failure to reach an agreement is providing the alternative of the formation of a two-state system.

Due to limited community interaction, politically, economically, and socially, the generation following the Cyprus crisis in 1963 have been alienated and have formed strong political cleavages that provide few options in settling the dispute peacefully that is satisfactory to all parties involved. Geostrategic-political issues, nationalism, dysfunctional relationships, and lack of trust have ultimately forced me to reach the same conclusion that many Cypriots have on both sides—that the best viable alternative is the permanent division of Cyprus. The events from 1963 to 1974 have not healed to usher in a peaceful coexistence and have been instrumental in the emergence of the idea of a two-state system. The recent peace talks reflect the lack of hope in the resolution of the disputes despite the efforts of the international community. The issues troubling the two Cypriot communities have sharply increased and have dramatically grown since 1963. It is, however, an illusion to assume that the building of partnership and return to Republic of Cyprus as existed from 1960 to 1963 will clear the way for a durable era of reconciliation and peace. The aim therefore is to use the historical lessons and political experiences in order to guard against the repeat of past mistakes and give way to the return of communal rivalry and the bloodshed that will accompany it.

The aim of this book is to present the harsh realities in Cyprus since 1974 and the existence of two self-governing sovereign states. The leaders of the two communities have missed many opportunities in negotiations for the reunification of the island. Both parties to the ongoing dispute have failed to display goodwill or willingness to compromise, but instead have opted to gain the international affirmation of its own legitimacy. Legitimacy is a bona fide symbol of authority, and the two communities have legislated laws that apply either in the south or the north of the island. The Turkish Cypriots in the north have a full governmental infrastructure in place and enforce their jurisdiction and legal authority. The Turkish Republic of Northern Cyprus is recognized only by Turkey but, in recent years, has engendered some international sympathy for the lifting of the economic embargo imposed on them by the Cyprus government since 1964. At the negotiating table, both community leaders have been at loggerheads in their game plan to gain major concessions for a settlement.

The Zurich-London Agreements of 1959 were reluctantly signed by the Greeks to establish the short-lived Republic of Cyprus. Greeks reneged on their pledge of shared governance with the Turkish Cypriots and launched a plan to nibble away at the constitutional rights provided to the Turkish Cypriots. On November 30, 1963, President Makarios proposed 13-amendments to the constitution that was vehemently rejected by the Turks. The game plan of Makarios alarmed the Turkish Cypriots, causing inter-ethnic skirmishes in December 1963. The Cypriots crisis of the 1960s and 1970s contributed to the abrogation of all governmental powers by the Greek Cypriots and to the exclusion of the Turks from all the established institutions that were agreed to under the Zurich-London Agreements in 1959. The incapability of the Greek Cypriots to subdue the Turkish Cypriots prevented the consolidation of their political authority in Cyprus. Cyprus government's draconian policies polarized the two societies, and the continued humiliation of the Turks elevated the crisis. The desire for *enosis* (union of Cyprus with Greece) by the Green nationalists and jingoism contributed to the alienation and separation of the ethnic groups.

The international efforts to prod the community leaders to achieve a settlement failed due to uncompromising stands and chartered unachievable desirable ends. Since 1964, the Turkish Cypriots have been determined not to be cowed in the shadow of the Greek Cypriots despite their economic and international isolation. The Greek Cypriot campaign of an all-or-nothing negotiated approach swayed the Turks to pursue a policy of self-government and independence. The invasion of Cyprus by Turkey in 1974 was generated in response to the Greek Cypriot plot to achieve *enosis* following the overthrow of President Makarios by the nationalist extremists on the island with the blessing of Athens. The *de facto* partition of Cyprus provided the two communities the ability to govern their affairs independently from each other. The Cyprus government applies its jurisdiction in the south while the Turkish Cypriots have authority in the north.

Since 1974, the Cyprus government positioned itself to sway the international community into thinking that it had the full sovereign and jurisdictional authority over the whole island and labeled the Turkish Cypriot authority as a "rebel." The hard realities are compelling many countries to acknowledge the presence of the two state systems on the island despite the zealous international campaign of Greece and the Cyprus government. The Greeks resorted to the United Nations, the European Union, and other international bodies, which gained them temporary support, but the global community has been appalled by their intransigence at the negotiating table. The overwhelming rejection of the Annan Plan in 2004 caused concern as to their credibility. International communities have become far more informed as to the ongoing Cyprus crisis and, as a result, are more willing to take an alternative diplomatic approach to resolve the issue.

The United Nations and international law can provide avenues to resolve conflicts between states by negotiating peaceful compromises. International law is the protector of the established principles and procedures based on customs, traditions, treaties, and the rules of peace and war, but it has no mechanism to enforce a settlement. When vital national interests of a state are at stake, a state's concern with the law is secondary. International law does not deter or restrain a powerful state when it chooses to ignore it to protect its interests due to the lack of a superior central enforcement agent. An acceptable political outcome at the negotiations will provide the remedy to resolve the Cyprus crisis, not law or litigation. The preservation of national interest and international law is a mere component in the power equation among nation-states.

The UN Security Council, under the leadership of the five major powers, is an international body and is bestowed with the responsibility to preserve the world peace and security, but since 1945, it has not lived up to the global expectations. The Cyprus government turns to the UN, international court, and the EU to have them be a catalyst to promote its own agenda by pressuring Turkey to withdraw its economic, political, and security alignment with the Turkish Cypriots and to recognize the Cyprus government as the sole legitimate authority over the island. It is a pervasive myth that the two Cypriot communities can reconstitute the state that existed between 1960 and 1963; however, that ignores the irreversible path that the two societies have taken since 1974. Most members of the international community have not been convinced by Greek arguments and continue to have diplomatic contacts with the Turkish Cypriots administration in Cyprus. Unsurprisingly, one of the key reasons marring the outcome of a communal settlement is the diplomatic campaign mounted by the Greeks to manage expectations ahead of an agreement as to the future of Cyprus. The Greek Cypriot leaders have been proactive in promoting negative references to TRNC (Turkish Republic of Northern Cyprus) as a "puppet regime," (the "so-called" chief justice, the "self-styled" minister, "illegal" university, "illegal" Bayrak television, "illegal" airport, and "occupied" part of Cyprus). The lack of response to the needs of the Turkish Cypriots has polarized the two communities. Reactive engagement further exacerbated the situation and contributed to the failure of peace-building projects. Instead of pursuing a more proactive stance in resolving disputes to restore confidence and trust, the rival decision-makers repeatedly flounder on the same sticky points.

In 1878, when Great Britain occupied Cyprus to protect the Ottoman Sultan against Russian expansionism, it soon faced the Greek Cypriot call for the Union of Cyprus with Greece (*enosis*) and the Turkish Cypriots call for partition (*Taksism*) as a defense against the Hellenization of the island. The goal for *enosis* was championed by the Greek Orthodox Church, which continues to play a pivotal role for the achievement of this goal. The *Megali Idea* (Greek for "Great Idea") is the Greek desire of establishing a Greek state that would encompass all ethnic Greeks in Epirus, Thessaly, Macedonia, Thrace, the Aegean Islands, Crete, Cyprus, parts of Asia Minor, and the city of Istanbul, that would replace

Athens as the capital. The *Megali Idea* is an irredentist concept to reestablish a Greek world that will be a dominant power in the region. The dream was shattered when the Turkish nationalists defeated and expelled the Greeks from Anatolia during the Greco-Turkish War (1919–1922). The Greek diplomacy to exclude Turkey from participating in any solution to the Cyprus issue and attempts to gain international recognition for the cause of *enosis* failed to achieve the expected support. Finally the Greeks were impressed upon to recognize Turkey's vital interest in the Cyprus dispute.

Cyprus' geostrategic geographical position explains its importance to Turkey, which is under its "soft-belly" forty miles away. The eastern Mediterranean has become a lucrative energy, commercial, and tourist hub for Turkey—the Baku-Tbilisi-Ceyhan (BTC), the Kirkuk-Yumurtalik[1] oil pipelines, Iskenderun is a major trade bridge between Asia and Europe, and Antalya region is attracting millions of tourists every year. Turkey's strategic location has become an important transit for Europe-bound Nabucco natural gas from Azerbaijan, Central Asia, Iraq, and eventually from Iran. On August 6, 2009, Russia's prime minister, Vladimir Putin, and his Turkish counterpart, Recep T. Erdogan, signed an agreement for the construction of South Stream pipeline that will supply Russian natural gas to Europe through the Turkish waters in the Black Sea. Russia will also ship crude oil from Turkey's Black Sea town of Samsun to the Mediterranean oil hub of Ceyhan as an alternative route to the congested Bosporus Strait.[2] Turkey is hoping that Egypt, Syria, and Qatar will connect their natural gas to Nabucco.[3] Turkey's strategic position as a gas supply route to Europe will give Ankara an increased influence for being an energy hub. France, Germany, Austria, Greece, and Cyprus continue to freeze and present obstacles in the EU membership talks for Ankara. The Greek course of action is to exercise their EU veto power leverage to exert pressure on Ankara and gain the desirable concessions on Cyprus negotiations, thus acting as a further hindrance to Turkey's accession to the EU. Turkey's application to join the EU and the Europeanization of the Cyprus issue have the perceived potential to be a catalyst for the reunification of Cyprus in line with Greek aspirations. The Greek endorsement of Turkey's accession into the EU is dependent on Turkish concessions in the Cyprus negotiations. Not surprisingly, it is unrealistic and a deeply flawed proposition that Turks will embark on such a venture conceding to *quid pro quo* to gain EU accession. Turkey's security interests cannot be compromised or overlooked. A settlement amicable to Greek political and territorial desires in the eastern Mediterranean will be rejected. The failure to divert attention from ethnocentric nationalistic policies will continue to block a negotiated settlement. A settlement must compliment the national interest of all parties. The current trend toward a two-state system is caused by the ethnic division that refuses to heal, and the more time that is allowed to pass kills the chances of a breakthrough in the negotiations. In the light of the conflict that is now raging in the Middle East, Turkey's role in the region for the Western security and economy is paramount for the free flow of oil and gas, in the containment of terrorism, and its geostrategic location is vital to the defense system of the West. Turkey's accession to the EU will appreciably contribute to the European economic and political security in tangible and intangible terms in our evolving world of escalating international terrorism and violence.

NOTES

ACKNOWLEDGMENTS

My appreciation and gratitude to my colleagues from many disciplines at Texas Wesleyan University who read parts of the manuscript and made valuable comments and recommendations to aid in the completion of the book. Likewise, I am especially grateful to Dr. Elizabeth U. Alexander, Dr. Linda Carroll, Dr. Carol J. Gerendas, Dr. Tim Grammer, Dr. Whitney Myers, and Dr. Stacia D. Neeley, for reading parts of the manuscript and making valuable suggestions on the final draft. I thank Dr. Birol Yesilada, professor of political science at Portland State University, for reviewing and suggesting useful, constructive ideas to improve the book. I extend my thanks to Greek and Turkish Cypriot friends who gave their time and expertise in discussing the Cyprus problem and their opinions as to the resolution of the crisis.

The ramifications of hard-line sentiments of both ethnic groups eroded the chances of peaceful coexistence desired by many friends in Northern and Southern Cyprus. I write this book for students, scholars, politicians, laymen, and anyone who wants to understand the complexity of the Cyprus crisis and explain the appealing notion to the Turkish Cypriots of the two-state system. Despite the prodding of the international community for an agreement, the hostile environment on the island transformed the former friends into enemies. In other words, paranoid nature of major decision-makers eroded the chances of a settlement.

In addition, many heartfelt thanks to Jessica Norman, graduate and employee of Texas Wesleyan University, for her suggestions in clarifying the issues presented, typing, and formatting the manuscript for print. Many thanks to the library staff of Texas Wesleyan University for requesting inter-library book loans across the nation and for assisting me in obtaining many documents relating to my research. I am personally responsible for any errors of facts, omissions, or interpretations.

H. Ibrahim Salih, PhD
August 2012

CHAPTER 1

CHALLENGES TO THE REPUBLIC OF CYPRUS

> Long before our time, the customs of our ancestors
> molded admirable men, and in turn those eminent
> men upheld the ways and institutions of their
> forebears. Our age, however, inherited the
> Republic as if it were some beautiful painting of
> bygone ages, its colors already fading through great
> antiquity; and not only has our time neglected to
> freshen the colors of the picture, but we have failed
> to preserve its form and outlines.
> —Marcus Tullius Cicero

The overarching problem that led to the collapse of ethnic cooperation in the established governmental system in Cyprus in 1960 was the conflicting political cultures, dysfunctional state, and competing ethnonationalism. From 1960 to 1964, neither the Greeks nor the Turkish Cypriots were engaged in nation-building, nor was the political machinery able to resolve the ethnonational conflict. Both ethnic groups view the state as an exploitable resource to enhance their personal interests, rather than a collective enterprise. As a result, ethnonationalist consolidation of political power favored the Greek Cypriots who played a crucial role in fanning ethnic passions. Likewise, the Turkish Cypriots made no effort to accommodate the Greek Cypriots interest. This favoritism only served to flare and magnify sectarian distrust and suspicion and was a prelude to an accelerated civil war that resulted in the disintegration of the

Republic of Cyprus. In April 1963, the Greek military had prepared tentative plans to aid the Greek Cypriots in their coordinated campaign to consolidate the Greek Cypriot control throughout Cyprus. By August, the minister of the interior of Cyprus, Polykarpos Yorgadjis,[4] a former *EOKA* leader, formed "The Organization of Greek Cypriot Patriots" for the armed clashes.[5] President Makarios unilaterally abrogated the Zurich-London Agreements of 1960 by his 13-Points Amendment proposals on November 30, 1963, precipitating the communal civil war. To protect the internal dominance of the Greek Cypriots, "they could all unite against the Turkish Cypriots who had served as the 'Trojan horse' to frustrate *enosis*, but also, after an independence they had not fought for, had been given a share in the power structure of Cyprus which seemed disproportionate."[6] Nicos A. Rolandis,[7] in an editorial in *Cyprus Mail*, on June 8, 2008, wrote the following:

> We endeavored in 1963 to amend the Constitution and strip the Turkish Cypriots of the rights we conferred on them in 1960 by our own signature. In other words, Makarios tried to change radically the very same Constitution which three years before he hailed with the word. "We have won." . . . We rejected the constitution which we had signed and which is considered today as a "blessing," even by people like Tassos Papadopoulos, who realized in 2005—that is 42 years later— that the constitution was a blessing (as he said) and that its provisions were constructive. In 1963, however, Tassos and almost all the others scuttled the provisions of the Constitution as if it were an anathema. . . . We partitioned the country.[8]

Richard A. Patrick, who served in Cyprus with the Canadian contingent in the United Nations peacekeeping forces, in respect to *enosis* wrote the following:

> An independent state did not satisfy the aspirations of the Greek-Cypriot community so they maintained their goal of *enosis* . . . it was decided to achieve Union with Greece by altering the constitutional status of the Republic, and various legal and political maneuvers and military preparations were undertaken to implement this decision. . . . Their failure to alter the status of the Republic did not induce Greek-Cypriots to change their political goal; instead they decided to force the

Turks-Cypriots into allowing *enosis* through the use of armed, economic and political coercion.[9]

Makarios's mission to consolidate the Greek Cypriot political power, and to contain and deprive the Turkish Cypriots of their constitutional rights, proved to be a failure, and the consequences were clear. Greece did not support the proposed constitutional amendments by Makarios and many feared that it might lead to a Greco-Turkish military confrontation.[10] The proclamation would remove the Turkish Cypriot constitutional safeguards, and all governmental institutions would have been under Greek control. Turkish air force attacked the Greek positions on Cyprus on August 7 and 8, 1964. Turkey threatened to invade the island but President Lyndon Johnson, in a letter on June 5, 1964, warned the Turkish president Ismet Inonu that the U.S. Sixth Fleet would stop it. The Acheson Plan on Cyprus presented on July 4, 1964, called for the union of Cyprus with Greece, and in return, Turkey would be granted a fifty-year lease on a military base in the Karpasia area of Cyprus; and in three cantons, the Turkish Cypriots were to have local autonomy. In addition, Greece was to make minor territorial concessions on its northeast frontier with Turkey and turn over to Turkey the island of Kastellorizon. Greece and Turkey rejected the plan.[11] When the *EOKA*'s founder, General George Grivas,[12] attacked the Turks in 1967, Ankara once again threatened to intervene under article 4 of the 1960 Treaty of Guarantee. Washington once again prevented the Turkish landing and Greece ordered Grivas to stop his onslaught against the Turks. After the death of Grivas on January 27, 1974, Greece put *EOKA-B* under Nicos Sampson and gave orders to overthrow Makarios on July 15 under the name "Operation Aphrodite." American diplomats referred to Sampson as "an irrational, psychopathic and dangerous opportunist, whom the Turkish Cypriots called the 'Butcher of Omorphits' on account of the Barbarous assaults carried out by him against the community during the 1963–4 crisis."[13] Under the presidency of Sampson, *enosis* would take phase under the *Akritas Plan*. With the assistance of the British forces on the island, Makarios narrowly escaped and fled to London. Turkey invaded the island on July 20, causing the military *junta* of Greece under Dimitrios Ioannides, and Nikos G. Sampson, called "The Turk Killer" in Nicosia, to be ousted from power. As to the role of the *junta* in Greece and *EOK- B* in Cyprus, Michael Attalkides writes as follows:

> A small, intense movement irrationally advocated Hellenic nationalism against the most fantastic international odds and internal interests. Since nationalism feed[s] on and are justified

---

by each other, this movement was one of the main means by which Turkey achieved the long-sought partition of Cyprus.[14]

The legacy of this disaster still haunts both communities. Makarios returned to Cyprus on December 7, 1974, as president of the Greek Cypriots, and the Turks formed their own state to govern the affairs of Northern Cyprus. A Turkish military intervention in 1974 resulted in the island's partitioning into two sections: Greek and Turkish. Subsequently, the two nation-states have accelerated the competing demographic claims and ethnonational ethnocentric agenda of each respective section.

The term *nation-state* in Cyprus will always be more myth than reality, and national divisions exist due to the distinctive culture that has spawned the partition of the island since 1974. The intermittent violence that lasted from 1963 to 1974 precipitated the island's division when the extremists nationalists among the Greek Cypriots created a strong sentiment to join Greece politically. In Athens, May 1965, Makarios failed to gain the endorsement of the Greek government to proclaim e*nosis* because Greece wanted to be drawn into a war with Turkey. When the Greek *junta* was in power in Athens (1967–1974), the methods to achieve *enosis* was substantially different from the policies pursued by Makarios.[15] Late in 1969, Greece and Turkey had secret talks, and an agreement was reached at the NATO foreign ministers' conference in Lisbon, June 1971. Both countries were agreeable to double e*nosis* or partition with the U.S. endorsement of the plan, but Makarios failed to support it. The events sparked a Turkish military invasion that prevented e*nosis* (union of Cyprus with Greece) after the coup d'etat against President Makarios. The driving force behind the partition has been ethnicnationalism. The internal conflict has become internationalized, and the difficulty to reunite the two parts is a challenge posing potential problems in the region. Jay Rothman considers the contested lands in Cyprus, Israel-Palestine, Lebanon, Sri Lanka, Eritrea-Ethiopia, and Northern Ireland as a "new class of conflicts in the world." He is of the opinion that these conflicts are not new but newly noticed:

> These conflicts are the technically rooted ones that rage primarily within states but also transcend their borders. . . . They stretch conventional ways of analyzing and addressing international conflicts; in fact, they pose important challenges to concepts about what constitutes "international." In a sense that they are contained within single states, or at least occur in situations in which two separate sovereign states are not yet

clearly defined, they may be called domestic disputes—and many are thus beyond the mandate of the United Nations. Yet, they are clearly about discord between contending nations, even if not embodied in sovereign states, seeking to perpetuate or change the status quo of the single state in which their conflict occurs.[16]

The divergent national identities continue to detract and derail the international forces trying to reestablish a state system with the institutional vehicles serving the interest of both Cypriot communities.

There is only one important fault line—the division between extremists and moderates in all camps. If extremists gain access to power, they will polarize and deepen whatever rifts they can feed on. Social peace, locally and globally, is secured only if moderates outweigh extremists.[17]

The mutual anathematization by the extremist on both sides make consensus on resolving the crisis highly unlikely in the near future. Evelin Lindner writes the following:

A nation is a group of people united by shared historical and cultural experiences and inspired by what Hans Kohn describes (in his definition of nationalism) as a unified "state of mind."[18] Powerful unifiers of a nation are people of common origins, and descent inhabiting a given territory that are bound by the same laws, common rights, duties, government, administration, and historical experiences.[19] William Bloom wrote that nationalism is a crucial ingredient in personal identity, and individuals seek to identify with a nation "in order to achieve psychological security."[20] According to Walker Connor, "Nationalism... does not connote loyalty to the state; that loyalty is properly termed patriotism. Nationalism should connote loyalty to one's extended family."[21] For David Miller, nationality provides a unifying common national identity, an identity a society inherited in large measure from the past, and it should not be fully open to rational scrutiny.[22] Professor Charles A. Kupchan wrote that nationalism should instill "a strong sense of belonging and allegiance—important in as much as the national state was soon to ask its citizens to die in its defense."[23] When the masses identify with the nation, "it then helped consolidate the construction of political community at the national level by drawing citizens into a collective mission that evoked passion and self-sacrifice."[24] Nationalism is simply an ethnocentric feeling of people that includes patriotism, a sense of community, and a sense of loyalty to your nation. Maurizio Viroli, in his book *For Love of Country*, contends that patriotism is focused on love of the political institutions, civic virtue, and the way of life that sustains common liberty within a republic.[25] A nation is composed of people identified politically within a specific boundary with a legal right to their own ideology, their own safety, and willingness to die for that cause—the nation-state. Philip G. Roeder, in his explanation as to the mobilization and emergence of a nation-state, wrote the following:

> The politicization of an ethnic group that galvanizes it into a nation, provides it a platform for nationalists mobilization, and finally empowers it with a state of its own.... The demand for a nation-state and separation arises from the awakening of ethnic self-awareness.[26]

The Turkish Cypriot community is a nation that has achieved the status of sovereignty and independence to produce a state of its own.

The Greek and Turkish Cypriots never had the opportunity to foster their own identity into a sense of nationalism nor to foster peaceful cohabitation; instead, they were given only a justification for the pursuit of ethnic self-interest. Greek settlement on the island started by Mycenaean-Achaean's around 1200 BC, and the Turkish migration followed the Ottoman conquest of Cyprus by Sultan Selim II in 1571. About 5,720 households were transferred to Cyprus from the Karaman, Icel, Yozgat, Konya, Alanya, Antalya, and Aydin regions of Anatolia. In addition, about thirty-six thousand Ottoman soldiers and their families settled in Cyprus, and by *firman* (decree) of the Sultan Selim II, they were given land and sustenance. Great Britain leased the island from the Ottomans in 1878, annexed it in 1914, and colonized it from 1923 to 1960. Zurich-London Agreements were signed in 1959 by Great Britain, Greece, and Turkey, and the Republic of Cyprus was established on August 16, 1960. The reality of true nation-building never occurred in Cyprus and the state-building, therefore, could only be imaginary—never a perfection. A nation is composed of people with cultural and demographic characteristics (language, race, religion, customs, values, traditions, similar patriotic sentiments, loyalty to state, and common historical and political experiences), as well as an adherence to common ideological principles. Nationalism is an ideology, a concept, a commonality of population with shared experiences such as a geographical area, self-determination, allegiance to a flag and national anthem, and even to the basic instinct of survival. The fault lines between the two communities were determined by their cultural background, biases, goals, religion, values, behavior, ideas, morals, interests, and deep-rooted desire for common actions and goals. Nationalism creates a sense of community, identity, and loyalty to self-government—a nation-state.[27] Nationalism is a fairly modern phenomenon, and nationalism took an important turn with the American (1776) and French (1789) revolutions that shifted the emphasis from the divine right of the rulers (king or queen) to governing by the consent of the people.[28] The belief in the right of a nation to self-determination was proclaimed in the doctrine of popular sovereignty with "liberty, equality, fraternity." Thomas Paine in *The Rights of Man* (1791) expressed the view that nations and democracy are inherently linked in the popularly governed nation-state. An ethnic group identity is relative to "long-standing association across generations, complex relations of kinship, common culture, and usually religious uniformity and common territorial attachments."[29] The difficult challenge facing both sides (Greek and Turkish Cypriots) will be overcoming deep-seated ethnic and social biases and prejudices in order to objectively and realistically resolve this seemingly endless crisis for the mutual benefit of all.

On Cyprus, the failure to promote a political community consciousness is mainly due to the lack of a shared claim to common ethno-cultural characteristics based on ethnicity, culture, race, language, and religion. Ernest Barker expresses ethnic nation formation in the following words:

> A nation is a body of men, inhabiting a definite territory, who normally are drawn from different races, but possess a common stock of thoughts and feelings acquired and transmitted during the course of a common history: who on the whole and in the main, though more in the past than in the present, include in that common stock a common religious belief; who generally and as a rule use a common language as the vehicle of their thoughts and feelings; and who, besides common thoughts and feelings, also cherish a common will, and accordingly form, or tend to form, *a separate state* for the expression and realization of that will.[30]

Promotion and protection of cultural diversity and expression has nurtured a psychological and physical wall between the two communities. As to cultural links among groups, Marc H. Ross wrote the following:

> Cultural identities, such as ethnicity, connect individuals through perceived common past experiences and expectations

of shared future ones. . . . People sharing a group identity possess, to a greater or lesser degree, a sense of common fate including expectations of common treatment, joint fears of survival/extinction, and beliefs about group worth, dignity, and recognition.[31]

Samuel Huntington has written that "cultural characteristics and differences are less mutable and hence less easily compromised and resolved than political and economic ones."[32] Joseph Rothschild postulates that "politicized ethnicity surfaces and hardens along the most accessible and yielding fault line of potential cleavage available" and that political institutions are powerful "in affecting the configuration of ethnic groups, the cutting edge of ethnic conflict, and the very content of ethnicity per se."[33] An ethnic community must embody a strong sense of belonging "with shared ancestry myths, histories and cultures, having an association with a specific territory and a sense of solidarity."[34] Although the two ethnic societies share distinct cultural characteristics and values that were borrowed and incorporated from the other, they continue to have a deep-seated sense of unique identity, which continues to keep them apart. A point of positive ethnic identification and pride has been reinforced with folkloric heritage, particularly with motherland Greece and Turkey. Culture, which has an influence on both the individual and ethnic identity, has emerged as a central arena of conflict along with the other intractable issues. This division has contributed to the exercise of discrimination, unfair treatment, rigid and intolerant, which prevented the development of a common identity or overarching loyalty for a common future. The cultural and political division continues to magnify the ethnic aspirations and claims to a particular identity. Peter Turchin's definition of ethnicity is as follows:

Ethnicity is the group use of any aspect of culture to create internal cohesion and differentiation from other groups. An imaginary boundary separates the members of the ethnic group from the rest of humanity. . . . The ethnic boundary can use a variety of *symbolic markers*—language and dialect, religion and ritualistic behaviors, race, clothing, behavioral mannerism, hairstyles, ornaments, and tattoos.[35]

The absence of respect of differences causes cultural and political fault lines to emerge and hinders the resolution of the inter-ethnic crisis by arbitration or mediation.

During the civil war in the 1960s and 1970s, the overwhelming reason the Greek Cypriots deployed military power was to humiliate the Turkish Cypriots. To arrogate superiority, the Greek Cypriots justified the use of full-scale collective punishment, destruction of homes, businesses, religious centers, and institutions. Thirty-thousand Turkish Cypriots were forced to abandon thirty-three villages destroyed by *EOKA* and settle in the predominantly Turkish sectors in the major cities. Most of the Greeks endorsed or acquiesced to the indiscriminate and violent methods of removal or expulsion of the Turkish Cypriots from their homes. The Greek Cypriot authorities have asserted the strength of the majority while confidently ignoring the treaties that it had signed in Zurich and London in 1959. A hierarchical order put in place bestowed special privileges, powers, and honors to Greek Cypriots, while subjugating the Turkish Cypriots to subordinated status by depriving them of their constitutional rights and representation in parliament. The stark inequality and biases were evident in businesses, employment, government bureaucracy, scholarships to study abroad, and building permits. In other words, the Turkish Cypriots were deemed as lower human beings and not worthy of higher status and good quality of life in Cypriot society. The process of subjugation reinforces internalized ethnic emotions, defiance, anger, and hostility, detrimental to peaceful coexistence. The Turkish Cypriots collective concept was being excluded from the governmental system put in place under the Zurich-London Accords of 1959. (For the full text of the 1963 *Akritas Plan,* see appendix A.) The principal author of the *Akritas Plan* was Tassos Papadopoulos, and he was assisted by the Interior Minister Yiorkadjis Polycarpos.[36] In an editorial in *Cyprus Mail,* on February 1, 2009, Loucas Charalambous wrote that "Makarios was the founder and figure-head of the Greek Cypriot 'extremist' organization known as Akritas."[37] The *Akritas Plan* was to dissolve the Republic of Cyprus and progressively, in stages, the Greek Cypriots would be expected to vote for *enosis.* There is little doubt that Makarios held the view that the enjoyment of political rights were to be based on an ethnic and religious doctrinal belief system in order to have the right to liberty, power, and equality. The secret document was published by a Greek Cypriot newspaper, *Patris,* on April 21, 1966. The threats and conspiracy of the *Akritas Plan* left deep scars on the Turkish Cypriot psyche. Papadopoulos was a major player in *EOKA* from 1955 to 1959, a prime promoter of *enosis,* and a crusader on retaining a firm hold on Cyprus for the exclusive domain of the Greek. As a result, he played a pivotal role in inflicting monumental suffering on Turks during the EOKA struggle and was a driving force in keeping them isolated economically and politically during his presidency from February 28, 2003, to February 28, 2008. The inevitable consequences have been smoldering resentment, high contempt, and rising animosity reflected in Turkish Cypriots fury toward Papadopoulos. The experience manifested deep frustration and an intense sense of disenfranchisement, injustice, hurt, humiliation, and violation of honor, which led to frequent and often violent confrontations.[38] Succumbing to economic, political, and military force was deeply humiliating to the Turkish Cypriots. Reaction to continuous suffering and humiliation in a relationship will result in a strong desire to humiliate in return. A victim of humiliation becomes preoccupied to reach for evidence to prove his victimhood.[39] It has become an obsession of the Turkish Cypriots to prove their Turkishness and entitlement to the northern part of the island, and as a statement, they have erected a huge Turkish Cypriot flag equal in size to eleven football pitches on the southern slope of the Besparmak Mountain range (the Greek call it Pentadaktylos), using stones and reflective white paint and illuminated at night with electric lights overlooking Nicosia and many villages, giving the area a psychological impact. A TRNC and a Turkish flag are placed on Besparmak Mountain in an area known as Ciklos. Each flag covers an area of 216 square meters and is on a 50-meter-high mast. The two flags are 12 meters in length and 18 meters in width and are illuminated at night. The flags irritate the Greek Cypriots and proclaim as to the Turkishness of the north.[40] President Demetris Christofias, in his Christmas message on December 23, 2009, extolled the Greek Cypriots mission "to remove the flag of the illegal Turkish Cypriot regime on Pentadaktylos Mountain range."[41] On the one hand, there is a contempt and opposition to "Turkish Cypriot regime," on the other hand, there is a coordinated effort to usher in reconciliation and trust for the reunification of the island. The Greek Cypriots in return refer to TRNC as an illegal puppet regime, with a self-styled government, self-styled president council of ministers, "Turkish rebels," and illegally established universities in the north. In addition, the Greek Cypriot administration is consistent in blaming TRNC for all its shortcomings as to animal foot-and-mouth disease in late 2007, and drug and sex trafficking and for the presence of the illegal immigrants in the south.[42] Symbolic demarcation that distinguished "us" from "them" clearly defines recognizable boundaries and is a glaring marker and promoter of national identities, which are associated with the nation-state. As Bogdam Denitch says,

> The political language used by nationalists almost always stresses unity against the outsider or the enemy, real or potential. Nationalism in modern politics establishes a boundary separating "us" and "them" and bases that boundary on inborn, that is to say national characteristics. You are born,

more rarely adopted, into a national group. There is no nonsense about individual choice.[43]

The rise of both identification and separate loyalty suggests the intensity of attachment and aspiration for permanent separateness. The stirring of nationalist sentiment will enhance the ethnic demands for a permanent division of the island.

Imbedded negative ideas and images of Cypriot ethnic groups contributed to the alienation that profoundly affected community relations and interdependence. The rift separated "us" from "them" and a condescending attitude polarized the two communities in a competitive mote. An editorial in *Cyprus Mail* on April 25, 2007, states as follows:

> In Cyprus, any questioning of the president's actions leads to a verbal onslaught by the pro-government parties, which cast aspersions on the patriotism of the doubter, routinely dismissed as a champion of the Turkish positions—in short, anyone who does not support the president's handling of the Cyprus problem is on the side of Turks. This simplistic thinking (or should we say lack of it?) has become the norm, with the majority of the media also embracing it.

A little humility would serve both communities' interests and would better lend itself to a win-win situation. Failure to nurture good neighborliness and social peace created rifts that led to hostilities, cutback in communication, lack of trust, and a campaign for dominance, which caused the labeling of the other as the "enemy." The security dilemma caused both the emergence of mutual distrust and the threat of preemptive attack forcing both sides to amass weapons.[44] However, the players did not possess the equal power to achieve their goals in a military confrontation. The Greek Cypriots were in a commanding lead to coercive power as well as in assets relating to both tangible and intangible power when assessing capabilities relative to the power of a nation-state. Turkey's intervention in Cyprus in 1974 was necessary in order to stop the overwhelming Greek military forces from overrunning the Turkish Cypriots enclaves. Professor Volkan wrote the following:

> Although it was the bitter enmity between two Greek elements on Cyprus [Before the outbreak of the war in 1974, the Greeks who supported Makarios fought against those who supported

---

11

Athens and Sampson] that triggered the war there, the war benefited the Turks by giving them inner peace and a new self-esteem.[45]

The Turkish Cypriot sees themselves as the victims of the *enosis*, and the oppressive humiliation of the Turks is accused as the villain. The proponents of *enosis* left behind bitter memories without any remorse, and many of its members continue to hold high positions in the Greek Cypriot government and are considered to be strong believers in their sacred Hellenic cause of joining motherland Greece.

The economic and political demise from 1963 to 1974 humiliated the Turkish Cypriots, and the trauma of rejection of the political partnership in the state system established under the Zurich-London Agreements of 1959 live in their minds and compels them to guard against their "former masters." The Turkish Cypriots' dignified future has led to political and economic interests, which have motivated them to "cleanse" themselves of their adversary. They have stood up to the challenges of nation-state building and their socioeconomic needs have been met. International recognition of TRNC by the international community could represent an ultimate solution to this seemingly unsolvable crisis; up to now, the lack of any constructive dialogue has contributed to the failure of the ultimate dream of a reunified Cyprus.

Competing manifestation of ethnic nationalism reinforced the schism between the two ethnic Cypriot groups; as a result, permanent barriers poisoned the climate of peaceful coexistence. Ethnic leaders cultivated the elements of distinct differences and inflamed the historical, religious, political, and cultural biases, further alienating the two ethnic communities. Frankly, Cypriot community leaders' political and cultural platforms have never been to strengthen the multiethnic bonds for cohabitation and peaceful coexistence. Rather, the cultivation and nurturing of insecurity, distrust, paranoia, and hate eliminated the prospects of a healthy ethnic relationship. Distortions and the pernicious communal isolation postulated by ethnic leaders further heightened distrust, leaving both communities as enemies. Community leaders' lack of joint partnership for the future was partly the result of untrained negotiating skills and diplomacy, but it was also duly influenced by religious and ethnic passions:

> Such a strategy is a response by ruling elites to shifts in the structure of domestic political and economic power: by constructing individual interest in terms of the threat to the group, endangered elites can fend off domestic challengers who

seek to mobilize the population against the status quo, and, can better position themselves to deal with future challenges.[46]

External conflict with other groups, "although justified and described in terms of relations with other ethnic groups and taking place within that context, has its main goal within the state, among members of the same ethnicity."[47] An unbridgeable difference between the two ethnic groups was skillfully manipulated in a complex game plan, which destroyed the formation of a Cypriot identity. The absence of the "ethos" of solidarity made social and political equality and emotional identification impossible under a common identity—Cypriotism. This great mistrust, nurtured for generations, can only be overcome through dialogue, education, the shedding of prejudices, and a show of goodwill.

The prejudicial stereotyping of the communities on Cyprus goes back to the fall of Constantinople (currently Istanbul, Turkey) after a shattering defeat of the Byzantium by the Ottomans in 1453. Following the conversion of the Roman emperor Constantine (r. 313–337) to Christianity, he ordered the construction of a new capital for the Byzantine Empire (New Rome) called Constantinople after himself. The Arabs, Persians, and Turks called the second Christian empire as "Rum" or the believers in Greek Orthodox Christianity. The collapse of the Byzantine Empire was confirmation of the rise and expanding of Islam and the decline of Christian Europe. The Greeks continue to claim Istanbul as their own and nurture the hope of liberation of the city in the future. *Megali Idea* is a Hellenic vision to reestablish a Greater Greek state (a restored Byzantine empire) that would extend from Sicily to Asia Minor, and from Thrace, Macedonia and Epirus, north, to Crete and Cyprus to the south. The capital of the Greek state would be Constantinople (Istanbul).[48] The Greek cultural phenomenon, the *Megali Idea,* is a grand old strategy launching a crusade to restore the greatness of Byzantium with the liberation of Constantinople. Yiannis Papadakis, a Greek Cypriot anthropologist in his book in 2005, expresses the belief of many Greeks that Istanbul will be liberated from the "infidel barbarians" and the *Megali Idea* (the Great Idea), will establish a state that will united the land that "rightfully" belong to Greece.

> For Greeks it always was, and always would be, Constantinople. Legends spoke of how one day Constantine, the last emperor, would be resurrected to liberate Constantinople, chase the Turks away and "there will be such a bloodbath that the cattle will have to swim in blood." We knew whose blood it would be.[49]

Harry Anastasiou, a Greek Cypriot scholar, writes that the Greek nationalist historiography ignores the fact that the Byzantium Empire was a continuation of the ideal of imperial Rome and not a Greek nation. "The Byzantine world was in fact a multiethnic empire, in which both the imperial leaders and their subjects saw themselves not as ethnocentric Hellenes but primarily as Romans."[50] He explains it further by saying,

> The Greek nationalist notion of a glorious past also overlooked the fact that the Byzantine world was not monoethnic nor did it embody the ideals of Hellenism.... Only by integrating certain facts in a mythological framework did nationalism create a history that suited its agenda.[51]

The military campaign of Greece to extend its borders into Asia Minor for the Great Idea culminated in the humiliating defeat of the Greek forces in 1922 by the Turkish army under the command of Gazi Mustafa Kemal Pasha. The ancient rivalry continues to overshadow Greek pride. Regaining the city thus evokes an intoxicating appeal to restore a glorious past by burying a humiliating defeat. The Greeks express strong conviction as to reconciliation and peaceful coexistence with the Turkish Cypriots by sidestepping the bloody events of 1964, 1967, and 1974 in Cyprus. At the same token, Greeks continue to harbor bitterness and dream of gaining control of Istanbul from the Turks, which has been under their control since 1453. How can coexistence and a healing process be applied to Cyprus by ignoring the profound abuses of power by the Greek Cypriots while refusing to accept reality that Istanbul is not Constantinople and is an integral part of Turkey?

Culture embodies a framework to support collective experiences, language, symbols, attitudes or images, myths, fantasies, and values. Cultural and political traditions encouraged the Greek Cypriots to deny the Turkish Cypriots equal economic and political opportunities and fair treatment. Language, symbols, political issues, racial ideology, schools, churches, media, business, and industry influence the ethnic groups' collective conscious. Learned behavior and attitudes permeated the whole society, which legitimized oppressive arrangements and accounts for ethnic conflicts. Hence, the Greek Cypriots emerged as the privileged and higher status economic and social class, while the Turks were relegated to a lower status.

In Cyprus, educational systems are designed as agents of political socialization to shape Greek and Turkish identities. Education Minister Andreas Demetrious's initiative in September 2008 was to rewrite the history curriculum to foster bicommunal reconciliation. It was characterized as a "self-castration of our Hellenic heritage: by the DISY deputy Andreas Themistocleous.[52] The history currently taught in Greek Cypriot secondary schools has remained "virtually unchanged since 1950"[53] and fails to address the brutal attacks against the Turkish Cypriots between December 1963 and the summer of 1964, and the periods are referred to as "The Turkish Revolt."[54] Archbishop Chrysostomos II warned the government on September 7 "to take their hands off education: or it will force the Church to react vigorously."[55] On November 6, Archbishop Chrysostomos said that the church would call on Greek Cypriot "children to throw away such books that contain a counterfeited history of our country."[56] The presence of solidarities of the "good old days" have been shattered as a result of hostilities between the two ethnic communities since 1964. The inability to reach a consensus to shared responsibility continues to erode trust and any hope for a settlement. The ethnic tension has enhanced divisions, complicating all initiatives for a solution. The Greeks and Turks do not share a common language, ethnicity, history, religion, flag, and are extremely ethnocentric. In the absence of shared psychological bonds or emotional identification, the barriers of ethnicity and nationalism have contributed to a continued deadlock in reaching a compromise to the crisis on Cyprus. A cohesive nation-state never developed; instead, the desired goal was to embrace enosis, which has long been the virtual preserve of the church. Still, the overall effect of the division of the island since 1974 has been characterized by some as the best solution with reciprocal benefits and peace.

Each community is united by a common dislike of the other. Respective distortions of one's own past must give way to depending differences in order to merge identities. The absence of a common identity is the curse of ethnicity; ironically, America is better than Europe in coping with the massive inflow of immigrants from around the globe. Canada, Australia, and the United States have been assimilating their diverse society into one nation-state, and those multicultural-multiethnic societies are proud of their inclusiveness in a representative pluralistic liberal democracy. Whereas Western Europe continues to lay claim to world civilization and culture, Judo-Christian values deeply divide the hearts and minds of their citizens.[57] A common political identity and allegiance to a nation-state will manifest itself with the absence of the fault lines that divide us. A new generation continues to reaffirm historical prejudices while inquiring into the reluctance of new immigrants' loyalty and reluctance to be assimilated.

The institutionalized distinction between ethnicity and culture tribalizes the society into a deeply conscious voice of resentment, disillusionment, and limited democratic privileges and economic opportunities. The decline in economic opportunities for the Cypriot Turks generated anxiety and resentment and contributed to the extreme condition of inequality. Ted Gurr, in his study on ethnic minority peoples, concludes that dominant elite groups would rather "give disadvantaged groups political rights and some access to power than to reduce economic inequalities."[58] The church and governmental officials desensitized the Greek society to the existing inequity and instead fueled the impulse to legitimize the established order. The concentration of wealth in Greek Cypriots' hands influenced shifts in political power and the formation of ideological arrangements associated with the uneven economic development, contributing to the marginalization of the Turks. This discourse alienated the Turks from the Greek community and contributed to the formation of an oppressive political arrangement. The impulse to exclude Turks was institutionalized and became more evident from 1964 to 1974. The arbitrary discrimination against the Turks was perceived as a serious obstacle to their individual advancement in the financial sectors of the economy, and business and governmental opportunities were designed primarily to benefit the Greek Cypriots. The economic and political institutions were structured to privilege the Greek Cypriots and, thus, were not conducive to the development of peaceful coexistence. At the same time, the economic gap between the two ethnic groups widened significantly, but since 2000, TRNC's economy has grown substantially. Tourism has been on the rise in Northern Cyprus by 6.2 percent annually since 2000. The Northern Cyprus economy grew by 10.6 percent in 2006, fuelled by construction and tourism. TRNC's economy has grown by about 10–11 percent per annum during 2003–2007.[59] Todd Gitlin, in his book *Twilight of Common Dreams*, writes, "Growing inequality erodes social solidarity."[60] The lack of cooperation between ethnic groups can only hinder that consciousness necessary for nationalism. Antonia Darder and Rodolfo D. Torres in their book *After Race: Racism After Multiculturalism* writes the following:

> The majority of people in this country continue to believe that they belong to a specific race, and this has an impact on the way they conceive of their social identity. Hence, it can be said that for many racism functions to define both Self and Other. This is apparent in racialized discourses of hierarchy, in which members of dominant groups assert their superiority over other groups, and in racialized discourses of solidarity, in which subordinated groups assert their unity and rights.[61]

The lack of advancement and ensuing financial stress contributed to the Turkish Cypriot frustration, resentment, and hostility. Europolitical structure compliments the immigrants' expectations, but this is no high degree of interdependence or favorable view of them as people. Aspiration to excel is a realistic expectation and can help overcome ethnic differences and will cultivate in Europeans and Cypriots alike the desire to become part of any nation-state.

The ethnic political crisis on Cyprus from 1963 to 2012 has shown that Greek and Turkish attempts to unite the islanders have led nowhere but have accelerated the rivalry to the point of splitting Cyprus (since 1974) down the middle. Edward Azar's analysis of protracted social conflict fits the Cyprus crisis that continues to derail a constructive political settlement.

> The process of protracted conflict distorts and retards the effective operation of political institutions. It reinforces and strengthens pessimism throughout the society, demoralized leaders and immobilizes the search for peaceful solutions. We have observed that the societies undergoing protracted social conflict find it difficult to initiate the reach for answers to the problems and grievances. As the protracted problem becomes part of the culture of the ravaged nation, it builds a sense of paralysis, which afflicts the collective consciousness of the population. An environment of hopelessness permeates all strata of society, and a siege mentality develops which inhibits constructive negotiation for any solution of the conflict.[62]

Sustaining and legitimizing a substantial advantage in the ethnic struggle for control of the state political system and maintaining an oppressive arrangement allowed the Greek Cypriots to relegate the Turkish Cypriots to a subordinate role. Behind this style of political discourse was an intent to dominate and capitalize political oppressive arrangements.

The absence of a unifying political culture, or common loyalty, compounds ethnic differences and reinforces the political schism between them. Description and prescription essentially divide and polarize the ethnic groups on cultural-political lines without serious considerations of a partnership to forge a common identity for a better future. The media in the north and south continued to whip up public passions and lay the groundwork for a polarized ethnicity to harden, which makes it more difficult to move forward on the peace process. A vision of harmony between ethnic groups must be translated into a policy of solidarity for the emergence of a common bond instead of rivalry. Ethnic integration into a nation is the product of enlightened self-interest designed to ensure the disappearance of condescending divisive walls. The termination of "us" versus "them" mentality, the promotion of shared values, social and economic equity, common national interests, aspirations, and a stronger sense of solidarity will heighten the sense of engagement for a common end.

The independence of Cyprus in 1960 did not bind the Cypriots because of lack of common goals and anticipated "ethos." The highly divided economically and politically structured relationship set the stage for change in ethnic attitudes and political behavior. A state system, as established under the Zurich-London Accords of 1959, managed to survive for a short period. The Zurich-London Agreements rejected *enosis* or *Taksim* (Partition), but Makarios did not relinquish his desire to unite the island with Greece. The imposed plan as to the partnership government was short-circuited by diverse nationalism and political goals. Glen Camp expresses the opinion that the Cyprus settlement was the result of *Realpolitik* and wrote as follows:

> Such a policy assumes that the role of diplomacy is to develop solutions to international problems that ratify an existing distribution of power rather than solutions that would change that distribution in the direction of greater equity. The statesman is thus a realist seeking a settlement based upon the existing balance of power, not an idealist seeking to rectify passionately felt injustices.[63]

Tragically, the Republic of Cyprus, dominated by the Greek Cypriots, became highly repressive toward the Turkish Cypriots. The political legitimacy of the Republic of Cyprus fundamentally influenced the Turks to withdraw from the partnership.

Relative tenuous ethnic peace in Cyprus had prevailed from 1878 to 1960 under a strong British colonial rule through the use of divide-and-rule and reward-and-punishment policies. After independence of Cyprus in 1960, the old animosities resurfaced, invoking the specter of *enosis*, thus forcing the two ethnic groups to regress to hostilities and violence. Great Britain was innovative in conjuring a venture to suit a special need, which equated the *enosis* containment with Turkish interests. The motivating force for the combined effort was intertwined with a divergent interest that acknowledged mutual benefits within North Atlantic Treaty Organization (NATO) defense structure. A viable alternative for the Turks in a future political settlement on the island was *Taksim* (Partition of Cyprus). To preserve the cozy relationship, the Turkish

Cypriots painfully depended on the British to check the Greek challenge to the status quo, which was vital to Turkish interests. The British assurance to the Turks helped solidify common interests, but their motivations were not aligned. The combined effort was intended to neutralize the *enosis* proponents. Compromise was crucial in achieving this goal. Strategic partnership effects were fragmented and often contradictory, but they also compelled the necessity to meet these challenges. British and Turkish motives in this engagement had obviously competing interests, but they were a means to serve higher ends for both partners.

Potent ethnic national consciousness promoted the development of jingoism and sectarianism. A common Cypriot identity or spirit of patriotic solidarity linking the two communities is an important aspect of nationalism that was never forged. Cypriots' national aspirations and patriotic feelings were focused on Greece and Turkey, or affectionately to Hellenism or Kemalism. The Greek Orthodox Church heightened the Hellenic identity of Greek Cypriots and blessed the denial of an equal role in the state system for Turkish Cypriots. Most Greek Cypriots considered independence of Cyprus in 1960 to be "only a first stage toward *enosis*."[64] The Greek Cypriots concluded,

> The *enosis* movement was part of Greek irredentism (*Megali Idea*), the prevailing ideology once the Greek state was formed, which entailed the vision of liberating those regarded as "Greek still under foreign yoke" and bringing them under one political roof.[65]

Markides, a Greek Cypriot sociologist, wrote that the *enosis* originated

> in the minds of intellectuals in their attempt to revise Greek-Byzantine civilization. However, being the most central and powerful of institutions, the church contributed immensely to its development.[66]

The Greek Orthodox Church is the wealthiest, most powerful organization and is very active politically in Cyprus. The church always has had a role in the Greek Cypriot political struggle on Cyprus and has been a strong public voice for *enosis*. Archbishop Makarios in the 1950s and 1960s was the architect for formation of *EOKA* (Ethniki Organosis Kipriakou Agonos or the National Organization of Cypriot Fighters), which contributed to the growing ethnic tensions on the island. Among the *EOKA* activities were handing out propaganda leaflets, writing slogans on walls, recruiting members, and organizing demonstrations against the British rule in Cyprus. An *EOKA* hit man assassinated the enemies of the *enosis* movement.[67] The church embarked upon a conflict in the 1960s with the hope that quick victory would prevail and that the enemy would be suppressed. All reasonable accommodation with the Turkish Cypriots was out of the question; the *enosis* struggle was to go on until victory was achieved. Rebecca Bryant wrote that the *EOKA* struggle was not to increase

> rights and opportunities, but for union [of Cyprus] with . . .
> mother Greece. . . . For Greek Cypriot nationalists, freedom was
> not a right but a duty, and enosis was not a future to be made,
> but a future to which one should concede.[68]

The church arrogated to itself the embodiment or custodian of Hellenistic ideals. Religion is inextricably tied to cultural and political ethos of Greek Cypriots. Makarios was the personification as to the destiny of the Greek Cypriots, and all were expected to give passionate loyalty to national ideas and Hellenistic "ethos." The British government's failure to suppress the Greek Cypriot insurrection compelled Athens and Ankara to engage in negotiations to grant Cyprus its independence on August 16, 1960. Ethnic rivalries intensified following Cyprus's independence in 1960, when the government's resources and institutions were geared to the benefit of the Greek Cypriots. The continued political conflict accelerated in 1963, and a compromise was difficult to achieve.

The Greek Orthodoxy not only is a spiritual force, but as a patriotic political instrument to reinforce ethno-nationalism, is also essentially the motivator and instigator of armed conflict on Cyprus. For a sense of ethnic and national identity, young Greek Cypriot children once a week attend Katichitiko lessons (religious instruction) conducted by the Greek Orthodox Church, which provides the priests the platform to emphasize religion and nationalism (the 1821 Greek war of independence against the Ottoman Turks, the *EOKA* struggle from 1955–1959 against the British colonial rule, the *Enosists* coup against President Markarios that contributed to the Turkish invasion in 1974, the destruction of the Orthodox Churches in Northern Cyprus by the "barbaric Turks," and the Greek superiority compared to other nations are all part of the message presented to children). Since 1974, the Greek Orthodox Church of Cyprus, in order to sustain the pain and suffering of the Greek Cypriot community, have mobilized the widows and mothers who have lost loved ones or family members during the conflict. These women, dressed in black, protest at the main checkpoint in Nicosia and are hyped up with nationalist's speeches reinforcing the ethnic polarization. The Greeks take great pride that ancient Greece is referred to as the cradle of Western civilization. The church continues to play a key role in the education of the Greek Cypriot children and influence and shape their ethnic and political identity.[69] Due to the strong protest of the Orthodox Church, on September 25, 2007, Cyprus, Greece, and historians were forced to withdraw a high school history book revised in 2006 because it failed to highlight the role of the church during the 1821 Greek uprising against the Ottoman rule. It objected to a reference to an event in 1922 of a Turkish attack on Izmir trying to drive out the occupying Greek forces, and it was critical of the reference as to the division of Cyprus and subsequent failed peace talks as the "Cyprus issue" rather than "Cyprus problem."[70] Religious ethno-nationalists succeeded in their endeavors to disintegrate ethnic coexistence by inhibiting the compromise of ethnic political differences at the state level. From the very inception of the independence of Cyprus on August 16, 1960, President Makarios embarked on an ambitious agenda for *enosis* that complimented the mission of *EOKA* from 1955 to 1960 and the Greek vision of *Megali Idea*. In June 1953, Makarios took an oath in Pahaneromeni Church in Nicosia not to give up the struggle for *enosis*, and he was to seek support from East or West in order to achieve his goal.[71] On March 14, 1971, Makarios in his speech in Yialoussa village during a memorial service to a fallen local *EOKA* hero said the following:

> Cyprus is a Greek island. It was Greek from the dawn of history and is shall remain Greek forever. We have taken it over as a wholly Greek island and we shall preserve it as an undivided Greek island, until we hand it over to mother Greece.[72]

The Turks were depicted as "uncivilized barbarians," "barbarian minority," or "infidel Turks" who had no claim to land or to partnership in the political system, and their extermination or forceful removal was thought essential by the *enosis* extremists. Almost universally the Greeks agree on their cultural superiority and Turkish inferiority. The Turkish Cypriots occupied the bottom rank in the hierarchy and discriminatory measures secured the Greek dominance to sustain their economic prosperity and political eminence. These ingrained attitudes of cultural, social, business, and economic superiority toward the Turks served to undermine virtually every major effort to reconcile communal standing in the negotiations to reach a formula for a peaceful settlement of the Cyprus problem.[73]

Based on empirical studies, the Greeks and Turkish Cypriots distinction and similarities are perceived to be as follows: the Turkish Cypriots are hierarchal, patriarchal, authoritarian, unemotional, self-denying, thorough, dependent, conventional, cohesive family structure, self-doubting, and reserved. The Greek Cypriots are competitive, individualistic, have high self-esteem, are cautious, suspicious, untrustworthy, and manipulative, believe in their cultural superiority, are supporters of *enosis* (Union of Cyprus with Greece), have strong family ties, distrust public officials and outsiders, and are dependent upon extended family and institution. Some of the similarities between the two communities are belief in natural phenomena, and until recently, male villagers wore baggy trousers with a sash around the waist (the Turks sash was scarlet and the Greeks blue), citizens coexisted in villages and towns, lack of toleration for child autonomy or aggressive behavior, internalize that which is "all good" and externalize that which is "all bad," the fear and distrust of each other due to the violence in 1963–64, 1967, and 1974, and the trauma of expulsion from their villages and towns. Distinct differences between the two communities still persist: shared "bad" experiences of each community, images of the other as "all bad," interethnic marriage as a taboo, no intimate friendships, and different customs and traditions. Also, Turks are Muslim and Greeks are Orthodox Christians, making each side suspicious and antagonistic toward the other. The secularization of the Republic of Turkey in 1923 under Mustafa Kemal Ataturk caused the Turkish Cypriots to make changes in the Sunni Muslim traditions and practices. Religion continued to play a major role in the Turkish Cypriot culture but not part of its daily life. The religious revivalism in the Islamic world had its impact on all Turks in Turkey and Cyprus. Since the 1980s, many mosques have been built in urban and rural areas, but the attendance to religious services is much higher among the Anatolian settlers than among the Turkish Cypriots. The psychological difficulties (survivor syndrome trauma) affecting the Turks can be attributed to their confinement to refugee camps in enclaves due to the tragic events in 1963–64 and 1968. The green line boundary continues to separate in Greek and Turkish sectors.[74]

A period of tentative peace from 1960 to 1964 was characterized by rationality in the ethnic interactions; however, the continued growth of tension, upheaval, and mistrust eventually led to bloodshed, which continued until the division of the island into two parts following the Turkish invasion in 1974. The expectation for an ethnic reconciliation with a strong rational vision, which is essential for the resolution of the crisis, has failed to materialize. The strained relationship between the two ethnic communities has heightened the nationalistic fervor of each, with the display of national flags, the singing of the national anthems, the celebrations of Independence Day, as well as other displays of pageantry and ritual glorifying all the symbols of each community's motherland. Strict adherence to ethnic nationalism promoted competitiveness, enhanced historical bonds with the motherlands, and produced a sense of cultural superiority, as schools and universities became the agents for national spirit by reaffirming ancestral myths.[75] Cypriots have marginalized the necessity for a collective political identity and instead have ostracized the other side to enhance their community's political interest. A constant tug-of-war between the community leaders contributed to the mobilized support for ethnic interests and sharpened the ethnic, religious, and political rivalry. At the Australian Open tennis tournament on January 15, 2008, the Greek Cypriot tennis star Marcos Baghdatis, joined by his Greek admirers, used the international stage to chant anti-Turkish slogans—"Turks out of Cyprus"—tacitly stoking animosity.[76] The common offensive chant of the Greek Cypriot National conscripts until 2008 was "A good Turk is a dead Turk."[77] DISY's nationalist deputy Sotiris Sampson, the son of Nikos Sampson, endorsed the racist slogan and called on the military superiors in charge to reinstate the chant. He said, "Slogans which are in favour of Greece and against Turkey cannot be considered either chauvinistic or racist."[78] Ethnicity continues to generate angry responses, and it is indicative of the fact that decades-long division help create a culture of hate and distrust that continues to be a troubling aspect of Cypriot society. An ethnic group that encourages hate cannot be the messengers of peaceful coexistence or ethnic healing under false pretenses.

Ethnic loyalties and religious affiliations solidified the bonds of Greekness and Turkishness to the detriment of both sides, destabilizing the strained political climate and adding the uncertainty of a common future. The absence of collective experiences failed to develop group consciousness. Each distinctive faith associated ethnicity and culture to foster a psychological unity, nationalism, and sectarian mind-set. To preserve ethnic purity, mixed marriages were shunned, and separate schools cultivated ethnic nationalism and prejudices. The prospects for harmony gave way to violence and deadlock, and the gulf of misunderstanding continued to widen, undermining all the international efforts for an amicable settlement and a lasting peace. Agreements calling for independence of a federal, bizonal, and bicommunal state were signed by Makarios-Denktash (1977) and Kyprianou-Denktash (1979), but the compromise failed to lead toward a comprehensive settlement. The Greek opposition to the Annan Plan (2004) contributed to the permanent division and a possible mergence of two states. President of Cyprus, Tassos Papadopoulos, and his party members in parliament, DIKO (Democratic Party), called the Annan Plan "Satanan Plan." A Greek Orthodox Cypriot bishop cautioned the YES supporters that "they would lose the Kingdom of Heaven," meaning that they would go to hell. The Greek Cypriots' mind-set of an "all-or-nothing" approach to negotiations made any compromise unlikely and helped shape the continued political deadlock that governs Greek and Turkish Cypriots relationships to this day.

The continued influx of estimated one hundred thousand farm settlers[79] from Turkey to Northern Cyprus would, according to the demographic predictions, in time be equal to the Greek Cypriot majority. This influx of settlers from Turkey has become problematic in the negotiations to maintain Cyprus under the Greek Cypriot majority rule. It certainly is a critical issue in face-to-face talks, with a growing tendency to compromise to reach a solution in regards to the Turkish settlers and ensuing land dispute. Of greater realism in the Cypriot public is the willingness to compromise on security arrangements, some form of demilitarization, bi-zonal federation, the settlers' controversy, and in good faith, the lifting of the economic embargo constricting the north since 1974. The continued stalemate and inability to reach a consensus on a plan brokered by the former secretary-general of the United Nations Kofi Annan will necessitate the emergence of a two-state solution. Despite the United Nations' efforts, the Greek Cypriot leadership is not amenable to political settlement, but grudgingly, under international pressure, may capitulate to a compromise and accommodation in the foreseeable future. The absence of a vision for the future, the need to take risks, and readiness for a peaceful coexistence, will tragically lead to dead-end outcomes and futile attempts to resolve the crisis.

Opportunity for a political settlement on Cyprus has been wasted over ethnic contest for domination at each other's expense. The intense disagreement stem from the following:

1. The inability to establish a trust as to security
2. Communal property in the north and south of the island abandoned as a result of the war in 1974
3. Inability to agree to coexist as politically equals
4. A workable arrangement as to a partnership in government
5. Provisions for equal economic opportunities
6. Consensus as to interests and values
7. Political freedom and rights
8. The establishment of a mechanism for the resolution of political and legal disputes
9. The permanent settlement of the majority of one hundred and sixty thousand Greek refugees in the south and sixty-five thousand Turkish Cypriots in the north

---

In the realm of security, each community guards it as a response to the tragedies in Cyprus from 1964 to 1974. The legitimacy of Turkish intervention in 1974 was viewed as falling within the purview of treaty obligation that was precipitated when the Greek Cypriot radicals resorted to arms for the Union of Cyprus with Greece (*enosis*). A strong case must be made to show promise of peaceful coexistence of the two ethnic communities on the island before the withdrawal of the major part of the Turkish troops to the mainland. Turkey will not withdraw its troops unilaterally before the resolution of long-festering Cyprus conflict unless a meaningful security is provided to the Turkish Cypriots.

The civil war on the island triggered the UN involvement and diplomatic efforts to bring about a cease-fire and negotiations to address the communal grievances with the hope of a settlement. The great challenge was to agree on the remedy acceptable for the emergence of consensus that defined and facilitated a Cypriot state. Since 1964, the UN peacekeeping has failed in transforming itself into peacemaking on Cyprus.

The ongoing property dispute must be linked to a comprehensive peace negotiation, and compromise as to territory is essential for peaceful coexistence. To reduce the tensions, an agreement must be translated into political, economic, and constitutional checks and balances. The improved security and trust will significantly facilitate a safer place for all Cypriots. The behavior of the protagonists is to persuade the international community as to their legitimacy with the expectation of perhaps to hasten the demise of the opponent. The goal is for a sustained political and economic growth while the opponent faces uncertainty as well as unresolved internal dispute and the challenge of unilateral decision to change the status quo. The claim of Northern Cyprus to an independent state is not recognized (expect by Turkey) by the international community and also it faces economic and political sanctions, which is designed to avoid the permanent partition in the promotion of reunification of the island. The isolation of Northern Cyprus is a collective international effort with the hope of promoting desirable outcomes to lay the foundation for the future of a federated Cyprus state.

A desirable arrangement is to maintain communal partnership and prioritize the demands that will be inconsistent with the overall goals of the radical nationalists. A meaningful partnership requires cooperation, consensus, commitment, respect for political rights and liberties, social, cultural, and religious tolerance and legitimacy are prerequisite to establish a viable state system or the alternative will be serious consequences. Both sides are to blame for missed opportunities that are due in part to so few face-to-face meetings that have been beneficial to the diplomatic efforts. More often than not, the talks have resulted in misperception, misunderstanding, misjudgment, which have only hardened preexisting attitudes as to the motives of the opponent. The opportunities to heal the wounds of the past and to unify and rebuild Cyprus have been squandered by the leaders of both communities. The continued political debacle would set back the prospect to tackle to common challenges and the opportunity at hand to come together have been missed. The political psychologist Vamik Volkan offers the opinion that

> the division of the island [is] an absolute reality in the minds of Turks, while this is an absolutely unacceptable for Greeks. However, I believe that if two culturally distinct groups are separated, especially after a long "togetherness" as is the case in Cyprus, it may be impossible for them to live together again. [80]

Vamik considers that the Cyprus solution has been achieved with the division of the island following the Turkish invasion in 1974. A viable option, as a result of the diplomatic failures, is to partition the island permanently, which has been since 1974.

The subject matter in this book remains of considerable controversy since 1964, which has polarized the two ethnic groups and contributed to the division of the island since 1974. The intention of this book is not sought to provide a comprehensive history or politics of Cyprus, but instead concentrates on events leading to the post Annan Plan. This book represents the proposition that the inability of community leaders to engage in serious negotiations, following the violent events of 1974, to reunite Cyprus diminishes the chances to win the "hearts and minds" of the new generation that has the potential to promote the permanent division of the island. Cultural and attitudinal differences that characterize the ethnic communities are contributing to alienation that has galvanized the argument to oppose unification. Diminishing efforts in consensus-building and "respectful give-and-take" is the prime cause in the failure to achieve desired political outcomes. The establishment of the Turkish Federated State of Cyprus in 1975, the formation of the Turkish Republic of Northern Cyprus on November 15, 1983, and the Unilateral Declaration of Independence reinforces the view that "the Turks have apparently lost interest in any settlement not based on partition." [81]

NOTES

CHAPTER 2

FAULT LINES IN THE UNITED NATIONS PEACE PLAN

> *The bane of philosophy is pomposity: people will*
> *not see that small things are the miniatures of*
> *greater, and it seems a loss of abstract dignity to*
> *freshen their minds by object-lessons from what*
> *they know.*
>
> —Walter Bagehot

The pros and cons of reunification of the island under the Annan Plan were intensely debated among the Greek and Turkish political hierarchy during 2003 and 2004. International efforts to reconcile political fault lines between the two Cypriot ethnic communities were widely seen as a mission that would both create a new political order on the island and accommodate conflicting interests and loyalties. However, great efforts to mold all the Cypriots into a cohesive political entity, which would then embrace common loyalties, failed to emerge. This failure is thought to be particularly a result of the national identities firmly established during thirty-six years of separation. Further, close ties maintained with the motherlands took on a new importance for many Greek and Turkish Cypriots during this period of separation. A new concept of citizenship that transcends ethnic, cultural, religious, and political divide never developed due to contentious troubles in Cyprus that blocked the realization of a common national identity. Between 1964 and 2004, a shift in loyalties promoted a sense of Greek and Turkish consciousness and subsequently retarded the development of "Cypriotism." As a consequence, the two communities existed under separate governments with quite distinct national identity and loyalty. Efforts, subsequently, to create a new political attitude had difficulty mustering sufficient ethnic endorsement without accommodating these communal interests.

The outcomes of the elections in Northern Cyprus, on December 14, 2003, provided that pro-unification parties resume the stalled peace talks and bring the status quo to an end. The left-wing Republican Turkish Party (RTP) of Mehmet Ali Talat won the elections. RTP acquired 35.18 percent of the votes with 19 seats in parliament, which dealt a resounding defeat for outgoing Prime Minister Dervis Eroglu's National Unity Party (NUP). Talat considered the election results a mandate for policy change and a renewed effort for the reunification of Cyprus.

Secretary-General Kofi Annan invited Greek and Turkish Cypriot leaders to New York on February 4, 2004, for emergency talks to negotiate an agreement to be submitted to an island-wide referendum on April 21. Annan ultimately hoped that Cyprus could join the European Union on May 1 as a reunited state. In 1995, Turkey accepted the start of European Union membership talks with the Republic of Cyprus in return for Greece's lifting of its objections to Turkey's customs union with the EU. Cyprus started accession negotiations with the EU in 1998 and joined it in the spring of 2004 with the exclusion of the Turkish Cypriots. The division of the island was not an obstacle of Cyprus's EU accession despite the arguments of Turkey that Cyprus's entry into the EU should be contingent on a political settlement on the island. Turkey, Greece, and the EU endorsed Kofi Annan's renewed efforts, and the U.S. urged both Cypriot leaders to seize the initiative and bring the long-running dispute to a positive conclusion. The Greek and Turkish newspapers in general were upbeat and optimistic about the outcome of the New York talks.

The New York talks began on February 10 at UN Headquarters. President Tassos Papadopoulos, Rauf Denktash, and the representatives of various party leaders attended the meetings. Annan stressed that without the ratification of the UN plan, negotiations could not proceed. The talks were to reconvene in Cyprus on February 19, with direct meetings between the two parties in the presence of the secretary-general's special advisor, Alvaro de Soto. The technical committees on laws and treaties were to reconvene on the same day. In the absence of an agreement, Greece and Turkey were to lend their collaboration in an effort to reach an agreement on a finalized text by March 29. President Papadopoulos came under EU and UN pressure to give evidence of its willingness to resume the process for a solution on the basis of the Annan plan. Both communities were committed to negotiation in good faith and wanted to reach a comprehensive settlement on the basis of the UN peace plan.

The UN-brokered talks resumed in Nicosia on February 19, and the negotiations were to continue until March 22, permitting both ethnic leaders to gain improvements for their respective sides. Before the first day's talks, a small bomb exploded in front of the Nicosia home of Turkish Cypriot Prime Minister Mehmet Ali Talat. After a second day of discussions, Denktash objected to the UN's request for a media blackout. Denktash's reasoning was that Turkish Cypriots had the right to be informed on the progress of a plan that would later become a referendum before them for a vote. The talks sparked unprecedented optimism among the Cypriots but also brought forth reservations about the sacrifices that might have to be made in order to reach a settlement.

The plan proposed a loose form of federation linking two largely autonomous regions. The Greek Cypriot leaders were also demanding from the Turkish National Assembly in Ankara for the ratification of the agreement after the referenda in Cyprus. The Turkish Grand National Assembly (TGNA) declared its readiness to give a positive response following the referendum by a majority vote in Northern Cyprus. A team of Swiss experts was to visit Cyprus in late February to advise the legal teams of the two sides on harmonizing the laws in areas of constitutional, administrative, economic, and public law.

As the Cyprus negotiations approached a critical stage, tensions between Erdogan and Denktash rose. Erdogan was critical of Denktash's insensitivity to the news blackout and continued detailed statements to the media. While Erdogan was drawing attention to the positive developments in the negotiations, Denktash was seemingly maintaining a negative approach. Denktash's obstructionism had essentially held the Turkish Cypriots hostage to a diplomatic impasse on the divided island and was obviously detrimental to Turkey's national interests. Erdogan's bold and constructive leadership wanted to settle the Cyprus crisis and clinch Turkey's long-stalled case for European Union membership. The Turkish armed forces endorsed Erdogan's policy agenda, but were supportive of Denktash's firm stand in the negotiations. The Cypriot leaders' proposals for changes to the UN Annan Plan were viewed by some as diverse and unyielding compromises. On February 28, Papadopoulos included the following proposals:

1. The territories vacated by the Turkish Cypriots would be placed under the supervision of the Security Council without any transition period (originally the plan called for a transitional period of 16 months).
2. Only those who cast ballots in the December 1963 elections and their children would be allowed to vote in the referendum.
3. Before the referendum, Ankara and Athens had to stipulate that they would accept the agreed plan.

Denktash insisted the following:

1. Bizonality must remain under the control of the two ethnic groups.
2. Based on Zurich-London Agreements in 1959, provisions should be made to protect the Turkish interests in Parliament, the High Court, and in other administrative areas.
3. People should be moved when rehabilitation programs can be put into effect.
4. The settlers from Turkey should have the right to vote at the referendum.

Denktash and Papadopoulos had their own agenda and were both set on achieving their political objectives, even at the expense of the other. The deadlock in negotiations compelled Washington to revive an aid package, discussed when President Ronald Reagan was in office, offering a $250 million grant for use in Cyprus's "peace and restructuring" process.[82] In Ankara on March 4, Denktash said that if his basic demands were not met in the Annan Plan, he would walk away from the negotiations and campaign against it in an April referendum.[83]

In Turkey, British Foreign Secretary Jack Straw's statement on March 3 was a warning to the Greek Cypriots who voted "no" in the Annan Plan referendum, as well as the Turkish Cypriots who voted "yes," that the southern part of Cyprus would be joining the EU, and the Republic of Cyprus would not represent the North and the Turks. A British foreign office spokesman said,

> The legal position remains clear. Cyprus' accession to the EU on May 1 is provided for by the Treaty of Accession, which was signed in Athens April 2003 and subsequently ratified by all EU Member States. In the absence of a settlement, a divided Cyprus will join the EU and the application of the Acquis would be suspended in the north.[84]

The New EU member's accession commits them to accept the entire acquis communautaire (the entire body of EU laws and policies) as their own, but waivers may be negotiated. Elizabeth Jones, U.S. assistant secretary for European and Eurasian affairs, testified on March 3 before the Subcommittee on Europe House International Relations Committee that by

> "March 22 Turkish and Greek Cypriots are to agree to the final text of an agreement" and should differences persist, "the

parties have agreed to allow the Secretary General to use his discretion to finalize the plan that will then be put to separate, simultaneous referenda on the island on April 21."[85]

Fileleftheros newspaper in Cyprus on March 7 reported that 62 percent of the Greek Cypriots would reply negatively to the referendum, while 24 percent would answer "yes." At the same time, 40.8 percent believed that the plan favored the Turkish Cypriots, 20.5 percent that it favored Turkey, while only 0.8 percent believed that it favored the Greek position. Furthermore, 31 percent considered security as the most important factor in the negotiations. The flag bearer in the Cyprus issues, George Papandreou's Pasok, was ousted after more than a decade in power in Athens on March 7, and Costas Karamanlis's New Democracy won in the general election by 46 to 40.5 percent.[86] Karamanlis stressed the continuity of normalization of relations with Turkey and the resolution of the Cyprus problem as facilitated by the UN. Before the national elections in Greece, George Papandreou supported the Annan Plan, whereas Karamanlis opposed it.

The peace talks on Cyprus displayed no signs for the resolution of the conflict or a significant commitment for the reunification of the island in a federation framework prior to its EU membership. The inability to bridge the differences between the two ethnic groups through the Annan Plan, and the tough negotiating posture of some participants, ruined chances of reunification of the island and resulted in a continuance of status quo. On March 17, Denktash decided not to attend the four-way meetings in Burgenstock, Switzerland, although other TRNC government officials planned to attend the talks. Greece and Turkey were to join the peace process from March 24 to 29 on the basis of the New York agreement from February 13. The enlarged Cyprus talks in Switzerland were attended by Karamanlis and Foreign Minister Petros Molyviatis, Erdogan and Gul, Mehmet Ali Talat and Serdar Denktash, and Tassos Papadopoulos. Prior to the new round of Cyprus talks, Greece and Turkey initiated discussions March 17 on security issues involving their respective roles and the reduction of troops on Cyprus. An initial meeting had been held in Ankara thirteen months before, but produced no breakthrough between Greece and Turkey as guarantor powers in Cyprus. Annan and De Soto joined the talks to finalize the UN plan, but in the event of a failure, the secretary-general would be empowered by the February 12 agreement (concluded in New York between Papadopoulos and Denktash) to fill in the gaps and put the plan to separate simultaneous referenda. During the high-level talks in Switzerland, Denktash launched his campaign to urge the Turkish Cypriots to vote against the Annan Plan. Erdogan and Gul were displeased with Denktash's decision not to participate and shocked by his insensitivity as to Turkish national interests. Denktash's scheme was to derail the peace talks without assessing the political consequences and backlash from Ankara. Denktash's persistence to chart a policy course unilaterally for Northern Cyprus provoked Erdogan and Gul to compel him to face the bitter realities in the management of Turkish foreign policy. Denktash's refusal to attend the talks in Switzerland was ultimately no loss, but an unexpected boon. A month of talks between Papadopoulos and Denktash concluded on March 22, but failed to forge a peace deal. The four-way talks, however, were expected to give more impetus to negotiations. The failure to bridge the gulf in the talks strengthened the opposition among the Greek Cypriots, and in spite of a public commitment to a settlement by Papadopoulos, the stalling tactics by his Democratic Party caused concern in Ankara and Athens.

The quadrilateral talks started on March 24, in Burgenstock, on the shores of Lake Lucerne, Switzerland, under UN auspices. Talat and Denktash's objective was to give the forty-seven-page text by the Greek Cypriots to the Turkish Cypriots, outlining terms for a settlement. Papadopoulos was given a nine-page document outlining the positions of the Turkish Cypriots for "strengthened bizonality" of the state and for permanent derogations from European Union rules and regulations, to be incorporated into the agreements, as well as a reduction in the number of Greek Cypriot refugees returning to Northern Cyprus. EU reaffirmed that the commission could not accept derogations of unlimited time from the acquis communautaire and incorporated these into an agreement for the reunification of Cyprus. The talks were also sidetracked due to a two-day EU summit in Brussels, Belgium, attended by Greece, Turkey, and the Greek Cypriot government. Furthermore, Papadopoulos refused to sit down with the Turkish Cypriot representatives.[87] The talks were held under a news blackout, but the Greek Cypriots had informed the media that the Turkish Cypriot proposals were merely a warmed-over repetition of their long-standing position, thus unacceptable. On March 26, the EU pledged to accommodate any peace settlement agreed upon by Cyprus before it joined the block on May 1, and in a draft statement, the EU said,

> The European Council reaffirms its strong preference for the accession of a united Cyprus to the EU and reiterates its readiness to accommodate the terms of such a settlement in line with the principles on which the EU is founded.[88]

Greece and Cyprus failed to gain the backing of EU for the Greek Cypriots' freedom of movement (explicitly extended to all areas of Cyprus) and to the right to own property. The Turkish Cypriots demanded restrictions on resettlement in Northern Cyprus, fearing that the wealthier and more populous Greek Cypriots could dominate them. The Greek Cypriot government wanted 180,000 of its community to have the right to return to Northern Cyprus.

On March 29, the fourth Annan Plan (over nine thousand pages including its addenda) was submitted to all parties. This plan established a fine balance between the vital criteria the Greek and Turkish Cypriots had submitted at the Cyprus negotiations and what is known as the *sine qua non* issues. The revised Annan plan on a comprehensive settlement in Cyprus included changes, additions, and alterations to his original plan. The plan included the following:

1. The Foundation Agreement
2. The Constitutions of the Greek Cypriot and Turkish Cypriot constituent states
3. The Treaty on matters related to the new state of affairs in Cyprus
4. The Draft Act of Adaptation of terms of accession of the United Cyprus Republic to the EU
5. The matters to be submitted to the UN Security Council for decisions
6. The measures to be taken during April 2004

The plan addressed territory reductions—the Turkish Cypriot territory was to decrease from 36 to 29 percent, and the Greek Cypriots were to settle in Rizokarpasso and Kokkina. The second alternative envisaged leaving the Turkish Cypriots with 24 percent of the territory and, in exchange, reducing the number of Greek Cypriots who would be allowed to settle in Northern Cyprus. Regarding the return of 180,000 Greek Cypriots to Northern Cyprus, the previous plan in February 2003 provided that they do not exceed 21 percent of the population in the Turkish constituent state. The new plan reduced this number to 18 percent (or 100,000 persons) in order to protect Turkish Cypriot homogeneity. The 45,000 Turkish settlers were to remain on the island and were to be recognized as citizens of Cyprus. Turkish troops were to be reduced from 35,000 to 6,000 by 2011, and Greece was also expected to reduce its troops' presence on Cyprus. The troops' numbers were to be reduced further by 2018 to 3,000 by both countries. Greek and Turkish contingents were to be stationed permanently on the island, even after Turkey's accession to the EU, in contrast to the previous Annan Plan, that provided for all troops to be withdrawn upon Turkey's accession. The provision was to be revised every five years and included the following:

1. It protected the security and identity of the Turkish Cypriot constituent state and the safety and dignity of its people.
2. The constituent states and the federal government were to exercise authority under the delegated and reserved powers.
3. The unified state will be vested in a co-presidency.
4. The federal government will be composed of a Council of Ministers of six members approved by the Senate and the Chamber of Deputies for a five-year term (three Greek and three Turkish Cypriots).
5. Presidents and vice presidents of the Chamber of Deputies and the Senate could not be elected from the same constituent state.
6. The executive power was to be executed by the presidential council, and for the first five years, a co-presidency of one Greek Cypriot and one Turkish Cypriot was to change posts every ten months.

During the second five-year period, a president and a vice president were to be elected and exercise their executive power for a twenty-month period. The first president would be elected by the Greek Cypriot community. The Senate was to be composed of forty-eight seats equally divided between the Greek and Turkish Cypriots, and the Greek Cypriot representatives were not to have the right to represent citizens in Northern Cyprus. The composition of the Chamber of Deputies was to be in proportion to persons holding internal constituent status, provided that each constituent state attributed no less than one quarter of the seats. The federal parliament could make decisions only with the approval of the Senate and Chamber of Deputies by simple majority. Presidents and vice presidents of the Chamber of Deputies and the Senate could be elected from the same constituent state. The central government, based on the Swiss model, gave unlimited authority to the alternating federal president in issues of foreign affairs, the banking system, taxes, immigration, shipping and fisheries, environmental issues, and other related matters. The Supreme Court would be comprised of an equal number of judges from each constituent state, and three non-Cypriot judges, until otherwise provided by law. The court was to uphold the constitution and enforce federal laws. Greece and Turkey were to continue to have effective and *de facto* guarantees on the island. Each constituent state was to have a separate government, a parliament, and courts. Cyprus was to have a new flag and national anthem. After examining the 204-page text, Annan asked the Greek and Turkish Cypriots for their reaction by the next day so that a final text could be formulated by March 31 and submitted to a referendum on April 24. Annan said that the text was an overall compromise for a comprehensive settlement and accommodated both community demands. He addressed Papadopoulos as follows:

The primary concern you have voiced has been to render the plan more functional and therefore more viable. I believe that this revised plan is significantly improved on this score, particularly in relation to the workings of the federal government, the updated transitional arrangements, the changes to the property scheme, the adjustments to ensure the financial soundness of the plan, and, of course, the completed laws and treaties.[89]

In addressing the Turkish Cypriot concerns, Annan said,

Mr. Talat and Mr. Denktash, your overarching theme has been the need to strengthen bizonality ... it covers the preservation of the security and identity of the Turkish Cypriot constituent state and the safety and dignity of its people. You will find the text has significantly improved in this regard, particularly if you examine the provisions on property, residency, and voting for the Federal State.[90]

After reactions of all concerned, the secretary-general Annan was to make an evaluation and further adjustments to the plan to accommodate the terms of the Cyprus settlement.

The revised Annan Plan, aiming at reunification of Cyprus before it acceded to the EU on May 1, did not satisfy the Greek Cypriot. The Turks received the new plan positively, but the acting head of the Holy Synod, the bishop of Paphos Chrysostomos, declared his opposition. The Bishop Pavlos of Kyrenia cautioned the Greek Cypriots that they would go to hell for supporting the Annan Plan.[91] Therefore, Papadopoulos failed to endorse the plan when he failed to convince Annan to incorporate the revisions proposed by the Greek Cypriots.[92] A frantic rush of diplomacy was unable to bring all parties to compromise for the greater good of the Cypriot people. Addressing the Greek and Turkish leaders, Annan said the following:

The choice is not between a settlement plan and some other magical, mythical solution. In reality, the choice is between this settlement and no settlement.... The process of negotiation is not a football match. It is not a question of keeping score of goals and own goals, of winners and losers. We have tried to accommodate the expressed concerns of both sides, so as to create a win-win situation ... my settlement plan offers the best and fairest chance of peace, prosperity and stability that is very likely to be an offer.[93]

The U.S., Great Britain, and the EU called on all Cypriots to seize the opportunity and implement the Annan Plan before it joined the EU on May 1. A written commitment was to be transmitted to Annan by Greeks and Turks by April 9.

Upon his return to Cyprus on April 1, Papadopoulos said that he was not going to sacrifice the rights of the Greek Cypriots in order to settle the Cyprus problem. After the government and the political leadership of the Greek Cypriots studied the UN proposals, Papadopoulos's stand on the Annan Plan was to be made public before the April 24 referendum. Greek Prime Minister Costas Karamanlis, in his address to parliament in Athens on April 2, said that his government continued to support the efforts of Cyprus President Tassos Papadopoulos for a viable and functional solution. Karamanlis was adamant that he would not impose a solution on the Greek Cypriots whose president had rejected the UN plan in Switzerland. Former Prime Minister Costas Simitis spoke in favor of the Annan Plan and cautioned the Greek Cypriots about the risks of a "no" on the April 24 referendum. On April 4, *Eleftherotypia* reported that the Pancyprian opinion poll conducted by VPRC declared that 84.7 percent of the Greek Cypriots and 61.7 percent of Greeks opposed the Annan Plan. It was a profound disappointment for the former president Glafkos Clerides, who supported the plan.[94] Erdogan, Gul, and Talat endorsed the plan and were ready to resolve the Cyprus deadlock once and for all. Denktash, who was at odds with Talat, stressed his opposition to the plan and considered it a "sellout." A survey by *Yeni Duzen* (a Turkish Cypriot daily) on April 1 put acceptance of the plan in Northern Cyprus at 59.5 percent. Talat campaigned for the Greek and Turkish Cypriot "yes" vote in favor of the UN plan.[95] On April 12, Denktash alleged that Erdogan had been "deceived" in Switzerland and he was "kowtowing to all of Greece's wishes just to get into the EU."[96] Erdogan refuted Denktash's contention by saying that the UN plan was not the best conceivable, but the optimal one, and one which could be agreed on.[97] TRNC Foreign Minister and Democrat Party (DP) leader Serdar Denktash endorsed his father's position and rejected the Annan Plan. Denktash, in his address to the Turkish parliament on April 15, harshly criticized the government, made disparaging remarks about the Annan Plan, prognosticated the union of Cyprus with Greece (*enosis*), and recommended that the plan referendum be rejected. Turkish armed forces' Chief of General Staff Hilmi Ozkok was reluctant to endorse Denktash's views and said, "If there is a reasonable solution, why would the army oppose it?"[98]

After a careful assessment of the Annan Plan, Turkey's leaders supported the implementation of the plan upon its approval on the April 24 referenda.

Cyprus President Tassos Papadopoulos wept in a televised address on April 7 and urged the Greek Cypriots to "say a resounding no" to the UN plan, saying that the consequences of voting for it were heavier and more onerous than rejecting it. Papadopoulos justified his "no" vote position by claiming that the Turkish Cypriot regime in Northern Cyprus could never be recognized by countries that "really count." The president said that the fifth and final Annan Plan contained improvements that "do not meet the minimum demands we had [already] submitted on the functionality of the plan as to the readiness to implement it the day after the referenda, [concerning] the substantive reunification of our country in the economic, public finance and monetary sectors." On the other hand, "the Turkish side submitted 11 demands that adversely affect the interests of Greek Cypriots and are all adopted in the final text of the Annan plan."[99]

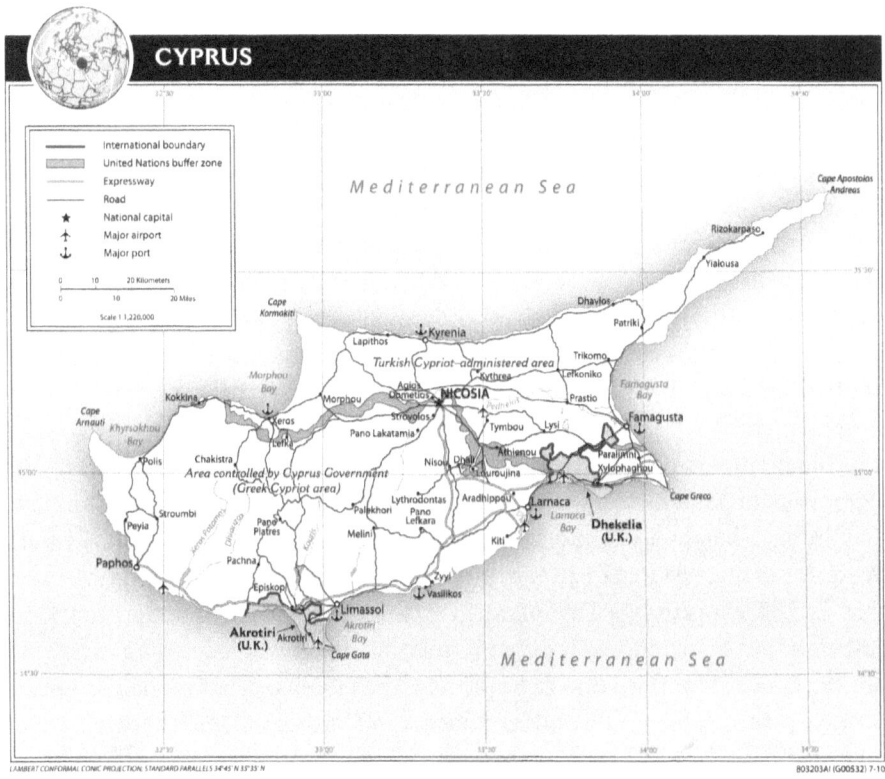

The Greek Cypriot Communist Party (AKEL) on April 10 asked the UN to postpone the April 24 referendum for a few months "in order to provide the possibility for objective presentation of the plan to the Cypriot people and for negotiations aiming at filling the gaps existing in the plan" or it "will be obliged to not support approval of the Annan Plan."[100]

The EU's Gunter Verheugen charged that the Greek Cypriot government "had taken him for a ride and [felt] personally cheated" by the President Papadopoulos. Verheugen said the following:

> We accepted at the request of the Greek Cypriots that the solution should not constitute a prerequisite for Cyprus' (EU) accession . . . but the Cypriot government had to do everything possible to find a solution to the conflict . . . the very least we could expect is a fair and balanced information campaign about the objective and the context of this plan.[101]

The EU officials were of the opinion that the Greek Cypriot public was being presented with biased information about the peace plan.[102] Papadopoulos refuted Verheugen's stinging rebuke and declared that he had never given any pledge to anybody. The UN decided to go ahead with the separate referenda on Cyprus on April 24, as scheduled, in which the Greek and Turkish Cypriot communities were to decide if they accepted Annan's plan of March 31 for a comprehensive settlement of the Cyprus settlement of the Cyprus issue. The preliminary predonors' conference in Brussels, on April 15, pledged financial assistance in the implementation of a Cyprus settlement plan, and the funds were to be made available to both ethnic groups on the island if both sides voted in favor of a UN settlement plan on the April 24 referenda. The U.S. pledged $400 million and the EU $385 million in aid to support the implementation of the UN plan.[103]

The members of the organization known as "Grey Wolves" terrorized the supporters of Annan Plan with death threats, and the bout between Denktash and Erdogan heightened the tensions among the Turkish Cypriots. U.S. Deputy Secretary of State Marc Grossman, in a conversation with Serdar Denktash, said that the U.S. expected the Democratic Party to contribute toward the process by casting a "yes" vote in the referendum, and the results would yield financial and political reward for the Turkish Cypriots if the Greek Cypriots failed to yield a positive result. The opinion polls conducted in Northern Cyprus showed a high rate of approval for the Annan Plan, despite the hard campaign of Denktash to defeat it, but opinion polls in the south suggested that 65 percent of Greek Cypriots would reject the plan.

The UN Security Council was given the report on Cyprus by Annan prior to the scheduled April 24 Cyprus referenda. He asked the council members to endorse the Foundation Agreement outlining the basic provisions of the settlement, which he had proposed to the parties. He also asked the council to "prohibit the supply of arms to Cyprus in a manner that is legally binding on both importers and exporters and on the operation of a new UN peacekeeping force on the island."[104] The fourteen members of the Security Council were in favor of Annan's request that the secretary-general's efforts and plan be passed before the referenda to provide assurances that security structures in the settlement would be in place before April 24.

Russia's deputy ambassador to the UN, Gennady Gatilov, said that Russia saw the U.S. and U.K. resolution on the matters of arms embargo and the operation of a renewed and strengthened UN operations as an attempt to influence the outcome of the twin referendums on Cyprus and vetoed it based on technical (not substantive) reasons. During the three-day visit of Erdogan to Russia, President Vladimir Putin, on January 11, 2005, told the press that Russia's veto of the resolution tabled by Britain and the United States was an effort to satisfy concerns over implementation of the plan. Putin said the following:

> The decision not to support the UN Security Council resolution was taken independently, bearing in mind that the acceptance of such a document on the eve of the referendum could have been interpreted by some critics as exerting pressure before the poll. . . . We voted against, after the Russian Foreign Ministry provided our Turkish colleagues with additional information. We did it deliberately, not to block the taking of this decision but to rule out any possible influence on the outcome of the referendum.[105]

Russia is an influential player in the Cyprus crisis, and it appears that with improved relations with Turkey, it will have leverage in prodding the Cypriots to strike a deal. Putin has stressed that Russia endorses Annan's effort regarding a Cyprus settlement, "including his plan to develop economic relations with Northern Cyprus, to remove the blockade that it has been in force there for many years."[106] Success in this regard would lend a tendency for the Greek Cypriots to engage constructively in a resolution of the disputes and abandon its embargo and trade sanctions on Northern Cyprus. These changes would dramatically improve the economic conditions in TRNC and force the adversaries to seek avenues for cooperation.

Annan, in a message to Cypriots on April 21, said that there is no magical way of accommodating the maximum demands of one side while at the same time accommodating the maximum demands of the other.[107] He urged them to approve the plan on April 24, and if either side on Cyprus rejected, the plan would be null and void, and his role as dealmaker would end.[108] The EU parliament in Strasbourg, in a resolution on April 21, called Cypriots to seize the historic opportunity to reunify Cyprus by accepting the Annan Plan.[109] The Greek-American lobby's last-ditch effort to derail the UN plan by pressuring President George Bush and U.S. State Department officials failed. One day before the referendum, about fifty thousand supporters of the Annan Plan gathered in the main square of the Turkish quarter urging a "yes" vote, and supporters and opponents of the plan rallied in the Greek Cypriot sector. In a final appeal to the Greek Cypriots to vote "yes," former pesident George Vassiliou and Glafcos Clerides said, "Cyprus will be isolated internationally and pay a heavy price for a 'no' vote."[110] Cyprus's government deployed intimidation and scare tactics by sending letters to 962 law enforcement officers and 3,500 civil servants that their job security and benefits were in jeopardy under the Annan Plan. Amnesty International, in its 2005 report covering the events from January to December 2004 on Cyprus, writes the following:

> During the pre-referendum period in the south, the government was accused of failing to show due diligence in carrying out its duty to protect the rights to freedom of expression, and there were allegations of attempts to intimidate individuals into rejecting the plan.[111]

The turnout among the Greek Cypriots was 428,587 (out of 480,557 eligible voters), and 143,636 Turkish Cypriots cast their votes in separate polling stations. The Greek Cypriots rejected the UN plan by 75.83 percent, which translates into 313,704 votes, and 24.17 percent or 99,976 persons cast a "yes" vote.[112] In contrast, 77,646 or 64.91 percent of Turkish Cypriots voted "yes," while 41,973 or 35.09 percent voted "no." Cyprus missed a historic opportunity to reunite the island after thirty years of division, and the island will continue to remain divided. The island's "Green Line" has effectively become a *de facto* EU border, a so-called "Taiwan solution," whereby TRNC is given everything short of full diplomatic recognition. Despite the Greek Cypriots' objections, EU officials in Brussels on April 25 considered ending economic sanctions on the Turkish Cypriots by removing tariffs on farm products and funds for infrastructure developments. On July 7, the EU Commission approved a decision lifting the commercial embargo imposed on the Turkish Cypriots and extended financial aid of 259 million euros, but EU Council endorsement was forthcoming.[113] For the economic development in Northern Cyprus, the U.S. earmarked $30.5 million in the fiscal year 2004.[114] As a result of the Turkish Cypriots' approval of the UN Plan, Turkey launched a vigorous campaign for the international community to lift the economic embargo on Turkish Cypriots. The Greek Cypriots' rejection of the plan was coming under a barrage of international condemnation, while the Turks were reaping political and financial benefits for their positive approach to the reunification of the island.

To ease the EU backlash for rejecting the UN plan, Papadopoulos stressed that his government would work for a bizonal, bicommunal federation, which is equitable and acceptable to the Greek Cypriots. In a speech at the Kennedy School of Government at Harvard University on June 2, Papadopoulos said that the Annan Plan was geared to satisfy Turkey's demands and "did not concern those areas where we felt that the compromises offered or imposed were simply not fair to us."[115] Annan, in his report to the UN Security Council on June 2, said that for the solution of the Cyprus problem, bold and determined political leadership was needed on both sides in order to compromise.[116] As for the future of his mission of good offices, Annan said, "I do not see any basis for resuming my good offices as long as this stand-off remains."[117] Annan also rejected the argument of Papadopoulos that Greek Cypriot concerns were ignored in the plan.[118] In the twenty-five-page report on Cyprus, Annan stressed that the international isolation of TRNC should be brought to an end and blamed Papadopoulos for the Greek Cypriots' rejection of the plan in the April referendum.[119] Annan's report to the Security Council asserted the following:

> The decision of the Turkish Cypriots [to vote in favor of the UN peace plan] is to be welcomed. The Turkish Cypriot leadership and Turkey have made clear their respect for the wish of the Turkish Cypriots to reunify in a bicommunal, bizonal federation. The Turkish Cypriot vote has undone any rationale for pressuring and isolating them. I would hope that the members of the Council can give a strong lead to all states to cooperate both bilaterally and in international bodies, to eliminate unnecessary restrictions and barriers that have the effect of isolating the Turkish Cypriot and impeding their development—not for the purpose of affording recognition or assisting recession, but as a positive contribution to the goal of reunification.[120]

Furthermore, the EU and the United States' promised direct financial assistance to the Turkish Cypriots was partially fulfilled due to Greek Cypriots resorting to diplomatic and legal obstruction of an aid package and trade with TRNC. Papadopoulos's aim was to block any direct aid to TRNC unless the disbursement of the money was channeled through the Republic of Cyprus.

Addressing a Greek gathering in New York on June 4, Papadopoulos said that he had no intention of bringing the Annan Plan in a new referendum to a vote because "this would be a heavy insult."[121] In a seven-page letter, with an annex of thirteen pages, Papadopoulos on June 7 responded to points raised in Annan's report, June 2, reaffirming the reasons why the Greek Cypriots could not accept the UN plan.[122] Papadopoulos was critical of Annan's special advisor Alvaro de Soto's role in the negotiations and charged that the UN plan had serious inaccuracies, fallacious assumptions, and erroneous interpretations. Papadopoulos said that he was "particularly offended" by Annan's "unfounded" remark that rejection of the UN plan amounted to rejection of a settlement. The Cyprus government was determined to lobby the Security Council to avoid adopting any resolution based on the UN report, claiming that it might undermine or weaken UN resolutions 541 and 550 adopted in 1983, which did not recognize TRNC. In a response to Papadopoulos's letter, Annan on June 17 responded by stressing "as you will have inferred from my report, I take a different view from you on most of the ground covered in your letter and its annex."[123]

The UN Security Council on June 11 extended the UN peacekeeping mission in Cyprus for six months[124] and asked the secretary-general to conduct a review as to the purposes of the force within three months. The resolution was adopted unanimously after a rancorous debate during which James Cunningham, the U.S. deputy ambassador, harshly criticized the Greek Cypriots for rejecting the UN plan on the April 24 referendum. Alternate U.S. representative in the UN for special political affairs, Stuart W. Holliday, said "that the rejection of the Secretary-General's settlement plan by the Greek Cypriot electorate raises fundamental questions regarding their commitment to a bizonal, bicommunal federal solution of the Cyprus problem."[125] The Security Council failed to reach consensus about adopting Annan's recommendations to end the Turkish Cypriots' economic isolation.

U.S. Secretary of State Colin Powell held a meeting on May 4 with the Prime Minister Mehmet Ali Talat of TRNC in Washington, D.C., during which the Turkish Cypriots were promised $311 million aid.[126] The Organization of Islamic Conference meeting in Istanbul on June 16 upgraded the status of the Turkish Cypriots with the organization as the "Turkish Cypriot State." At the 32nd OIC Foreign Ministers' Meeting at Sanaa, Yemen, on June 28, 2005, Serdar Denktash represented TRNC with a nameplate in front of him as "Turkish Cypriot State."[127] The bill also called on OIC members to establish direct communication, trade, tourism, investment, and sports ties with the TRNC. The OIC stressed that their decision was not *de jure* recognition of TRNC but to help Turkish Cypriots to overcome the inhumane isolation until the Cyprus problem is solved.

As "confidence-building measures," Papadopoulos's government proposals on July 16 included as follows:

1. The opening of eight additional crossing points along the ceasefire line
2. Disengagement of 2,000 soldiers from the walled part of Nicosia and from the wider Dherinia Famagusta and Strovilia areas
3. Demining of landmines by both sides inside the UN buffer zone
4. Curbs on war games and establishment of a 1.2 miles military-free area either side of the "Green Line"
5. Common operation of the Famagusta port by both communities and to cede Varosha to the Greek Cypriot administration[128]

Turkish Cypriot Prime Minister Mehmet Ali Talat dismissed the proposals and labeled them an attempt to deflect attention from the fact that Greeks had rejected the UN reunification plan. The Greek Cypriots' endeavor was to improve its sullied image and take out the sting of strong international criticism after an overwhelming rejection of the Annan Plan.

On July 30, the Cyprus government announced that it would allow the Turkish Cypriot vehicles to carry goods to the south and would exempt them from paying value-added tax (VAT) on goods sold directly to Greek Cypriot consumers.[129] The measure's intent was to avert direct trade or political interaction of the EU with the Turkish Cypriot north and derail the possibility of transcending the interaction to legitimating the *de jure* recognition of the divided island.[130] On August 23, the formal trade under the "Green Line Regulations" as adopted in July by the European Commission, between the two sides, resumed after thirty years of economic isolation, enabling the Turkish Cypriots to sell their goods produced in TRNC to EU countries, over the Greek Cypriot sector.[131] All goods from TRNC have to comply with EU standards on food safety and plant health, and all animal and agricultural products are excluded from the regulation as are goods originating from Turkey. In addition, Turkish Cypriot businessmen need a Greek Cypriot partner who will buy and sell their product in the south.[132] The move is politically symbolic to end the isolation of the north, because expectation of flourishing trade between the two ethnic groups across the Green Line remains an unrealistic hope.[133]

On September 28, 2004, two daily Greek Cypriot newspapers, *Fileleftheros* and *Alithia*, reported that Secretary-General Kofi Annan had assigned Deputy Undersecretary Kieran Prendergast to initiate a new resolve for the reunification of Cyprus. Denktash's reaction to the news was "if Annan undertakes new initiatives to revive the [UN] plan, he contradicts himself...and would necessitate holding a new referendum."[134] The Turkish foreign minister and deputy prime minister Abdullah Gul denied the reports that Annan was undertaking a new initiative on Cyprus, but he reiterated that the UN should lift the economic embargo on TRNC. In New York, Serdar Denktash stated that the UN should "take a specific decision regarding the international status of TRNC" and lift the provision in regard to the nonrecognition and the economic embargo of the Turkish Cypriot regime. Mr. Denktash also called on the UN to withdraw the UN peacekeeping forces on the island.[135] Based on the recommendation of the four-member UN team who spent a week on Cyprus for a fact-finding mission in August, the UN peacekeeping force was downsized by 30 percent (860 soldiers) as a result easing of tensions along the 110-mile ceasefire line and mobile units were to be deployed.[136] On October 22, the UN Security Council unanimously approved Resolution 1568 to cut back the UNICYP force on Cyprus.[137] The Greek Cypriots expressed their satisfaction with the resolution, but TRNC considered it unacceptable because it referred to the "government of Cyprus."[138] UNFICYP were to retain its original mandate, and Annan had no plans to send another envoy to carry on his "good offices" mission to reunify the island.[139]

The organization of the Islamic Conference (OIC) and EU Foreign Ministers Joint Forum, scheduled to be held on October 4 and 5 in Istanbul, was derailed due to the lobbying efforts of Greece and the Republic of Cyprus in Brussels. Turkey was persistent in having the TRNC represented as "The Turkish Cypriot State" (previously called "The Turkish Muslim Cypriot Society"), as described by the fifty-seven OIC members, which was rejected by the EU Term President of the Netherlands' Foreign Minister Bernard Bot. The international symposium entitled "Civilization, Harmony, and Values of Global Order" was to initiate a dialogue between the EU and the Muslim world as a response to the thesis of "a clash of civilizations"; but unfortunately, EU and OIC could not compromise over nameplates. On October 2, *Hurriyet* reported that Turkey had succumbed to EU pressures and accepted customs union with the Republic of Cyprus, but Turkish Foreign Minister Gul (to appease the critics) said that the decree "is not tantamount to recognition of the "Greek-Cypriot administration." Nevertheless, for Greeks, it was a dual diplomatic achievement conjured by Athens.

On October 11, the EU Council of Ministers, by a unanimous vote, approved what was agreed to in Brussels on September 29, in regard to 259 million euro as an annual financial assistance to the Cypriot Turks. A compromise was reached after EU accepted a series of amendments protecting Greek Cypriots' property in TRNC. Furthermore, the Parliamentary Assembly of the Council of Europe (PACE) in Strasbourg adopted a resolution on October 4 allowing Turkish Cypriot parliamentarians as representatives of Cypriot community, not TRNC, to participate in all its sessions[140] with the right to vote but not to participate in debates. The Cypriot Turks would have observer status in the General Assembly and would be permitted to explain their views.[141] The two Cypriot Turks, one associate member and one alternate member, would participate along with two Cypriot Greeks in PACE sessions and would be on the list of representatives of the Greek Cypriot parliamentary delegation.

On February 3, 2005, Cyprus and the European Commission agreed to broaden the transport of goods from the north to the south without the Turkish Cypriots paying VAT to the Cyprus government. All Turkish Cypriot imports were to come through Cyprus's government-controlled areas, with assent to raising the ceiling on purchases allowed by individuals from the north to south. Papadopoulos previously had refused to approve the direct trade regulation proposed by the commission. The European Commission draft declaration, released on December 7, 2005, explicitly modeled by the Greeks to decouple the 259-million-euro aid package that would have directed trade across the Green Line, agreed to the concession's demands on Varosha, directed trade through the Famagusta Port, and established a moratorium on the sale of Greek properties in TRNC. Releasing the impounded funds in return for the concessions not considered valid quid pro quo, it was quickly rejected by the Turks. The EU's designed proposal had unfavorable connotations for the Turks, revealing that the Greeks are an indispensable actor in all areas of policy-making.[142] The angry reaction of the Turks forced the EU to back down and shelve the declaration. This development suggested that the EU was not vested with the authorization to link the financial aid to specific concessions.[143] The European Commission intended to facilitate trade and economic links across the Green Line and to allow direct trade between the north and the EU.[144] To improve the political climate in the negotiations for a Cyprus settlement, Kofi Annan enforced the lifting of the economic and political embargo imposed on the Turkish Cypriots by the Cyprus government. The EU was supportive of the UN efforts and agreed to extend 259 million euros in financial assistance to the Turkish Cypriots—to spread from 2004 to 2006. In addition, the EU proposed freeing up trade between the north and south. Freeing up internal trade on Cyprus between the north and south would have lifted the air and maritime embargoes upon the north, and would have enabled direct commercial air and maritime traffic to enter ports and airports of the Turkish Cypriots. The Greek Cypriots were opposed to the simultaneous adoption of the aid package; neither the direct trade regulation nor the direct aid regulations were adopted. The money for 2006 (139 million euros), however, was adopted on February 27, 2006, by the EU Council. Nevertheless, the Cyprus government demanded that the direct trade regulation would require a unanimous vote in the council, rendering the prospect of the adoption of the regulation doubtful.[145]

On October 6, the thirty-person European Commission gave the green light for Turkey to commence EU accession talks, but not to set a date to start full membership negotiations.[146] Gul hailed the news as "a historic decision for Turkey and for Europe."[147] On December 17, the EU summit by a unanimous approval of the twenty-five heads of member states was to decide whether to start membership talks depending on Turkey's adoption of EU Commission's recommendations. In a September 2004 editorial, *The Economist* endorsed Turkey's final status negotiations on full accession to the EU and wrote, "a no to Turkey could have catastrophic consequences. If the EU were to turn its back on Turkey now, not only might Turkey's own reforms be under threat, but it would be widely interpreted in the Muslim world as a blow against all Islam."[148] A Turkish scholar writes the following:

> Failure to enter the EU could derail Turkey's transition from authoritarianism and abort the vital broader example it represents of a leading Muslim country's successful adoption of liberal democracy and advanced capitalism.[149]

The eighteen-page report envisaged three pillars and included a series of recommendations for monitoring and verifying the future performance of Turkey. The annual report of the commission included areas on economic development, human and minority rights, political and judicial reforms,[150] civil-military relations, corruption, torture, freedom of speech and religion, gender equality, child labor, and regional disparities. The report had many reservations and concerns, including the following:

1. Turkey's accession would be different from previous enlargements because of the combined impact of Turkey's population, size, geographical location, economic, security and military potential.[151]

2. With over three million, Turks constitute by far the largest group of third-country nationals legally residing in today's EU . . . a permanent

safeguard clause can be considered to avoid a serious disturbances on the EU labour market.[152]

3. The Commission will recommend the suspension of negotiations in the case of a serious and persistent breach of the principles of liberty, democracy, respect for human rights and fundamental freedoms and the rule of law on which the Union is founded.[153]

4. There is a clear need to strengthen the dialogue on a number of issues ... where concerns and perceptions can be discussed in a frank and open manner. This includes a dialogue on difference of cultures, religion, issues relating to migration, concerns on minority rights and terrorism.[154]

5. The EU will need to define its financial perspective for the period from 2014 before negotiations can be concluded.[155]

6. On civil-military relations, the government has increasingly asserted its control over the military ... the armed forces in Turkey continue to exercise influence through a series of informal mechanisms.... Civilian control over the military needs to be asserted.[156]

7. On Cyprus, over the last year Turkey has supported and continues to support the efforts of the UN Secretary General to achieve a comprehensive settlement of the Cyprus problem.[157]

Turkey is expected to be an EU member in the next ten to fifteen years, providing that it overcomes all the hurdles. European Union Agriculture Commissioner Franz Fischler, an Austrian, in a nine-page letter to the twenty-nine other members of the commission, criticized the EU's approach to possible Turkish membership. He wrote, "There remain doubts as to Turkey's long-term secular and democratic credentials," noting that secularism might not last, and that Turkish EU membership could cost 11.3 billion Eurodollars a year in agricultural subsidies.[158] EU's competition commissioner Frits Bolkestein, who is Dutch, warned that Turkish accession could lead to an "Islamisation" of Europe and could make the EU "implode."[159] Panhellenic Socialist Movement (PASOK) President George Papandreou in an article in the Belgian daily *La Libre Belgique*, on October 8, wrote the following:

Denying Turkey a European future based on religious reasons

would be tantamount to denying the EU's diversity. Democracy is a worldwide value and under no circumstances does it belong only to certain religions. Accepting a country that shares our democratic values and human rights, regardless of nationality or religion, is a positive indication towards the Muslim world and will relieve the increasing tensions between Christianity and Islam, which are being fuelled by international terrorism and nationalism.[160]

Samuel P. Huntington, who considers the Greeks as anti-Turkish and "spear-carriers of Christianity," was supportive of Turkey joining the EU.[161] On October 20, German Foreign Minister Joschka Fischer, in regard to Turkish entry to the EU, said, "To modernize an Islamic country based on the shared values of Europe would be almost a D-Day for Europe in the war against terror."[162]

"The future of the European Union as a peaceful community is at stake," said Hans-Gert Pottering, a conservative German affiliated with the European People's Party, who opposes Turkish membership.[163] On November 10, Former German Chancellor Helmut Kohl alleged that EU leaders were deceiving Ankara with the promise of EU membership. Kohl said that he was in "favor of special partnership with Turkey, because this is the most rational way."[164] French President Jacques Chirac declared that such a momentous decision could only be decided by a popular referendum in his country on Turkey's full EU membership. EU public opinion continues to have serious reservations and an unfavorable posture toward Turkey's membership, which could doom Turkey's application. Despite Turkey's objections, EU states are determined to impose requirements on Turkey that did not apply to other EU candidates.

Following the resignation of Prime Minister Mehmet Ali Talat of TRNC on October 20, Denktash two days later asked Dervis Eroglu, leader of the National Unity Party (UBP), to form a new government. Talat's Republican Turkish Party (CTP)–Democratic Party (DP) coalition government was paralyzed after losing its slim parliamentary majority in April. The UBP was the majority party in parliament with nineteen deputies, but Eroglu failed to form a government within fifteen days, and Talat did not take the initiative to form a coalition government. Under the TRNC Constitution, early elections can be called either by parliament or the president within sixty days.[165] Eroglu had to garner the support of twenty-six deputies in order to form a coalition government. Talat's resignation was due to his failure to table the budget bill in the National Assembly controlled by the twenty-seven opposition members who were determined to kill the budget bill when put to a vote in parliament.[166] On October 21, *Afrika* wrote that TRNC had "gone through 18 governments in 30 years. . . . The only one who has not gotten up from his seat is Denktash." An editorial, Istanbul *Radikal* newspaper, on October 22, alleged that Denktash, whose term was to end in April 2005, conspired the resignation of Talat so that Eroglu could succeed to the presidency while Serdat Denktash would become prime minister. Talat resigned to force new elections that would give his party the majority of parliamentary seats and reinstall him as prime minister. A strong support for Talat, at the polls, would strengthen his candidacy for the presidency. Eroglu's failure to form a coalition government forced him to relinquish the task on November 1, and Denktash gave the task to Talat on November 8.[167] After failing to form a new coalition government, Talat, on November 22, returned his mandate to Denktash, which boosted the possibility for early elections.[168] Early elections were held as determined after a month under the constitutional guidelines. The political crisis in TRNC further complicated Turkey's EU prospects on December 17.[169] Papadopoulos threatened the right to veto Turkey's request to get a date to start accession negotiations with the EU, if it did not recognize the Republic of Cyprus and pull its forces from the island.[170]

Not surprisingly, in an interview with Greek Cypriot daily *Fileleftheros* on November 1, Talat said that he was ready to discuss certain changes and additions to the Annan Plan, but Ankara was disturbed by the announcement.[171] To fully grasp the enormity of the task at hand, one must appreciate the controversy over land, security, and trust, with neither side willing to capitulate or take risks. In a statement on November 2 in Ankara, General Ilker Basbug, deputy chief of the general staff, argued that there were "two peoples" on Cyprus and that one did not have the authority to represent the other.[172] Open involvement and excessive influence of the generals in politics will not improve Turkey's image in the West, and the Turkish leaders yearning to start accession negotiations with EU on December 17 may be impeded.

At a state dinner given in honor of Greek Prime Minister Kostas Karamanlis, who was in Cyprus for a two-day visit on November 12, Papadopoulos's speech focused on Turkey's EU accession and Ankara's recognition of Cyprus as a condition for him not to exercise the veto.

> Part of this obligation is the recognition of the Republic of Cyprus, the withdrawal of the occupation troops and settlers, the end of the organized new wave of settlers, avoiding hostile actions against Cyprus, like the obstruction of the participation of the Republic in international organizations and international treaties . . . we have sent a message to the government of our

neighboring country that we are ready for a dialogue to explain our positions.[173]

Papadopoulos's move was a direct negotiation invitation to Turkey, whose administration Ankara does not recognize. Papadopoulos sketched the design with the basic purpose of compelling Turkey to deliver a list of political demands or be subjected to a veto in its EU accession mission.[174] Even a dedicated friend of the Greek Cypriots was a strong critic of Papadopoulos's course of action. Former prime minister of Greece Constantinos Mitsotakis, during a television interview in Athens on November 10, accused President Papadopoulos of leading Cyprus to complete isolation from the international community and following a dead-end stance.[175] Mitsotakis seemed to stress that Papadopoulos's policy would damage the Greco-Turkish convergence of interests cultivated in the last five years. Papadopoulos had openly blackmailed EU and Turkey before reasonable options were exhausted and launched a campaign that was unproductive. Given the carefully crafted dramatic changes between Greece and Turkey, Athens applied variable pressures on Papadopoulos to engage in negotiations more moderate in their terms and based on persuasion rather than coercion. The stakes were high, and it would have been a grave mistake to end a growing convergence of interests benefiting Greco-Turkish relations.

In the intensive search for a level of economic and political integration in Cyprus, sacrifices must be made by all participants for the common good, or expected results are extremely unlikely to be realized and will yield only disappointment. Political policies in the future should not be based on ethnic interests, but rights-based interests that will enhance common ground in a new partnership. Both community leaders have failed to secure a higher level of trust, which is essential in a political partnership in shared governance. The failure to overcome the cultural, political, psychological chasm will not bring the Cypriots to a realistic appraisal of the opportunity offered in terms of the beneficial outcomes to contending parties.

The draft report prepared by Dutch member of the European Parliament Camiel Eurlings on Turkey's accession negotiations to be opened was approved by the European Parliament Committee on Foreign Affairs on November 29 by 50 votes to 18, with 6 abstentions. An amended report said a December 16–17 summit should "open the negotiations with Turkey without undue delay" if conditions are met.[176] The following are selected recommendations of the commission:

1. The Commission will recommend the suspension of negotiations to the Council, who will decide by a qualified majority, in the event of a serious

and persistent breach of the principles of liberty, democracy, respect for human rights and fundamental freedoms, and the rule of law.

2.   The new Penal Code and the Law on Intermediate Courts of Appeal have not yet entered into force, while the decision on the Code of Criminal Procedure, the legislation establishing the juridical police and the law on execution of punishments and measures are still to be adopted.

3.   The Turkish authorities are still discriminating against religious minorities and protecting the Alevites as a Muslim minority.

4.   The Greek Orthodox Halki seminary has not been reopened.

5.   The border between Turkey and Armenia has still not been reopened. Calls on Turkey and Armenia to start a process of reconciliation.[177]

6.   The international community remains concerned about the non-recognition by Turkey of the Republic of Cyprus and the fact that more than 30,000 Turkish troops are stationed in Northern Cyprus.

7.   The Turkish government is to limit the political power of the army.

8.   Turkey needs to resolve outstanding legal issues with EU Member States, including legal recognition and a settlement of common interests.

9.   Specific arrangements in areas such as structural policies and agriculture and permanent safeguards for the free movement of workers in the accession agreement should not have a negative impact on Turkey's efforts to align with the acquis.[178]

The National Security Council at its meeting in Ankara on November 30 said, "There are things that need to be done in the short term before recognition [of Cyprus]."[179] Erdogan was critical of the document, which tacitly demanded the recognition of Cyprus. He said, "We have done our best in order to find a solution on the island. The Greek Cypriots, however, declined to sit down at the negotiating table. It is now their turn to take a step."[180] The draft had gone beyond the executive European Commission's recommendation issued on October 6 and gave one-third of EU member states the right to seek a suspension of the talks if Ankara failed to honor the expected reforms.

The draft did not address the alternatives to membership sought by Austria and France, but imposed permanent restrictions on free movement of Turkish labor. Austrian Chancellor Wolfgang Schuessel and Vice Chancellor Hubert Gorbach, and Valery Giscard de'Estang of France, proposed to offer Turkey "privileged partnership" and "strengthened cooperation" as an alternative to full EU membership. It was rejected by the Foreign Affairs Committee. Turkey, along with Great Britain, has rejected any special conditions that did not apply to previous EU candidates.

A total of 483 riders were submitted for changes in the draft; many of them concerned the Cyprus issue, the Greco-Turkish Aegean disputes, the Copenhagen Criteria, human rights issues, social issues, economic policy, recognizing the Armenian genocide, minority rights, and political reforms.[181] The report was voted on by the European Parliament plenary session in Strasburg on December 13 before it was forwarded to the EU Summit in Brussels on December 16 and 17.

To respond to concerns raised by the Committee on Foreign Affairs, Turkey embarked on a review process to mitigate the potential harm to its EU accession process. A top-level meeting was called by President Sezer on December 3 in Ankara. Denktash and Talat were in attendance to discuss the recognition of Cyprus by Turkey before the December 17 EU summit. The president of the European Parliament, Josep Borrell, in his address that same day to the Turkish parliament, said the following:

> The very process of opening negotiations between the 25 member states and Turkey implies recognition of Cyprus. It is not possible to negotiate with someone that you don't recognize. I would suggest both to you and to the authorities in Nicosia that if the opening negotiations in itself means recognition of Cyprus and Turkey, then, perhaps, there may be less of a political problem for both governments.[182]

During his press conference in Istanbul on December 6, Borrell said that the recognition of Cyprus "is not a new condition set by the EU on Turkey, but something mandated by logic, given that when negotiations take place, there must be recognition of the other side."[183] Greek Cypriot Prime Minister of Foreign Affairs George Iacovou in a speech before the 12th meeting of the Organization for Security and Cooperation in Europe (OSCE) Ministerial Council in Sofia, Bulgaria, on December 7, said, "We are convinced that a process of normalization will engender further positive developments for all concerned."[184] Turkey agreed to custom union (Ankara Agreement) with all the

EU members, including Cyprus, but all exports to Greek Cypriot administration will be noted as "Cyprus" rather than the "Republic of Cyprus."[185] Washington endorsed Turkey's EU accession negotiations without the need for Ankara to recognize Cyprus, which was not part of the Copenhagen criteria.[186]

The second draft report of the European Commission on Turkey, on December 2, spelled out the benchmarks that Ankara had to meet to start the membership negotiations on December 17. The Commission did not propose a date for opening accession negotiations, but addressed the following:

1. The international community's concerns as to the non-recognition by Turkey of the Republic of Cyprus and the presence of 30,000 Turkish troops in Northern Cyprus.
2. Turkey should resolve any outstanding disputes with neighboring states in accordance with the UN Charter and relevant Treaties.[187]

Ankara's major objections were as follows:

1. Recognition of the Greek Cypriot Administration on Cyprus.
2. Austrian, Denmark, and France's "privileged partnership" proposal.
3. Greece's demand for settling the Aegean Sea issue at the EU Court of Justice at The Hague.

The Turkish press considered the second draft of conclusions more negative in comparison to the first draft. The Turks were outraged by all the requirements stipulated in the final draft; specifically, the recognition of Cyprus was a repugnant prospect as a precondition to gain entry to the EU. Turkey was engaged in a battle of wits not only with the Greeks but also with the maneuver of the coalition of opponents intending to derail the negotiations.[188]

On December 15, the European Parliament, by 407 votes to 262 with 29 abstentions, backed Turkey's bid to open accession with the EU. The nonbinding resolution reflected the views of the EP prior to the EU-Brussels summit, which no doubt influenced the twenty-five heads of government in their final decision on December 17. The EP resolution also recommended initiatives in the following areas:

1. Free movement must not disadvantage Turkey
2. Resolution of the Greco-Cyprus crisis by Ankara
3. The opening of the Greek Orthodox theological seminary on Heybeli Island

4. Alawi faith to be recognized by Ankara
5. Armenian border to be opened
6. The acknowledgement by Turkey of the Armenian Genocide

However, the EP rejected the "privileged partnership" proposal. The Cyprus issue was removed from the text and placed in the appendix." The EU would meet with pleasure Turkey's acceptance of signing the protocol, which would expand the Ankara Agreement in a manner that would also include the new members of the EU.[189] Ankara neither committed itself nor rejected signing of the protocol, but Papadopoulos threatened to veto Turkey's membership if Cyprus's government was not recognized as the legitimate authority over the whole island. Erdogan and Gul refused to cross the "red line" but were in agreement with a negotiated settlement on the Cyprus crisis.[190] The Economist wrote, "The Cypriot government, already in bad odour because it encouraged the Greek-Cypriot rejection of the UN's unification plan in April, will come under huge pressure not to cast its veto now."[191] Papadopoulos took a gamble, and his failure in diplomatic arm-wrestling with Turkey made him the obstacle to a settlement regarding Cyprus.

Intensive diplomatic haggle started in Brussels on December 16 between the EU and Turkey over the Cyprus issue. EU required Turkey to initial a new protocol to the 1963 Ankara Agreement with the ten newest member states and offered Ankara, October 3, 2005, to begin its accession talks with no guarantee of membership. The new political conditions greatly disturbed Erdogan, and there were speculations that the Turks were ready to walk out. After hours of wrangling between Erdogan and Dutch Prime Minister Jan Peter Balkenende, holder of the EU presidency, Turkey verbally pledged unilaterally to sign a protocol, extending the Ankara Agreement to the ten new members, including Cyprus, prior to the actual start of the accession negotiations. The draft approved by the European Council includes the following:

> The Turkish government confirms that it is ready to sign the protocol on the adaptation of the Ankara Agreement prior to the actual start of the accession negotiations and after reaching agreement on and finalizing the adaptations, which are necessary in view of the current membership of the Union.[192]

The final text took into account the special situation on the divided island, and it was not designed to facilitate the *de facto* recognition of Cyprus. British Foreign Secretary Jack Straw played down the political significance of Ankara protocol and said, "It does not involve formal or informal recognition of the government about that."[193] President Papadopoulos, in a meeting with the press in Nicosia on June 22, 2005, said that Turkey, by signing the protocol to the customs union, would not signify the recognition of the Republic of Cyprus.[194] The compromise formula as a condition for opening EU membership talks would grant effective *de facto* recognition of the Greek Cypriot–led government, and it could take ten to fifteen years for Turkey to join the EU. Straw expressed the view that signing the protocol was not a binding legal acknowledgment of the Cypriot government under international law.[195] British Prime Minister Tony Blair called it an "historic event" and said the following:

> It shows that those who believe there is a fundamental clash of civilizations between Christians and Muslims are actually wrong, that they can work together, that we can cooperate together. And I think that is of fundamental importance for the future of peace and prosperity.[196]

Turkey's EU membership is widely opposed in Austria and France, and both countries intend to put the issue to the voters in a referendum. Papadopoulos had not ruled out using a veto to block Turkey's entry into the EU on October 3 unless his administration was recognized as the legitimate government of Cyprus.[197] On March 30, 2005, Turkey marked its agreement on the draft text of the protocol prepared by the European Commission, but anything that constitutes recognition of the Republic of Cyprus will be rejected by the Turkish parliament and will set in motion the grounds to overthrow the government. On June 13, the EU approved the agreement expanding the customs union with Turkey to the ten new EU members, and Ankara signed it on July 29, which opened the membership talks on October 3.

The Brussels results did not measure up to the Greek Cypriot expectations, and Papadopoulos came under a strong criticism for not using the veto against Turkey.[198] On the other hand, Denktash was outraged that Erdogan had compromised the future of TRNC by capitulating to EU demands to strike a deal rather than strengthening the forces to block Turkey's European accession prospects.

Denktash and his son, Serdar, in eagerness to strike back, asserted that if Turkey were to abandon the Turkish Cypriots, "they will engage in armed resistance similar to the PLO." The thrust of Denktash's message was to secure the aid of the military to attach conditions to negotiations and unequivocal assurance that Erdogan, in embracing a settlement, will not forsake TRNC's independence and sovereignty.[199] In an editorial in *Cumhuriyet*, on December 20, Professor Mumtaz Sosyal, Denktash's henchman, was harshly critical of Erdogan and readily embraced an appeal to the patriotic feeling of the military to "speak out loudly" and to intervene. It is hard to imagine that Turkish armed forces would find virtues worthy to be propelled to take an active part in such a preposterous idea. Talat, detesting Denktash's policies, on December 28 expressed the view that "the TRNC's independence was a dream, and the struggle had failed."[200] The next day, he alleged that he was misquoted: "I did not say that the independence of TRNC was a dream, but I said that recognition of TRNC as an independent and sovereign state was dream."[201] He knew that the future of TRNC depended absolutely on an intimate attachment with Turkey and wanted to keep the channels of negotiations and initiatives open. Talat realized that cold-shouldering Erdogan would be an act of humiliation. He had no wish to be drawn into a confrontation but was prepared to submit with a combined effort to negotiations.

In an interview with *Imericia* (Athens) on December 25, Papadopoulos laid down four points as preconditions for the resumption of a new attempt at negotiations.

1. No time limit linking a settlement before the opening of the EU-Turkey entry talks on October 3, 2005.
2. Annan should not be an arbitrator or fill in the blanks during talks.
3. No imposed settlement on a "yes" or "no" basis.
4. No new referendum, unless the two sides reach a settlement and this is then put for approval before the people.[202]

The Greek Cypriot leaders were also reconsidering Annan 3 Plan (March 2003) with substantial changes before its approval by a referendum.[203]

Because of the absence of a dialogue on the Cyprus settlement, Erdogan's Justice and Development Party (AKP) decided to invite DISY leader Nicos Anastassiades to Ankara for exploratory talks on the resumption of negotiations with Cyprus.[204] President Papadopoulos was not enthusiastic about DISY's travel to Ankara and objected to Anastassiades probing the Cyprus issue with Erdogan. On the eve of his arrival to Ankara on February 9, Anastassiades, in an interview with *Milliyet*, suggested that Turkey should withdraw some of its troops from Cyprus as a good gesture. Gul described the remarks as "ugly and inappropriate," believing they could dampen the expectations in the pursuit of dialogue to return to the bargaining table.[205] Perhaps anticipating the possibility of sharp differences on issues, Anastassiades passionately targeted the presence of the Turkish military on Cyprus—a topic attuned to Greek Cypriot primary demands and linked to collective grievances. The political debate probed questions such as the following:

Territorial adjustments, the abolition of intervention rights in Cyprus, full demilitarization of the island, the return of Varosha to the Greek Cypriots, the resolution of the missing persons, lifting movements' restrictions, and the withdrawal of the Turkish troops and settlers from the island.[206]

> Anastassiades's trip to Turkey failed to transcend the twin ethnic nationalism generated by the political leaders, but the dialogue is indicative of a desire for a settlement. During their meeting on February 13, Erdogan extended his invitation to President Papadopoulos "to sit down face to face . . . and solve the Cyprus problem" through Anastassiades.[207] On June 13, Erdogan rejected the invitation of Anastasiadis to visit Southern Cyprus because accepting might have been misconstrued as the recognition of the Greek Cypriot administration.[208]

A collective effort is needed to redefine the mission, to embrace the promotion of reconciliation, to give way to fostering community outreach, and to explore ways of strengthening and facilitating the process of transition from hostility to peaceful coexistence, which is essential for a political settlement. The failure to replace obsolete political attitudes will prevent decision-makers from embracing and implementing plausible alternatives necessary for political transformation. There is a growing anxiety among the Cypriots that the continued stalemate has metamorphosed into *de facto* partition of Cyprus. It is time for the Cypriots to forge a genuine partnership and learn to live together as coequals.

In a speech on January 12, Papadopoulos said that he was committed to the preservation of the Cyprus Republic, as established under the Zurich-London Agreements of 1960, "even though he had been vehemently opposed to the agreements at the time."[209] Papadopoulos, on March 21, told a group of students from Athens, at the Presidential Palace in Nicosia, that he "will not accept arbitration from the UN," neither would he accept any time constraints for any new talks, nor would he outline the changes desired in the Annan Plan before any negotiations.[210] Any hope of a settlement under the Annan Plan during his term of office was shattered. Papadopoulos's vacillating political stance and nuance strongly suggested that he was neither committed to playing an important role in facilitating and agreement, nor was there clear evidence of preconditions to negotiate an agreement. Papadopoulos was an ideologue with deep personal convictions about the justness of the Greek cause, with a tendency of indifference to commitments initiated by his predecessors. His behavior since coming to power did not suggest that he was interested in a compromise mutually agreed upon, or straightforward with a plausible alternative to achieve a just outcome for both sides. The passion with which he was driven ignored the somber realities of divergent ethnic, cultural, religious, and national interests; the result increased the permanency of a divided island.[211]

A delegation of twelve American businessmen, accompanied by the commercial attaché of the U.S. embassy in Ankara, visited TRNC on February 17. The U.S. State Department spokesman Richard Boucher described the visit as follows: "This delegation is consistent with our goal of easing the economic isolation of the Turkish Cypriots by expanding business contacts on and off the island."[212] U.S. Secretary of State Condoleezza Rice, during her trip to Turkey, said that the isolation of the Turkish Cypriots must be eased because of the failure to reunify the island prior to Cyprus's EU accession. Papadopoulos condemned the U.S. business delegation visit to TRNC and stressed that it would have a negative effect on Cyprus-U.S. relations. The visit emphasizes mounting frustration among the international community, whose pursuit is to break down barriers that limit trade and tourism to TRNC.[213] Hoping to capitalize on the urgency to end the economic isolation of TRNC and to overcome the continued Greek Cypriot entrenched opposition to the Annan Plan, U.S. Congressman Edward Whitfield (R-KY), accompanied by an eleven-member delegation, including two other members of the U.S. Congress, Nathan Deal (R-GA) and Eddie Bernice Johnson (D-TX), flew from Istanbul directly to Ercan airport in Northern Cyprus on May 30, 2005, despite Greek-American community protest and lobbying. Still, this hardly meant that the United States was ready to recognize the legitimacy of TRNC, but it was a calculated effort by the State Department to overcome the Greek Cypriot foot-dragging for a negotiated settlement. Papadopoulos's intention of achieving unilateral advantage was evident by his refusal to negotiate further, and the divided island continued to mar any efforts for a comprehensive settlement. His disingenuous assurances about the reunification of Cyprus failed to yield significant results and his intentions were open to question by the international community.[214]

Fifty-three Turkish Cypriot companies participated in the 30th Cyprus International Fair held in the south from May 20 to 29. The Green Line Regulations approved the Turkish products that appeared at the fair—an opportunity for TRNC to introduce goods to potential consumers abroad and to the Greek Cypriots.[215] Despite Papadopoulos's nationalistic policy, international effort would facilitate a coordinated planning to grasp the complicated political conditions, to accommodate the economic needs and isolation of the Turkish Cypriots. On June 30, 2005, Azerbaijan declared that it would accept Turkish Cypriot passports, which gives TRNC a degree of diplomatic recognition. Azerbaijani President Ilham Aliyev said that his country would work to end the international isolation of TRNC and plans to start direct charter flights and business investment in Northern Cyprus.[216] On July 17, 2005, eight Azerbaijani parliamentarians attended the Peace Operation's 31st Anniversary Celebrations in TRNC.[217] The first commercial passenger aircraft flew from Baku to Ercan airport in TRNC on July 27, bringing a delegation of eighty-two Azerbaijani businessmen, journalists, and artists for a four-day visit, and on August 29, a delegation led by Rauf Denktash flew to Baku from TRNC, defying an international embargo. Azerbaijani declared that its policy was to end the economic isolation of TRNC, and it was not an extension of diplomatic recognition.[218] Reliance on nationalists' mind-set will not facilitate a climate of trust, but will reinforce suspicions of Greek motivations and increase Turkish incentives of continued self-reliance.

Ethnic political turmoil manifests itself in self-gratifying patriotic slogans accompanied by self-righteous arrogance by ignoring and distorting the reality of economic disparities, social injustice, domination, hostility, and fear-mongering, instead of focusing on shared convictions to promote an enduring common interest that entails a balance of benefits and responsibilities. Professor Corey Robin, in his book *Fear: The History of a Political Idea,* writes that "it is freedom and equality that inspire us to oppose political fear, and it is freedom and equality that underwrite our struggle against it. . . . Fear is an obstacle and a stumbling block, but it is not, and cannot be, a foundation for politics."[219] Responsible leadership calls for a conscious effort with a realistic vision to overcome the complexities and choice facing two ethnic groups. Communities working together will transcend parochial concerns and narrow interests by articulating a common vision. EU members of the south have lured over thirty thousand Turkish Cypriots to apply for Greek Cypriot passports in order to have access to job opportunities and studies in Europe, which has given false expectations to the Greek Cypriots that, "in the long run, the island will be reunited not under a careful UN plan, but through effective Greek domination."[220] Adriaan Van der Meer, the head of the EU delegation in Cyprus, said that the EU's priority was a Cyprus settlement under UN auspices. Another European diplomat said the following:

> The government [Republic of Cyprus] is very effectively spinning the outcome of the discussions in Brussels and creating battles

and arguments where they are none and creating victories out of compromises and that's par for the course. . . . There is constant spin on EU involvement and talk of fundamental principles on which the EU was founded.[221]

The Greek Cypriots are having

a problem over power sharing with the Turkish Cypriots. . . . Cyprus, which represents 0.2 percent of the EU's population, expects to have an equal say with European giants as Britain, Germany and France. . . . The danger is that Cyprus, relishing its power as a member state, seeks to use it in a negative way to bash Turkey over the head, to make demands and to assert itself to the fullest extent possible. . . . They saw the EU as the savior that would stop Turkey messing with them anymore.[222]

The U.S. deputy assistant secretary for European affairs Laura Kennedy, on May 5, was in Cyprus to urge the Greek Cypriot leaders to make a "realistic contribution" to the Cyprus peace process by specifying the changes it wants to the Annan Plan. Kennedy's intended mission on the island was to "meet with a broad cross-section of leaders in both communities," and to assert that Washington supported the Annan Plan.[223] The Greeks continue to underestimate the determination and the will of Ankara as to the future of Cyprus and the island's geostrategic importance relative to its security.[224] The Greek nationalists envision that by perseverance, an opportunity will emerge to facilitate and shape their political aspirations and will serve to invalidate the necessity for reconciliation or an embracing of the political equality of the Turkish Cypriots. The nationalists are the elites in control of political apparatus, enabling them to pursue their agenda while intimidating and coercing opponents who do not heed their directives, embrace their goals, or submit to their stated purpose.

On February 20, the Turkish Cypriots went to the polls for a third time in just over a year to elect a fifty-deputy parliament. The electoral contest was between Talat and Eroglu; the former endorsed Annan Plan, while the latter strongly opposed it. The Western powers favored Talat for endorsing the reunification of the island, and the pursuit of that vision brought him an invitation to visit Brussels for talks with European Commission President Jose Manuel Barroso and the visit of a U.S. and British trade delegation to TRNC. Immediately at issue was the resolution of the economic isolation of TRNC and a fair and viable formula for peaceful coexistence of Greek and Turkish Cypriots,[225] but a triple benefit will be to better position Greece and Turkey to deal with issues relating to the Aegean.

Talat's Republican Turkish Party emerged as the winner in the parliamentary elections by capturing twenty-four seats. The National Unity Party of Eroglu took nineteen seats. The Democratic Party of Serdar Denktash lost one seat and was left with six, and the Movement for Peace and Democracy led by Mustafa Akinci received one seat. Talat acknowledged that a coalition government would form and that he "aims at a solution to the Cyprus problem and the unification of Cyprus."[226] Talat's victory demonstrated the desire for settlement despite the efforts of Papadopoulos to tag him as Ankara's puppet, bent on partitioning the island.

On March 16, 2005, Talat declared his candidacy for the presidency, and on April 17, he was elected by 55.6 percent of the votes cast (102, 853 voted out of 147,823 that had registered). The low voter turnout emanates from voter fatigue as a result of four elections held in TRNC in 2004–2005. Dervis Eroglu, the leader of the National Unity Party, won 22.73 percent of the votes. The general secretary of the Republican Turkish Party (RTP), Ferdi Sabit Soyer, became the new prime minister within the framework of the agreement reached between RTP and DP. Democratic Party Leader Serdar Denktash continued to serve as foreign minister.[227] Republic of Cyprus spokesman Kypros Chrysostomides described the outcome of the elections as "a positive development" and went on to say that the elections were neither democratic nor free but "an act of secession that could lead to consolidating the division."[228] Talat,[229] who resumed the reign of power on April 24, was considered by Denktash to be "a man cold-blooded like a snake, may God preserve him from evil. He also has patience that will frustrate the Greek Cypriots."[230] Despite the negative remarks, Talat enjoyed a far greater confidence from the international community and Ankara, making it possible to facilitate the resumption of negotiations for a Cyprus settlement. What propelled Talat to the presidency was his pragmatic-realist approach to the Annan Plan, commitment to moderation, and genuine political creativity for the resolution of the Cyprus crisis. The Turkish Cypriots were tired of Denktash's vociferous opposition to the Annan Plan and his inability to actually deliver results. Reflecting upon his thirty-year burden of leadership, Denktash's source of fury is the unprecedented isolation at home and from Ankara, who has championed the solution of the island's partition and EU membership.

Under Denktash's patrimonial authority, the loyal individuals and groups were rewarded to strengthen their social, economic, financial, and political positions, and were a major source of expansion of political power for a select group. Denktash's desire to advance his political agenda failed to generate enthusiasm among the Turkish Cypriot masses because it suffered from the illusions of realism. Yet, whatever one may think of Denktash, he undoubtedly grasped the colonial legacies, complex ethnic divisions, political culture, Turkish national interests, and achieved mixed success at different periods. Unfortunately his leadership failed to produce a breakthrough in the negotiations for a Cyprus settlement. Following his succession to the vice presidency in 1973, Denktash emerged as a key player in Turkish Cypriot politics, and succeeded in solidifying popular leadership on the island and in Turkey. His reputation depended on the *de jure* recognition of TRNC by the international community and the gradual rapprochement between the two communities, but was entrapped in attempts to derail the process for the reunification of Cyprus under the Annan Plan.

A brief social encounter at the Kremlin in Moscow, in the framework of Victory Day celebrations marked the 60th anniversary of the end of World War II in Europe. On May 9, in a tripartite exchange between Annan, Papadopoulos and Erdogan expressed an interest to start "exploratory talks" on resuming negotiations to reunify Cyprus. The tripartite positive stance in Moscow brought an unexpected positive dimension to the meeting held between Greek Prime Minister Costas Karamanlis on May 20, and Turkey's Prime Minister Erdogan on June 8, with President George Bush in Washington, D.C., where the issue of Cyprus was high on the agenda.[231] Tassos Tzonis, director of the president's diplomatic office, on May 13, was appointed to participate in the discussions to be held at the UN in New York on May 16 to clarify the negotiating framework for the resumption of the new talks on Cyprus, and it was also agreed that the consultations would be kept confidential. Annan, in his semiannual report to the UN Security Council, on May 27, 2005, states the following:

> The overall situation in Cyprus remained stable, although the official contacts between the leaders of the Greek Cypriot and Turkish Cypriot sides, which had ceased since the April 2004 referenda, have not been resumed and there is little sign of improvement in relations. . . . In the area of property, it has opened up new fronts of litigation and acrimony. . . . The prospect of an increase of litigation in property cases on either side poses a serious threat to people-to-people relationships and to the reconciliation process. Only a comprehensive settlement of the Cyprus problem can bring closure to the property issue. . . . On 19 May 2005, the Turkish Cypriot side lifted the restrictions imposed on UNFICYP in July 2000 by the Turkish forces/ Turkish Cypriot security forces. . . . Official contact between

sides is hampered by a high degree of mistrust.... The presence of the UNFICYP on the island remains necessary for the maintenance of the ceasefire and in order to foster conditions conducive to a comprehensive settlement of the Cyprus problem.... The mandate of UNFICYP [to be extended by the Security Council] for a further six-month period, starting on 16 June 2005 and ending 15 December 2005.... I do not believe that the time is ripe to appoint a full-time person dedicated to my good offices.[232]

The interlocutors of the two communities need to engage in serious negotiations and make the necessary concessions without capitulating in order to break the deadlock and produce an acceptable agreement. The erosion of trust, the increased cynicism, the emerging debacle over property issues, and the gloomy prospect for compromise have sabotaged all international efforts in the quest to restart the negotiations. Skeptical mood, along with the community leader's ineptitude and lack of will to engage more actively in substantive issues, has resulted in the emergence of pessimism among the principal players. The involvement of the UN and various outside powers will dramatically improve the prospect and conditions for negotiations provided the Cypriot leaders exhibit flexibility on various crucial points to forge a compromise. If the community leaders continue to strive for unilateral advantage, the prospect for a settlement is bleak with adverse consequences for all Cypriots. The recalcitrance of Cypriot leadership has done little to hide the failure of their political strategy, and furthermore, it has managed to further erode the shaky trust, which has exacerbated the peace process.[233]

UN Deputy Secretary-General for Political Affairs Sir Kieran Prendergast participated in the exploratory talks on Cyprus with Tasos Tzonis in New York and was sent to Nicosia by Annan on May 30 to June 2 to meet with Papadopoulos and Talat.[234] Prendergast briefed the UN Security Council on June 22 about his meetings in Cyprus, Greece, and Turkey between May 30 and June 7 for consultations on the future of his mission of good offices in Cyprus. He reported that it was "premature and inadvisable" to relaunch an intensive new process on Cyprus, because "the gap between the stated positions of the parties on substance appears to be wide, while confidence between them does not seem high; rather the contrary."[235] Due to the chasm between positions of the two communities and the lack of mutual confidence, Annan did not reengage in another negotiation unless the parties were able to bridge their differences and showed a willingness to compromise in order to reach an agreement. On May 18,

Prendergast announced that he was retiring at the end of June and had accepted an appointment as a Goodman Fellow at Harvard University.[236]

Papadopoulos on May 15 reiterated that "no talks will start if the prerequisites for success are not there,"[237] and no conditions, restrictions, or other predetermined issues were to be part of the deal. Papadopoulos's demand for changes in Annan Plan, and the list of concessions continue to paralyze and deepen the controversy. Papadopoulos's tough-game approach was to gain a significant modification of the Annan Plan at the detriment of the Turkish Cypriots. The challenges appear insurmountable, and inconclusive negotiations made Secretary-General Annan the whipping post for all the frustrations of the Cypriots. The prolonged division of the island continued to cause consequences. Moreover, the UN Security Council continues to extend the deployment of the UNFICYP on the island for the purposes of peace and security.[238]

The Greek Cypriot leadership's continued interest in negotiations with the Turks was not to concede by offering specifics but to prepare the ground to make their task easier at the negotiations. Adding to the complications, the European Union and the Greek Cypriot justice system resorted to issuing arrest warrants for building contractors or buyers of Greek Cypriot property in TRNC. Talat expressed the view that the properties will be settled within the framework of an overall Cyprus agreement.[239] Papadopoulos wanted to send an unmistakable signal to the international community of his willingness to join a new initiative for a comprehensive peace conference in return for major concessions from the Turks. Thus, should the negotiations fail to yield dividends, it will clearly enhance Papadopoulos's image with expected political benefits at home and abroad. High-stakes diplomatic initiatives were calculating the international ramifications in case the step in breaking the stalemate over the Annan Plan failed to achieve a breakthrough. Many issues continued to plague Annan's efforts to broker an agreeable alternative solution acceptable to both sides, and despite a commendable initiative, no breakthroughs or dramatic shifts emerged. The chances for progress demanded a willingness to accept a compromise to break the continuing deadlock in the negotiations.

On May 29, 2005, the French electorate by 55 percent, and on June 1 the Netherlands by 61.6 percent voted to reject the proposed European Union constitution. President Jacques Chirac's reassurance that Turkey's EU admission would be put to a referendum was to no avail. In an editorial, George Will wrote that it was a "backlash against Chirac's championing of EU membership for Turkey."[240] The outcome of the elections in France and the Netherlands, plus the opposition of the new pope, Benedict XVI, and the elections of the Christian Democrats in Germany on September 18, has definitely influenced the pace of

Turkey's EU course.[241] Valery Giscard d'Estaing, a former French president and the architect of the EU constitution, who is a fierce opponent of EU membership for Ankara, said that the possibility of full membership for Turkey contributed to the rejection of the constitution in France.[242] The major contributing factors to the defeat of the EU constitution were the disenchantment and frustration of the public with the political elites' inability to cope with the economy, unemployment, prospect for a better future, immigration policy, and Turkey's full EU membership. *The Economist* writes that "the French and Dutch does . . . . reflect growing hostility around Europe to further enlargement of the EU . . . specifically . . . big and Muslim Turkey."[243] The rejection of Turkish membership caused Ankara to reorient itself to the EU, ease up on reforms required as part of its membership drive, and try to restore strong ties with the U.S.[244] James Ker-Lindsay of *Civilitas*, a think-tank in Nicosia, says that "in the longer term no state has more to lose from a bout of Turkish disenchantment with the EU than Cyprus."[245] In an editorial on June 2, *Cyprus Mail* questioned the political strategy of Papadopoulos to squeeze more concessions from Turkey on every step on its way to accession to the EU under the threat of Greek veto. European public opinion has founded Turkey's EU prospects and Papadopoulos's plan "lies and Tatters." Linking the Cyprus issue with Turkey's EU accession negotiations has been counterproductive, and any prospect for a breakthrough has severely hampered expectations for an early settlement.

After Turkey signed the customs union protocol on July 29, Papadopoulos took a tougher stance due to his disenchantment with the Turkish declaration that this action did not mean the recognition of the Greek Cypriot government. Furthermore, Papadopoulos was encouraged by French Prime Minister Dominique de Villepin, whose statement openly questioned Turkey's refusal to recognize the Cyprus Republic. De Villepin told a radio station the following: "It does not seem conceivable to me that a negotiation process of whatever kind can start with a country [on October 3, 2005] that does not recognize every member state of the EU, in other words all 25 of them."[246] In an editorial in *International Herald Tribune*, on August 18, Philip Gordon wrote, "One wonders whether his [Villepin] true goal is to bring about recognition of Cyprus or to score easy points with French voters by scuttling the start of Turkey's negotiations with the EU."[247] The spectre of the veto appeared on the horizon once again with the encouragement of France to block Turkey's path to start the accession negotiations with the EU as decided on December 17, 2004. During a July discussion in London, Papadopoulos had assured British Prime Minister Tony Blair he would not insist on recognition of Cyprus by Turkey, and similar assurances were given to Karamanlis in Athens. Papadopoulos, buoyed by anti-

Turkish sentiments in Europe, was in the saddle to single-handedly block the start of talks, since the negotiations require a unanimous mandate from the twenty-five-member states.[248] Reneging on promises made by EU to Turkey has seriously undermined the credibility of the member states, with consequences more far-reaching to Greek Cypriot government.

In Brussels and at the EU foreign ministers meeting in Newport, Wales, on September 1 and 2, 2005, Turkey rejected the diplomatic pressures to establish normal relations with the Greek Cypriot administration. Abdullah Gul, Turkey's foreign minister, stated that the opening of the Turkish ports and airports to Greek Cypriot administration was not covered by the customs union agreement between Ankara and Brussels since Turkey was not a full EU member. Gul qualified his argument by saying that Turkey would recognize the Republic of Cyprus following the Greco-Turkish Cypriot political settlement on the island.

France and Austria latched onto the Cyprus issue to justify their opposition to Turkish EU membership, and furthermore, President Chirac's *modus operandi* was to boost popular support for his government in the elections. As to Angela Merkel's proposed "privileged partnership" for Turkey instead of full EU membership, Gul said that the idea was "illegitimate and immoral. . . . I regret to see that a long-term issue as crucial as Turkey's future integration with Europe is being exploited for short-term domestic political calculations by some circles."[249] Danish foreign minister Per Stig Moeller said that the EU had never demanded that Ankara recognize Cyprus as a condition for opening accession talks.[250] In Naples, Italy, on September 2, Erdogan declared that Turkey had no more concessions to make to EU.[251] British and German foreign ministers were supportive of Ankara EU accession talks on October 3, despite the Greek political scheme to extract more concessions from Turkey relative to their interest in Cyprus. Gul said, "Should they [EU] propose anything short of full membership, or any new conditions, we will walk away, and this time it will be for good."[252] Italian Foreign Minister Gianfranco Fini said, "It would be wrong to set new conditions for Ankara because [last year's] European Council of heads of state agreed Turkey met all conditions that were set."[253] Cyprus and France kept on putting pressure on Turkey and demanded "*de jure* normalization of relations between Turkey and all EU member states and the removal of all obstacles to the free movement of goods, including restrictions on means of transport."[254] Foreign Secretary of Britain Jack Straw, in an article in the *International Herald Tribune*, on September 8, stressed Turkey's

> strategic importance and the momentous consequences that
> will follow from that decision. . . . Stopping enlargement would

only weaken Europe's ability to compete with emerging Asian economies.... To do otherwise would not only compromise the credibility of the EU but it might also endanger the considerable progress already made in Turkey.... If we get it wrong now we could find that we have a crisis on our doorstep.[255]

Greeks characterized Straw as biased, imperious, and intemperate, whereas the majority of EU members were convinced that raising the ante so high would force Turkey to walk out of the negotiations, which would precipitate a tragic course of events.

On September 12, Britain and France agreed on a formula with Turkish recognition of Cyprus as a condition before full EU membership in fifteen to twenty years. London and Paris Accord, which had angered Nicosia, states the following:

> Prior recognition of all member states is necessary component of accession. Accordingly, the EU underlines the importance it attaches to the normalization of relations between Turkey and all EU member states as soon as possible. In the context, the EU and its member states agree on the need to support the efforts of the UN Secretary General to bring about a comprehensive settlement to the Cyprus problem and that just and lasting settlement will contribute to peace, stability and harmonious relations in the region.[256]

The following day, the Greek Cypriot government spokesman Kypros Chrysostomides cautioned that Cyprus could prevent Turkey's entry talks as scheduled on October 3, "if there is no agreement,"[257] but criticized the veto option as premature. The rejection of Turkey could compel the parliament to shelve the reforms, strengthen the Islamists and the nationalists, and draw the country away from the West.

On September 19, the Committee of Permanent Representatives of the EU (COREPER) failed to formally approve a hotly debated joint declaration on Turkey's refusal to recognize Cyprus, muddying the waters for Ankara's membership talks on October 3. The text of the draft declaration stated that Turkey must formally recognize Cyprus at anytime in the accession process, which could last ten to fifteen years.[258] The next day, ministers from the twenty-five EU member states pulled the declaration from its agenda in Brussels at Cyprus's request. Papadopoulos said, "We have no illusions that Turkey will recognize us as soon as possible, but the rejoinder does contain a provision that this will be reviewed in 2006."[259] The counter-declaration, approved on September 21, which lacked both legal standing and binding character, lobbied for by the Greeks, made no reference to the Annan Plan or to the Cyprus settlement under the UN auspices.[260] Furthermore, the recognition of Cyprus was made as part of the negotiating process and not linked to the solution of the Cyprus crisis. The counter- declaration supports UN efforts, but any resolution of the Cyprus problem will be in line with Security Council resolutions and principles of the EU. EU rejected Turkey's unilateral declaration that it does not recognize Cyprus—"does not form part of the Protocol"—and the Republic of Cyprus and its elected Greek officials were to be recognized as the legitimate government of the whole island, but it sets no specific deadline for Turkey to recognize Cyprus. EU's counterstatement constituted a *de facto*, and foundations are laid for *de jure* recognition of Cyprus by Turkey.[261] It also created a mechanism to monitor the full implementation of the protocol for the customs union declaration in 2006, and if Turkey failed to fulfill its obligations, it would have a negative impact on its accession negotiations. The political maneuvering of the Greeks was to bind the recognition of Cyprus in its current structure by Turkey in a shorter period during its accession. Papadopoulos objected to an appended clause that the EU will not "reopen" issues agreed in the declaration. In the final analysis, Papadopoulos's strategy was fashioned to serve the political objectives of the Greeks and demonstrate to his Greek Cypriot constituents that on the substantive points, no concessions were made to the Turks.

On September 22, Turkey's foreign ministry spokesman Namik Tan described the EU declaration as follows:

> We regret the publication of this counter-declaration. It has a style which does not accord well with the traditional spirit of co-operation that has existed between Turkey and the EU over a period of more than 40 years . . . ignored the rights and expectations of the Turkish Cypriot people . . . one-sided and politically motivated.[262]

On the same day, the Turkish newspapers reflected a frustration and bitterness with the EU and predicted that the suspension of relations with the EU would have the backing of the people. Besides the counter-declaration, Austria still kept pushing the argument that Turkey should be offered a "privileged partnership."

The EU parliament voted 311–285 to delay ratifying Turkey's customs union on September 28 because of Ankara's refusal to recognize the Greek Cypriot administration and for not acknowledging the killings of Armenians by the Ottomans during the 1914–1918 war.[263] The two issues did not affect Turkey's accession talks on October 3, because it was a nonbinding resolution. Erdogan forewarned the EU that he would not accept the counter-declaration to be included in the negotiation framework document, and Austria's proposed option of "privileged partnership" was rejected.[264] A provision in the declaration that particularly irked the Turks was a demand for Ankara not to obstruct the membership of EU countries (Cyprus) in other international organizations (e.g., Cyprus should not be blocked by Turkey from joining NATO).[265] The additional conditions imposed on Turkey contributed to deadlock the EU ambassadors in seeking agreement on a joint negotiating framework on September 29, forcing UK to call for an emergency meeting in Luxemburg on October 2 with an attempt to break the logjam. Straw told the Labour Party conference, "It would now be a huge betrayal of the hopes and expectations of the Turkish people and of Prime Minister Erdogan's reform progamme if, at this crucial time, we turned our back on Turkey."[266] Martin Schulz, chairman of the Socialists in Parliament, accused the conservatives of not wanting Turkey in the EU. He said, "It would be better for you to say clearly: We don't want Turkey in the EU. You're skirting the message."[267] *The Times* editorial "Eastern Promise: There Must Be No Alternative to Talks on Full Turkish EU Membership" on September 29 declares,

> The conditions as provocative as they are politically disingenuous pander to an increasingly hostile EU opinion by citing issues that appear reasonable but are calculated to anger Ankara . . . talking of "privileged partnership" as a substitute for full EU membership. The phrase may sound emollient, but it signifies a dishonorable reneging on past promises and a humiliating rejection of Turkish aspirations for the past 42 years. . . . What politicians in Strasbourg, Paris and Berlin are hoping is that a piqued Turkey will itself flounce out of the talks. . . . Beneath the rumblings in France, Germany, Austria and the Netherlands also lie popular hostility to Islam and a rejection of any more Muslim immigration. To reject Turkey on these grounds is not only dishonorable but wrong; it is to ignore the entire Ataturk legacy and the huge strides that Turkey, as a secular nation . . . has made towards democracy.[268]

Gul refused to travel to Luxemborg for membership talks without the EU foreign ministers' consensus to withdraw the additional conditions on Turkish accession talks.[269] The different interest groups in the EU launched a campaign to skew Turkey's accession process, by adding demands contrary to the terms of the agreement that only serve the narrow interests of few states, while contributing further to the paralysis of Western Europe.

The frantic diplomatic negotiations at the emergency meeting, held on October 2 over admitting Turkey to the EU, failed to resolve a standoff over Austria's insistence that Ankara be offered a "privileged partnership" as an alternative to full membership. Erdogan told Turkish television, "Either the EU will decide to become a world force and a world player, which would show its political maturity, or it will limit itself to a Christian club."[270] After marathon talks and intense diplomatic negotiations, on October 3, Straw succeeded in persuading Austrian Foreign Minister Ursala Plassnik to lift her objections, clearing the way for accession talks with Turkey to begin.[271] Another thorny issue was Paragraph 5 of the negotiating mandate, which forced Ankara to cease blocking Cyprus's accession to international bodies, including NATO, which Turkey had the right to veto. Ankara's concern was the membership of Cyprus in NATO, and its right to invoke the "self-defense" clause compelling the U.S. to come to her defense against Turkey's military presence on the island and the right to demand the withdrawal of the British from the two sovereign bases. The U.S. intervened regarding the controversial paragraph, and Ankara was assured that it would not affect its voting power in NATO. Straw issued a clarifying statement that read, "Irrespective of whether a country is an EU Member-Sate or not, its policy within the international bodies is not at all affected."[272] Ankara's objections to the inclusion of Paragraph 5 in its negotiating mandate with the EU were removed with American assurances that the clause had no impact on security arrangements within NATO. A month of brinksmanship between Turkey, France, Austria, Cyprus, and Greece averted a rift between Christian Europe and Muslim nations in the East. Failure to start the talks would have undermined the economic and political reforms in Turkey and would have deepened the crisis in Europe, after the defeat of EU constitution in France and the Netherlands, and the failure in June 2005 to agree on a long-term budget. The accession negotiations were scheduled to start with the ratification of the additional protocol by the Turkish parliament, and Ankara has to adapt EU *acquis communautaire* fully to its laws.[273]

Despite the misgiving of EU members, on October 3, 2005, Turkey, a relatively less-developed nation, a predominately Muslim nation, was given the green light to start the EU entry negotiations. EU Enlargement Commissioner Ollie Rehn, on June 29, said that Turkey's entry talks must be "open-ended . . . we cannot guarantee that we certainly reach the conclusion of them."[274] Furthermore, Rehn said that he could not see Turkey joining the EU before 2014 and implied that Ankara may be given a "special relationship" with the European bloc rather than full membership. In his address to the leaders of EU in the Czech capital, Prague, on April 5, 2009, President Barack Obama urged EU to accept Turkey as a member. President of France, Nicolas Sarkozy, declared his continued opposition to granting EU membership to Turkey.[275] In his address to the Turkish parliament in Ankara on April 6, President Obama said, "Europe gains by diversity of ethnicity, tradition and faith—it is not diminished by it. And Turkish membership would broaden and strengthen Europe's foundation once more."[276] The comments of Obama drew an immediate rebuff from President Sarkozy of France who declared that it was up to the EU member states to decide Turkey's membership, not the United States.[277] During the campaign for the European parliamentary elections on June 4 to 7, 2009, about 375 million European citizens in 27 countries voted and the 736-member parliament was elected for a five-year term. During the campaign, anti-Turkish sentiments were promoted by the European conservatives and far-right leaders under the slogans "No to Turkey and Islam." Even though the campaign rhetoric against Turkey was expected to fade once the elections were over, opposition to Turkey's membership by many of EU member states was strong, and a public survey in France showed that 67 percent of French voters objected to Turkish membership.[278] The European conservative's stance is based on the premise that EU's common root of Judeo-Christian religious and Greco-Roman political heritage absence in Turkey makes the Turks an unsuitable member. On cultural, political, and religious reasons, a significant number of EU members declared Turkey's EU membership as impractical.[279]

Belgian Prime Minister Herman Van Rompuy, a Roman Catholic and Christian Democrat from the center-right, on November 19, 2009, was appointed to be the EU's first full-time president. He is a firm opponent of Turkey's EU membership bid, and in a speech, the following remarks were made in Belgian parliament in December 2004:

> Turkey is not a part of Europe and will never be part of Europe. An expansion of the EU to include Turkey cannot be considered as just another expansion, as in the past. The universal values which are in force in Europe, and which are also fundamental values of Christianity, will lose vigour with the entery of a large Islamic country such as Turkey.[280]

Rompuy's speech compliments the voices of Nicolas Sarkozy, France's president, and Angela Merkel, Germany's chancellor, both of whom are willing to offer Turkey a "privileged partnership" but not EU membership. In 2012, Germany was floating a new proposal for Turkey referred to as "sectoral membership" in the EU that will prevent the accession process from derailment and it will include Ankara in the EU's decision-making process in a number of areas and leave the prospect of full membership open.[281]

The greatest failure of Western Europe has been their shortcomings in integrating millions of Muslims into their society, and aggravating the Christian-Muslim relationship by the possibility of outlawing the burka and the niqab in France and banning of building minarets in Switzerland. The continued opposition to Turkey's accession into the twenty-seven-nation EU bloc is an arbitrary decision to exclude a country with 70 million Muslims from joining a "Christian Club." Western European states, instead of facilitating and promoting religious tolerance, reconciliation, and trust, are reinforcing Islamophobic fear and prejudice toward Islam and Muslims. Radical religious right-wing xenophobic nationalists in Europe are propagating negative images as to Muslims and Islam, and are effective in mobilizing public opinion in validating their version of religious and political ideology in a multicultural and pluralistic society. Islam, in the final analysis, has become a shibboleth for terror and Muslims have become synonymous with terrorists. Demonizing Muslims in Europe and around the globe hampers peaceful coexistence and religious harmony, but strengthens the conviction inspired by the "clash of civilizations" thesis.

In a survey conducted on 6,465 people by the Turkish Board of Statistics (TUIK) on July 5, 2009, only 51.9 percent voted for EU membership, 29.5 percent voted against it, and 18.6 percent did not express an opinion. The survey indicated that 58.5 percent of men and 45.6 percent of women would back EU membership in a possible referendum.[282] According to the Ankara Anatolia News Agency, May 30, 2012, Turkey's EU accession has stalled and strengthened the opposition against the EU support among the young Turks plunged to 47.2 percent in 2011 from 74 percent in 2005. Opposition to EU membership among the young Turks almost doubled from 16.8 percent to 30.8 percent. Among the adults, the support dropped from 63 percent to 44.3 percent. Turkey has lost enthusiasm for the EU bid because its accession remains ambiguous, and because of the continued opposition of France, Germany, and Austria. Nevertheless, the EU continued to add demands on Turkey:

1. The recognition of the Republic of Cyprus
2. The acknowledgment of the Armenian genocide
3. Opening the border with Armenia

4. Special agreement as to annual agricultural subsidies
5. Protection of religious minorities
6. Resolution of outstanding legal issues with EU Member States (Greece and Cyprus)
7. Special agreement on the free movement of (Turkish) workers to EU Member States
8. Human rights issues
9. Political reforms
10. The withdrawal of Turkish troops and settlers from Cyprus

To break out of the cycle of deadlock, a new initiative on a whole range of issues had to be included to achieve a political settlement. Something external needed to happen that would demonstrate the value of negotiations and reconciliation to resolve the ongoing Cypriot crisis.

Despite the strong objections of the Greek Cypriots and Greece, U.S. Secretary of State Condoleezza Rice, on October 17, 2005, extended an invitation to Talat to Washington for an official visit on October 28. Talat's visit was mostly symbolic in nature and sends a goodwill message to Ankara, but Papadopoulos charged that Washington was promoting division and tension on the island. The U.S. was not ready for groundbreaking moves to end the isolation of the Turkish Cypriots by the international community, but it was an important message to Papadopoulos that efforts must be made for the peaceful resolution of the crisis on Cyprus.[283] Dr. Rice reiterated that the United States supported the Annan Plan, which continues to remain as the most suitable basis for a comprehensive solution to the Cyprus problem.

British Foreign Secretary Jack Straw's visit to Cyprus to assess prospects for a new initiative to reunite Cyprus sparked Greek Cypriot hostility and negative publicity. Straw's decision to visit Mehmet Ali Talat in his presidential office was strongly objected by the Greek Cypriot administration, and President Tassos Papadopoulos refused to see him. Kofi Annan hailed Straw's mission to Cyprus, Greece, and Turkey to resolve the Cyprus crisis and said that it complemented UN engagement on the island. Straw defied Papadopoulos's protest and met Talat at his presidential office in Nicosia on January 25, 2006. A lower-ranking foreign ministry official greeted Straw at the airport, and he was not allowed to use the VIP lounge. The visit was greeted by protesters as a "divide and rule all over again."[284] Straw's comments in the House of Commons on February 7 sparked a political furor in Cyprus by accusing President Papadopoulos as follows:

I suspect, the government of Cyprus are now seeking to use

———

their membership of the EU to try unacceptably to seek progress on their United Nations-related issues. . . . Moreover, because of their unhelpful approach towards the aid proposals for the north from the European Union, they are in my judgment seeking to marginalize the Turkish Cypriot community and not in any way to assist in their economic development.[285]

Papadopoulos lodged an official protest over Straw's remarks in parliament and accused him of "fueling tension" between the two countries.[286] The Greek Cypriots prefer a European solution in place of a UN resolution to the crisis.

On January 24, Turkish Foreign Minister Gul unveiled Turkey's New Action Plan for Cyprus:

1. Opening of the sea ports of Turkey to Greek Cypriot vessels serving the trade of goods in accordance with the EU-Turkey Customs Union.

2. Allowing Greek Cypriot air carriers to use the Turkish air space for over-flights and to land at the Turkish airports in accordance with relevant international rules and procedures.

3. Opening of the ports in North Cyprus, including Gazimagosa, Girne, and Gemikonak to international traffic of goods, persons, and service under Turkish Cypriot management.

4. Opening of Ercan airport for direct flights under the Turkish Cypriot management.

5. Special arrangements for the practical inclusion of North Cyprus, as an economic entity, into the European Union's customs union. Unhindered direct trade between both sides of the island as well as with the outside world.

6. Participation of the Turkish Cypriot side in international sports, cultural, and other social activities.

A high-level meeting was to convene no later than May or June 2006 under the auspices of the UN with the participation of Greece, Turkey, and the two communities on the island to finalize the draft action plan. The results of the meeting were to be submitted by the UN secretary-general to the UN Security

Council.[287] U.S. Ambassador to Ankara, Ross Wilson, on January 30, considered Turkey's initiative to be an important step in the peace process; however, the Greek Cypriot administration rejected the plan as "reheated food" and expressed the desire that a UN envoy be appointed for Cyprus.[288] Straw expressed the view that Gul's proposal deserved to be taken seriously in order to break the deadlock.[289]

Russian President Vladimir Putin, on January 31, delivered unexpected praise for the Turkish Cypriot's side for its commitment to a Cyprus settlement. Putin said Russia's policy had not changed but added,

> We would, however, very much like our policy to be balanced and for all these involved in the process, the Turkish Republic and the northern part of Cyprus and Greece and the Republic of Cyprus as a whole, to have confidence in what Russia is doing on the international scene in general and specifically on settlement in Cyprus. . . . We believe that the northern part of Cyprus is also making its desire for a settlement clear and this should be encouraged, in any event in joint economic activity. . . . We hope that compromises acceptable to the north and south of Cyprus will be found.[290]

While the Turks welcomed the U-turn policy of Moscow, the Greek Cypriots were scrambling to insist that there was no change in Russia's policy on Cyprus.

The Paris meeting of Papadopoulos and Kofi Annan on February 28 was described as "substantive and productive" by the Greek Cypriots, but Annan confined himself to saying that "as long as you are talking you are making progress."[291] Annan reiterated that he would appoint a special envoy "when the time is ripe."[292] Papadopoulos insisted that he had achieved all its targets with Annan and described the outcome of the meeting in Paris as highly positive. Greek Cypriots claimed that technical committees "on the ground" would explore confidence-building measures between the two communities, including the disengagement of forces on the island, gradual demilitarization and demining, and the possible return of Varosha under Greek Cypriot administration. Papadopoulos was putting a positive spin on the Paris meeting to bolster the pro-government parties' chances in the coming election in Cyprus. In an editorial in *Cyprus Mail*, on March 7, Loucas Charalambous wrote the following:

> I am under the impression that the scam has, more or less, worked, Annan had been used by Papadopoulos and Christofias, who

have already began boasting that they have paved the way for a settlement. . . . All this fuss we are witnessing now is nothing more than a pre-election publicity stunt.[293]

In a letter sent to Talat on March 20 by Undersecretary-General for Political Affairs Ibrahim Gambari clarified the issues discussed at the February 28 meeting in Paris between Annan and Papadopoulos. Gambari's letter to Talat states that there was a common sentiment for progress if an agreement could be achieved on disengagement of forces from the island, saying "it would be beneficial for all concerned."[294] His letter went on to say,

> Without relating these issues to the Technical committees, it was agreed that further work needed to be done on them at a time and in a manner to be determined by both sides in order to progress to be achieved towards a comprehensive settlement.[295]

The creation of technical committees was agreed to by both sides prior to the Paris meeting, which was to include issues relating to waste management, water resources management, and traffic congestion, but it did not include withdrawal of troops or Varosha or the Famagusta port.[296] The letter stated, "There was no unilateral agreement on issues that quite clearly have to be agreed by both sides."[297] The letter clearly expressed the continued gap between the two communities, which prevented the resumption of full-fledged talks to reach a comprehensive settlement. The Paris meeting was to review the situation in Cyprus and to discuss ways of moving it forward; and that the statement issued afterward was not necessarily a "join statement" by Papadopoulos and Annan.[298] The letter reassured the Turks that their role in the negotiations was not diminished, but that they were full-time partners.

The leaders of both communities continue to struggle to enlist sympathizers to their ranks in order to achieve outcomes that will advance their political interests in the contest. The envisioned total victory will create the inevitable outcome— the partitioning of the island. It is the heartfelt wish of many Cypriots that in future negotiations, the concerted expertise will usher in a collective courage and deliver a final settlement. Both community leaders have been reluctant to engage in achievable results and tend to show no urgency to resolve the political crisis or close the gap to bridge their difference. A defiant posture or stalling of the negotiations is not an option, but the absolute height of the saga of the ongoing tragedy will lead to the realization of permanent division of Cyprus.

NOTES

CHAPTER 3

THE FAILURE TO FORGE A NEW SETTLEMENT

If you can dream—and not make dreams your master, If you can think—and not make thoughts your aim; If you can meet with Triumph and Disaster and treat those two imposters the same.
—Rudyard Kipling

The entrenched political rhetoric of the communal leaders has not laid the foundation for what could be considered the heroic period of Cypriot history, but instead has demonstrated a complete lack of any real desire for reconciliation and peaceful coexistence. Negotiations have merely been grand political duels emblematic of the emotional intensity of the ethnic hostility of both sides. Reckless political attitudes as well as the lack of foresight have resulted in communal leaders who are too preoccupied with their own ethnocentric interest. These leaders must certainly understand that this stalemate cannot be broken without concessions from both sides.

The international community continues to make a joint effort to mobilize diplomatic pressure in an attempt to bolster UN efforts and resolve the Cypriot crisis.[299] Short of diplomatic recognition, the Organization for the Islamic Conference Parliamentarians Union meeting in Istanbul, on April 13, 2006, decided to recognize TRNC as the Cypriot Turkish state.[300] During her two-day visit to Athens and Ankara on April 25 to 26, Condoleezza Rice called on the Greeks to facilitate Turkey's accession to the European Union and urged the Cypriots to resolve the Cyprus crisis.[301]

The May 21 parliamentary elections in the south did not usher in a more conciliatory attitude. Papadopoulos demonstrated that he would not be intimidated and continued to chart a hard-line policy to secure desired concessions and outcomes. The prevailing mood continued to endorse polarization instead of reconciliation: the boundary between the north and the south has not shifted since 1974. The stark fact has been a diplomatic stalemate as a result of leadership intransigence rather than cooperation in exploration of deliverable outcomes. The two Cypriot communities view each other as an Achilles' heel for purposely wrecking the attempted diplomatic efforts of a negotiated settlement. The irrationality of both sides trying to orchestrate maximum gains has dominated the relationship since 1964. Most intriguingly, the absence of a settlement has created a stalemate that continues to block results that would serve shared interests. What is also striking is that the continued division of the communities has alienated the new generation, and according to the April 30, 2006, census, the population in the north stands at 264,172, which is a 31.7 percent rise from 200,587 in 1996.[302] The consequences will produce irreversible trends and are likely to ensure permanent partition, thereby confirming the prospects of an eventual development that few people on either side would have foreseen. The ultra nationalists have created a perverse logic to the illusion by refusing to accommodate the realities that confront them.[303]

The international community is gradually becoming cognizant of the reality of the existing division on Cyprus, and on June 9, Talat was in Germany for talks with the German Foreign Minister Frank Walter Stein Meier.[304] Furthermore, despite Greek objections, a deal was clinched by the EU foreign ministers, on June 12, on a common position to start membership talks with Turkey. The nineteen-page document urged Turkey to speed up its reform process; normalize civilian-military relations; more freedom to non-Muslim minorities; extend the customs union agreement to the EU's ten new members, including Cyprus; and normalize relations with neighboring countries; otherwise, it will affect its progress in the membership negotiations.[305] The Greek manipulation of Turkey's EU accession process has caused the Turkish people to feel not wanted, and many are losing faith in the successful outcome of the negotiations. Turkey is the only candidate country with no firm date to accession, and Erdogan has cautioned EU that "our attitude will change accordingly if politics becomes involved in the process."[306] Cyprus's issues will continue to hinder Turkey's EU accession process, and Europe's harsh messages on the Kurdish issue, Cyprus, and human rights, had adverse public reaction to Brussels conditions. Cyprus continued to reap benefits from its EU membership and continued to threaten Turkey with the veto. EU Enlargement Commissioner Olli Rehn warned of a looming train crash: "If such a train crash is to be the case, the crash would not be on one side and the responsibility would not lie with the one side."[307] Cyprus's issue will dog Ankara's accession marathon every step of the way, and Turkish press expressed the view of all the Turks by claiming that Turkey has turned into a "toy" of the Greeks.[308] Luxembourg Prime Minister Jean-Claude Juncker, on June 15, recommended that the EU should freeze membership talks with Turkey if Ankara continued to refuse to open its ports and airports to traffic from Cyprus in 2006.[309] Air and sea ports were closed to Greek Cypriot traffic in 1992.[310] Erdogan replied to the threat by saying that Turkey was prepared for a possible suspension of membership talks with the EU.[311]

The grandstanding by Cyprus at the EU foreign ministers' meeting in Luxembourg was embarrassing for the Greek government, which desired to ease the tensions with Turkey over the midair collision in the southeastern Aegean between Greek and Turkish F-16s, an accident that resulted in the death of a Greek pilot. Athens had no desire to endorse the confrontational policy of Papadopoulos. Athens papers quoted unnamed sources at the prime minister's office as saying, "The interests of Greece are above the interest of any other country, irrespective of how friendly it is."[312] Foreign Minister Dora Bakoyannis, of Greece, on June 18 heralded a new plan for the reunification of Cyprus as an alternative to the Annan Plan that would place greater association of the two parts of Cyprus with EU. Cypriot Foreign Minister Giorgos Lillikas rebuffed the idea, stressing that Cyprus's government had not been informed of the plan.[313] Annan admonished the EU for admitting the divided island to the EU that contributed to the difficulties in resolving the Cyprus crisis.[314] Papadopoulos was defiant to all alternatives suggested as a remedy to the Cypriot crisis and prefers the use of chutzpa to put into effect a grand strategy under EU auspices.

For two years (2004–2006), no discernible progress for the settlement was registered due to the flawed strategy of measuring success by the prolonged isolation of the adversary, which instead deepened political fault lines. Papadopoulos and Talat met on July 8 for one hour to discuss the fate of the 1,500 missing persons' issue with bristling distrust, determination to match any challenge, and repeated incantations by defending the adopted political posture to maintain the status quo.[315] Real communication cannot be with coldness bordering on hatred, unresponsive, unimaginative; it cannot take on the character of a stone-faced sphinx. Yielding in the negotiations is considered a sign of weakness, which would gravely jeopardize rightful claims to "legitimate" demand. Papadopoulos, unlike his predecessor, had developed his idiosyncratic way to legitimize his rigid version of diplomacy—the Sinatra doctrine "My Way." By consolidating his power, Papadopoulos was ambivalent to suggestions to modify his position or partition could be regarded as inevitable. All kinds of suggestions were unable to resolve this dispute, and it could hardly be expected for the Turks to dismantle TRNC's autonomy without respecting their demands in support of a settlement. The Turkish Cypriots cannot forget the past sufferings before setting in motion the termination of the two-state systems. Leaders must take the initiative by acknowledging that the recent past cannot continue to shape the future and devise the means they hope to be acceptable to all. Policies' choices help reach a consensus to break down the determinism or run the risk of a distant future to confirm division of the island. Community leaders have no vision of the whole, but continue to cling to previous choices that continued to intensify the desire of separation.[316]

After his consultation with the Greek and Turkish leaders in Athens and Ankara, UN Undersecretary-General Ibrahim Gambari had meetings with Papadopoulos and Talat in Nicosia from July 6 to 9, 2006, in order to gauge the prospects for another UN initiative to resume negotiations toward a comprehensive settlement to the Cyprus issue.[317] In a joint meeting on July 8, the leaders of the two communities agreed to a five-point declaration outlining the framework for a future settlement "based on a bizonal, bicommunal federation and political equality."[318] They also agreed to establish technical committees that would tackle "day-to-day" issues, and Papadopoulos and Talat agreed to meet "from time to time as appropriate"[319] to "evaluate [and] review the work of the technical committees."[320] Turkey declared its opposition to discussion on the substance of the Cyprus issue by the technical committees. The future of the island would be based on the Annan Plan.[321] By the end of July 2006, Papadopoulos and Talat drew up a common list of items vital to the Cyprus issue. Their advisors worked on the core issues, and the technical committees focused on "soft" issues.[322] The Varosha issue was to be resolved as part of a comprehensive settlement of the Cyprus problem. The two sides have been unable to reach an agreement on the establishment of a technical and working group as it was agreed on July 8.[323]

Greece was not to derail the Greco-Turkish rapprochement in place since 1999 and invited Papadopoulos to Athens on July 10 to formulate a strategy to compel Turkey to make concessions under the UN resolutions and the European *acquis communautaire*. Papadopoulos was restrained by Athens not to veto Turkey's EU course and to ease the economic restrictions of TRNC with EU. Athens and Ankara grasp that harmful rivalry might precipitate unexpected crises and the damage both were unwilling to embrace.

In an attempt to avert a crisis on Turkey's EU bid, a Finnish initiative was introduced to facilitate discussions for the resolution of the Cyprus crisis.

Ankara responded to the plan positively, whereas the Greeks rejected the plan. The formula provided for the opening of the Famgusta port to facilitate Turkish Cypriot exports under the administration of the EU for twenty-four months, with a simultaneous opening of the Turkish ports to Greek Cypriot ships, and the transfer of Varosha to the UN for two years. Greece and Cyprus, backed by other EU members, continued to threaten to derail Turkey's membership talks if Ankara failed to implement the full customs union with all the EU member states. Turkey was steadfast in its decision to not allow the Greek Cypriot shipment to its ports until the economic embargo against the Turkish Cypriots was lifted. Cyprus continued to put formidable obstacles in the way of Turkey's progress in joining the EU, and continued to threaten that with its veto, it would derail Ankara's EU progress. In an editorial *Sunday Mail*, on October 22, 2006, the author wrote the following:

> These negative tactics have not won Cyprus many friends in the EU, but more importantly, they had nowhere, apart from advertising a lack for good will. Our primary objective at the EU seems to be to block any move relating to the Turkish Cypriots, unless we can dictate the terms.

Turkey was adamant in its determination not to make further compromises on Cyprus unless the isolation of TRNC was terminated. Finnish initiative failed to yield results due to the uncompromising stand of the Greeks and Turks. Turkish government was not in a position to take major political risks due to the impending elections in Turkey. In addition, Turkey was already embittered by France's move to legislate a law, making it a crime to deny that the Ottomans had committed genocide against the Armenians in 1915–1917.[324] For the purpose of gaining French Armenian votes in the coming elections in France, Prime Minister of France Nicolas Sarkozy, presidential candidate in May 2007 elections, declared that Turkey should never be allowed to join the EU. He said, "We have to say who is European and who isn't. It's no longer possible to leave this question open."[325] France provoked a nationalist backlash and contributed to alienating the Turks in Ankara's relationship with the EU.

Finland's effort to stave off the collapse of Turkey's bid to join the EU failed over acute concern about freedom of speech, "cases of torture," penal code, and its refusal to open up ports to Greek Cypriot vessels. The criticism provoked a backlash in Turkey, and Turks accused Europe simply in an attempt to humiliate them by coming up with never-ending new demands. The toughest critics of Turkey have been Austria, Cyprus, France, and Greece. France declared that it would hold a referendum before admitting Turkey, and the French parliament passed a law making it a crime to deny that Turks committed genocide against the Armenians during the First World War. The total collapse of Turkey's membership bid with the EU "would confirm suspicions across the Islamic World that the union is a Christian club."[326] In the *Wall Street Journal*, November 2, 2006, an editorial reads as follows:

> Turkey's rejection by the EU would be seen by many Muslims as further evidence that the West is hostile to Muslims and seeks to subdue them. The West's regional image is already tarnished by the U.S.-led war in Iraq. The Israeli bombing of Lebanon and Pope Benedict XVI's recent critical comment about Islam, which inflamed anger that is likely to resurface when the pope visits Turkey [from November 28 to December 1, 2006].

The opponents of Turkish membership focused on the shortcoming in Kurdish minority rights, the Armenian genocide, demands over Cyprus, the military influence in politics,[327] freedom of expression, Article 301 of Turkey's penal code, which were reasons to block Turkey's EU prospects. The European Commission report on November 8, 2006, was very critical of Turkey and, with the added required concessions, help reduced Turkish public support, trust, and contributed to the disillusionment of the Turks with the twenty-five-nation bloc.

The European Commission on November 8, 2006, released its seventy-five-page ninth Progress Report for Turkey, rebuking Ankara for its slow pace of political reforms. EU gave Turkey a December 14 to 15 deadline to open its air and sea ports to Cyprus by extending the Ankara protocol and, furthermore, cautioned Ankara that no link could be made to end the international isolation of TRNC. Turkey rejected any link between the Cyprus issue and its EU accession, but pledged its commitment to reform. The report added to the widespread skepticism among the Turks that the West will never accept an overwhelmingly Muslim nation of 70 million into the midst of the Christian club. The collapse of the EU talks will give fodder to nationalists and Muslim conservatives to suspend the accession negotiations due to the never-ending demands imposed on Ankara. The Turkish people's support for the EU continues to plummet from 23 percent in 2005 to 12 percent in 2006, and the two-thirds majority was calling for the suspension of the talks. On November 20, the EU set a deadline for Turkey to normalize its relations with the Republic of Cyprus or face a setback at the EU foreign ministers' meeting on December 11 and at the European

Commission summit on December 14–15, 2006.[328] Erdogan and Gul ruled out any concessions and did not respond to the EU deadlines or "blackmail."[329] Emboldened, Erdogan, never doubting public support, rejected compromises that failed to grant the Turkish Cypriots equal treatment, while the Greek Cypriots shoved their agenda through.

The list of consequences heightened the level of engagement to avoid a potential political pitfall that could damage the wider Greco-Turkish national interests. To cope with this problem, a concerted international effort was to adopt a coherent policy designed to restore moderation that would surely enhance comparative advantages and provide a valuable service to the international community. Intense political struggles are often counterproductive because the adversaries' commitment to their goals makes them rigid and inflexible, and as a result, it overshadows achievable balanced alternatives. The two Cypriot ethnic groups cannot use each other as a political lightning rod to deflect anger from the popular discontent and world community. Entrenched hostile attitudes contribute to unfavorable views and negative sentiments that had given rise to violent conflicts and sometimes redirect attention and energies to help to rearrange mutually unacceptable compromises. The ultimate responsibility of the protagonists is to reconcile their differences or face the new century with a permanent partition of the island. Without reassurance of partnership, security, and the well-being of the citizens, neither side would surrender its sovereign prerogatives for the purpose of an agreement without desired guarantees. Ethnic rivalry must be replaced by a commitment to peaceful coexistence and the promise of equitable benefits regardless of ethnicity or religion. Since 1964, the ethnic performance has not matched its rhetoric; above all, the overriding concern has been competing priorities. The parties must derive benefits from a settlement and failure to exhibit that concern, to optimize the chances for success, would maximize the proposition of permanent division.

On November 27, the Finnish initiative failed to broker a Greco-Turkish compromise on Cyprus. The deadlock over Cyprus dimmed Turkey's hopes for EU accession. The Ankara protocol, the return of Varosha to the Greek Cypriots, can only be resolved, Gul said, as part of a comprehensive solution to the problem on a UN basis. On November 29, the European Commission recommended a partial suspension of Turkey's negotiations to the EU (eight of the thirty-five policy chapters not be closed, into which accession talks are divided) until the Cyprus issue was resolved.[330]

German Chancellor Angela Merkel, who is not supportive of Turkey's EU membership, said, "There cannot be a simple 'let's carry on as we are' in the negotiations with Turkey."[331] Cypriot President Papadopoulos expressed his frustration with the recommendation and said, "We believe it does not offer any form of pressure on Turkey to comply with its obligations. . . . This is not helpful at all."[332] Cypriot government spokesman Christodoulos Pashiardis said, "If we are not satisfied with the EU conclusions . . . we will revert and exercise our right not to permit the opening of chapters of Turkey's accession course."[333] Erdogan's defiance of EU threats meant bold leadership that was crucial in mobilizing domestic support for his party in the coming elections in 2007. The grand strategy was to project confidence and expectations of a stirring call to end the international embargo that has been in place on the Turkish Cypriots over twenty years and overcome the many forces resisting Turkey's accession. To mobilize support for Turkey, Erdogan broadened his personal campaign at home and abroad to forge an effective support for Turkey's accession the EU member state. Before Cardinal Joseph Ratzinger became a pope in April 2004, Pope Benedict XVI declared to *Le Monde* in 2004 that Turkey did not belong to EU. Pope Benedict XVI, instead of highlighting the common religious bonds of Judaism, Christianity, and Islam, expressed the conviction that the European Union represented the Christian spiritual community, and the Church (Christ's body), to stay pure, must derail Turkey's (a Muslim nation) application for membership. Contrary to this proclamation, diversity of religious orientation should be accepted and tolerated in an atmosphere of mutual respect and should form an essential part of creative political change. But during his four-day visit to Turkey, on November 28, 2006, Pope Benedict gave support for its bid to enter the EU.[334] The Rev. Federico Lombardi, in a brief statement, said that the Vatican has "neither the power nor the specific political task" of getting Turkey admitted to the EU.[335] The Vatican has said that it "views positively and encourages the road of dialogue and of moving toward integration of Turkey in Europe on the basis of common values and principles."[336] It was a shrewd maneuver by the Pope to repair relations with the Islamic world after his remarks at Germany's Regensburg University, in Bonn, on September 15, 2006, quoting Byzantine Christian Emperor Manuel II Paleologus in a conversation with a Muslim intellectual in which the emperor said the prophet Muhammad's contributions to religion were "evil and inhuman, such as his command to spread by the sword the faith he preached."[337] The Islamic world was incensed by the remarks, and the pope's trip to Turkey provided him the platform to energize dialogue and goodwill with the Islamic world.

On December 7, Turkey proposed a three-pronged plan to avert a partial suspension of its EU membership talks. The concession included the following:

1. Open one port and one airport to traffic from Cyprus for one year.
2. The EU must take steps to ease the isolation of the Turkish Cypriots. Turkey's expectation was the opening of Ercan Airport to international flights, and the Port of Famagusta would be used for direct trade under the EU Direct Trade Regulation of July 7, 2004.
3. Under the patronage of the UN, Turkey wanted a comprehensive Cyprus settlement within 12 months.

The offer failed to narrow the sharp division between Greece and Cyprus, and both adamantly rejected Ankara's offer and refused to link the Cyprus issue with Turkey's obligations to enforce the customs union. The Greek Cypriots signaled that they would block all EU membership talks with Ankara if attempts were made by some EU members to let Turkey "off the hook."[338] The Turkish overture was seen largely as an act of political stagecraft aimed at influencing the outcome of the EU meeting on December 14–15, 2006, to decide whether to freeze negotiations on about a quarter of the chapters required for EU membership.[339] EU Commission President Jose Manuel Barroso called it "an important step" toward breaking the deadlock over Turkey's EU membership application.[340] Finland called Turkey's offer a "positive indication" of progress, but "not a solution."

The EU foreign ministers agreed unanimously, on December 11, to freeze eight chapters (on trade, financial services, agriculture, and transport) related to the customs unions out of the thirty-five total, and not to close any other chapters until the EU Commission verified annually until 2009 that Turkey had fulfilled its commitments related to Cyprus. Despite the Greek demands that a date (2008) be set at which the sanctions could be toughened if Ankara make no progress, no ultimatums or deadlines were endorsed by the EU.[341] In a *New York Times* editorial, "Obstacles in Turkey's Path," on December 30, 2006, the author purported the following:

> The E.U. blundered when it allowed a divided Cyprus to join the union in 2004. Reunification—of Greek Cypriots in the south and Turkish Cypriots in the north—should have been a precondition . . . some are using the stalemate [to reunite the island] as an excuse to hamstrung Turkey's entry. Opposition to Turkey fails the test of Europe's values of tolerance and political compromise . . . it's up to the European Union to mend the Cyprus divide and clear the way for a dispassionate recognition of Turkey's vital role in Europe.[342]

EU also reiterated a promise to end the economic isolation of the Turkish Cypriot community. The foreign ministers' decision was endorsed formally at an EU summit in Brussels on December 14 to 15, 2006. The EU decision will slow down Turkey's membership talks, but Ankara vowed to press ahead with reforms. Despite the humiliation of Turkey by the EU, Ankara contemplated their dilemma and opted to pursue its economic and political alignment with the West.

The EU, under the leadership of Germany, committed itself to respond to dire needs of the Turkish Cypriots and plans slowly emerged around the principle to provide TRNC access to international markets. On January 22, 2007, the General Affairs Council of the EU reached a decision to start working on direct trade with TRNC. The United States endorsed the EU's policy to reduce the economic isolation and the economic disparities between the two Cypriot communities. On March 6, the Enlargement Commissioner, Olli Rehn, declared that the EU was determined to pursue direct trade with TRNC regardless of Nicosia's objection by recourse to Article 133, which allows the implementation of the decision without the unanimous approval of all member states. Papadopoulos threatened that he would appeal the case to the European Court of Justice if the commission approved the direct trade regulation through harbors and airports under the control of TRNC, as this would lead to the "dismemberment" of Cyprus.[343] Despite the European Commission–drafted regulation in 2004 to kick-start direct trade with TRNC, Papadopoulos was totally intransigent on direct trade and, as a result, progress was put on ice until after the presidential elections in Cyprus in 2008.[344]

On March 31, 2007, Papadopoulos submitted a new proposal to EU as an alternative to direct trade regulations that allowed TRNC exports and imports only through the Greek Cypriot–controlled ports. The diplomatic goal of Papadopoulos, as in 2006, was to block and suspend EU's direct trade proposals and the continued economic isolation of TRNC from the international community. The Greek Cypriot parliamentarians reminded the EU that the direct trade regulations could not be implemented without the approval of the Republic of Cyprus.[345] Despite the economic embargo in place since 1974, TRNC has gone through remarkable industrial and development transformation. By an overwhelming majority, the Bundestag on May 28, 2007, approved a resolution for Germany to take the initiative to push for a Cyprus settlement and direct trade with TRNC. The resolution calls on the Cyprus government to lift its ban on parliament, administration, public organizations, and educational institutions in TRNC. The nonbinding resolution, which irked the Cyprus government, calls for direct ties between TRNC and the EU.[346] Turkey and the United Kingdom signed a Strategic Partnership Agreement in London on October 23, 2007. The agreement stresses a joint cooperation against terrorism, support for Turkey's entry negotiations with the EU, facilitation of an end to the international and economic isolation of the Turkish Cypriots. Greece and the Greek Cypriot administration in Cyprus strongly objected to the cooperation pact, and Cyprus issued a veiled threat against the presence of the British bases on the island.[347]

Ethnic leaders failed to project a vision to tackle the root of the problem: willingness to compromise in order to develop close relationships to shape their political future. Lack of trust continues to divide them even more deeply, and each exploits the vulnerabilities of the other in floundering European political circles. Ardent supporters of the radical elements are eager to exploit the frustration of both ethnic members by tightening the political grip to promote their agendas. The tragic experiences of the past continue to be reinforced at every political event, and the political agenda is aimed to exploit the frustrations of both groups, contributing to the irreconcilability of their differences. The political strategy of aiming to promote ethnic agendas has created contentious fracas and feuding about political interests and predominance over all governmental institutions. The minority exclusiveness backfired and added to the conflict with competing ideologies and determination for political survival.

EU members are proud of their claim of inclusivity, cultural diversity, religious tolerance, universal human rights, and peaceful coexistence. But the vote against Turkey on December 14 to 15, 2006, reinforces the radical view that the Christian West continues to discriminate against the Muslims and the Jews. The merging consensus is that Christian Europe has a sense of superiority, being discriminatory against minorities, intolerant of immigrant population and their religion, and anti-Semitic. The vote demonstrated that the European vision is a union of Christians and an exclusion of other religions, which poses a risk that limits the pursuit of peaceful coexistence.

This European mind-set manifested itself once again when French President Jacques Chirac, on October 3, 2005, remarked that Turkey would need a "major Cultural Revolution before joining the European Union."[348] In an interview with French daily *Le Figaro* on March 23, 2007, EU Term President Germany's Chancellor Angela Merkel compounded the offence in her skeptical remark by calling for a "privileged partnership" that would fall short of membership. She went on to say, "The question about full membership won't seem so pressing in fifty years' time because the relationship of neighbor states to the EU will be that much more attractive." Erdogan, seeking answers to the exclusion of Turkey from the EU 50th anniversary celebrations in Berlin in March 2007, said, "If the EU has negative thoughts about Turkey, it should make its decision so that we can continue our own course. Let's not waste money or energy."[349] Chirac and Merkel have effectively thwarted Turkey's desire for full EU membership in the Berlin Declaration by avoiding a positive gesture to Ankara. The election of Nicolas Sarkozy as president of France on May 6, 2007, dealt a further blow to Ankara's hopes of becoming an EU member. Sarkozy, a staunch opponent of Turkey's entry to EU, reaffirmed his decision by saying that "Turkey does not have its place in the EU" and proposed that Turkey be included in the creation of a "Mediterranean Union." [350] Foreign Secretary David Miliband, in a speech on the UK's relationship with Europe on November 15, 2007, said that the EU should keep its promises to Turkey, adding, "If we fail . . . it will signal a deep and dangerous divide between east and west."[351] On January 8, 2008, President Bush, in his remarks to President Gul at the White House, endorsed Turkey's bid to join the EU and called it a "constructive bridge" between the West and the Muslim world.[352] Turkey was the first Muslim country to gain admission to the European community of nations in 1856, and hence it was treated as an equal with full rights under international law. U.S. President Barack Obama attended the meeting of the Alliance of Civilizations held in Istanbul on April 7, 2009, as his commitment to forge new relations with Islamic countries. The U.N.-backed Alliance of Civilizations was launched in 2005 in a bid to help overcome prejudices and misunderstanding between different cultures and religions. Obama is keen on reconstructing good relations and "anchor[ing] Turkey more firmly in the West"[353] to help reverse anti-Americanism. Turkey's relations with the U.S. were strained following the Turkish parliament's March 2003 decision to block U.S.-led coalition forces from launching an invasion of Iraq through Turkey. Turkey has been conceptualized as a critical ally of the U.S., but Obama's visit on April 6 and 7, 2009, laid the groundwork for a renewed partnership and the goodwill that will serve America's interest in the Muslim world and help resolve issues in Afghanistan, Iraq, Iran, Israeli-Arab relations, and the energy security for Europe. Obama's speech to the Turkish parliament on April 6 was well received by the Turks and helped strengthen ties and heightened Turkey's emergence as a regional power. Turkish-American relations, as a strategic partnership, are expected to facilitate the removal of the economic isolation of the Turkish Cypriots. Despite ongoing debate, Western governments hesitate to admit a Muslim nation to the EU under the argument that the major part of Turkey is in Asia Minor. Far-right parties' sweep in the European Union parliamentary elections on June 7, 2009, slowed the accession talks with Ankara and privileged partnership for Turkey instead of membership as proposed. Conservative parties are not proponents of a strong European Union, immigration, enlargement, or Turkey's membership.[354]

Professor Niyazi Berkes, a Turkish Cypriot-Canadian sociologist, wrote the following:

> Throughout [Turkey's] history, in respect to its economy and politics, it has been more western than eastern. The dominant direction of Ottoman history has tilted more toward the west than toward the east. But its adherence to an eastern cultural reference has prevented Turkey's inclusion in the western world. . . . Europe has never considered itself as including Turkey, and if we think the contrary, no one but ourselves believe it.[355]

But since Ataturk, Turkey continues to push westernization as a state policy, and despite all the obstacles, Turkey is determined to succeed in the long and bumpy journey to the EU. The EU is hesitant to allow Turkey's integration due to possible Turkish immigration to Western Europe in huge numbers. The following are the contributing factors of the Greco-Turkish conflict: Cyprus; the Aegean Sea dispute over the extension of territorial waters; the economic exploitation of minerals (oil) beyond Greece's territorial limit of six miles; the questions regarding sovereign airspace; the remilitarization of the eastern Greek islands in the Aegean, which is considered by the Turks in violation of the Lausanne Treaty (1923); the Montreux Convention (1936); and religious distinctions (Greeks are predominantly Greek-Orthodox Christians while Turks are Sunni Muslim). The Turkish government is highly cognizant of the challenges it faces.

The politics of oil off Cyprus added to the tensions in the region. On February 1, 2007, Turkey sent warships to international waters off Cyprus amid growing tensions over the oil and gas agreement signed between Cyprus and Lebanon on January 17, 2007, to facilitate undersea exploration. Similar accords were signed with Egypt in 2003, and Israel in 2010, which has been divided into thirteen exploration blocks covering about 51,000 square kilometers, but Syria declined to join the negotiations. On January 30, 2007, Turkey warned Egypt and Lebanon not to press ahead with the oil and gas exploration agreement without considering the legitimate and legal rights of the Turkish Cypriots. The 120-mile-wide seabed separating Lebanon and Cyprus is believed to hold $400 billion worth of crude oil and natural gas deposits. Cyprus considers the natural reserves in its exclusive economic zone under the Law of the Sea.

Turkey is poised to challenge the oil exploration plans by the Cyprus government and is moving ahead with plans to carry oil exploration with an offshore area that Greeks plan to open for explorations. A Turkish oil company, TPAO, conducted seismic studies in a 2,485-mile area in the Mediterranean.

Despite Turkish warnings, Cypriot Foreign Minister Giorgos Lillikas declared that Cyprus as a sovereign nation has the right, according the *acquis communautaire* and international law, to conclude bilateral agreements, and at the end of 2007, the first licenses for oil explorations were to be issued. On March 21, the European Council urged Turkey to avoid any action that could negatively affect the peace in the region and that the benefits accrued from the offshore area on the continental shelf should enhance the prospects for reunification rather than cause military confrontation.[356] On August 14, the state-owned Turkish Petroleum Corporation (TPAC) opened the tender for oil and gas exploration in a four-thousand-kilometer area in the eastern Mediterranean.[357] Foreign Minister of Cyprus Erato Kozakou-Marcoullis declared that Turkey's stance on oil exploration was in violation of international law and "may affect the country's EU membership process negatively."[358]

On August 16, 2007, the Cyprus government received two applications submitted by a consortium consisting of the three companies from the United Kingdom, Norway, and the United Arab Emirates and from a company based in Texas to search and exploit oil in three out of the eleven exploration areas open for tenders.[359] On November 13 and 24, 2008, two Panamanian-flagged Norwegian vessels conducting an exploratory survey twenty-seven nautical miles southwest of Paphos coast and south of Larnaca related to oil and gas, working for the Greek Cypriot administration, were ordered by a Turkish warship to cease operations and withdraw to Cyprus's twelve-mile territorial waters.[360] In Ankara, foreign ministry spokesmen said the following:

> We consider it an adventurist move to carry out activities on Turkey's continental shelf at a time when negotiations for a comprehensive settlement are underway in Cyprus.[361]

There was no indication that Ankara would ever change course regarding its Cyprus policy despite the tough Greek rhetoric that it will block Turkey's EU accession course. The Turkish Petroleum Corporation, in a partnership with an Italian company, has launched explorations for oil and gas in the areas around Antalya, Mersin, Iskenderun, and the TRNC.[362]

On May 26, the U.S. ambassador to the Republic of Cyprus, Frank Urbancic, told the media that an American company was expected in the near future to start exploring for oil and natural gas in the island's southwest coast. The reserves are in international waters at 2,500 meters depth, and it is estimated to be worth about $400 billion. Ankara was shocked and infuriated by the news and considered the move "provocative" because it "will harm the equal rights and interests of the Turkish Cypriot people vis-à-vis the natural resources of the island."[363] Turkey warned that it will not allow the American company slated to undertake exploration for oil and gas in Cyprus waters. Burak Ozugergin, spokesman of the Turkish foreign ministry, said the following:

> Such moves are inconsistent with the ongoing substantial negotiations between the two sides on the island. Such moves create the dynamics for tension and are devoid of legal standing; in addition they infringe equal rights and the interests of the Turkish Cypriot people that are related to the natural wealth of the island. Turkey has basic rights and interests in the marine areas that are on the west of the equator. It is natural that our country will protect these rights.[364]

As a stern warning to Greek Cypriot administration, Turkish warships staged two-day search and rescue drills starting on June 17, 2009, in the disputed waters off the northern town of Famagusta, where exploration for oil and gas were to be carried out by an American company. The Greek Cypriots reacted acidly to Turkish naval exercises and decried them as a violation of its territorial sovereignty under international law. Christofias lambasted Ankara's claim to legitimate rights and interests in the Eastern Mediterranean.[365] The United States and Russia sent naval forces to patrol Eastern Mediterranean waters around Cyprus and both states supported the Greek Cyprus's right to explore for undersea oil and gas in its territorial seas under the UN Convention on the Law of the Sea that entered into effect in 1982 and was signed by 162 nations.

In October 2012, the Republic of Cyprus with the help of Israeli energy company DELEK and Noble Energy Inc., of Houston, Texas, discovered a gas reservoir in block 12 ranging from 8 trillion cubic feet in an 800,000 acre (3,237 square kilometer) southeast of the island, in Leviathan field bordering Israeli waters that will make the island energy independent for two hundred years. The drilling started September 18, 2011, and reached 19,225 feet in water depth of about 5,540 feet. The maritime boundaries of Syria, Turkey, Lebanon, Cyprus, Israel, and Gaza continue to be disputed. The UN has been reluctant to assume the responsibility to establish the sea boundaries between the countries. Turkey declared Cyprus's maritime agreement with Israel null and void. Turkey declared that the Turkish Cypriots have rights and jurisdiction over maritime areas of Cyprus. Cyprus claims the underwater gas reservoir is under its exclusive economic zone under the 1982 United Nations Convention on the Law of the Sea, which Turkey has not signed.[366] The Turkish Cypriots objected to drilling because they felt excluded from any potential revenues from oil and gas. Solon Kassinis, director of the Cyprus Energy Services, dismissed claims that the Greek Cypriots would monopolize any revenue from oil and gas. Kassinis said, "What we find will not only be for the Greek Cypriots. . . . It is for legal residents of Cyprus."[367] Nicos Rolandis, who served as minister of commerce, industry, and tourism from February 23, 1998, until February 28, 2003, in an editorial in *Cyprus Mail* on June 13, 2012, wrote, "I always thought that this potentially huge oil and gas wealth might constitute the catalyst for a solution to the Cyprus problem and of any issues between Greece, Turkey and Cyprus."[368] Turkey warned the international companies "that if they had any commercial involvement in the Cyprus offshore gas deals, they would be denied to take part in any of the energy projects in which Turkey is involved."[369]

The Turkish government on July 16, 2009, authorized the state-owned Turkish Petroleum Corporations (TPAO) to explore for oil beyond Turkish territorial waters in international waters in the Mediterranean for one year.[370] The Koca Piri Reis research vessel started geophysical surveys and seismic data collection on September 19, 2011, in Block 12, a zone where the Greek Cypriots were claiming exclusive economic zone. Piri Reis was escorted at sea by frigates and by fighter jets. Greece urged "restraint" on the part of all countries, but considered any deal signed between Turkey and the Turkish Cypriot administration as invalid under international law.[371] Turkey continued to step up its threats against the Greek Cypriots by strengthening its naval and air power in the disputed region. Greek Cypriot Foreign Minister Erato Kozakou-Marcoullis said that "Cyprus is taking turkey's threats seriously, and is doing everything possible to find a solution."[372] Turkish Prime Minister Recep Erdogan said, "We will try all channels of peace, but we will also protect our country's interests until the end."[373] The UN's envoy Alexander Downer urges for restraint to avoid derailing the Greco-Turkish Cypriot peace talks and the UN would consider mediating a resolution to the drilling dispute. Cyprus government rejected the offer and declared that the drilling was unrelated to the peace talks.[374] On February 13, 2012, Cyprus invited license applications to search for minerals inside twelve of thirteen sections that together make up the island's 19,700 square miles (51,000 square kilometers) exclusive economic zone off its southern coast. Israel has proposed a partnership with Cyprus to build a facility on the island to process and export gas to Europe, but Russia is exerting pressure on Cyprus to be given license to develop some of the fields for having backed the Greek Cypriots' position on the natural gas issue with the Turks.[375]

Minister of Foreign Affairs Dr. Erato Kozakou-Marcoullis, in a forum in Washington, D.C., on May 3, 2012, said that "single drilling indicated an estimated gross resource range of 5 to 8 trillion cubic feet (Tcf) of natural gas, with a gross mean of 7 Tcf."[376] Marcoullis, in regard to recent discoveries, said that "the U.S. Geological Survey has estimated a mean of 1.7 billion barrels of recoverable oil and a mean of 122 trillion cubic feet of recoverable gas in the Levant Basin Province, as well as 1.8 billion barrels of recoverable oil, 223 trillion cubic feet of recoverable gas and 6 billion barrels of natural gas liquids in the Nile Delta Basin Province in the Eastern Mediterranean."[377] The Turkish Petroleum Corporation (TPAO) on April 26, 2012, began drilling for oil and gas in TRNC under an agreement signed in September 2011. Turkey's state-run oil company started drilling for oil and gas as deep as 3,000 meters (9,850 feet) in Gazimagusa, and an agreement was signed with Royal Dutch Shell for operations in the southeastern region of the island.[378] Turkish Energy Minister Taner Yildiz, who attended the drilling ceremony, said, "The Turkyurdu-1 well could be a force for peace in Cyprus. . . . While energy has produced wars in other parts of the world, here it will be a force for peace."[379] The drilling was to be completed in August 2012 at a cost of $400 million, and the profits were to be divided halfway between Turkey and TRNC. On September 21, 2011, Turkish Prime Minister Erdogan and Turkish Cypriot President Dervis Eroglu signed an agreement in New York on the delineation of the continental shelf between Turkey and TRNC, and the following day, and exploration license was given to TPAO to explore for oil and gas around the island.[380] Turkish President Abdullah Gul on July 13, 2012, approved the Continental Shelf Delineation Agreement signed with TRNC on September 21, 2011.[381] TPAO has license for land explorations for oil and gas in Morfou in TRNC.

The early parliamentary election was called by Erdogan due to AKP's nomination of Foreign Minister Abdullah Gul to the presidency. The nomination precipitated strong opposition by the nationalists' secularists and the Turkish military hierarchy. The military, backed by the secularists in the major cities, sees its role as the guarantor of Kemalist ideals to maintain as a secular state.[382] Turkish general elections on July 22, 2007, gave Erdogan a resounding victory by capturing 46.5 percent of the votes and a second five-year term to Justice and Development Party (AKP) by capturing 341 seats in the 550-member parliament. Erdogan's election victory was welcomed by the EU, and he vowed continued reforms and efforts to resolve issues relating to "concrete progress" on freedom of expression and religion, Iraq, Kurds, and Cyprus. The election results were a stinging rebuke to the Turkish old guard in the military (it made veiled coup threats in May 2007 to overthrow AKP), judiciary, bureaucracy, and the main opposition party (the Republican People's Party [CHP] won 20.9 percent of the votes or 112 seats in parliament). The resounding victory of AKP strengthened the ruling Republican Turkish Party (CTP) under the leadership of Talat in TRNC.

Following the AKP's triumph in the elections, on August 28, Gul secured 330 votes in the 550-seat parliament to win the presidency at a third round of voting. Gul needed a simple majority of 276 votes in the third round. Despite the opposition of the Turkish military chief General Yasar Buyukanit and secularist Turks, Gul's presidency would usher in a new democracy under moderate Islamists. Gul's selection was wholly democratic, and AKP will demonstrate that Muslim religious values can be incorporated in democratic politics within a secular constitutional system. AKP continues to be faithful to liberal democratic values and to the continued economic growth of Turkey despite the coup threat by the military establishment and the secularist Turks whose party agenda failed to attract the voters. Among the major issues facing the new government in Ankara was Turkey's bid to join the EU, the constitutional revisions that would limit the powers of the president over appointments and ease a rule against "insulting Turkishness," Kurdish separatism, and the Cyprus crisis. Chief of Turkish General Staff, General Yasar Buyukanit, in a speech at the Turkish War Academies on October 1, 2007, and Lieutenant General Hilmi Akin Zorlu, head of the General Staff Planning and Principles Department, at a meeting in Ankara in September, warned Erdogan's government not to take the fast lane in the EU reform process as demanded by the European Commission. The military staff is opposed to any amendments to change or abolish Article 301 of the Turkish penal code, the law that punishes the offenses of insulting Turkishness, or increasing the rights of religious foundations. The military has also shown keen interest in the property dispute in Cyprus.[383] Nobel laureate writer Orhan Pamuk, slain Armenian journalist Hrant Dink, Ragip Zarakolu, Arat Dink, and Serkis Seropyian are among those tried under Article 301 but never convicted. The AKP intends to review the law that has damaged Turkey's bid to join the EU.[384]

Turkish President Gul visited Northern Cyprus on September 18, which was his first foreign visit since taking office, and he urged the international community to end the economic isolation of TRNC. In his address to the TRNC parliament, Gul said, "The reality on the island is that there are two states, two democracies, two languages, and two religions. It is difficult to find a settlement without taking these into account."[385] Cyprus's government condemned the visit of Gul and threatened that it "will create obstacles to Turkey's accession course to the EU."[386] Gul's visit to TRNC demonstrated Turkey's solidarity and support for the Turkish Cypriots' overtures for the peaceful settlement of the Cyprus crisis. Turkish Prime Minister Erdogan, on September 19 at an *Iftar Dinner* (the celebration that breaks the Muslim fast during Ramadan), hosting a group of foreign diplomats serving in Ankara, said that his country "will not make any concessions on Cyprus" even if these concessions are required by Turkey's EU course.[387] In his address to the UN General Assembly on September 28, 2007, Erdogan said that a comprehensive settlement in Cyprus is only possible "under the good offices mission of the UN secretary-general on the basis of the well established UN parameters." He also called for the lifting of all economic embargoes imposed on TRNC by the Greek Cypriot government.[388] Former German Chancellor Gerhardt Schroeder visited TRNC on February 1, 2008, as the guest of the Turkish Cypriot authorities to boost trade. Papadopoulos described the visit as "a very sad development." Greek Cypriots in general were outraged and expressed the view that Schroeder's visit was "another episode in the serial of upgrading the occupied areas" that caused acute embarrassment to Papadopoulos's government. The international community was determined to ease the economic isolation of the Turkish Cypriots, and EU Enlargement Commissioner Olli Rehn declared that ports and airports of TRNC could be used by ships and aircraft of third countries, even though Papadopoulos's government has declared them illegal ports of entry.[389] The 5th Conference of the Organization of the Islamic Conferences Inter-Parliamentary Union in Cairo approved a draft resolution to lift the isolation implemented on TRNC and provided for the strengthening of cooperation in the fields of culture, politics, economy, and sports.[390] UN Secretary-General Ban Ki Moon's report on November 23, 2007, called for the ending of the Turkish Cypriot economic isolation.[391] The UN Secretary Council adopted Resolution 1789 on December 14, 2007, renewed the mandate of UNFICYP until June 2008, but left out the controversial reference to the isolation of the Turkish Cypriots.[392] The organization of Islamic Conference in 2007 adopted a resolution encouraging closer economic cooperation with TRNC.

On August 21, 2007, Greek and Turk representatives met to discuss the arrangements for the meeting between Papadopoulos and Talat after fourteen months on September 5. The meeting reaffirmed the gap between the two leaders, and neither side was receptive to the other side's proposals. Papadopoulos insisted on the unconditional implementation of the July 8 Gambari agreements, while Talat proposed the launching of comprehensive talks at once to reach a solution by the end of 2008. Papadopoulos reacted to Talat's proposals as follows: "Mr. Talat wanted changes to the [deal] ... which could not expedite the process, but would on the contrary expedite the realization of deadlocks."[393] Talat's reply was that "the Greek Cypriot side is not psychologically ready to start full-fledged negotiations."[394] The meeting was arranged to bolster the presidential candidacy of Papadopoulos on February 17, 2008, because no substantive progress was made toward setting up the working groups and the technical committees. *Cyprus Mail*, on August 17, 2007, in an editorial, wrote the following:

> Papadopoulos wants a meeting purely to disprove opposition accusations that the Cyprus problem is not in the deep freeze on the eve of an election, while the Turkish Cypriots may go along with it, reluctantly, if only to avoid being seen as the party sabotaging talks.[395]

A successful negotiation is not elusive if it extends beyond ethnicity and religion, but acknowledges equal opportunity for Greek Turkish Cypriots for a better life, security, justice, education, and representation in all governmental institutions. Lack of a genuine commitment to the peace process has not allowed community leaders to cooperate and cultivate their own virtues in devising the political institutions to govern themselves under protected human rights.

Greek Prime Minister Costas Karamanlis's three-day visit to Turkey on January 25, 2008, did not produce a breakthrough on Cyprus, the ongoing dispute over the Aegean Sea that brought the two countries to the brink of war three times since 1974, or on the issue of minority rights in both countries. Nevertheless, the visit was an important step to improving relations and enhancing economic cooperation. His uncle, Constantine Karamanlis, was the last Greek premier to visit Turkey in 1959. Greek economic interests in Turkey are growing, and the two countries have opened a joint gas pipeline, and the normalization of relations with Turkey is no longer conditional on a Cyprus settlement.[396] In his remarks, Karamanlis stressed the resolution of the Cyprus problem, the airspace and sea boundaries between Greece and Turkey, the reopening of the Halki Theological School on Heybeliada Island near Istanbul, and the protection of the human rights of religious minorities. Erdogan, on the other hand, emphasized the resolution of the Cyprus issues based on the Annan Plan, while his Greek counterpart Karamanlis stressed the need to tear down the wall that has divided Cyprus since 1974, and the implementation of the July 8, 2006, agreement between Papadopoulos and Talat that was to contribute to a comprehensive settlement to the Cyprus crisis. The failure to achieve a comprehensive reunification settlement has accelerated the process of "Taiwanisation," which will inevitably speed up the process to the partition of Cyprus.

The Greek Cypriots went to the polls on February 17, 2008, to elect a president for a five-year term. The three presidential hopefuls were incumbent president Tassos Papadopoulos, the candidate of the center-right Democratic Party (DIKO), the Social Democrat (EDEK), the European Party, and the Environmentalists; Demetris Christofias,[397] the leader of the Communist Party (AKEL); and Ioannis Kasoulides, the right-wing Democratic Rally (DISY) party candidate. AKEL endorsed its own candidate in its eighty-two-year history for the presidency, and its campaign promise was to press for the reunification of Cyprus. In the last presidential elections in 2003, AKEL supported Papadopoulos, but in recent years, it has been critical of his handling of the Cyprus problem. Papadopoulos's stress on reunification and the resolution of the complex Cypriot crisis is not out of honest conviction for reconciliation but a political theatrical performance for the international community. With the UN's growing impatience with the lack of progress on the Cyprus issue, the option for the permanent partition of the island is gaining the support of the international community.[398]

Hard-line President Papadopoulos was eliminated in a first-round presidential election after taking 31.79 percent of the vote:

> In what is seen as a no-confidence vote for the policies of a man who led the rejection of the Annan Plan in 2004, calling for and receiving a "resounding no." . . . He was unwilling to take any initiative or to show the slightest hint of good faith in dealing with the other side.[399]

Most Greek Cypriots rejected Papadopoulos's uncompromising approach to solving the Cyprus crisis and voted in favor of progressive-minded candidate. Ioannis Kasoulides, fifty-nine, a former foreign minister and member of the European Union, ran as an independent backed by the right-wing DISY party, and won 33.51 percent of the vote. Demetris Christofias, sixty-two, AKEL secretary-general and the speaker of parliament, received 33.29 percent of the vote. Since none of the two leading candidates secured more than 50 percent of the vote, Kasoulides and Christofias competed in the runoff election, held on February 24. The two candidates pledged to bring new flexibility and commitment to peace negotiations with the Turkish Cypriot community.

The center-right DIKO party of ousted president Papadopoulos and the Socialist EDEK endorsed the candidacy of Demetris Christofias in the runoff elections on February 24 against Ioannis Kasoulides. Kasoulides refusal to repent and show remorse for his "yes" vote on the Annan Plan contributed to DIKO's decision to back Christofias. The outgoing president Papadopoulos "had a big hand in the final decision, despite his earlier declaration of neutrality" on election runoff.[400] AKEL offered three ministerial positions to DIKO against the five cabinet posts offered by Kasoulides in order to gain their endorsement. Christofias has a doctorate degree in history from a Russian university, he has strong ties with the nonaligned countries, and his party is wary of NATO and was against the admission of Cyprus into the euro zone on January 1, 2008. AKEL leader has cultivated good relations with President Talat by crossing over the green line to promote bicommunal contact and trade union movement. Kasoulides, a medical doctor, who specializes in geriatric medicine, was foreign minister in the Glafcos Clerides government from 1997 to 2003. In June 2004, he was elected as Cyprus's first member of the European Parliament, and as an independent candidate, he was endorsed by the island's Orthodox Church amid concerns about the communist party rule scrapping religious education from the school curriculum. Christofias charged that the comments of Archbishop Chrysostomos II were a slur and that he never contemplated abolishing religious education.

The Greek Cypriots elected Christofias as Cyprus's first communist president by 53.37 percent of the votes casted on February 24, making him the only communist in the twenty-seven-member EU. His rival, Kasoulides, received 46.63 percent of the votes. AKEL supporters hailed the election victory by wielding flags with the image of Ernesto "Che" Guevara, a red flag emblazoned with a hammer and sickle, Greek flags, and party flags. At Nicosia Eleftheria stadium, Christofias said the following:

> You know well we have a clear vision . . . a noble vision to reunite
> Cyprus . . . rid it of the occupation [and] unite all its people,
> Greek Cypriots and Turkish Cypriots.[401]

AKEL leader was quick to stress the need for unity and cooperation with Talat in a bid to stop the "slide to partition."[402] AKEL, DIKO, and EDEK alliance played a pivotal role in Christofias's victory, and he acknowledged their help by saying, "I am standing before you as the elected President of the Cyprus Republic."[403] Christofias vowed to accelerate the negotiations with the Turkish Cypriots, but had given assurances to DIKO and EDEK that he "would never accept a solution based on provisions of the Annan Plan."[404]

Will the new president be a hostage to the hard-liners who supported him in the elections, or fulfill his campaign pledge to secure a Cyprus settlement? His failure to respond to the Turkish Cypriot demands at the negotiations will give cause to establishment of a two separate state system.

NOTES

CHAPTER 4

SHATTERED ASPIRATIONS BETWEEN
COEXISTENCE AND SEPARATION

If only we lived on the reverse side would we see
things straight on?
— Odysseus Elytis, "Maria Nephele"

Will President Christofias seek to explore the roots of the Greco-Turkish conflict and identify creative solutions in handling the differences to find a win-win outcome instead of advocating entrenched radical positions? John P. Lederach writes the following:

> Conflict transformation must actively envision, include, respect, and promote the human cultural resources from within a given setting. This involves a new set of lenses through which we do not primarily "see" the setting and the people in it as the "problem" and the outsider as the "answer." Rather, we understand the long-term goal of transformation as validating and building on people and resources within the setting.[405]

In the transformation of ethnic conflict, the two protagonists must be motivated to establish constructive peaceful relationships in reconciliation and nonviolent resolution of disputes. An honest exchange of views through dialogues to resolve conflicts have been forced into the background by the hard-line Greek Cypriot leaders. The moderate representatives of the Greek Cypriot parties are giving acknowledgement to the necessity of a dialogue to resolve the substance of the Greco-Turkish differences in the negotiations. Norbert Ropers writes as follows:

> Conflict resolutions deals not only with obvious conflicts over matters of substance, but also with troubled relations between parties in order to set the substantive conflicts themselves in a new context and tackle them as a shared problem.[406]

What this means is that a constructive dialogue process between protagonists should build up consensus in order to facilitate honest discussions about the conflict in a new context and provide new impetus for conflict resolution.

Before the inauguration of President-elect Christofias on February 28, he declared his determination to resume the dialogue with President Talat, only on the condition that all the Security Council resolutions and the agreements reached between the leaders of the communities were not revoked by future negotiations. He wanted the talks to focus on UN-brokered agreements of July 8, 2006, also known as the Gambari Process, and was prepared to secure an agreement by accepting a bizonal, bicommunal federation form of governance. He also demanded the withdrawal of all foreign troops from the island. Upon his arrival to TRNC, on March 26, the Turkish chief of the general staff Yasar Buyukanit stated that the Turkish troops were to stay on the island until "a just and lasting peace is secured."[407] Talat's proposal advocated two states, known as the virgin birth of a new state, using the Annan Plan as the basis for negotiations. Talat stressed that the Annan Plan would be used as a fundamental reference during the talks, and that Turkey was not ready to open its ports to Greek Cypriot registered vessels before the removal of the international economic isolation of TRNC. Furthermore, Talat underlined the need for Great Britain, Greece, and Turkey's approval for any alterations to the Treaty of Guarantee and Alliance, and that EU would not be a "guarantor of anybody."[408] The opposing sides' contestations over these issues set the stage for unachievable political goals and unleashed fuel against the legitimatization of the two-state system.

A zero-sum attitude prevails in the ethnic conflict negotiations when it comes to sovereignty, power-sharing, the restructuring of the security forces, security dilemmas, property, return of the refugees, withdrawal of Greek and Turkish troops, Anatolian settlers, citizenship, and political equality of the two ethnic groups. There is no easy solution to the Greco-Turkish dilemma on the island. The negotiations could not proceed in the direction intended to conform to the perceived interests of either community. To produce an agreement, neither side should doggedly defend causes that have little chance of success, or that systematically and endlessly create impossible preconditions for the start of negotiations. A genuine change of positions in the contested ethnic conflict offers a mechanism for bridging some degree of reconciliation that will deepen commitment in pursuit of a shared political agenda. The appearance of intransigence renders the political action less plausible, allowing the parties in conflict to produce a parallel impasse. It is naïve to think that a settlement is possible if the contending parties' positions are incompatible with those of the opponent, diminishes the chance of accommodation.

Christofias and Talat met over three hours on March 21, 2008, at the residence of the UN secretary-general's special representative in Cyprus, Michael Moller.[409] They managed to agree for their advisors, George Iacovou[410] and Ozdil Nami, to meet subsequently to arrange the working groups and technical committee's necessary for preliminary face-to-face talks, and in three months Christofias and Talat were to meet to review the results before starting the full-fledged negotiations.[411] An agreement was reached on March 26 for the creation of six working groups and seven technical committees. The working groups were assigned to deliberate on governance and power-sharing, EU matters, security and guarantees, territory, property, and economic matters. The technical committees were responsible for matters relating to crime, economic and commercial, cultural heritage, crisis management, humanitarian concerns, health, and the environment. The working groups were not to engage in negotiations but to prepare the ground for substantive direct negotiations between the two community leaders. To avert the recurrence of the catastrophic miscalculations of 1974, the decision-makers must be realistic as to attainable goals and capable of utilizing a peaceful means to defuse political tensions. The peace process was overshadowed by the inflammatory remarks of Archbishop Chrysostomos who said that some of the Greek Cypriots' views on the technical committee were identical to those of Turkey: "The only fear we have as a church is the presence of a few fortunately people on the panels whose views are identical with those of the Turks." The prelate was referring to some team members who supported the Annan Plan in the referendum.[412] Arrangements intended to advance and consolidate political power as a means of subduing and neutralizing the opponent yielded ominous results. The surge of international support helped lure the leaders of both communities to seize the opportunity in creating a realistic mechanism to achieve agreements and arrangements in the quest of a comprehensive settlement or lose the opportunity forever.

Christofias relied on presidential leadership, personal diplomacy, and compromise in dealing with the Cyprus crisis. He did not yield to his critics and devoted considerable energy to strengthening ties with Talat. The simultaneous achievement of the establishment of the working groups and the April 13, 2010, opening of Ledra Street[413] (Turks call it Lokmaci Street), whose barricade had been in place since 1963 to pedestrians, indicated a sure-footedness on the part of both leaders in dealing with their single biggest challenge: Cyprus settlement. On June 16, 2008, the EU eased the economic isolation of the Turkish Cypriots by adopting new amendments to the Green Line Regulation designed to "enhance[e] trade and economic integration on the island" and help "support" confidence and integration between the two communities. The rules would lift duties on a variety of agricultural products from the north and ease restrictions on companies that carry services across the Green Line border when providing services in the south. The 135 euros ceiling on personal goods carried by visitors crossing the line was first adopted in April 2004 was raised to 260 euros to encourage economic integration.[414] To achieve breakthroughs on a settlement, Christofias slowly and deliberately seized the opportunity to discuss cooperative measures with Talat in an effort to broker a compromise. This provided an impetus for promoting trust necessary to extract concessions.

On April 22, 2008, the Greek Cypriot Foreign Minister Markos Kyprianou,[415] in an interview with ANA-MPA, warned the Turks of a "red line" that the Greeks would not cross. He went on to say that "the new Cypriot state will result from a solution and should be a continuation of the Republic of Cyprus"; further, he noted the reintroduction of the Annan Plan would constitute a setback in the negotiations. Kyprianou reiterated the Greek demands as to territory, security, property, settlers return to Turkey and the return of the Greek Cypriots to their homes in the north. The unexpected remarks before the May 1 meeting between Christofias and Talat cast a shadow over the negotiations and were counterproductive to a comprehensive settlement. Most astonishing is Kyprianou's presumptuous and rigid outlook that puts boundaries on counter-proposals and, left to its own, would prove disastrous for the negotiations.[416] Former President Glafcos Clerides forewarned Christofias's government that what happens in the peace process negotiations will determine if "there will be partition."[417]

Ozdil Nami, advisor to Talat, in an interview with the Greek Cypriot newspaper *Phileleftheros*, on April 23, to the consternation of the Greeks, said that the negotiations for a solution will be on the basis of the Annan Plan. Before the community leaders engaged in the negotiations to resolve their differences through a mutually acceptable arrangement, the state subordinates were focusing on competing claims to yield particular outcomes. Lynn M. Wagner in his book expresses the view that the negotiation process entails compromises between the negotiating parties' positions, where neither party is entirely satisfied on all accounts. A problem solving process should create an outcome that integrates the parties' positions, respecting the needs of all and dissatisfying no one.[418]

By agreeing to negotiate a settlement, the parties must achieve a compromise over incompatible positions in order to provide outcomes that will satisfy the interests of both parties. Some issues proved to be very contentious for immediate resolution, but a failure to identify joint benefits will not encourage accommodation of one's own position. In the bargaining process, both parties must work with the other to find a solution through an exchange of concessions. The Greek and Turkish Cypriot negotiators desire to resolve the outstanding matters to reach a settlement and a final agreement, but failure to recognize the other's needs on a range of issues contributes negatively to the negotiation process and outcome. One negotiator cannot dictate the terms, and neither precludes the other's needs in an effort to maintain their own ethnocentric interest. Lack of flexibility and intransigence in the negotiations will set the tone for futility. Conciliatory actions are indicative of the negotiators' resolve for the successful resolution of disputes and set the tone for compromise. Hard bargaining tactics, or scripts, slow the process without eliciting concessions, and the negotiations once again adjourn in failure.

At the request of Christofias, the two leaders met on May 23, 2008, to assess progress and exchange views concerning the difficulties experienced by the working groups and technical committees. Both reaffirmed their commitment for the formation of a bizonal, bicommunal federation based on two equal constituent states with a single international identity. Christofias's critics nitpicked on the political equality reference, and the fact that the two sides would discuss civilian and military confidence-building measures reversing a long-held position that security issues must be discussed with Turkey. It was agreed that they would meet again in the second half of June to clarify differing opinions regarding the start of extensive negotiations and to discuss the difficulties faced by the working groups and technical committees, which impacted the talk's resumption date. The gap between the two sides remained huge, but both sides reaffirmed their commitment to work through the difficulties despite the acknowledgment of disagreements.

The thirteen bicommunal teams were to lay the groundwork for June 21 negotiations between the leaders of the two communities, but the Greek Cypriots were frustrated by the Turkish side's inability to engage on fundamental issues, to facilitate a compromised proposal before direct dialogue ensued between the two leaders. The groups and committees had no mandate to negotiate on substantive to sensitive issues. The Greek parliamentary House President Marios Garoyian expressed the view that a negotiated settlement must be based on the High Level Agreements of 1977 and 1979 Ten-Point Agreement, as well as the pertinent UN resolutions, under which Cyprus was to be reunited under a "United Republic of Cyprus as one state and not two states."[419] The hard-liners were opposed to a compromise solution and advocated an all or nothing proposition and were critical of Christofias's handling of the Cyprus peace process. The barrage of criticism came from DIKO president Marios Garoyian, former president Tassos Papadopoulos, EDEK leader Yiannakis Omirou, the European Democratic Party (EDP) vice president Nikos Koutsou, and the Green Party leader George Perdikis. The quintet had made no attempt to heal the ethnic divide; in fact, they had exacerbated them. The hawks were naïve to think that negotiations were going to be held outside the framework defined by the 2004 UN peace plan. Loucas Charalambous, in an editorial in *Cyprus Mail*, May 25, 2008, wrote the following:

> I find it impossible that there are in Cyprus today politicians who are so naïve to believe there is even one change in a million for the Greek Cypriots to secure a settlement that is significantly better than the settlement outlined in the Annan plan. On the contrary, the reality shows that the best we [Greeks] could hope for would be to secure some limited improvements on a few issues. . . . If he [President Christofias] genuinely thought that the Turkish Cypriots were so stupid to agree that their starting point for negotiations would be the Annan plan while ours would be the 1997 High Level Agreement then he must be living in the realm of fantasy.[420]

Christofias was furious with his coalition partners in DIKO and EDEK and let them know that they cannot remain in government and sow confusion in order to build public opposition to the peace efforts. Despite the concessions to enable progress in the negotiations, the political environment was too thoroughly permeated with distrust to bring matters to a suitable conclusion.

The question arose as to the competing motivations of the working groups and the clash of perspectives on the part of Christofias and Talat. The inability of the two leaders to rise to the challenges of overcoming the deadlock on the most complex issues—governance, territory, property, and Turkish settlers' issue—rendered the purpose of the joint enterprise initiative a failure in spite of the international engagement harnessed to ensure a sweeping reconciliation and a settlement. Given what was at stake, it was gross negligence caused by thoughtlessness, especially the failure to facilitate those goals indispensable to the interests of both parties. The ethnic leader's tactics were driven by justified fears, arguments, and motives, causing them to be less respondent to the needs of the other. For this reason, the negotiators were unable to stop the slippery slope resulting from their failure to overcome the hurdles relative to acceptable choices to warrant realistic outcomes. The parties interested in the reconciliation between the two communities and Cyprus settlement were overly swayed with optimism by the election of Christofias, believing that a serious debate and consensus had finally recognized the moral quest for a comprehensive agreement. Of course, one can argue that the change of Greek leadership gave the international community good reason to think that any incentive to get out of the bind demanded major concessions that reflected the common will of the community leaders to help resolve the crisis. Unfortunately, fresh optimism was quashed by deep distrust and the lack of a common vision for the future did not present the expected breakthroughs in the negotiations.

At the diplomatic front, Christofias initiated fundamental changes by venturing abroad to bolster the backing of the international community in the Cyprus negotiations. He succeeded in recruiting the British government to join him in his effort to unify Cyprus under one state. A memorandum of understanding was signed in London by Christofias and Prime Minister Gordon Brown of Great Britain on June 6, 2008, for the two states to work together to reunify the island under a "single sovereignty, international personality and a single citizenship." The Turks slammed the compact as unacceptable and declared that the memorandum was contrary to the agreements of March 21 and March 23, stating it would have a negative impact on the negotiations concerning the Cyprus settlement. In return, the British support for the Greek Cypriots in return succeeded in neutralizing the Greek Cypriot hard-liners' call for the closing of the two British military bases on the island.[421] Another issue adding to the controversy was relative to the extension of the UFICYP's mandate. On June 13, UN Security Council approved the extension of UFICYP's mandate for another six months.[422] Despite the acceptance of the draft three days earlier, the U.S. permanent representative to the UN, Zalmay Khalilzad, moved to amend the text that would have added the words "constituent states" to reflect the joint statement agreed to by Christofias and Talat on March 23, which reaffirmed their commitment for a bizonal, bicommunal federation of politically equal states. The Greek Cypriots were incensed by the U.S. motion because it was tantamount to "a tacit recognition of TRNC."[423] The U.S. motion was in reference to a partnership of two politically equal constituent states as it was agreed to in Nicosia between the two leaders on March 23, but since the debate on the resolution was already closed and accepted, the motion failed.[424] The UN undersecretary-general for political affairs Lynn Pascoe arrived in Cyprus for two days on June 16. The next day, the plans developed at a dinner hosted by UN mission chief Taye-Brook Zerihoun were to set a date for Christofias-Talat to meet, but Talat declined the invitation. Talat was irritated by the joint pact signed between Cyprus and the United Kingdom and over the wording on June 13 of the UN Security Council resolution on UNFICYP.[425] On June 18 at the "breakfast policy briefing" of the European Policy center in Brussels, Christofias remarks caused adverse reaction in Turkey and Cyprus. Christofias reverted to the sterile tactics of the past and publicly stated the Greek positions.

1. Turkey should remove half of its soldiers from Cyprus.
2. Turkey should not be a "guarantor" of the Turkish Cypriots security, but the European Union.
3. Leaders should create a reunited Cyprus under a single sovereignty and citizenship.
4. There should be a demilitarization of the island.
5. Greeks should continue to strongly oppose the two-state systems, even while Turkish Cypriots have been promoting the "virgin birth" and "new partnership state."[426]

Christofias's rhetoric against the Annan Plan was intended to satisfy EDEK and DIKO leaders, and his insistence for an endorsement of the July 8, 2006, agreement between Papadopoulos and Talat as a condition for a Cyprus solution had become a zero-sum game.

In the presence of the UN secretary-general's new special representative to Cyprus, Taye-Brook Zerihoun, on June 1, 2008, Christofias and Talat met for four and a half hours to review the progress of the bicommunal teams with all aspects of the Cyprus crisis. The two leaders agreed in principle on the issue of single sovereignty and citizenship, and both gave their approval to the appointment of Australia's former foreign minister Alexander Downer as UN special envoy.[427] The top advisory body to President Christofias, the National Council, expressed their confidence and support for the handling of the Cyprus negotiations. Talat's commitment in principle to a "single sovereignty and citizenship" came under harsh criticism by Turkish Cypriot party leaders and retired Turkish diplomats and generals.[428] Their joint statement in particular regarding the phrase "a single sovereignty and citizenship" was considered selling out Turkish interests and called on Talat to resign from office. Sovereignty and citizenship evoked the idea of a unitary state under the Republic of Cyprus based on the 1960 agreement that would render the TRNC illegitimate rather than a partner under a loose federation set out in the Annan Plan.[429] Talat defended the agreement by saying that there was no state in the world with two sovereignties or two citizenships. In an interview with Greek Cypriot daily *Alithia* on July 3, 2008, Talat said that a federation will be made up of Greek Cypriot Republic and TRNC, and the new constitution would be compromised of elements of both parties. A policy driven by a real politick view of interests tells us more about ethnic nationalism than about humility or good intentions.

Turkey's official stance is based on "equal sovereignty equal partnership" while the Greek Cypriot plan is single sovereignty and single citizenship under the Republic of Cyprus. Under the Greek Cypriot proposals, the Turkish Cypriots will be extended a minority status with some privileged rights. According to Strategic Forecasting Inc.'s report, "Cyprus: A Breakthrough for the Greek Side" on July 1, 2008, the two leaders "[have] produced deals on crucial demands of the Greek Cypriot side, paving the way for future progress on Greek terms." Strat Fore noted that "reunification still rests on the Turkish Cypriot ability to give in to all the demands of their Greek counterparts. The Greek Cypriots hold all the cards." The report underlined that the single citizenship and single sovereignty consensus of the two leaders "illustrates just how little room for the maneuver the Turkish Cypriots in the North have ... [toward] Reunification on Greek terms; therefore, will see the end of the separate Turkish political entity." The Turkish Cypriots cannot ignore Turkey's interest to favor an arrangement with the Greek Cypriots because it would put them at a great disadvantage vis-à-vis the Greeks and probably cause the severing of their economic lifeline to Ankara. Talat refuted the allegations that "single sovereignty" meant an end of TRNC nor was it acceptance of the minority status for the Turkish Cypriots in a Greek Cypriot state. But this explanation of Talat's political skill helped reduce deep political division by reaching across party lines to craft a strategic policy in the negotiations. Talat became more assertive and less conciliatory to break the dysfunctional political dynamics in a divided island not out of international pressure but out of confidence coupled with the reassurance of Turkey.

An agreement may bring certain distinct economic advantages to the Turkish Cypriots, but it drew vigorous opposition to Greek Cypriot efforts to assert their political dominance over the whole island. The Turkish Cypriots discovered the key to unlock their economic potential and built political institutions to secure their self-governance over the last two and a half decades. TRNC continues to operate under severe constraints in a complex geopolitical environment faced with the deep challenges concerning matters of security, economics, and politics. Absence of skillful diplomacy and uncompromised posture bogged down the negotiations by the hard-liners on both sides.

To bolster Talat's negotiating posture on July 25, 2008, Prime Minister of Turkey Erdogan, accompanied by eight cabinet members, attended the 34th anniversary celebrations on July 20 in Nicosia of the Turkish invasion of Cyprus. During his three-day visit, Erdogan reiterated Turkey's unconditional support for the Turkish Cypriots and said the following:

> We support the position of two equal constituent states in Cyprus.... Turkish Cypriots are no longer a minority.... The solution of the Cyprus [issue] would be in the framework of a new partnership relation which would be formed between two equal communities and two founder states under the umbrella of the United Nations and the goodwill mission of the UN General-Secretary, based on the realities of the island.... The Turkish government had been displaying remarkable efforts in order to find a fair and lasting solution to the Cyprus issue.... A comprehensive solution could only be achieved with a new partnership in which Turkish Cypriot people participate equally and as a founder element. Such new partnership will be established on the principles of bizonal structure, political equality and Turkey's effective status as guarantor state. We do not and will not accept the continuation of the isolation imposed on Turkish Cypriots.[430]

President of Turkey Gul, in his message to Talat, reaffirmed that Turkey, as a guarantor state, backs the establishment of a new partnership on Cyprus, adding, "There are only two politically equal nations, democracies and states on Cyprus."[431] In his remark, Talat called for a just, urgent, and lasting settlement to the Cyprus problem and said, "Turkish Cypriot people aim at a solution in which its equal partnership in sovereignty will be registered through using its inherent constitutive power.... [Indeed, a] solution of Cyprus problem is a must for regional and world peace."[432] Christofias accused Erdogan of being divisive, a major obstacle, and not in harmony with the commitments for the peaceful coexistence of the two Cypriot communities. Erdogan and Gul reaffirmed to the Greek leaders that a final negotiated settlement must protect the legitimate interests of the Turkish Cypriots and cannot constitute an unacceptable threat against Turkey's security. The securities of the Turkish Cypriots are inseparable from the national security of Turkey.

The fourth meeting between Christofias and Talat took place in Nicosia on July 25, and consensus was reached on many issues, but key disputes relative to sovereignty, governance, and guarantor system were left to be tackled by the two leaders at their September 3 meeting under the UN umbrella. Success of the cooperative efforts were on issues relating to the environment, cultural heritage, crisis management, wildfires, conservation of scarce water supplies, and information sharing on crime. The final agreement was to be put to separate simultaneous referenda. One could say that there was a glimmer of hope for a comprehensive agreement due to the flexibility and dedication of the two leaders with mutually acceptable outcomes.[433]

The Greek Orthodox Church leaders were strategizing to undermine a negotiated agreement without their approval or input. On August 19, 2008, Bishop of Paphos Georgios, in a speech on behalf of Archbishop Chrysostomos II, vehemently criticized President Christofias for mishandling the Cyprus problem at the negotiations. Bishop Georgios declared his strong opposition to the system of rotating presidency and rebuked the government's decision to allow 1,100 Turkish Cypriots to go to Kokkina through the Limnitis (Yesilirmak in Turkish) crossing on August 8. Each year, the Turkish Cypriots cross to visit the Kokkina enclave to mark the anniversary of the Turkish air force aerial bombardment that stopped the Greek Cypriot siege of the enclave in 1964. Until 2004, the Turkish Cypriots had access to Kokkina by boat, but a crossing was opened in Nicosia, allowing them to cross by land through Limnitis for the first time since 1974. On August 29, the Turkish Cypriot authority denied Kato Pyrgos villagers permission to pass through Limnitis (Yesilirmak) crossing on an organized pilgrimage to Saint Mamas church.[434] President Christofias, in response to Bishop Georgios, cautioned the Greek Cypriots that to pursue patriotism "in the name of religion, in the name of our cultural heritage and our heroes then we will be completely destroyed. . . . I won't accept lessons in patriotism."[435] Archbishop Chrysostomos II, in his Christmas message in 2009, cast doubts on President Christofias's patriotism and warned his Christian flock to keep vigilant and be wary of efforts to impose an unfair Cyprus settlement, which would be worse than the Annan Plan of 2004.[436] The church leaders persisted in playing a pivotal role in the Cyprus negotiations and opposed any partnership plans of Christofias with the Turkish Cypriots.

To complicate matters, Foreign Minister of Cyprus Markos Kyprianou deployed his predecessor's policy of threatening to block Turkey's EU bid unless Ankara capitulated to Greek demands at the negotiations. Absence of good intentions to find an amicable solution during the talks hindered pragmatic resolutions and exacerbated the Greco-Turkish relations.[437] On August 26, 2008, Kyprianou continued with his uncompromising rhetoric and claimed that the island was under a unified state, and the Green Line that divides the two communities was a temporary "cease fire line." Since 1974, anyone who visited Northern Cyprus could not dispute the jurisdiction or the authority of TRNC. The Greek Cypriot attempt to suppress reality was bumping up against good faith and trust, and the Turks had no incentive to embark on a partnership plan that drained their political power base or set the stage for Greek Cypriot dominated state.[438] Consciousness of the past communal hostilities gave the Turkish Cypriots a visionary perspective on their future with the Greek Cypriots.

Kosovo's independence from Serbia on February 17, 2008, and South Ossetia and Abkhazia's choice for independence from Georgia on August 26[439] created a new opportunity for the Turks to map out a new strategy to resolve the Cyprus issue. The long-standing position of the Turkish Cypriots as to political equality and Turkey's guarantorship were uncontestable issues that deepened strains at the negotiations. Rival leaders met on September 3 at the UN-patrolled buffer zone, the old Nicosia airport, the official residence of the UN special representative and UNFICYP chief mission Taye-Brook Zerihoun, to address matters of procedure while substantive negotiations were set to begin on September 11. In a statement on the commencement of direct negotiations, Christofias stressed that the issues relative to settlers, properties and territory, virgin birth, and confederation remained as topics that the two sides were unable to agree on and had to be revisited. Christofias's remark that the Greek Cypriots's "major concession" were stipulated in the 1977 Makarios-Denktash agreement and nothing more was to be offered met an unfavorable response by Talat as "unfortunate and weird."[440] Christofias's offer was not a new partnership of two states through virgin birth, but a partnership of two communities in the Republic of Cyprus as founded in 1960. The statement of Christofias was designed to advance the Greek Cypriot interests by extracting further concessions from the Turkish Cypriots, which had a substantial negative effect on the negotiations.

Christofias and Talat, along with their advisors in the presence of the UN representatives, began their first substantive talks on power-sharing in a reunited state on September 11, 2008, at the abandoned UN-controlled buffer zone in Nicosia. Following the four-hour meeting, UN special envoy Alexander Downer said that the two leaders agreed to resume their meeting on September 18 and no comments were to be made to the press.[441] The second substantive meeting was held in Nicosia on September 18 for five hours on the chapter "Governance-Power-Sharing." The pending issues of executive power, central government, legislative authority, judicial authority, and resolution of disputes were scheduled for discussion on October 10. They continued to be at odds about the power of the central government—Christofias advocated a strong central government to prevent Cyprus from sliding back into partition or secession after post-settlement and Talat favored a loose federation, fearing dominance by the Greek Cypriots, who outnumber them roughly four to one. In an address to the general assembly of the Parliamentary Assembly of the Council of Europe (PACE) in Strasbourg on October 1, Talat said that the biggest obstacle in the negotiations was the unwillingness of the Greek Cypriots to recognize the political equality of Turkish Cypriots. Talat said, "We want to establish a new partnership in Cyprus . . . composed of two constituent states of equal status."[442] He also criticized the isolationist policies of the Greek Cypriots against TRNC and said the following:

> We stand on our feet at a time of isolations, only through the support of Turkey extends. . . . Had it not been for Turkey's support, there would remain no Turkish Cypriot on the island. The Turkish Cypriots are faced with political, economic and social isolation.[443]

After his speech to PACE on September 30, Christofias said that he had the political will to solve the Cyprus problem, but he would never accept the recognition of a second state in Cyprus.[444] Despite the news blackout agreement, both sides continued to make public statements underscoring competing news of a settlement.[445] Christofias was reservedly optimistic but continued to be distracted by the demands of the hard-liners Garoyian, Omirou, Koutsou, and Perdikis for assurances relating to the negotiations. On September 20, *Phileleftheros* and *Simerini* had bleak prognosis as to peace talk prospects and accused Talat of promoting a two-state system. The two sides had still to exhaust the issues in reaching a common understanding, but the talks continued to be distracted by squabbling and exploration of options to sabotage a settlement.

Talat's speech to PACE parliamentarians attracted the attention of about thirty members, but the invitation provided the first Turkish Cypriot leader a platform to air his views before a European audience. PACE Resolution 1628 adopted on October 1 praised the Greek Cypriot initiative, but it was very critical of Turkey and TRNC's political stands in the negotiations. The resolution called upon the Turkish Cypriots to reaffirm their commitment for a reunified Cyprus and to abandon their stand as a two-state system. Prior to the October 10 scheduled meeting, a consensus was reached on seven chapters that included meteorology, citizenship and passport formalities, asylum, extradition of fugitives from justice, terrorism, smuggling of drugs or narcotics, money laundering, organized crime, amnesty and general amnesty for crimes perpetrated to the founding state, appointment of federal officials including diplomats, copyright laws, and standards and measures. The remaining chapters included foreign relations, international agreements, defense, European Union, central bank functions, federal financial issues, aviation, electronic communication, transport and natural resources, Law of the Sea (1982), and antiquities.[446] The adversaries elevated semantics above substance by arguing for the preferences designed to allocate benefits, privileges, and political power on the basis of ethnicity, which were viewed with deep resentment as the exercise of a zero-sum game. Serious doubts and cynicism on matters of substance tragically transformed the 2008 negotiations, creating such adversity and barriers that it was sufficient corrosive element working against the progress to a permanent solution.[447] Once again it became evident that the opportunity for a settlement would be denied due to the inflexibility of the community leaders to adjust their clashing interests in order to render an agreement for the good of the whole.

To help shift ethnic antipathy and contention, the international community was once again focused on promoting confidence building measures to create a climate for resolving differences in the Cyprus negotiations. On October 8, three distinguished international personalities arrived on the island in the hope that an atmosphere would be created to open the way toward a comprehensive settlement. Former U.S. President Jimmy Carter, age eighty-four; Archbishop Demond Tutu, seventy-seven; and Lakhdar Brahimi, seventy-four, called the Global Elders, offered their collective experience to urge a peaceful resolution to the Cyprus conflict. The Global Elders, formed on July 18, 2007, in Johannesburg, South Africa, formed by Nelson Mandela, of South Africa; Graca Machel, of Mozambique; and Desmond Tutu, to contribute their wisdom and leadership to resolve the world's toughest issues. Jimmy Carter, the former U.S. president from 1977 to 1981, has been a champion of human rights around the world. Archbishop Tutu was active in the struggle against apartheid in South Africa, and in 1994, he was appointed as chairman of South Africa's Truth and Reconciliation Commission. Lakhdar Brahimi, a former Algerian ambassador, is a lecturer at the Institute for Advanced Study in Princeton on conflict resolution. They were not involved in the negotiations, but the trio was to garner more international support for a lasting settlement in Cyprus. The trio was acutely aware that the Cyprus issue had reached a point that unprecedented measures had to be taken to resolve the contentious, long, and complex political debacle. After meeting the representatives of political leaders, civil society representatives, and young people of both communities, the trio left Cyprus on October 9, firmly convinced that they did not see failure ahead in the negotiations.[448]

Christofias and Talat had their third meeting on October 10, 2008, at the site of Nicosia airport in the presence of special adviser of the UN secretary-general on the Cyprus issue Alexander Downer and UN secretary-general's special representative in Cyprus Taye-Brook Zerihoun. After three and a half hours of talks, they agreed to meet on a weekly basis starting on October 13 to continue their negotiations on power-sharing and governance. In an effort to reduce tensions, both sides cancelled their annual war games Nikiforos and Taurus as a sign of goodwill. House Defense Committee member Zacharias Poulias and political party RUROKO denounced the cancellation of National Guard military exercises, Nikiforos.[449] Christofias was irked over Turkey's election as a nonpermanent member of the UN Security Council seat for 2009 to 2010. The ten nonpermanent seats are filled by the UN General Assembly, with five countries elected each year with a two-year nonrenewable mandate.[450]

A thorny irreconcilable difference between the two sides was over the executive council, which is similar to the Federal Council of Switzerland. Talat's proposed council consisted of seven members, four Greek Cypriots, and three Turkish Cypriots. The council needed two votes from each community to make a binding decision on any issue. In Switzerland, seven-member executive council constitutes the federal government and serves as the Swiss collective head of state. The entire council leads the federal administration of Switzerland, and each council heads one of the seven federal executive departments. Christofias, on the other hand, proposed a presidential system where the president and vice president run on a joint ticket and are elected by direct vote of the people. The presidency was to rotate between a Greek Cypriot president and a Turkish Cypriot vice president. The vice president was to serve half the term of the president. The president and vice president were to appoint the members of the federal government who would serve a six-year term. Talat's proposal was unacceptable to Christofias because it deviated significantly from a past UN plan to reunite the island and the proposed three-to-four ratio in federal council. It did not reflect the population ratio of Greek and Turkish Cypriots on the island. Fundamental disagreements over the exercise of federal authority included as follows:

1. The ownership of property and the operation of airports.
2. Defense and foreign relations. The Turkish Cypriots wanted the two constituent states to have the authority to make international agreements within their own spheres of authority.

3. The Turkish Cypriots wanted equal participation of the two constituent states in the regulation and supervision of the banking sector, regulation and supervision of the financial sector, and the oversight of competition by the federal authority.
4. Control over international navigation and maritime areas.
5. Federal government should decide whether its laws should be implemented by the constituent states.

The Turkish Cypriots proposed that the constituent states should be able to implement the federal laws in appropriate situations within the framework of the principle of "subsidiaritry."[451] The lack of progress at the peace talks gave way to pessimism and for the nationalists to call for border closures between the north and the south. According to a Brussels-based organization, the Center for European Policy Studies (CEPS) survey released on October 30, 2008, only 18 percent of Greek Cypriots and 13 percent of the Turkish Cypriots were hopeful for a Cyprus solution. Seventy-five percent of the Turkish Cypriots considered mutual recognition of two states preferable, and 99 percent of the Greek Cypriots did not trust Turkey or the Turkish Cypriot leaders.[452] The survey uncovered deep disdain and continued lack of trust between the two communities that intensified pessimism as to a reconciliation poisoned by disagreements and full of hollow rhetoric.

On November 20, in Moscow, Christofias and Russian President Dmitry Medvedev signed seven agreements covering financial, commercial, and political spheres. On his official Russian visit, Christofias publicly disparaged NATO and declared that alliance had no reason to exist any longer, but promoted Russia's proposed security system for Europe at the EU. He ignored the fact that twenty-one of the twenty-seven EU member states were members of NATO. AKEL General Secretary Andros Kyprianou described NATO as "an aggressive organization that has scattered death and destruction in many corners of the world, and continuously violates international law and the UN Charter."[453] AKEL has been against joining NATO's Partnership for Peace program, and Cyprus does not have bilateral ties with NATO through its (PfP). Turkey has prevented Cyprus from participating in the European Security and Defense Policy (ESDP) missions abroad, where they involve NATO intelligence and resources, and in return, Cyprus has vetoed Turkey from engaging in the overall development of ESDP "to an extent commensurate with Turkey's military weight and strategic importance to Europe and transatlantic alliance."[454] Despite hopes of a peaceful resolution of the Cyprus crisis, the Greek Cypriot administration decided to spend 200 million euros on military hardware from Russia.[455] Naturally, Turkish observers felt that the Greek Cypriot leaders were starting to alter their policies as a form of leverage over the Turks rather than engaging in substantive dialogue on topics of mutual interest. Such moves added to a growing skepticism with consequential consequences and cast a shadow over the feelings of goodwill and rapprochement between the two communities. In addition, it undermined the efforts of those who tried to promote greater understanding and goodwill that started in the aftermath of peace negotiations.[456]

After the 19th meeting on February 4, 2009, Christofias voiced his disappointment over the results of the negotiations with Talat. Christofias upheld the original owner's right to property, while Talat argued for compensation and land swaps.[457] On April 28, the European Court of Justice (ECJ) in Luxembourg, on an appeal from a British court, ruled that Meletis Apostolides's property in Lapithos (Turkish: Lapta) village on Cyprus's northern coast sold by a Turkish Cypriot to David and Linda Orams from the UK, who built a holiday home on the land, were to recognize the judgment of the Greek Cypriot district court in Nicosia. In 2005, the Greek Cypriot court ruling could not be enforced in TRNC and Apostolides pursued the matter in the UK and the European Court of Justice to demand compensation from anyone using their property. The EU court ruled, "The fact the land concerned is situated in an area over which the government does not exercise effective control . . . does not preclude the recognition and enforcement of those judgments in another member state [UK]."[458] Turkey rejected the ruling of the European Court of Justice and declared that the Greek Cypriot administration did not have any jurisdiction over the Turkish Cypriots or the authority to represent the entire island.[459]

The European Court of Human Rights (ECHR) on March 5, 2010, in the case of *Demepoulos v. Turkey*, recognized the Immovable Property Commission (IPC) in TRNC as an effective domestic remedy of Turkey. (The Law on Compensation, Exchange and Restitution of Immovable Property was approved in Northern Cyprus on December 19, 2005.) As a result of the ruling, the Greek Cypriots seeking compensation or restitution, approximately 1,500 property cases pending at the European Court, will now have to exhaust all domestic remedies in TRNC before applying to the ECHR in Strasbourg. For the first time, a Turkish Cypriot commission has been recognized by a major European human rights court.[460] *Today's Zaman*, March 6, 2010, reported that

as of November 2009, the number of cases brought before the IPC stood at 433. Of these, 85 had been concluded, the vast majority by means of friendly settlement. In more than 70 cases, compensation had been awarded. Some 361,493 square meters of property had been restituted and approximately 47 million Euros paid in compensation.[461]

Many Greek Cypriot refugees are expected to start accepting the IPC ruling as to the property settlement in the north and renounce their ownership rights in return for monetary compensation. In an editorial in *Cyprus Mail*, on June 24, 2012, Hermas Solomon wrote the following:

> From March [17] 2006 until June 2012, 3,365 applications had been lodged by Greek Cypriots with the Immovable Property Commission (IPC), yet only 241 have been concluded. . . . The Commission has paid out over 77 million pounds sterling in compensation and ruled in favor of exchange and compensation in two cases, for restitution in one case and for restitution and compensation in five cases.[462]

The alternative for a property owner is to wait for a political solution. It is estimated that about 1,600 applications to the European Court of Human Rights will be dropped. According to the Turkish officials, the court's decision saved Turkey 23 billion euros.[463] President Christofias urged the Greek Cypriot property owners not to resort to IPC in TRNC to settle their claims in Northern Cyprus.[464]

The Council of Ministers of the Republic of Cyprus on July 12, 2012, approved the decision of the "Immovable Property Commission" of TRNC in the case of a Greek Cypriot, Mike Tymvios, to exchange his property in the north with a Turkish Cypriot property in the south of the island. A new airport will be built on land acquired from Tymvios south of the Ercan airport in the north. The ruling of the European Court of Human Rights in March 2010 supported the IPC 2007 decision to swap a Turkish Cypriot 27 donums in Larnaca in exchange for 550 donums in Girne (Kyrenia). The land swap set a *de facto* precedent arrangement in resolving the property disputes. The swap or purchase of land in the north is not recognized by the Republic of Cyprus Land Registry, but the decision of the Council of Ministers in Tymvios's case is anticipated to bridge reconciliation on all issues relating to property. From March 17, 2006, until June 2012, 3,429 applications have been submitted by Greek Cypriots with IPC, but to date, only 241 have been settled and 103 cases were withdrawn by the applicants. The IPC paid out over 78 million pounds sterling in compensation and in two cases, ruled in favor of exchange. IPC will accept applications until the end of 2014. Since 2004, out of 347, only 78 Turkish Cypriots have been compensated for their property in the south.[465]

The Orams case had a negative impact on the talks between Christofias and Talat, and could spur more judicial rulings about the real estate on the island owned by 22,000 foreigners. The peace talks once again regressed to a stalemate and the unresolved crisis dragged on in interethnic relations. On February 5, 2009, in his most categorical statement, Christofias said, "It's not possible for Turkey to be accepted as a member of the [European] Union while continuing the occupation of Cyprus."[466] When the acceptable results floundered, Christofias expressed confidence that Turkey's EU accession would be a catalyst in achieving a Cyprus settlement. On February 6, Deputy Prime Minister–Foreign Affairs Minister of Turkey Turgay Avci called on Christofias to stop tying to pressure Turkey and TRNC and to not place preconditions and obstacles for Turkey's entry into the bloc.[467] Greece and Cyprus's obstructive attitude to use the veto card to block Turkey's accession to the EU reinforced the Turkish people's perception that the Greeks were not inclined to agree to a Cyprus settlement. Despite the high expectation by the international community of a Cyprus settlement, by the end of 2009, Talat said that the negotiations were not moving forward as expected. Due to the impartiality of the EU to Greek causes, Talat stressed that the bloc leaders should not interfere in the Cyprus negotiations.[468] The underlying motivation and stimulus for the Greek Cypriots's indulgence in their political rhetoric has been to restore the governmental power base as it existed from 1960 to 1963, which would undermine the negotiations. The sole power to judge as to the division of power or alliance is by common consent of the coequal and cosovereign status of both ethnic groups, and therefore, contemplation of imposition of a unilateral decision by Greeks would precipitate resistance to and collapse of the talks.

During a secret document handed to Greek Cypriot politicians by President Christofias, the National Council meeting at the Presidential Palace on February 27 was capriciously leaked to the press in less than twenty-four hours. On February 28, 2009, excerpts from the thirty-five-page document was published by *Simerini* newspaper, which stated that the Turkish Cypriots were proposing a weak central government and listed the points of convergence and disagreement on key issues of a reunited Cyprus. Furthermore, "the relationship between the Federal Government and the constituent states shall not be one of dominion, supremacy or hierarchy."[469] Moreover, "the Federal Government shall entrust the implementation of federal laws, including the collection of specific taxes, to the constituent states,"[470] and "any measure enacted by Federal organs shall not supersede measures enacted by the competent authorities of the constituent states."[471] A confederation system rather than a federal system was anathema to Greek Cypriots.

The Turkish Cypriots favored a Swiss-style presidential council to be elected by the Senate on the basis of a single list for a five-year term. The presidential council would consist of nine members, six from the Greek Cypriot side, and three from the Turkish Cypriot community. The rotation would take place based on a four to two ratio that favors the Greek Cypriots. The president and vice president (one from each community) could not be chosen from the same constituent state during the same term, and both posts would be subject to rotation every twelve months. The Greek Cypriots proposed that the president and vice president be elected on a single ticket by the citizens of the Federal Republic. Needless to say, the Greek Cypriot majority will end up deciding the president and vice presidential candidates of the state. Cyprus would have a parliament that consists of a Senate and a House of Representatives with equal members of Greek and Turkish Cypriots. The Greek Cypriots favored the elections of both houses by the permanent residence of the island; whereas, the Turkish Cypriots favored election on the basis of community citizenship for the Senate and based on founding state citizenship for the House. As to the sovereignty of the federal state, the Turkish Cypriots demanded the approval of the constituent states in regard to international agreements that could affect its internal affairs, but the Greek Cypriots rejected it as a breach of the single-sovereignty principle and held the view that the founding states can only make agreements on cultural and commercial issues, with mediation from the federal government.[472]

On security guarantees, the Turkish Cypriots called for Cyprus to "maintain the special bonds of friendship [with Turkey and Greece] and to respect the balance between Greece and Turkey.... Cyprus shall afford these two countries equal treatment until such time as Turkey becomes a member of the European Union. Issues of equal treatment shall be regulated by enacting relevant laws."[473] The sharp divisions between the two communities were so intractable and overwhelming that they bordered on paralysis with no chance to forge an agreement between Christofias and Talat.

In an interview with *Sabah* newspaper on March 6, Talat said that he would not run for president in 2010 if there was no solution to the Cyprus problem by the end of 2009.[474] On March 9, *Phileleftheros*, a Greek Cypriot newspaper, accused Talat of resorting to "blackmail" in order to expedite a Cyprus settlement. The ideas proposed by Christofias for a negotiated settlement were a political relic of the 1970s and did not create new hopes and prospects for political arrangements to mobilize the support of both communities. In an editorial in *Cyprus Mail*, March 15, 2009, the author wrote the following:

He [Christofias] is trying to make progress at the talks while also resorting to the same sterile rhetoric used by Papadopoulos against "suffocating time-frames," arbitration and other such nonsense, in the belief that this will keep the hard-liners happy. . . he has become a hostage to his brinkmanship and cannot persuade anyone about his intentions.[475]

President Abdullah Gul of Turkey on July 13, 2009, at a news conference in Ankara with Turkish Cypriot leader Mehmet Talat, said, "We want the negotiations to be concluded speedily. If possible, we want to see [the results of the negotiations] submitted to the public through a referendum by the end of this year."[476] Turkey's entry to the EU partly hinged on the reunification of the island, but there was little expectation of real progress by the end of the year. Christofias on July 13 rejected any peace agreement that would empower Turkey with the right to intervene militarily as a condition of reunifying the island.[477] The gulf between Christofias and Talat severely undermined the emergence of a new political order, and the spirit for a cooperated effort in the resolutions of the crisis brought a resumption of the ethnic tensions.

Turkish Cypriots, on April 19, 2009, held general elections in which 161,373 voters cast their ballots to elect 50 new parliamentarians out of 345 candidates from 7 political parties and 8 independent candidates. Before the humiliating defeat, Talat was invited to Washington, D.C., to meet with Secretary of State Hillary Clinton, members of Congress, and the Jewish lobby. The visit did not translate into boosting Talat's chances at the parliamentary elections, because the U.S. and the EU failed to persuade the Greek Cypriots to agree to a power-sharing based on the political equality and an end to the international isolation of TRNC. The elections results directly affected Talat and limited his ability to negotiate a settlement that would be approved by a referendum in early 2010. Parties defending "no solution is the solution" won the elections, and as a result, the Cyprus stalemate will continue due to lack of substantial progress in peace talks. The media in Turkey expresses the view that Turkey's national interest and European Union aspirations could be better served in supporting a negotiated Cyprus settlement. Turkey is conciliatory to a negotiated settlement within the parameters of the UN-led initiatives, but ignoring the legitimate geostrategic concerns of the Turkish military and the security of the Turkish Cypriots cannot create favorable conditions leading to a sustainable outcome.

The right-wing National Unity Party (UBP) garnered 50.38 percent or 121,982 of the votes while the ruling leftist Republican Turkish Party (CTP) of Talat stood at 42.85 percent, which provided Eroglu a shaky majority with enough seats in parliament for a single-party government. About 164,000 voters cast their votes, and the turnout was stronger than five years ago, up from around 69 percent in 2005 to 76.37 percent in 2010.[478] Eroglu served as prime minister of TRNC from 1985 to 1994 and from 1996 to 2004. The Democratic Party (DP), of Serdar Denktash, ranked third with 5 seats or 10.73 percent of the votes, center-left communal Democracy Party (TDP) with 6.83 percent of the votes, and Freedom and Reform Party (ORP) with 6.31 percent of votes, winning two seats each. A political party must capture 5 percent of the votes cast in order to win a seat in parliament.[479]

UBP advocates two-state settlement contrary to the federal model discussed by Talat and Christofias, and the talks would have collapsed, but Turkey pressured on Eroglu to take a pragmatic approach and continue with the negotiations. A UBP representative was to accompany Talat to the negotiation that will severely restrict his ability to steer negotiations as he wishes.[480] In his victory speech, Eroglu said, "We are supporting the continuation of negotiations and a settlement deriving from those negotiations."[481] Turkey's Prime Minister Tayyip Erodgan, on April 21, said the following:

> It would be very wrong for the new government to end the negotiations or to continue the negotiations on a basis different than the one that has been followed so far. . . . The process must continue exactly as before. . . . We will never support a move that would weaken the hand of Talat.[482]

Turkey's annual $500 million subsidy to TRNC's economy gives it a strong leverage in all aspects of Turkish Cypriot life.

Talat's ability to maneuver and make concessions in the negotiations has been compromised as a result of the elections. Reunification is no longer a top priority; EU leverage on Turkey is a poor option, and solidified Turkish Cypriot resolve on the two-state system was verified by the elections. UBP changed the framework of the talks, because Eroglu does not favor a federal solution but has called for a confederal solution based on "equality of sovereignty." Talat, agreeing to "single citizenship and sovereignty" demands of the Greek Cypriots at the start of the talks, cemented the perception of a large segment of the Turkish Cypriots that he would surrender to the Greek Cypriots. Turkish Cypriot daily *Bakis* newspaper on June 1, 2009, reported that on May 30, Talat reminded the journalists that Denktash and the TRNC parliament had approved to retain 29 percent of the territory and transfer the remainder to the Greek Cypriots as part of the final Cyprus settlement. Talat sought to facilitate and agreement and a new beginning by acknowledging a commitment by returning land to Greek Cypriots. Support for Talat over the years continued to decline in public opinion polls, because of his willingness to make concessions without getting an inch in return regarding Turkish Cypriot demand of full political equality of the two ethnic groups in a future federation of "two equal constituent states." The Greek Cypriot nationalists reject political equality of the two ethnic groups and argue that the Greek Cypriot ethnic majority have the legitimate right as to popular sovereignty and state power in a democracy and express the view that the Turkish Cypriots minority rights will be secured before the law. The ethnocentric majoritarian democracy will absorb the ethnic minority into a state system dominated by the ethnic majority, and the minority will only be entitled to equal rights as to communal affairs. Compounding the problem was the fact that both Christofias and Talat were vacillating between hope and despair in trying to bridge their differences on the core issues to reunify the island. Talat seized the initiative, made bold concessions, pursued full discussions, both the Greek Cypriot leadership instead of taking advantage to reach a reconciliation they took every opportunity to confuse public opinion and transformed every initiative into a failed policy. Talat's administration was also accused of nepotism, corruption, the continued international isolation of TRNC, and the growing economic difficulties.

In an interview, Eroglu, leader of UBP, said, "We have our own state, and our main duty is to maintain and strengthen our state. Everything will be easier if it is universally accepted that we are a nation that we have a state."[483] Eroglu is a strong advocate as to sovereignty of TRNC as a constituent state in a federal settlement, but his preference of a two-state model could hamper efforts to reunite Cyprus. Talat on May 16, 2012, expressed the opinion that the Turkish Cypriots have the right to establish a separate independent state and that right was created after 1974.[484] In an editorial in *Cyprus Mail*, on April 26, 2009, Loucas Charalambous wrote, "The Cyprus problem was solved on April 24, 2004. [The Annan Plan to settle the Cyprus dispute was put to a referendum on that date.]"[485] The first official trip abroad of the newly appointed foreign minister of Turkey Ahmet Davutoglu was to TRNC on May 6, 2009. The visit was a gesture of support to Talat and a warning to UBP not to block the ongoing negotiations on Cyprus. Davutoglu said, "We believe . . . that the international community, the Greek Cypriot administration, [and] Greece and Britain as guarantor powers, will continue to play a positive role in talks."[486] Ahmet Sozen, director of the Cyprus Policy Centre at the Eastern Mediteranean University in Gazimagusa, said that Ankara grants $600 million annually to TRNC and "no Turkish Cypriot leader can afford to decide on things in the negotiations despite

Turkey."[487] The efforts to negotiate a final and comprehensive settlement are likely to persist indefinitely amid debates as to token concessions and trying to place fault as to who forfeited the opportunity for the peaceful coexistence of the two communities on the island.

As a boost to the ongoing bilateral talks, the UN Security Council approved Resolution 1873 on May 29, 2009, extending the mandate of the 1,100-member UNFICYP, which was due to expire on June 15, to December 15. The resolution strongly urged Christofias and Talat to increase "the momentum of negotiations, improving the current atmosphere of trust and goodwill, and engaging in the process in a constructive and open manner. "[488] It also referred to the "rare opportunity to make decisive progress"[489] in the resolution of the Cyprus crisis and the "important benefits for all Cypriots that would flow from a comprehensive and durable Cyprus settlement."[490] Despite the proactive effort of the United Nations, the bilateral peace talks lacked the commitment to engage and in power-sharing of coequal of fellow citizens, and their unwillingness to face up to realities continued to dampen the chances for a reunited Cyprus. A *Cyprus Mail* editorial, "It's Time to Change," on June 13, 2009, stated that many Greek Cypriots would support a two-state solution.

> They [Greek Cypriot politicians] openly say that they do not want to share power with the Turkish Cypriots but nobody dares to repeat this view in public. . . . Some politicians have implied that partition was better than the type of federal settlement on offer. . . . All the hardliners [are] opposed to power-sharing and the demise of the Cyprus Republic. . . . Separation and two states is a legitimate a political option as a bi-zonal federation.[491]

Trying to put a positive spin on the peace talks without significant leaps forward provided the extreme right to capitalize on any possible excuse to derail attempts to narrow a growing divide. Giving in to extremism instead of compromise will lead to a two-state solution, a stark alternative. The hard-line stance of the nationalists constitutes an important political force that shapes ethnic patriotic pride and political attitudes. Even more pointedly, the Turkish Cypriots are worried that a peaceful solution that addressed their needs and rights were apt to be derailed by the *enosists*.

To nudge the two Cypriot leaders to bridge the gap to advance the peace process, Vice President of the EU Commission Gunther Verheugen and President of the European Commission Jose Manuel Berroso visited Cyprus in late June 2009. Verheugen's statement that guarantees were no longer a valid concern for the Turkish Cypriots security was strongly disputed and dismissed. Both representatives failed to address the EU unanimous April 2004 commitment to end the economic isolation of the Turkish Cypriots, but in a harsh judgment, Verheugen chose to chastise Turkey for not opening its ports and airports to the Greek Cypriot vessels. Verheugen should have realized that the political will of the countries party to the conflict will bring about a breakthrough in the peace process but extortion will not bear any results. EU officials' expectations of imminent breakthrough in the talks lacked the realization that the rivals did not have a complete consensus on major issues.

An agreement was reached on June 26, 2009, to open the controversial Limnitis (Turkish: Yesilirmak) crossing in the island's northwest, linking the Greek and Turkish Cypriot communities. The context of the agreement included the following:

1. Persons wishing to visit Kokkina will be escorted by UNFICYP.
2. The visits will be made by minibuses on Wednesdays, Saturdays, and Sundays.
3. One or two extra minibuses a week may be requested with UNFICYP escort.
4. Reasonable quantities of food, water, and other supplies of nonmilitary nature will be delivered to Kokkina under UN escort.
5. Kokkina will be connected to the nearest electricity grid.
6. Ambulances will be able to visit Kokkina to move sick persons.
7. Turkish Cypriot fire engines and accompanying water tanks will cross to Kokkina.
8. There will be reciprocal arrangements from time to time for specific events at this and other crossings in the opposite direction.

Under the agreement, Kokkina had to be connected to the nearest electricity grid before the opening of the Limnitis crossing.[492] The opening of Limnitis crossing was a constructive step forward, but the crucial issues as to land and security continued to plague the negotiations.

The fate of the peace talks continues to linger on at the conclusion of the 41st meeting on September 10, 2009,[493] and Christofias's three-way coalition government lacks the consensus essential on the major outstanding issues to bring a solution for a settlement sharing power

> in the new virgin birth partnership: with the Turkish Cypriots on
> the basis of political equality, security arrangements, territorial

compromise, refugees, migration,[494] and compensation and permanent derogations. The Greek Cypriot National Council, on September 18, ended its four-day meeting with a joint resolution endorsed by all the political parties. Once again, the National Council warned Turkey that if it failed to comply with the Greek Cypriot goals it won't be left unhindered to continue its accession process, without sanctions.[495]

The demands include the following:

1. Cyprus must have one sovereignty, international personality, and citizenship, and must be an evolution of the Cyprus Republic.
2. The departure of Turkish forces and settlers from Cyprus.
3. Cyprus demilitarization and closure of the British bases.
4. The restoration of the basic freedoms and human rights of all Cypriots, including refugees' right to return to their homes and properties.
5. It "rejects and excludes any form of a solution that will lead to the legalization of status quo or a solution for two separate states."[496]

Not surprisingly, Christofias's chief aims were to sustain the Greek Cypriot position, as best he could, and at the same time, to keep the peace talks going. Therefore, he offered minor concessions to Talat. By communicating such excessive stipulations for an agreement with the Turkish Cypriots, Christofias invokes the skeptic's projections that Cyprus peace negotiations are in vain.

Talat submitted the Turkish Cypriot proposals to Christofias on January 4, 2010, and included the following:

1. Both communities will vote to elect the president and the vice president of the United Federal Cyprus Republic. The elections would be based on a cross-voting system whereby both the Turkish Cypriots and the Greek Cypriots would vote for their respective candidates. If a candidate received 40 percent of the Turkish Cypriot vote, he/she could be elected with ten percent of the Greek Cypriot vote.
2. The president and the vice-president will have the authority to veto decisions made by the council of ministers.
3. The Turkish and Greek Cypriot founder states would have their own Flight Information Region (FIR).
4. In order to maintain the balance between the two Cypriot communities, the citizens of Turkey would keep their existing rights to work, buy

property and settle since the citizens of Greece already have been given this right.[497]

Christofias submitted to Talat the thirteen-page Greek Cypriot proposals on "Governance and Power Sharing" on January 12, which contained the previously submitted points that included the following:

1. Single sovereignty, one state, one citizenship in a United Cyprus.
2. Strong central government with intent to establish a unitary state with two communities having a certain degree of autonomy in internal affairs.
3. The two federated units will have no competence in foreign affairs or defense.
4. The central federal government will have power over external relations, EU affairs, defense policy, meteorology, regulatory high boards, finance, natural resources, aviation, navigation, communications, internal security, federal justice, labor rights, intellectual property, antiquities, and family affairs.
5. A two-chamber legislature, a senate with equal representation from the two federated units, and a house of representatives with "a minimum representation of 25 percent for each federated unit." Each chamber will elect a president and a vice-president, one from each federated unit and the president of the two chambers shall never come from the same community. No decision can be adopted without at least 25 percent of senators from each of the two federated units present and voting. A required quorum [for amending the constitution or laws] will be present and voting in parliament of at least two-fifths of senators from each community. Representation in both houses will be on the basis of permanent residence.[498]

The proposals as to "governance" were to be presented to Talat later. The Greek Cypriot proposals made no reference to the existence of two self-governing entities, two ethnic communities, cultures and religions, no acknowledgment as to the equality of the two communities, no "special ties" with Greece and Turkey as to the 1960 founding treaties of the Republic of Cyprus.

The two proposals constituted the entrenched positions of the two communities and a major setback to the dreams of bridging the ethnic divide. The Greek Cypriots continue to demand restoration of a unitary government, while the Turkish Cypriots are proposing a confederal governing system. Christofias rejected the Turkish Cypriot proposals on January 15, 2010, and during his consultations with the Greek government in Athens on January 17, a team of legal experts from Greece was appointed to assist him in the negotiations. A fundamental difference in the proposals provided a bleak prospect for concession for a compromise. Failure to usher in a new and more hopeful era reinforces the disaffection and disillusionment among growing sections of the population with the peace talks and contributes to the permanency in the division of the island. Negative response to proposals, skepticism expressed continues to reinforce the harsh realities from *de facto* to *de jure* division. The 1963 to 1974 events left a profound and long-term impression and deep psychological scars on both communities and can be considered a decisive turning point in the ability of the two communities to coexist under one political system. The permanent separation of the two ethnic governmental entities will be legitimized as it transpired under the Velvet Revolution with the dissolution of Czechoslovakia as a nation-state into Slovakia and the Czech Republic in 1993.

UN Secretary-General Ban Ki-moon's thirty-six-hour first visit to Cyprus, on January 31, 2010, was to dispel the public gloom on both sides of the divided island and in a bid to inject momentum to the slow-moving talks. On his arrival to Larnaca airport, Ban said the following:

> I am here to encourage the two leaders to bring these talks to a successful conclusion. Reaching a mutually-acceptable solution will require courage, flexibility and vision as well as a spirit of compromise.[499]

The Greek Cypriot leaders of DIKO, EDEK, EVROKO, and the Greens boycotted the reception at Ledra Palace Hotel on February 1 in honor of Ban in protest of his meeting in Talat's presidential office in northern Nicosia. In an editorial, *Cyprus Mail*, on February 3, wrote the following:

> Why did they snub the Secretary-General who had come to Cyprus to help the peace procedure . . . ? No, their knee-jerk reaction was part of the Cyprus problem theatre that we have been witnessing for years, with party leaders competing over who will be perceived by the public as the most courageous patriot. Patriotism is now measured by the degree of negativity a politician could record in slamming the peace procedure and efforts to improve the political climate between the two sides.[500]

Christofias's own party members joined the obstructionists to create a treacherous political climate by distancing themselves from the peace process instead of cultivating a climate of optimism and the support for a settlement. Wide differences still remain in the talks over power-sharing and property, and no significant progress has been achieved in more than sixty meetings over the seventeen months. The real difficulty, of course, lies in trust, security, geostrategic interests of Greece and Turkey in the region, and the peaceful settlement of the Aegean maritime disputes.

Ethnic proposals on the major issues remain unchanged and the status quo continues since 1974. The Greek Cypriot coalition government uses international frameworks to pursue a campaign of delegitimization of TRNC and pursues a policy

> to reunite the country, the people, the institutions and the economy, a federal state with a single sovereignty, a single citizenship, and a single international personality . . . free Cyprus from occupation and foreign guarantees . . . the right to return back [of the Greek Cypriot refugees] to the homeland and the right to property.[501]

The Turkish Cypriot leaders have little interest in losing control over Northern Cyprus, and Christofias's version of a settlement is unacceptable, and even a moderate would much rather see a two-state solution. Turkish Foreign Minister Ahmet Davutoglu, on July 21, 2009, said, "Either the status quo will change, which is what we want, or we all together will be forced to think about alternatives . . . they [Greek Cypriots] are trying to get a solution that will only meet their expectations."[502] The warmed-over political rhetoric of the past thirty-five years continues to hinder, nor to provide, any new alternatives to reach an agreement in the peace process.

On the occasion of the 35th anniversary of Turkey's military "Peace Operation" in 1974, Talat, on July 19, 2009, pledged that he would not allow the peace talks to make Turkey's status as a guarantor state a matter of discussion in any future settlement.[503] On a TV program, *Son Durum* (Latest situation), on July 16, Talat declared that the withdrawal of the Turkish army from Cyprus without an overall agreement will present the Greek Cypriots an opportunity to seize the whole island by force.[504] In the absence of a substantive progress toward a Cyprus settlement, Talat, who is expected to seek reelection, faces a humiliating defeat in the presidential elections on April 18, 2010. Prime Minister Dr. Dervis Eroglu declared his candidacy on January 18 and will challenge Talat

---

who champions the cause of two states for two people.[505] A combative stance taken by both sides to play to their hard-line supporters failed to set the stage to narrow their political position to break the deadlock to agree on a peace plan for the reunification of the island.[506]

The European Union has been struggling for years to respond with sound ideas to address the Cyprus problem, but the results have been disappointing. The admission of the divided Republic of Cyprus into the EU on May 1, 2004, has made Turkey's accession process hostage to the Greek Cypriots veto and succeeded in blocking the EU direct trade and financial assistance to the Turkish Cypriots. In addition, the prospect of Turkey's EU bid has been crippled by the opposition of France and Germany, and the Turks are scolded as to their lack of compliance with European rights and democratic standards.

The EU Parliament on February 10, 2010, endorsed an annual report evaluating Turkey's progress in 2009. The report, penned by Dutch Christian Democrat Ria Oomen-Ruijten, calls on Turkey

> to facilitate a suitable climate for negotiations by immediately starting to withdraw its forces from Cyprus by addressing the issue of the settlement of Turkish citizens on the island and also by enabling the return of the sealed-off section of Famagusta (Varosha or Maras in Turkish) to its lawful inhabitants in compliance with Resolution 550 (1984) of the United Nations Security Council.[507]

At a luncheon on February 11, 2010, for EU ambassadors accredited to Turkey, Turkish Prime Minister Erdogan said that the EU Parliament was "acting like a spokesperson for the Greek Cypriot side."[508] The Turkish foreign ministry described the report as

> unilateral and not in compliance with facts. . . . The fact that promises given to Turkey by the EU are not mentioned in the report, while expectations from Turkey are listed, is additionally thought provoking. In the report, ongoing comprehensive negotiations and the Turkish Cypriot side's constructive efforts toward resolution are virtually disregarded, while facts concerning those who have responsibility in emergence of the Cyprus issue have been ignored.[509]

Turkey labeled the EU report as unbalanced.

The report should be penned through objective and encouraging approach. We see one-sided, unrealistic and unacceptable elements in the report which may negatively affect the accession process. It is thought-provoking that the report stressed what are expected from Turkey but ignored what commitments EU had failed to carry out towards Turkey.[510]

The EU Parliament report had a counterproductive effect on the peace talks by entirely ignoring the expectations of the Turkish Cypriots but bolstered the Greek Cypriots' confidence of reunited Cyprus under their control. As a consequence, the reality illustrates that the *Modus Vivendi* will usher in new rationale, arguments, and conviction that a viable alternative is the permanent division of the island.

Not surprisingly, Yiannakis Omirou, leader of the Movement for Social Democracy (EDEK), withdrew his party from the coalition government on February 8 2010, due to its "total disagreement" with President Christofias's strategy on the Cyprus negotiations.[511] This highlights the fundamental difference between the Greek Cypriot political parties in considering the future political relationship between the two Cypriot communities. Christofias was not surprised by EDEK's decision and said, "Unfortunately, throughout our collaboration, while participating in government, EDEK effectively ran as the opposition, both regarding the Cyprus problem and on many issues of domestic governance."[512] As a result of political fracture in the coalition government, the Greek Cypriot communist newspaper, *Haravghi*, on July 26, 2009, claimed that the extreme right-wing organization *Chrysi Avgi* (Golden Dawn) has been coordinating efforts to overthrow President Christofias.[513]

As a consequence, the Turkish Cypriots are weary of the Greek Cypriot–proposed political partnership arrangement because EDEK and the Democratic Party (Dimokratiko Koma [DIKO]) leader Marios Karoyian are not cooperating with Christofias to usher in an era of peace, reconciliation, and trust, but their coordinated effort is to facilitate the Greek Cypriot dominance over the whole island. The harsh realities are that the events from 1964 to 1974 remain an open wound for the Turkish Cypriots as if it had happened yesterday. As a direct consequence of refusal to be more imaginative and proactive to change direction, the path toward an amicable goal may mark a major turning point in the negotiations, paving the way to two political systems. The peace talks have been effectively paralyzed, offering little other than more of the same.

Following the Cyprus crisis in 1963, Greek Cypriots' coordinated diplomacy with Greece had been the isolation of the Turkish Cypriots and sustained support and the recognition of the Republic of Cyprus as the sole legitimate sovereign authority in Cyprus. In a letter to twenty-six EU member states, Christofias protested that the accredited EU ambassadors to his government had attended a dinner hosted by Talat in TRNC on November 24, 2009, and furthermore, served notice that at the Brussels European Council summit in December, he intended to block further progress in Turkey's EU accession bid. The EU parliament on November 26 approved a draft European Council document without recommending sanctions against Turkey despite the failure of Ankara to normalize relations with the Republic of Cyprus. On December 9, the EU summit, despite the Greek objections, adopted the recommendations of the EU foreign ministers. Greeks were anticipating major gains and concessions from the Turks, which failed to transpire. Eight chapters, out of a total of thirty-five needed for Turkey's EU accession, had been frozen by France since 2006 due to the refusal of the Turks to honor the 2004 Customs Union to Cyprus (also known as the Ankara protocol) that includes the opening of the Turkish ports and airspace to Greek Cypriot traffic and the normalization of diplomatic relations. Despite the ongoing negotiations in Cyprus, the Greek Cypriot government declared that in 2010, it would unilaterally block six policy areas (labor mobility, fundamental rights, the justice system, education, foreign policy, and energy) in Turkey's EU accession negotiations as a punitive measure, unless Ankara changed its stance on the Cyprus dispute.[514] According to the outgoing EU Enlargement Commissioner Olli Rehn, the chapter on the environment is to be opened before the end of 2009.[515] Swedish Foreign Minister Carl Bildt, whose country served as president of the EU until January 2010, rebutted the rhetoric used by certain EU members who oppose Turkey's accession into the EU.[516] Egemen Bagis, Turkey's chief negotiator for EU accession, stressed Ankara's standing policy as to the normalization of relations with the Republic of Cyprus. Bagis stated the following:

> Turkey made a promise to open its ports [to Greek Cypriots] in exchange for ending the isolation of the Turkish Cypriots. We are behind our promise. If EU countries decide to have direct trade with Northern Cyprus, we will be more than happy to open our ports, and keep our part of the promise.[517]

Athens and Nicosia's lobby efforts at the Brussels summit blocked Turkey's EU accession process and the adoption of punitive measures to force the resolution of the Aegean and the Cyprus issues compatible with Greek national interest failed, but it compounded the fragility of Greco-Turkish relations. When

Cyprus took over EU's six-month rotating presidency on July 1, 2012, President Christofias offered to open several chapters for Turkey along with allowing the Turkish Cypriots to use Gazimagusa port for foreign trade in exchange for opening Varosha to Greek Cypriot residence, and in addition, Turkey open its air and naval ports to the Republic of Cyprus.[518] The UN Security Council Resolution 550 in 1984[519] called on the Turkish army to hand over Varosha to UN Administration and to its lawful residents. Christofias was anticipating that his EU presidency will be a catalyst to navigate the Greek agenda to reach a negotiated agreement in line with Greek national interests. Turkey's Foreign Minister Ahmet Davutoglu, on June 7, 2012, said, "The relations and contacts with the EU will continue, but none of the ministries or institutions on the Turkish Republic will be in contact with the EU Presidency in any of the activities related to the Greek Cypriot Presidency."[520] The Turkish minister of EU affairs and chief negotiator Egeman Bagis said that Turkey would recognize the Greek Cypriot EU presidency if there is a mutually acceptable solution before July 1, 2012. Turkey froze relations with the EU the day Cyprus took over the EU presidency on July 1.[521] Given the complexity of the two problems, the parties in the conflict had to face the harsh political reality and face the task of adjusting their countries' expectations because the unyielding negotiating posture gives the reason to remain skeptical as to a settlement. The UN Security Council, on December 14, 2009, approved Resolution 1898 that extends the UNFICYP peacekeeping operations for another six months and highlights the UN engagement in the communal negotiations to reach a comprehensive settlement.[522]

Talks resumed on May 27, 2010, but the slightest manifestation of independence under a federal system aspired by Eroglu needed a divine providence to bridge the gap and reconcile the new proposition put forth to Christofias. By early June, the talks reached an impasse and UN Special Advisor Alexander Downer asked the two Cypriot leaders whether they wanted a solution or not. On November 18, 2010, first tripartite meeting at the Greentree was arranged by the UN Secretary-General Ban Ki-moon in New York, but there were no agreements between Christofias and Eroglu on the main issues. On January 26, 2011, the second tripartite meeting occurred in Geneva, Switzerland, but the communal leaders once again failed to reach an agreement. Ban Ki-moon's failure to prod the two leaders to reconcile their differences prompted him to say the negotiations were not an open-ended process and talks for the sake of talks could not continue. The UN Security Council, on June 15, 2010, Resolution 1930;[523] on December 14, 2010, Resolution 1953;[524] on June 13, 2011, approved Resolution 1986;[525] and on December 14, 2011, approved Resolution 2026[526] to extend the UNFICYP peacekeeping forces for another six months with the belief that a solution will be reached in Cyprus with the cooperation of the two communal leaders. On July 7, 2011, the third tripartite meeting occurred in Geneva, Switzerland, on October 30–31, the fourth tripartite meeting in New York, and in January 23–24, 2012, and the fifth tripartite meeting took place in New York with the urgency to reach a comprehensive Cyprus resolution and an end to negotiations before Cyprus took over the EU presidency on July 1, 2012. All tripartite meetings failed to achieve convergences on the major issues within the chapters of governance, power-sharing, property, security, economy, and European Union–related matters, which was a major disappointment for Ban Ki-moon.[527] In January 2012, Ban Ki-moon noted "the longer the talks have been drawn out, the more disillusioned the public has become and the harder it has become to conclude agreements."[528]

Christofias and Eroglu met on March 29, 2012, which focused on property, but no new meeting was agreed on. After forty-two months, the negotiations collapsed. In late February 2012, Eroglu forewarned that "if the talks fail this time, the Turkish Cypriots will decide their own future. July 1 [2012] marks the end of the peace talks . . . we will design policies to strengthen the existence of the state in the north."[529] Eroglu called for an international conference to resolve the deadlock on Cyprus peace talks, but Christofias opposed the idea and suggested first that agreements must be reached to the internal issues relating to Cyprus and its citizens. Eroglu said the following:

> If he [Christofias] has intention to agree let him come to a five-party conference this time. Let us sit at equal level in a five-party conference where Turkey and the other guarantor powers will participate and solve the Cyprus problem with the three guarantor powers. This is the last call which I will make. If he rejects this as well, let everyone take his own way.[530]

On April 20, 2012, Ban Ki-moon, over the phone, informed the Greek and Turkish leaders that there was no sufficient progress on core issues of the Cyprus problem that provided a basis for calling a multilateral conference at the end of April that would have included Greece, Turkey, and the UK.[531] Eroglu informed the Turkish Cypriots that he will not be meeting with Christofias anymore.[532] Eroglu also set terms for future talks that the reunification talks can resume with the introduction of a deadline for the negotiations and the lifting of embargos imposed on the Turkish Cypriots.[533] During the Cyprus EU term presidency, the Cyprus negotiations were suspended, but the technical meetings continued.

President Christofias on May 14, 2012, announced that he will not stand for reelection in February 2013. According to an opinion poll published in *Simerini* (Greek Cypriot newspaper) on May 13, 2012, Christofias would have won 20 percent of the votes in the presidential elections and AKEL's lack of support for his candidacy forced him not to seek a second term. An immediate effect was to strengthen the candidacy of Ioannakis Omiriu, the leader of the Movement for Social Democracy (EDEK), against Nicos Anastasiades, the leader of the center-right Democratic Rally Party (DISY) who endorses a loose federation bordering a confederation. An electoral coalition is aimed at preventing the election of Anastasiades because his views complement those of the Turkish Cypriots.[534]

On July 19, 2012, the UN Security Council extended UNFICYP's mandate until January 2013 with Resolution 2058, despite the failure of the UN-brokered peace initiative.[535] The resolution reiterated a call for the Greek and Turkish Cypriot leaders to accelerate the pace of the talks at unifying the divided island since 1974. The UNFICYP has been deployed on the island since 1964, and the UN has been facilitating the communal talks with a view to the eventual establishment of a federal government with a single international identity consisting of equal Greek and Turkish constituent states. Negotiations have not achieved significant desired ends, and in the absence of a settlement, it has enhanced the prospect for *de facto* partition of the island and recognition of that reality beyond what they ever before had been. Lack of convergence of viewpoints and diminishing credibility could not withstand repeated frustration confronted by the negotiators. A long-term patient was not capped with success but disillusionment and detestation as well. All of which sum up the lack of faith in the negotiations and diminishing prospect of unification of the island.

Even though the talks are Cypriot-owned and Cypriot-led, under the auspices of the UN, the talks may drag on for years because of no time frames. The Cyprus negotiations have made it painfully obvious that there are no intentions on both sides for the convergence on the core issues. To exert political pressure on the Greek Cypriots, the Turks are embarking on plan B, which will allow Turkish settlers into Varosha and annex it as part of TRNC. Failure reconciliation will inhibit the emergence of new attitudes that will engage both ethnic groups to have a meaningful political partnership, and the harder it will be to reach a breakthrough for a permanent settlement.

Since 1964, the Greek Cypriot leadership has been committed to preserve, safeguard, enhance, and defend the enjoyed political liberties and economic privileges by their compatriots. During his tenure, President Makarios set a dangerous precedent of presidential power by unilaterally usurping the constitution and steering a course away from the Turkish Cypriot involvement in governmental affairs. The gross violations of the Turkish Cypriots economic and civil liberties, and the unresolved political issues from 1964 to 1974, ultimately led to a coup d'état led by Sampson against Makarios. Makarios ventured for the erosion of constitutional rights of the Turkish Cypriots, and Grivas's and Sampson's disastrous offensive against the Turks, designed to facilitate *enosis*, had unintended consequences that precipitated Turkey's military intervention in 1974. Serious blunders, miscalculations, and oppressive treatment of the Turkish Cypriots brought the resumption of "ethnic cleansing" in which Makarios, Grivas, and Sampson deserve most of the blame. In sum, the Greek Cypriot leadership's severe and counterproductive policies toward the Turkish Cypriots should get credit for the division of the island and for their resistance in settling disputes through international arbitration.

All the Greek Cypriot leaders have envisioned a strictly limited role or a "privilege minority" for the Turkish Cypriots in any future government. Turkey's proposal for a quintet summit on the Cyprus crisis, including the two communities and the three guarantor powers, under the UN supervision, was rejected on November 18, 2009, by Christofias and the Greek Cypriot political parties.[536] The Greek Cypriots continued to safeguard their traditional economic and political superiority and continue their wish to be the most important player in all governmental affairs. The spirit for a cooperative effort in the resolution of the Cyprus crisis gradually dissipated due to serious blunders and squabbling of the extreme nationalists' bickering, backbiting, and continued embryonic assumption that the disproportionality of the political system can be imposed by sheer will power. The Greek Cypriots' proposals giving them greater weight in an envisioned federal system and allocation to the Turkish Cypriots autonomy within their own enclave will never be an acceptable proposal. In addition, the draconian economic embargo created horrendous economic difficulties for the Turkish Cypriots, but the strategy has failed to achieve the anticipated expected results. The failure of the two ethnic groups to exhibit viable alternatives to accommodate the interests of both will be a catalyst for the permanent division of the island.

NOTES

CHAPTER 5

THE FAILURE OF POLITICS AND DIPLOMACY OF PEACEMAKING

International law is based by nature upon this principle: that the various nations ought to do, in peace, the most good to each other, and, in war, the least harm possible, without detriment to their genuine interests.
—Charles Louis Montesquieu

This chapter covers the international efforts following the tragic events of the 1960s and 1970s to bring the two Cypriot leaders together to reach an amicable comprehensive settlement relative to Cyprus. Diplomats struggled to come to grips with national interests of Greece and Turkey, while trying to be sensitive to the security and shared governance priorities of the two ethnic groups on the island. Diplomacy that transpired since 1964 has failed to achieve a peaceful reconciliation of the disputes, and the tense adversarial relations has provided no chance for agreement. The UN efforts have been peacekeepers along the Green Line, while prodding the leaders of the two ethnic groups to reconcile their differences through a negotiated settlement instead of continued armed confrontations. The efforts of the international community have failed to make dramatic breakthroughs in the communal negotiations. Diplomatic maneuvering to achieve the goals of one player at the expense of the other has not presented a formula for either side that will ensure success. A study on peacemaking puts it: "Wars are seldom a struggle between total virtue and vice. . . . But when so conceived, they become crusades that remove the possibility of finding common ground after the battles are over."[537] The diplomatic approaches utilized in the Cyprus crisis have failed to induce the trust and the expected evenhandedness in the "good offices of the United Nation, and the lack of political will to freely engage in facilitating an agreement continues to be a major obstacle to progress."

Since 1963, Cyprus has been on the agenda of the Security Council and the General Assembly in an effort to resolve the crisis. On December 21, 1963, the intercommunal violence flare-up (the Turkish Cypriots call it "the bloody Christmas massacre") in Nicosia contributed to the escalation of the hostilities on December 23. The London peace conference, attended by all the interested parties, caused the UN Security Council in March of 1964 to authorize an international peacekeeping force to maintain peace and security in Cyprus. President Makarios's political motives and objectives were to involve the UN to protect the Greek Cypriot interests in Cyprus. The intentions of Makarios were to neutralize the Treaty of Guarantee (1960), to prevent Turkey's right under the international law to unilaterally intervene in Cyprus, and to protect the Turkish Cypriot interests as provided under the Zurich-London Agreement of 1959. Turkey's threat to militarily intervene in Cyprus was blocked by the United States with the backing of Great Britain

The ethnic crisis of 1963 was precipitated by Makarios's thirteen-point constitutional amendment initiative, which intended to unilaterally abrogate Turkish Cypriots partnership in governance. The conflicting ethnic crisis in Cyprus was internationalized when Turkey threatened to intervene in 1964 to neutralize the superior Greek force attacks against the Turkish Cypriot enclaves under the command of General George Grivas. United States Undersecretary of State George W. Ball's mission to London and Nicosia in February 1964 helped ease the Greco-Turkish tensions, but failed to bring a peaceful resolution to the Cyprus crisis. On June 5, President Lyndon B. Johnson, in a sharp letter to the Turkish premier, declared his opposition to the Turkish invasion of Cyprus and cautioned Turkey of possible consequences of potential direct Soviet involvement in the conflict. As a result of Johnson's letter, Turkey abandoned the invasion plans of the island. The Greek Cypriots, emboldened by the American ultimatum note to Ankara, accelerated the attacks against the Turkish Cypriot enclaves. In August 1964, the Turkish air force bombed the Greek military positions to prevent them from destroying and exterminating the Turkish Cypriots. The bombing halted the conflict temporarily, but caused heavy damage to homes, and thousands of Turkish Cypriots were forced to flee to Turkish sectors as refugees. The Turkish Cypriots enclaves were placed under the protection of the UN peacekeeping force. As long as the Turkish military intervention was in check by the international community, Makarios had no difficulty whipping the Turkish Cypriots into shape.

President Makarios bolstered his diplomatic position with the support of Athens and Moscow while trying to extract UN resolutions favorable to the legitimacy of his government. Makarios's political maneuvering was to settle the fate of Cyprus outside of an Anglo-American setting. He gained the endorsement of the Afro-Asian and Eastern bloc countries, which greatly increased the backing of the international community to reshape the events on the island in line with Greek national interests.

The UN peacekeeping force was preferred by Makarios in place of the British or NATO troops to preserve the peace on the island. The UN force was to serve as keeper of the ceasefire, but for Makarios, they were also to deter and prevent the Turkish invasion of the island. Time was the essence for Makarios to neutralize the Turks, gain international endorsement as to his political arguments, and improve his military posture to effectively eliminate the Turkish Cypriot threats for the achievement of *enosis*.

The UN was to be a forum for political debate to enhance Makarios's arguments as to external invasion threat from Turkey, and he expected the international community to bless his plan to unilaterally revise the Zurich-London Accords. A major victory of Makarios was the placement of the government of Cyprus under the full control of the Greek Cypriots and to secure its legitimacy in the international arena. Anglo-American plans to settle the Cyprus crisis were rejected, and Makarios favored UN involvement for the resolution of the conflict.

Shrewd diplomatic maneuvering of Makarios at the UN extracted the UN Security Council resolutions to marginalize the Geneva Conference in August 1964 where Acheson's "double *enosis*" was proposed. While ignoring the Western plans and mediation efforts, the UN submitted the Ecuadorian mediator Galo Plaza's report on March 26, 1965, endorsing most of the views of Makarios.[538] Plaza's report was critical of the Treaty of Guarantee and Treaty of Alliance and the "constitutional oddity" of 1960.[539] He recommended self-determination and negotiations between the two ethnic communities under UN auspices. The sixty-six-page document recommended a unitary state under majority rule, provided the Turkish Cypriots minority status, and abolition of the 1960 treaties. Plaza's recommendations included the following:

1. *Enosis* and *Taksim* should be renounced.
2. The island should be demilitarized.
3. No attempt should be made to restore the political arrangements as it existed before December 1963.[540]

Plaza's report was enthusiastically endorsed by Makarios, but the Turks rejected it and accused Plaza of biased reporting and argued that he had exceeded his mandate and authority as a mediator. Plaza resigned his post on December 22, 1965.

Makarios referred the Cyprus problem to the UN General Assembly to further involve the UN and, furthermore, to obtain the backing of the nonaligned and emerging underdeveloped states. Makarios reminded the members of the international body of their struggle to exercise the right of self-determination and liberation from the yoke of imperialism. International politicization of the Cyprus crisis invoked arguments of neocolonialism and designs of Western imperialist conspiracy on a strategically located island. Furthermore, in his political rhetoric, Makarios invoked the UN Charter articles relative to peace and security, calling upon states to refrain from the threat or use of force against the territorial integrity of an independent state and the Security Council's responsibility to preserve international peace and security. The right of self-determination by the majority served the Greek interests, but nullified all the constitutional rights and privileges given to the Turkish Cypriots. In October 1965, Cyprus government presented a set of proposals to the UN on minority rights for the Turkish-Cypriots, but eliminated their special position as guaranteed by the Zurich-London Agreements.[541] The political gains of Makarios at the UN contributed to his risky venture to achieve the ultimate premeditated political goal of *enosis*.

In the 1960s, the universal mood was to condemn any secession movement whether it be in the Katanga province of Congo or Cyprus. The Turks were labeled as rebels, and the universal view was to protect the unity, sovereignty, self-determination, nonintervention, and the territorial integrity of Cyprus. The nonaligned countries rallied in support of Makarios and partition of Cyprus was not an alternative solution. Makarios succeeded in articulating his message effectively and mastered the majority consensus in the UN. The repeated adoptions of UN resolutions and "mini" proposals have not provided the Greeks the expected results since 1964. Additionally, they have prevented the two communities from reaching an amicable settlement. Extracting UN resolutions is not an alternative or substitute for an agreement, and failure to generate a political settlement is a hollow victory.

President Makarios used the UN as a political platform to neutralize the proposals made by Great Britain, Turkey, and the United States to resolve the Cyprus issue. Makarios continued to interject the premise that as a sovereign and independent state it had the right to unilaterally abrogate the 1960 Treaties that validated the guarantor powers the authorization to intervene in Cyprus to restore peace and a settlement. Makarios expected the international community to present him with a license to amend the constitution, disenfranchise the Turkish Cypriots, abrogate the international treaties, advance Greek Cypriot interests, prevent the use of force by Turkey, and recognize the independence of Cyprus under Greek rule.

The UN Security Council resolutions adopted on March 4, 1964, brought a great satisfaction to Makarios and bolstered his confidence in his political struggle with the Turks. The UNFICYP in Cyprus was to cooperate with the "government of Cyprus to preserve international peace and security"[542] and to cooperate with the Greek Cypriot administration to restore law and order. A UN mediator was appointed to promote a "peaceful solution and an agreed settlement of the problem confronting Cyprus in accordance with the Charter of the United Nations."[543] Makarios used the UN as an instrument in his struggle to achieve the full Greek dominance of Cyprus and scrap the Zurich-London Accords of 1959. The UN involvement in the island politics delayed the urgency for an early settlement and contributed to the catastrophic events of 1967 and 1974.

On December 17, 1965, Greek and Turkish foreign ministers met in Cyprus, and an agreement reached provided for *enosis*, in return for the cession to Turkey of Dhekelia. The agreements were never implemented. Greek and Turkish prime ministers met on September 9–10, 1967, in Kesan, Turkey, and Alexandropoulos, Greece, but the proposals offered as to the Cyprus settlement were rejected. Greco-Turkish talks in Lisbon on June 3–4, 1971, on partitioning Cyprus was aborted, but Athens warned Makarios to bring his policy in conformity with Greek and Turkish positions. Greek *junta* instituted a plan for EOKA-B to assassinate Makarios and the new regime under Sampson was to implement *enosis* shortly after the coup. When Makarios regained the presidency, the U.S. presidential emissary Clifford Mission to Cyprus, in February 1977, failed to convince the Greek leader to accept a bizonal federal for Cyprus in return for American engagement in the negotiations. November 10, 1978, Canada, Great Britain, and the U.S. plan for the creation of a bicommunal, bizonal federation was unsuccessful.

The threat of Turkish military intervention in Cyprus was put on ice but failed to gain the serious attention of Greece as to the geopolitical security interests of Turkey. Western mediation efforts were derailed in anticipation of *enosis* and lack of Ankara's resolve to block it. Escalation of ethnic violence in November 1967 subsided with Turkish air attacks on heavily armed Greek position on the island, and the scramble for solutions intensified. Greek military forces under the command of General George Grivas attacked the Turkish

Cypriot enclaves in Ayios Theodoros and Kophinou to reassert Greek Cypriot government's authority and disarm the Turkish paramilitary forces. Turkey mobilized its armed forces for a military confrontation with Greece, and on November 17, 1967, the Greek ambassador to Ankara was presented with an ultimatum containing the following demands:

1. The withdrawal of 12,000 Greek troops in Cyprus.
2. The immediate recall of Grivas to Athens from Cyprus.
3. The disarming of Greek Cypriot irregulars and national guards. (Makarios did not disarm the National Guard.)
4. Compensation to the Turkish Cypriots in Ayios Theodoros and Kophinou for loss of life and property. (No compensation was supplied to rebuild the two villages.)
5. The end of economic sanctions on the Turkish Cypriots. (Not removed until March 8, 1968.)
6. The right of Turkish Cypriots to govern and police their own enclaves. (Makarios refused to recognize the *de jure* existence of Turkish Cypriot government or police force.)
7. UNFICYP's mandate should include coercive powers. (UNFICYP's powers were not increased.)
8. Intercommunal talk to resolve constitutional issues on Cyprus. (Makarios did not agree to inter-communal negotiations.)

Greece decided to accede to Ankara's demands and the invasion threats were halted. A military confrontation between Greece and Turkey was averted by the successful mediation efforts of Cyrus R. Vance and his associates in the international organization.

In 1977, President Spyros Kyprianou and Denktash, under the auspices of UN Secretary-General Kurt Waldheim, met in Nicosia and signed a ten-point agreement. The major issues agreed on were as follows:

1. The basis for the talks will be the Makarios-Denktash guidelines of February 12, 1977, and the UN resolutions relevant to Cyprus question.
2. Priority was to be given to Varosha, the constitutional and territorial issues.
3. *Enosis*, partition or secession, was not to be an option.

The talks ended due to basic disagreement over the same fundamentals issues that plagued the negotiations from its inception.

In August 1984, the UN Secretary-General Javier Perez de Cuellar invited Kyprianou and Denktash to New York to discuss his "working points." The two Cypriot leaders agreed to engage in "proximity talks" for eight days. Since the two Cypriot leaders refused to sit in the same room for the talks, Cuellar served as a go-between in the round of indirect talks. On December 17, 1985, Kyprianou and Denktash had face-to-face talks in New York and agreed to discuss issues relating both to territorial and constitutional issues. The irreconcilable negotiations posture of the two representatives' caused the talks to collapse. The 1986 proposals of Cuellar to President George Vassiliou and Denktash failed to achieve any headway.

To ease the Greco-Turkish political tensions, President Ronald Reagan, in a confidential letter on November 22, 1984,[544] urged Turkish President Kenan Evren to hasten a Cyprus settlement. Denktash was pressured by Ankara to adopt a more conciliatory approach toward the Greeks to form a federal state. Land concessions by the Turks were not adequate to satisfy President Spyros Kyprianou, who succeeded Makarios after his death on August 3, 1977, and the talks failed.

On March 29, 1986, the secretary-general made a new set of proposals suggesting the more than 29 percent of the territory in the north be returned to Greeks and described the functions of the central government. The Greek Cypriots were cold to the idea, and the Greco-Turkish Aegean Sea crisis over oil explorations poisoned the climate for talks. The demarcation of the Aegean Sea is the most contentious issue between Greece and Turkey involving the continental shelf, the territorial sea, and sovereign airspace. Greece and Turkey have come to the brink of war over Cyprus and the Aegean Sea at least seven times—over Cyprus, in 1963–64, in 1967, and July–August 1974, oil explorations in the Aegean in May 1974, February 1976, March 1987, and in 1996. The war tensions eased between Greece and Turkey in 1988 as a result of the talks at Davos, Switzerland, and at Voukagmeni, Greece.[545] Papandreou-Ozal dialogue on détente led to the resumption of Vassiliou-Denktash talks on August 24, 1988, but the discussions collapsed over the Greek demands for "three freedoms": freedom to travel, freedom to settle, and freedom of property ownership.[546] The second round of Vassiliou-Denktash talks was on December 19, 1988, in Nicosia, the third round was with the UN secretary-general in New York in June 1989, the fourth was in July, and the last meeting was on March 2, 1990, before the talks collapsed. Talks on the formation of a federation of north and south Cyprus failed, and the island continued to be separated by a "green line."

In 1992, UN Secretary-General Boutros-Ghali proposed the "set of ideas"[547] but failed to achieve the expected results for resolving the Cyprus crisis. Boutros Boutros-Ghali, as secretary-general of the UN (1991 to 1996), used power politics to exert pressure on both Cypriot leaders, President George Vassiliou and President Rauf Denktash, to resolve the Cyprus crisis. Boutros's non-map divided the island between the Greek and Turkish Cypriots to two equal constituent states and each state will exercise extensive self-government. The Turks were to make major land concessions and a limited right to return of the Greek Cypriot refugees, demobilization of local and armed forces, and set up a reconciliation commission. Cyprus was to be considered as a single entity under the Zurich-London Accords of 1959. The Security Council Resolution No. 789 was approved in November 1992 despite the objections of the Turks. Denktash's refusal to endorse Boutros's idea as to single sovereignty, single citizenship, territorial changes, and the return of all the Greek Cypriots refugees to the north was not endorsed by Turkey. Newly elected president of Cyprus republic Glafkos Clerides failed to support Resolution 789. The rightist Greek Cypriots demanded the return of all Greek Cypriots refugees to the north and their homes and the free movement of the two communities on the island. Furthermore, all the Turkish settlers from Anatolia in the north and the Turkish troops were to return to Turkey. On March 30, 1993, the UN secretary-general met with Clerides, leader of Democratic Rally (DESY) party, and Denktash. An agreement was reached to resume the talks in New York on May 24, 1993.[548]

The withdrawal of foreign troops is not a realistic proposition when it fails to address the security concerns of both communities and the strategic geopolitical interest of Turkey. Despite the failure of the Turkish Cypriot administration in the north to gain international recognition (Turkey is the only country that recognizes it), the subsequent *de facto* division of the island is *fait accompli* and many Turkish Cypriots have become accustomed to being independent since 1974. The political, economic, and social alienation of the two communities crippled the prospects for rapprochement and world public opinion in time will be receptive to the existence of two-state systems on the island.

On November 22, 1993, a *Report of the Secretary-General in Connection With the Security Council's Comprehensive Reassessment of the United Nation's Operation in Cyprus* (S/26777) informed the council that:

> in the past two years, there has been an intensification of efforts to achieve an overall settlement. The process has yielded a "set of ideas" for an overall framework agreement, endorsed by the Security Council as the basis for reaching a settlement but not yet accepted by both sides and an important package of confidence-building measures, which also has won the support

of the Council, but has not yet received the backing of both sides.... [The Council] also insisted ... on a positive approach by both sides ... to accelerate and intensify the negotiating process.[549]

The lack of progress in the peace talks was unacceptable to the international community and neither was giving in the continuation of the status quo. Joe Clark, the former Canadian prime minister, was appointed by the secretary-general to be his special representative for Cyprus and Deputy Special Representative Gustavo Fiessel who would reside on the island. The "extensive meetings of 1992 were not successful" and the "set of ideas" presented in Nicosia and New York failed to achieve any progress. The Turks were accused of not showing "the necessary goodwill and cooperation required to achieve an agreement!"[550] No breakthrough in settlement was achieved in the 1992, 1994, and 1995 talks. Meanwhile, Greece exploited its EU membership to pressure Turkey to soften its stance while Turkey continued to be satisfied with the status quo.

In July 2000, Alvaro de Soto, the Peruvian diplomat, UN Secretary-General Kofi Annan's special advisor on Cyprus, as to the Proximity talks said his mission was to facilitate a comprehensive Cyprus settlement. In November 2002, the first version of the Annan Plan was circulated. Four subsequent versions proposed a confederation of Cyprus (loose federal union based on the Swiss Confederate model)[551] providing the ethnic territorial units' maximal autonomy and limited joint institutions at the federal level would operate on the basis of consociational norms. The constituent states would have jurisdiction over foreign policy, EU affairs, central bank functions, and a 9 percent transfer of territory to Greeks (72:28 formula). The Greek Cypriots would control a portion of the Karpas peninsula, including Argaki and Varosha. A moratorium as to the number of Greek Cypriots residency in the north for six years and population transfer were to proceed under the UN supervision. Transfer of population from the south to north set a limit of 7 percent of Greeks in any one village in 7 to 11 years; a limit of 14 percent for 12 to 15 years; and a limit of 18 percent for 15 to 19 years. The remainder of Greek refugees who had migrated to the south was entitled to compensation for lost property. About 45,000 settlers from Turkey would receive Cypriot citizenship. Greece and Turkey would be allowed to station 6,000 troops each on Cyprus until 2011, reducing it to 3,000 each until 2018. Cyprus would be demilitarized and all Greek and Turkish Cypriot military forces, including reserve units, were to be dissolved.

Under the federal system, the parliament would be bicameral—the upper house (Senate) would consist of forty-eight members, equally divided between

Greek and Turkish Cypriots, and the lower house (the Chamber of Deputies) would consist of forty-eight members divided on the basis of population of each constituent state (with no fewer than twelve for the smaller communities). Parliamentary decisions required a simple majority in both houses but "specified matters" required cross-community majorities in the senate. Both chambers concurrent majorities would elect a federal copresidency with a rotating chairmanship. A president and vice president would be chosen by the presidential council from among its members, one from each community to alternate in their functions every twenty months during the council's five-year term of office. The copresidency would act by consensus and lack of consensus by simple majority as long as that majority included at least one representative from both constituent states. The six-member federal council of ministers would be allocated according to population and selected and voted in by parliament. An additional three nonvoting members would be assigned two to one (four Greek Cypriots and two Turkish Cypriots). The six representatives in the European parliament would be four Greek and two Turkish Cypriots. The Supreme Constitutional Court consisted of equal number of judges from each constituent state and three non-Cypriot judges, to be appointed by the presidential council. The court would resolve disputes between the constituent states and between one or both of them and the federal government, and resolve on an interim basis deadlocks within the federal institutions. The constitutional structure was modeled on the Swiss system, the status and relationship of its federal government and its cantons. The plan included a federal constitution, constitution for each state, a united Cyprus flag, and a national anthem. A reconciliation commission was to resolve outstanding disputes from the past and help bring the two communities together. The agreement affirmed the political equality of the two communities under a bizonal partnership, similar to the confederal and consociational Dayton agreement that ended the Bosnian war at the end of 1995 as well as the Northern Ireland agreement reached on Good Friday in April 1998.

On February 13, 2004, Tassos Papdopoulos and Rauf Denktash met in New York to close the gaps in the Annan Plan with the joint efforts of Greece, Turkey, and UN Secretary-General Kofi Annan. The amended plan was to be endorsed by separate simultaneous referenda by the two electorates in the north and south on April 24. The Turkish Cypriots endorsed the plan by 64.90 percent, but Greek Cypriots resoundingly rejected it by 75.83 percent. In his rejection, Papadopoulos departed from his acceptance of the Annan Plan and before Cyprus television launched a tearful rejection of it. Papadopoulos challenged the validity of the acceptance of a bizonal, bicommounal federation and demanded the restoration of Greek territories to their owners. He strongly opposed the presence of Turkish troops on Cyprus and the granting of citizenship to Turkish settlers in the north. AKEL (Anorthotikon Komma Ergazomenou Laou/ Progressive Party of the Working People), the communist party, that endorsed the election of Papadopoulos at February 2003 elections, and DISY, the party founded by Glafocs Clerides in 1976, who were supportive of the Annan Plan reversed their decision to kill the UN-brokered settlement when they failed to secure the postponement of the referendum "for a few months" for negotiations aimed at proposing changes in the Annan Plan. Greek desire was to achieve a unitary state and avoid a bizonal solution as preferred by the Turks. The UN spokesman reminded the two communities that there was no plan B, and EU Commissioner Gunter Verheugen accused the Greek leaders of "cheating" him. The UN-brokered Annan Plan was a major substantive political settlement that was rejected by the Greek Cypriots.

Kofi Annan's comprehensive plan on Cyprus was revised five times before it was presented to the Cypriots for their approval on April 24, 2004. At The Hague meeting on March 10–11, 2003, Papadopoulos and Denktash agreed to submit Annan III Plan to a referendum after changes relative to the Treaty of Guarantee, as demanded by Turkey, were met. The prior meetings where revisions were made occurred on November 11, December 10, 2002, and February 26, 2003. The final result, Annan V Plan (Annan IV Plan was revision-based only), included nearly ten thousand pages.[552] The financial assistance to mitigate the cost of the reunification under Annan V Plan was estimated to come to $15 billion. Annan V Plan provided for the Turkish Cypriot autonomy under confederation; Turkey, as a guarantor power, had intervention rights; expanded Britiain's right in the sovereign base areas; granting of citizenship to Turkish settlers; transfer of limited number of Greek Cypriots to the north and the compensation for lost property; and the plan deleted the ratification by Cyprus of the July 20, 1936, Montreux Convention on navigation through the Turkish Straits. Greek leadership charged that Annan V Plan provided for the *de facto* partition of Cyprus. On the other hand, the Turks declared that they would not renegotiate Annan V Plan, and they had accepted it without preconditions.

One of Makarios's greatest achievements was unilateral initiative in forming political alliances in the national organizations that backed his ongoing effort for *enosis*. As to the question of political power versus ethnic partnership, the two communities drifted apart revealing a permanent split. Neither the UN nor the EU has acted as a unifier to stop the erosion and the crisis intensified the desire by the Turkish Cypriots for a permanent division, which will continue to grow. EU failed to act as a catalyst, as expected by the Greeks, for the reunification of Cyprus. The international community's flawed theoretical approach in the resolution of the ethnic conflict was an exercise on pontificating on matter of grand politics adding more than subtracting from the Cyprus quagmire. An adversarial contest does not provide a means of rescuing the available options to accommodate the interests of two societies. The problem-solving tasks delegated to the United Nations in the contest between the Greek and Turks has led some observers to speculate prematurely for the quick resolution of the underlying conflict, but instead, the UN has become an issue in and of itself. The perception of the UN's fundamental weakness and ineffectiveness is due to the long-standing failures over Palestine, the Korean Peninsula, Kashmir, the Cambodian and Rwanda genocide, the Iraq war, Darfur, and Cyprus. The essential weakness of the UN is due to the limitations placed on its task of legitimizing its international actions and how to apply them in particular circumstances for the peaceful resolution of disputes. A grand vision of reunifying Cyprus is unsustainable ambition to facilitate a "comprehensive" agreement in a polarized society. Since 1974, seven international initiatives on Cyprus failed to bring the two communities to address the complex issues and the obstinate and insatiable stance of the Cypriot leaders would eventually lead to partition. They were the Galo Plaza report (1965), the Anglo-American-Canadian Plan (1978), Kurt Waldheim initiatives (1981), Perez de Cuellar plan (1983, 1985–86), the Set of Ideas of Boutros-Ghali (1992), and Kofi Annan initiative and Plan (1997, 2002, 2004). However, the election of a president on February 24, 2008, for a five-year term presented a positive prospect for the breakthrough to the Cyprus crisis, but those hopes diminished by July 2012. On February 19, *Cyprus Mail* wrote, "The U.N. was making plans to extricate itself from the Cyprus quagmire had Tassos Papadopoulos been re-elected." The UNFICYP denied the allegation and said that it will continue to keep the peace as long as the Greek Cypriot administration and "the international community deem it necessary."[553]

The international community had failed to bridge the gap between the two communities to reach a settlement. Czechoslovakia model (Czech Republic and Slovakia) or the Rambouillet Kosovo peace conference agreement on February 23, 1999, the international community should offer a similar two-state political arrangements to settle the ongoing Cyprus crisis since 1963. The Turkish Cypriots' full autonomy and self-government, under democratic institutions, should be agreed on with a pledge to peaceful coexistence and a commitment to settle all issues relative to the interests of their citizens.

NOTES

APPENDIX A

THE 13 POINTS: NOVEMBER 1963

The amendments to the constitution proposed by Makarios were fundamental in every respect, essentially altering the basis of the "ethnic" arrangement for political governance. In this sense, then, the 13 Points must be seen as rewriting the treaties and governing instruments for all of Cyprus. Makarios, who certainly had legitimate complaints about the political paralysis that the 1959 accords had produced, acted unilaterally, without consultation with the Turkish Cypriot leadership, and this itself became a source of friction. In a note attached to these points and the accompanying memorandum, Makarios said he was taking this radical step because the constitution as written by Greece and Turkey had created "difficulties in the smooth functioning of the State and impede the development of the country. In this respect I transmit herewith for your information a Memorandum setting out the immediate measures, which I consider necessary, to meet the situation. I have today conveyed the attached Memorandum to the Vice- President, Dr. Kutchuk, inviting him to talks with a view to resolving the various difficulties set out in the Memorandum. I have arrived at the decision to take this initiative in my earnest desire to remove certain causes of anomaly and friction between Greeks and Turks which prevent them from co-operating, to this grave detriment of the country. It is hoped that the Turkish Cypriots, after carefully studying this Memorandum, will agree that my proposals are both realistic and constructive." They did not.

One reason Makarios acted so peremptorily was because he had consulted with Sir Arthur Clark, the British high commissioner (ambassador) in Cyprus, who apparently had signaled his approval. Makarios believed this meant that the British government would back his constitutional overhaul, which turned out to be a false expectation.

Below are the 13 Points, with an explanation following, contained in the text of letters Makarios sent to the prime ministers of Greece, Turkey, and Britain on November 29, 1963.

Suggested Measures for the Removal of Causes of Friction Between the Two Communities

1. The right of veto of the President and the Vice-President of the Republic to be abolished.

2. The Vice-President of the Republic to deputise for or replace the President of the Republic in case of his temporary absence or incapacity to perform his duties. In consequence, therefore, all the constitutional provisions in respect of joint action by the President and the Vice-President of the Republic to be modified accordingly.

3. The Greek President of the House of Representatives and its Turkish Vice-President to be elected by the House as a whole and not as at present the President by the Greek Members of the House and the Vice-President by the Turkish Members of the House.

4. The Vice-President of the House of Representatives to deputise for or replace the President of the House in case of his temporary absence or incapacity to perform his duties.

5. The constitutional provisions regarding separate majority for enactment of Laws by the House of Representatives to be abolished.

6. The constitutional provision regarding the establishment of separate Municipalities in the five main towns to be abolished. Provision should be made so that: (a) The Municipal Council in each of the aforesaid five towns shall consist of Greek and Turkish Councillors in proportion to the number of the Greek and Turkish inhabitants of such town by whom they shall be elected respectively. (b) In the Budget of each of such aforesaid towns, after deducting any expenditure required for common services, a percentage of the balance proportionate to the number of the Turkish inhabitants of such town shall be earmarked and disposed of in accordance with the wishes of the Turkish Councillors.

7. The constitutional provision regarding Courts consisting of Greek Judges to try Greeks and of Turkish Judges to try Turks and of mixed Courts consisting of Greek and Turkish Judges to try cases where the litigants are Greeks and Turks to be abolished.

8. The division of the Security Forces into Police and Gendarmerie to be abolished, (Provision to be made in case the Head of the Police is a Greek the Deputy Head to be a Turk and vice versa).

9. The numerical strength of the Security Forces and of the Army to be determined by Law and not by agreement between the President and the Vice-President of the Republic.

10. The proportion of the participation of Greek and Turkish Cypriots in the composition of the Public Service and of the Forces of the Republic, i.e. the Police and the Army, to be modified inproportion to the ratio of the population of Greek and Turkish Cypriots.

11. The number of the members of the Public Service Commission to be reduced from ten to either five or seven.

12. All the decisions of the Public Service Commission to be taken by simple majority. If there is an allegation of discrimination on the unanimous request either of the Greek or of the Turkish members of the Commission, its Chairman to be bound to refer the matter to the Supreme Constitutional Court.

13. The Greek Communal Chamber to be abolished.

Suggested measures to facilitate the smooth functioning of the state and remove certain causes of inter-communal friction

The Constitution of the Republic of Cyprus, in its present form, creates many difficulties in the smooth government of the State and impedes the development and progress of the country. It contains many sui generis provisions conflicting with internationally accepted democratic principles and creates sources of friction between Greek and Turkish Cypriots. At the Conference at Lancaster House in February, 1959, which I was invited to attend as leader of the Greek Cypriots, I raised a number of objections and expressed strong misgivings regarding certain provisions of the Agreement arrived at in Zurich between the Greek and the Turkish Governments and adopted by the British Government. I tried very hard to bring about the change of at least some provisions of that Agreement. I failed, however, in that effort and I was faced with the dilemma either of signing the Agreement as it stood or of rejecting it with all the grave consequences which would have ensued. In the circumstances I had no alternative but to sign the Agreement. This was the course dictated to me by necessity. The three years' experience since the coming into operation of the Constitution, which was based on the Zurich and London Agreements, has made clear the necessity for revision of at least some of those provisions which impede the smooth functioning and development of the State. I believe that the intention of those who drew up the Agreement at Zurich was to create an independent State, in which the interests of the Turkish Community were safeguarded, but it could not have been their intention that the smooth functioning and development of the country should be prejudiced or thwarted as has in fact been the case. One of the consequences of the difficulties created by certain constitutional provisions is to prevent the Greeks and Turks of Cyprus from co-operating in a spirit of understanding and friendship, to undermine the relations between them and cause them to draw further apart instead of closer together, to the detriment of the well being of the people of Cyprus as a whole. This situation causes me, as President of the State, great concern. It is necessary to resolve certain of the difficulties by the removal of some at least of the obstacles to the smooth functioning and development of the State. With this end in view I have outlined below the immediate measures which I propose to be taken.

1. **The right of veto of the President and the Vice-President of the Republic to be abandoned.** The right of veto given under the Constitution of the Republic to the President and the Vice-President can be exercised separately by each one of them against: (a) laws or decisions of the House of Representatives concerning foreign affairs, defence and security; and (b) decisions of the Council of Ministers concerning foreign affairs, defence and security. It is a right of final veto and, therefore, different from any other measure provided in certain Constitutions whereby the President of the country has a right of limited veto in the sense that he is entitled not to promulgate a law immediately, but to return it for reconsideration. Provisions for the return of laws and decisions for reconsideration exist in the Cyprus Constitution independently from the provision of final veto. The Constitution of Cyprus has been based on the doctrine of separation of powers between

the Executive and the Legislature. The balance between them must be carefully maintained and friction avoided, if it is to work. The right of veto cuts right across the principles involved and could bring the President and Vice-President into direct conflict with the Legislature. The exercise of the right of veto is a negative power in the sense that it does not enable the President or the Vice-President to take decisions, but it gives them the power to prevent a decision of the Council of Ministers or the House of Representatives on matters of foreign policy, defence, or security from taking effect. It is obvious that it cannot be considered as a power which affords the President or the Vice- President the opportunity to deal with an existing situation in a constructive manner. More difficulties are encountered because of the fact that the right of veto is not vested only in one person but in two persons, the President and the Vice-President of the Republic, thus increasing the occasions when a deadlock may occur. An example in point is the use of veto by the Vice-President on the subject of the composition of the units of the Army of the Republic. Under the Constitution the Army of the Republic must consist of 60% Greeks and 40% Turks. The Council of Ministers, by majority, decided that the organisational structure of the Army should be based throughout on mixed units comprising both Greeks and Turks. The Vice-President, who wanted the structure to be based on separate units of Greeks and Turks, exercised his right of veto against the above decision of the Council, with the result that there is no decision on this mat- ter and the Army has remained ineffective. In the case of the Army, no great harm has resulted, since it is doubtful whether the Republic can really afford its expansion to 2,000 men at present and cope simultaneously with her heavy financial burdens of economic development and expansion of educational and social services. But it is easy to envisage situations where exercise of the veto could result in more far-reaching and damaging repercussions. Therefore, the right of veto should be abandoned and reliance placed instead on the provisions for the return of laws and decisions for reconsideration, and the various other relevant safeguards.

2. **The Vice-President of the Republic to deputise for the President of the Republic in case of his temporary absence or incapacity to perform his duties.** Under the provisions of the Constitution, the Vice-President of the Republic does not deputise for the President in the event of his absence or incapacity to act, but the President of the House of

Representatives does so instead. This provision created the impression that a person belonging to the Turkish community and elected by it cannot deputise in a post the nature of which bears responsibility to Cyprus as a whole. It produces a situation whereby, in the absence of the President of the Republic, the Vice-President is overlooked and the President of the House of Representatives steps above him. The practical effect of this is that it binders the continuity of the smooth functioning of the executive power. The Vice-President of the Republic is a member of the Executive, he participates in the deliberations of the Council of Ministers, he knows the reasons and background of decisions taken and is, therefore, in a much better position to continue with the implementation of such decisions than the President of the House of Representatives, who is not a member of the Executive, and on whom the burden of acting as Head of the Executive is suddenly thrust. It is for the above reasons that the Vice-President should deputise for the President of the Republic during his temporary absence or incapacity to perform his duties. As a result of the new status of the Vice-President certain consequential or relative amendments have to be made.

3. **The Greek President of the House of Representatives and the Turkish Vice-President to be elected by the House as a whole and not as at present the President by the Greek Members of the House and the Vice-President by the Turkish Members of the House.** Under the provisions of the Constitution the President of the House of Representatives, who must be a Greek, is elected by the Greek Members of the House and the Vice-President, who must be a Turk, is elected by the Turkish Members. Further, the Turkish Vice-President cannot deputise for the President in case of his temporary absence or incapacity. The function of the President of the House, who presides over the entire Assembly, is one which bears responsibility to the House as a whole and not to a particular section of it. It is, therefore, improper that the election of the President of the House should be carried out by the Greek Members only. As far as can be ascertained there is no other Constitution where the President of the Legislative Assembly is elected by one section of the Assembly. The participation of Representatives of both communities in electing the President of the House will also create conditions which will gradually train the two communities to co-operate in electing persons to political offices. It will lead both Greek and Turkish Representatives to closer contact with the office of the

President of the House and will facilitate the solution of problems which arise in considering legislative measures. For the same reasons the Vice-President of the House should be elected by the House as a whole and not by the Turkish Members only.

4. **The Vice-President of the House of Representatives to deputise for the President of the House in case of his temporary absence or incapacity to perform his duties.** Under the provisions of the Constitution the Vice-President of the House cannot deputise for the President of the House of Representatives. In case of temporary absence or incapacity of the President of the House his duties are entrusted to the oldest Greek Representative or to such Greek Member of the House as the Greek Members may decide. In the case of the Vice-President his duties are performed by the oldest Turkish Representative or by such other Turkish Member as the Turkish Members may decide. The fact that the Vice-President never presides over the House and never deputises for the President creates a situation whereby neither does he feel that he owes responsibility to the whole House nor do the Greek Members feel that they owe any duty or responsibility towards the Vice-President. Apart from the fact that this provision of the Constitution tends to show that the Vice-President is a figure Vice-Head it also affects the smooth functioning of the House. It may occur that the oldest Greek or Turkish Member is not the right person to per form the duties of President or Vice-President of the House. If on the other hand, the Greek or the Turkish Members of the House nominate other Greek and Turkish Representatives to act as President and Vice-President, respectively, by decisions taken on each occasion, there will be no experienced Acting President or Vice-President to take over at a given time. Finally, in view of the non-existence of a permanent Vice-President of the House entitled to deputise for the President, there is no one familiar with the work involved either in regard to the political aspect of the functions of the President or to the duties connected with the administration of the House.

5. **The constitutional provisions regarding separate majorities for enactment of certain laws by the House of Representatives to be abolished.** The Constitution provides that any law imposing taxation and any law relating to Municipalities and any modification of the Electoral Law requires separate majorities of the Greek and Turkish

Members of the House of Representatives taking part in the vote. This provision is obviously contrary to all democratic principles. Its effect is that, though a Bill may be unanimously approved by the Council of Ministers and though it may receive the overwhelming majority of votes in the House of Representatives, nevertheless it is defeated if it does not receive the separate majority of the Greek or Turkish Representatives taking part in the vote. The House of Representatives consists of 3 5 Greek Members and 15 Turkish Members. If, for example, 35 Greek Members and 7 Turkish Members vote in favour of a Bill, i.e., the Bill receives a total of 42 votes in favour, it can be defeated by 8 Turkish votes. Even 2 Turkish Representatives can defeat a Bill if only 3 Turkish Representatives take part in the vote. This provision obstructs the enactment of vital legislation, generally, and impedes the development of the country. In particular, it has already caused serious adverse effects on the State by preventing or delaying the enactment of taxation legislation. Thus, on one occasion by the exercise of the right of separate majorities, the State remained completely without taxation legislation for several months. When, subsequently, an Income Tax Bill was introduced to the House the Turkish Representatives again used their right of separate majority to defeat the Bill with the result that the State remained without an Income Tax Law. In an attempt to minimize the grave consequences of the situation thus created, an unorthodox system has been devised whereby one Income Tax Law was enacted by the House imposing taxation on non-citizens of the Republic and two separate Income Tax Laws were enacted by the Greek and Turkish Communal Chambers imposing a form of income tax on Greeks and Turks, respectively. Thus, the Republic has three income tax systems, which cause administrative dislocation and give rise to a multitude of legal contentions. Further, in view of the fact that the Government has no control over the Communal Chambers, any amendment may at any time be made by the respective Communal Chamber in its income tax legislation, thereby creating incalculable difficulties for assessment purposes. The existence of three separately controlled tax systems requires separate accounting; the consequent slow rate of assessment and collection of the income taxes encourages tax evasion to a level unknown before in Cyprus. Past experience has shown that the right of separate majorities was not exercised by the Turkish Representatives because of disagreement with provisions of the taxation legislation before the House. The Turkish Members used this right against taxation Bills neither because they disagreed with their provisions nor because such Bills were discriminatory against their community, but for matters unconnected with taxation legislation. A further difficulty in the enactment of taxation legislation, arising out of the separate majorities provisions, is demonstrated by the fact that such legislation submitted to the House requires months of frustrating negotiations. Even if one assumes that in the future a more prudent use will be made of the right of separate majorities, the application of this procedure will always cause serious difficulties. It may well make it impossible for the Government to effect proper development of the direct taxes as revenue procedure and also as unified instruments of social and economic policy. No Government is able to carry out a programme of development unless it can also plan and control its resources. There is no justification at all for the provision of separate majorities. If such provision were intended as a safeguard against discriminatory legislation, then it is completely unnecessary because there are other provisions in the Constitution affording adequate safeguards and remedies. Any legislation which is discriminatory can be challenged before the Constitutional Court by the Vice-President of the Republic. Furthermore, Article 6 of the Constitution provides that no law or decision of the House of Representatives shall discriminate against any of the two communities or any person as a person or as a member of a community. Any citizen has a right given to him by the Constitution to challenge any law or decision which discriminates in such a manner as to affect his interests directly.

6. **Unified Municipalities to be established.** The Constitution provides that separate Municipalities shall be created in the five main towns of the Republic. Not only does this provision not serve any useful purpose but it has also proved to be unworkable. The impossibility of finding a way to define geographical areas and create separate Municipalities, based on communal criteria, is due to the fact that never before did the Greek and Turkish Cypriots contemplate living in separate areas. A factual examination will show that there are many areas in which Greeks and Turks live side by side and that the ownership of property by the two communities does not follow the pattern of communal areas. This fact is clearly apparent from the proposed principles formulated by the Vice-President of the Republic for determining which streets will fall within the Greek Municipality and which will fall within the

Turkish Municipality. The Vice-President proposed that: "The frontage of all property abutting on any street will be measured and if the total length of the frontage of the property belonging to the members of the Greek community in that street is greater, then that street will be included in the sector of the Greek Municipality. The same principle will apply in the case of a street where the total length of the frontage of the property belonging to the members of the Turkish community is greater." It should be observed that by this proposal the Vice-President has tried to find a solution by distinguishing ownership of property on the basis of communal criteria without taking into consideration the occupants of such property. It is an undisputed fact that there are many properties belonging to Turks which have Greek tenants and vice versa. Many streets abutting on or leading into each other will fall in the area of one or the other Municipality and thus the resulting two municipal areas will not have any territorial cohesion. This fact alone demonstrates the impracticability of the division of the towns into separate areas on the basis of communal criteria. Apart, however, from the fact that geographical separation is not feasible, the separation of Municipalities will be financially detrimental to the townsmen. There would be duplication of municipal services and the cost of their running might become so prohibitive as to render their proper functioning almost impossible. The impossibility of agreeing on the separate areas became apparent during the year-long deliberations of the Constitutional Commission. In view of the inability of the Constitutional Commission to reach agreement on this point, the responsibility was transferred to the President and the Vice-President of the Republic by the insertion of Article 177 of the Constitution, whereby the President and the Vice-President were empowered to define boundaries of the areas of each Municipality. Owing to the above difficulties, however, they failed to reach an agreement on the determination of the boundaries. Under the proviso to Article 183(1) of the Constitution the President and the Vice-President of the Republic have a duty, within a period of four years from the date of the coming into operation of the Constitution, to examine the question of whether or not the separation of the Municipalities in the five main towns shall continue. It is obvious that the reason why this provision was inserted was that, even at the time when the Zurich Agreement was drafted, doubts were entertained as to the desirability or practicability of such an arrangement and it was, therefore, thought necessary to give the President and the Vice-President power to reconsider the position within a specified period from the date of Independence. If it were put forward that the separation of the Municipalities in the five main towns was provided for in order to protect the Turkish inhabitants of such towns against any discrimination, other safeguards may be provided in this respect such as: (a) The municipal council in each of the five main towns should consist of Greek and Turkish councillors in proportion to the number of the Greek and Turkish inhabitants of such town by whom they shall be elected respectively; (b) There should be earmarked in the annual budget of each such town, after deducting any expenditure for common services, a sum proportionate to the ratio of the Turkish population of such town. This sum should be disposed of for municipal purposes recommended by the Turkish councillors.

7. **The administration of Justice to be unified.** The Constitution separates the administration of Justice on the basis of communal criteria by providing that in all cases, civil and criminal, a Greek must be tried by a Greek Judge, a Turk by a Turkish Judge and that cases, however trivial, involving both Greeks and Turks, must be tried by a mixed Court composed of Greek and Turkish Judges. This division is not only entirely unnecessary but what is more important, is detrimental to the cause of Justice. The very concept of Justice defies separation. The mere fact that a Greek must be tried by a Greek and a Turk by a Turk is in itself a slur on the impartiality and integrity of the Judges. It is inevitable that when a Judge assumes jurisdiction on the basis of communal criteria he begins to think that the interests of his community stand in danger of being jeopardized and that he is there to protect such interests. The Judge will, therefore, gradually lose the sense of being a judge above communal criteria. This is particularly so in mixed cases, where each Judge will eventually come to feel that his presence is necessary in order to protect the party belonging to his community from possible injustice by his brother Judge. As a consequence of this, Judges will lose their respect for each other, will begin to regard each other with suspicion and may develop the mentality, not of a judge, but of an arbitrator appointed by one of the parties to a dispute. This mentality will inevitably seep into the minds of the people as a whole, who will consider Judges as advocates in the cause of their community and expect them to act as such. It is another consequence of the dichotomy of Justice that the public is bound to compare sentences imposed by Greek Judges on Greeks and by Turkish Judges on Turks and to draw conclusions from such comparisons. In view

of the fact that the jurisdiction of Judges is based on communal criteria, the result of such comparisons will be to foster the belief that there exists separate Justice for Greeks and Turks. This will diminish the respect of the people for the administration of Justice. Thus Justice will not only cease to be done but will also cease to be seen to be done. Nothing is more certain to undermine Justice and to bring it into disrepute than the situation described above. Apart from the aforesaid most important considerations, the system which has had to be devised in order to implement these provisions of the Constitution is also unnecessarily costly. In view of the fact that Greek cases are more numerous than Turkish cases, the Greek Judges are burdened with a much larger volume of work than the Turkish Judges. Due to the separation imposed by the Constitution, Turkish Judges, even if not fully occupied and although willing, cannot relieve their Greek colleagues by taking cases in which the parties involved are Greek. There must, therefore, be maintained a greater number of Judges than would be warranted by the number of cases if they could be evenly distributed. The fact that even a trivial case, as well as a preliminary enquiry, must be heard by two Judges if the parties belong to different communities results in un- necessary waste of time and money, delay and hardship to the litigant, and is yet another reason for having a greater number of Judges than would otherwise be necessary. A further result of the separation of the administration of Justice is the duplication of registry work and therefore of court personnel, thus creating an additional financial burden. The measure of civilization of a country and its stability greatly depend on the fair administration of Justice and on the confidence enjoyed by its Judiciary. If the principle of Justice is undermined the consequences to the State cannot but be serious and, in Cyprus, if the present system continues. Justice is certain to suffer. Before the Constitution came into force, the court system prevailing in Cyprus had been operating extremely well for many years. Justice being administered by Greek and Turkish Judges, honourably and impartially, irrespective of community. There can be no greater proof of this than the fact that even at the height of intercommunal strife, when Justice was still unified, never was a shadow of doubt cast on the integrity of the Judges or any complaint made about their impartiality. There is, therefore, no reason for the imposition of restrictions on the jurisdiction of the Judges of the Republic, on communal criteria, thus establishing a system which is bound to undermine justice and is most impracticable in its application.

---

8. **The division of the Security Forces into Police and Gendarmerie to be abolished.** Since the establishment of Independence the Security Forces of the Republic have been divided into Police and Gendarmerie and operate as two separate and distinct Forces in defined areas and under separate command. This division of the Security Forces is entirely unnecessary and should be abolished for the following reasons: (a) With the existence of two Forces under separate command, separate Headquarters for each Force had to be established. This has led to unnecessary financial expenditure; (b) The creation of separate commands necessitates concentration of many officers at Headquarters and causes a waste of manpower, especially in the higher ranks. At least 200 officers are engaged in additional administrative posts due to the division and duplication of the administration. There now also exists a greater ratio of officers vis-a-vis men without a corresponding increase in the total numerical strength. This increase in personnel costs the State an additional expenditure of at least £150,000 per annum; (c) Due to the division of the Security Forces and their command into two, both at Headquarters level and at Divisional level, the cohesion and strength of the Security Forces is adversely affected and results, inter alia, in lack of uniformity of discipline and in friction between the two separate Forces; (d) In case of an emergency or other grave situation neither Force will have readily available for immediate use the full strength of the Security Forces and their reserves. Finally, the experience gained in having only one Force, the Police Force, which worked efficiently and effectively for so many years proves that there is no valid reason for the division of the Security Forces into Police and Gendarmerie, a course not even warranted by the size of the Island.

9. **The numerical strength of the Security Forces and of the Defence Forces to be determined by a Law.** The Constitution provides that the Security Forces of the Republic shall consist of the Police and the Gendarmerie and shall have a contingent of 2,000 men which may be reduced or increased by agreement of the President and the Vice-President of the Republic. This is an unworkable provision because, even if the President and the Vice-President agree to increase the numerical strength of the Security Forces, such agreement will be completely ineffectual unless the House of Representatives approves the resulting increase in budgetary expenditure. Under the Constitution the President and the Vice-President cannot, by agreeing to increase the Security Forces, create a charge on the Consolidated Fund. The

question of increasing or decreasing the numerical strength of the Security Forces should, in the first instance, be decided by the Council of Ministers in the normal way and legislation be introduced to the House for enactment. The Constitution also provides that the Republic shall have an Army of 2,000 men. This provision is impracticable as no implementation of the numerical strength of the Army can take place unless the House of Representatives approves the financial expenditure required. Furthermore, no provision exists for the increase or decrease, depending on ordinary requirements, of the numerical strength of the Army. Constitutional provision should, therefore, be made that the Republic shall have such Defence Forces as may be regulated by Law.

10. **The proportion of the participation of Greek and Turkish Cypriots in the composition of the Public Service and the Forces of the Republic to be modified in proportion to the ratio of the population of Greek and Turkish Cypriots.** The Constitution provides that 70% of the Public Service shall be com- posed of Greek Cypriots and that 30% shall be composed of Turkish Cypriots. It further provides that this ratio shall be applied, as far as practicable, in all grades of the Public Service. The Constitution also provides that the Security Forces shall be composed of 70% Greek Cypriots and 30% Turkish Cypriots and that the Army shall be composed of 60% Greek Cypriots and 40% Turkish Cypriots. It is an accepted fact that the proper administration of a country depends on the efficiency of its Public Service. This is of particular importance in Cyprus owing to the fact that, as a result of independence, new institutions have been created adding further complexities to the normal problems of administering the country. Furthermore, the Government, by undertaking a five-year development plan which provides for a Government expenditure of approximately £10 million per year, is casting an additional burden on the Public Service. The percentages of participation of the two communities in the Public Service as fixed by the Constitution bear no relation to the true ratio of the Greek and Turkish inhabitants of the Island which is 81.14% Greeks and 18.86% Turks. Generally speaking any provision the effect of which is that certain posts in the Public Service or a certain percentage of such posts are reserved for persons belonging to a community, religious group or ethnic minority is contrary to the internationally accepted principles of Human Rights. Thus under Article 21(2) of the Universal Declaration of Human Rights of the United Nations it is provided that "Everyone has the right of equal

access to the Public Service of his country." It can, of course, be argued that the fixing of a percentage of participation of a community in the Public Service of a country is for the purpose of securing to the citizens constituting such community a right of equal access to the Public Service of the country. The best way of securing the right of equal participation in the Public Service is not by fixing a percentage, but by provisions in the Constitution giving the right to citizens who applied and were not appointed to the Public Service to challenge the decision of the appointing authority before the competent court on the ground that they were discriminated against. If, however, the method to be followed for securing equality of access is by fixing the ratio of participation of a community in the Public Service, then, in order to minimize discrimination, such ratio must be a fair one so as to afford an equal opportunity to the community constituting the minority to participate in the Public Service, without at the same time preventing the majority of the population from having an equal opportunity of participation in the Public Service of the country. The present constitutional provision, by specifying that 70% of the Public Service shall be composed of Greek Cypriots, when in fact the Greek Cypriots constitute more than 81% of the population, and that 30% of the Public Service shall be composed of Turkish Cypriots, when in fact the Turkish Cypriots constitute less than 19% of the population, does not afford an equal opportunity to the majority of the citizens of the Republic to participate in the Public Service. It is, therefore, clearly discriminatory. The implementation of the above provision of the Constitution creates serious problems for the State. It makes it necessary, in considering appointments and promotions, to use criteria other than those universally accepted, such as qualifications, efficiency and suitability of the candidate, because the appointing authority has to take into consideration the community to which the candidate belongs. As a result the best candidates cannot always be selected. Further, particular hardship is created in the case of promotions. Public servants who possess all the required qualifications and experience/or promotion to higher grades may haw to be overlooked in favour of less qualified or efficient public servants, solely in order to give effect to an artificially fixed communal ratio of participation in the Public Service. The result of the situation thus created is that the efficiency of the Public Service is adversely affected. If the provision is to be implemented without affecting the promotion of public servants, the alternative is to create unnecessary posts and impose a further financial burden on the State. The Government now spends 31% of its Ordinary Budget for salaries and other allowances to public servants, not including pensions. It is clear, therefore, that any increase or unnecessary expenditure in expanding the Public Service would be highly detrimental to the economy of the country. In addition to what is stated above this provision cannot be implemented for the following reasons: In many cases in which the Public Service Commission decided to allocate posts to the Turkish community, it was found that no qualified Turks were available for appointment, with the result that a number of posts remained vacant and in some cases the Commission had to ap- point Greeks on a temporary basis until qualified Turkish candidates might become available. In some instances the minimum qualifications specified in the schemes of service were lowered in order to enable Turkish candidates to enter the Public Service, but even with such lower standards no Turkish qualified candidate could be found. The fact that the Commission had to draw from a population forming less than 19% of the population of the Island in order to f ill the 30% of the posts in the Public Service made it very difficult to find qualified Turks for many posts. Further, the exigencies of public business and the pattern of business and professional activity in the Island require that the Public Service should contain an adequate proportion of Greek officers. The language problem of itself demands this. It can be seen from what is stated above that not only is the provision that the Public Service shall be composed of 30% Turks unjust and discriminatory against the Greeks, but it is also impracticable, it creates serious difficulties and impedes the efficient functioning of the Public Service. The reasons given above regarding the ratio of participation of the two communities in the Public Service apply to a great extent to the ratio fixed for the participation of the two communities in the Security Forces. It must be stated that the 60:40 ratio of participation of Greeks and Turks in the Army discriminates to an even greater extent against the Greeks. Nevertheless, in so far as the present ratio of Greeks and Turks in the Public Service, the Security Forces and the Army exceeds the population ratio, no abrupt steps should be taken to reduce it. The proper balance can be achieved over a period of time through normal appointments, thus avoiding hardship or unfairness to existing members of the Services of the Republic.

11. **The number of the Members of the Public Service Commission to be reduced from ten to five.** The Constitution provides that there shall be

a Public Service Commission consisting of a Chairman and nine other Members appointed jointly by the President and Vice-President of the Republic and that seven Members of the Commission shall be Greeks and three Members shall be Turks. Practical experience has shown that, for the purposes/or which the Public Service Commission is intended and bearing in mind the nature of the duties it has to perform, it is too large a body to work efficiently. A smaller body will have a better chance of securing closer co-operation and understanding amongst its Members, and valuable time, wasted in lengthy arguments resulting from the divergence of opinion of its many Members, will be saved. Generally, a more constructive approach to the problems facing the Commission will result.

12. **All decisions of the Public Service Commission to be taken by simple majority.** The Constitution provides that any decision of the Public Service Commission shall be taken by an absolute majority vote of its Members. The general provision, however, is qualified by other provisions making it necessary that in matters of appointments, promotions, transfers and discipline such majority must include a certain minimum number of Greek and Turkish votes depending on whether the decision relates to a Greek or a Turk. In short, a power of veto is given to a section of the Greek or Turkish Members to negative majority decisions. It is obvious that this procedure/or taking decisions by the Public Service Commission creates a situation whereby the Greek and Turkish Members feel that their paramount purpose, as Members of the Commission, it to protect Greek and Turkish interests and not to serve the true interests of the Public Service. Thus, even in the mode of deciding an issue communal criteria are superimposed on the universally accepted criteria adopted by similar bodies elsewhere. This is of particular significance in view of the fact that the Public Service Commission in addition to being the appointing authority, is also the disciplinary body for the Public Service. Furthermore, the procedure laid down in the Constitution creates situations leading to deadlock, resulting in a state of uncertainty amongst the public servants and often preventing the speedy appointment of officers to vital posts. If this situation is allowed to continue it will result in undermining the efficiency of the Public Service. It may be argued that, in taking decisions, the Public Service Commission may act in a discriminatory manner. In such a case there is adequate remedy provided by Articles 6 and 146 of the Constitution. The former Article prohibits discrimination against any of the two communities or

any person as a person or by virtue of being a member of a community, while the latter article provides that any person may make a recourse to the Constitutional Court against any decision, act or omission contrary to any of the provisions of the Constitution, one of which is Article 6, if any legitimate interest, which he has either as a person or by virtue of being a member of a community, is adversely affected.

13. **The Greek Communal Chamber to be abolished.** The Constitution provides that there shall be two Communal Chambers, one Greek and one Turkish, each having jurisdiction in matters of religion, education, cultural affairs and personal status over members of its respective community, as well as control over communal co-operative societies. This provision appears to have its origin in the concept that the Republic ought not to interfere with religious, educational, cultural and other cognate matters, the administration of which should be regarded as a safeguarded right in the case of the minority. When this concept was extended to the Greek majority the result was to place the entire education of the country outside the sphere of government economic and social policies and to create financial problems and other difficulties for the Communal Chambers, reflecting adversely on the State. With a view to minimizing these difficulties the Communal Chambers should be abolished and a new system should be devised providing/or their substitution by appropriate authorities and institutions. Should the Turkish community, however, desire to retain its Chamber, in the new system, such a course is open to it. I have dealt with certain of the difficulties created by our Constitution. In conclusion I would stress that it is not my intention by any of these proposals to deprive the Turkish community of their just rights and interests or proper safeguards. The purpose is to remove certain causes of friction and obstacles to the smooth working of the State. The main object of a Constitution should be to secure, within its framework, the proper functioning of the State and not to create sources of anomaly and conflict. Experience has proved that our Constitution falls short of this object, and certain of its provisions have created great difficulties in practice. In the interests of our people we must remedy this. I earnestly believe that the proposed settlement of the various points of difficulty will be to the benefit of the people of Cyprus as a whole. I hope that the Turkish Cypriots will share this view.

ARCHBISHOP MAKARIOS, President of the Republic of Cyprus

———

APPENDIX B

THE AKRITAS PLAN

TOP SECRET HEADQUARTERS

Recent public statements by Archbishop Makarios have shown the course which our national problem will take in near future. As we have stressed in the past, national struggles cannot be concluded overnight; nor is it possible to fix definite chronological limits for the conclusion of the various stages of development in national causes. Our national problem must be viewed in the light of developments which take place and conditions that arise from time to time, and measures to be taken, as well as their implementation and timing, must be in keeping with the internal and external political conditions. The whole process is difficult and must go through various stages because factors which will affect the final conclusion are numerous and different. It is sufficient for everyone to know, however, that every step taken constitutes the result of a study and that at the same time it forms the basis of future measures. Also, it is sufficient to know that every measure now contemplated is a first step and only constitutes a stage towards the final and unalterable national objective which is the full and unconditional application of the right of self-determination. As the final objective remains unchanged, what must be dwelt upon is the method to be employed towards attaining that objective. This must, of necessity, be divided into internal and external (international) tactics because the methods of the presentation and handling of our cause within and outside the country are different.

A. **METHOD TO BE USED OUTSIDE** In the closing stages of the (EOKA) struggle, the Cyprus problem had been presented to the world public opinion and to diplomatic circles as a demand of the people of Cyprus to exercise the right of self-determination. But the question of Turkish minority had been introduced in circumstances that are known, inter-communal clashes had taken place and it had been tried to make it accepted that it was impossible for the two communities to live together under a united administration. Finally the problem was solved, in the eyes of many international circles, by the London and Zurich Agreements, which were shown as solving the problem following negotiations and agreements between the contending parties.

(a) Consequently our first aim has been to create the impression in the international field that the Cyprus problem has not been solved and that it has to be reviewed.

(b) The creation of the following impressions has been accepted as the primary objective:

(i) that the solution which has been found is not satisfactory and just

(ii) that the agreement which has been reached is not the result of the free will of the contending parties.

(iii) that the demand for the revision for the agreements is not because of any desire on the part of the Greeks to dishonor their signature, but an imperative necessity of survival of them.

(iv) that the co-existence of the two communities is possible, and

(v) that the Greek majority, and not the Turks, constitute the strong elements on which foreigners must rely.

(c) Although it was most difficult to attain the above objectives, satisfactory results have been achieved. Many diplomatic missions have already come to believe strongly that the Agreements are neither just nor satisfactory, that they were signed as a result of pressures and intimidations without real negotiations, and that they were imposed after many threats. It has been an important trump in our hands that the solution brought by the Agreements was not submitted to the approval of the people; acting wisely in this respect, our leadership avoided holding a referendum. Otherwise, the people would have definitely approved the Agreements in the atmosphere that prevailed in 1959. Generally speaking, it has been shown that so far the administration of Cyprus has been carried out by the Greeks and that the Turks played only a negative part acting as a brake.

(d) Having completed the first stage of our activities and objectives we must materialize the second stage on an international level. Our objective in this second stage is to show:

   (i) that the aim of the Greeks is not to oppress the Turks but only to remove unreasonable and unjust provisions of the administrative mechanism;

   (ii) that it is necessary to remove these provisions right away because tomorrow may be too late;

   (iii) Omitted

   (iv) that this question of revision is a domestic issue for Cypriots and does not therefore give the right of intervention to anyone by force or otherwise;

   (v) that the proposed amendments are reasonable and just and safeguard the reasonable rights of the minority.

(e) Generally speaking, it is obvious that today the international opinion is against any form of oppression, and especially against oppression of minorities. The Turks have so far been able to convince world public opinion that the union of Cyprus with Greece will amount to their enslavement. Under these circumstances we stand a good chance of success in influencing world public opinion if we base our struggle not on ENOSIS but on self-determination. But in order to be able to exercise the right of self-determination fully and without hindrance, we must first get rid of the Agreements (e.g., the Treaty of Guarantee, the Treaty of Alliance, etc.) and of those provisions in the Constitution which will inhibit the free and unbridled expression of the will of people and which they carry dangers of external intervention. For this reason, our first target has been the Treaty of Guarantee, which is the first Agreement to be cited as not being recognized by the Greek Cypriots.

When the Treaty of Guarantee is removed no legal or moral force will remain to obstruct us in determining our future through a plebiscite.

It will be understood from the above explanations that it is necessary to follow a chain of efforts and developments in order to ensure the success of our Plan. If these efforts and developments failed to materialize, our future actions would be legally unjustified and politically unattainable and we would be exposing Cyprus and its people to grave consequences. Actions to be taken are as follows:

(a) The amendment of the negative elements of the Agreements and the consequent de facto nullification of the Treaties of Guarantee and Alliance. This step is essential because the necessity of amending the negative aspects of any Agreement is generally acceptable internationally and is considered reasonable (passage omitted) whereas an external intervention to prevent the amendment of such negative provisions is held unjustified and inapplicable.

(b) Once this is achieved the Treaty of Guarantee (the right of intervention) will become legally and substantially inapplicable.

(c) Once those provisions of the Treaties of Guarantee and Alliance which restrict the exercise of the right of self-determination are removed, the people of Cyprus will be able, freely, to express and apply its will.

(d) It will be possible for the Force of the State (the Police Force) and in addition, friendly military Forces, to resist legitimately any intervention internally or from outside, because we will then be completely independent.

It will be seen that it is necessary for actions from (a) to (d) to be carried out in the order indicated. It is consequently evident that if we ever hope to have any chance of success in the international field, we cannot and should not reveal or proclaim any stage of the struggle before the previous stage is completed. For instance, it is accepted that the above four stages constitute the necessary course to be taken, then it is obvious that it would be senseless for us to speak of amendment (a) if stage (d) is revealed, because it would then be ridiculous for us to seek the amendment of the negative points with the excuse that these amendments are necessary for the functioning of the State and of the Agreements.

The above are the points regarding our targets and aims, and the procedure to be followed in the international field.

B. THE INTERNAL ASPECT

Our activities in the internal field will be regulated according to their repercussions and to interpretations to be given to them in the world and according to the effect of our actions on our national cause.

1. The only danger that can be described as insurmountable is the possibility of a forceful intervention. This danger, which could be met partly or wholly by our forces, is important because of the political damage that it could do rather than the material losses that it could entail. If intervention took place before stage (c), then such intervention would be legally tenable at least, if not entirely justifiable. This would be very much against us both internationally and at the United Nations. The history of many similar incidents in recent times shows us that in no case of intervention, even if legally excusable, has the attacker been removed by either the United Nations or the other powers without significant concessions to the detriment of the attacked party. Even in the case of the attack on Suez Canal by Israel, which was condemned by almost all members of the United Nations and for which Russia threatened intervention, the Israelis were removed but, as a concession, they continued to keep the port of it in the Red Sea. There are, however, more serious dangers in the case of Cyprus. If we do our work well and justify the attempt we shall make under stage (a) above, we will see, on the one hand, that intervention will not be justified and, on the other hand, we will have every support since, by the Treaty of Guarantee, intervention cannot take place before negotiations take place between the Guarantor Powers, that is, Britain, Greece, and Turkey. It is at this stage, i.e. at the stage of contacts (before intervention) that we shall need international support. We shall obtain this support if the amendments proposed by us seem reasonable and justified. Therefore, we have to be extremely careful in selecting the amendments that we shall propose. The first step, therefore, would be to get rid of intervention by proposing amendments in the first stage. Tactic to be followed: (Omitted)

2. It is evident that for intervention to be justified there must be a more serious reason and a more immediate danger than simple Constitutional amendments. Such reasons can be:

(a) The declaration of ENOSIS before actions (a) to (c)

(b) Serious intercommunal unrest which may be shown as a massacre of Turks. The first reason is removed as a result of the Plan drawn up for the first stage and consequently what remains, is the danger of intercommunal strife. We do not intend to engage, without provocation, in massacre or attack against the Turks. Therefore, (section omitted) the Turks can react strongly and incite incidents and strife, or falsely stage massacres, clashes or bomb explosions in order to create the impression that the Greeks attacked the Turks and that intervention is imperative for their protection. Tactic to be employed: Our actions for amending the Constitution will not be secret; we would always appear to be ready for peaceful talks and our actions would not take any provocative and violent form. Any incidents that may take place will be met, at the beginning, in a legal fashion by the legal Security Forces, according to a plan. Our actions will have a legal form.

3. (Omitted)

4. It is, however, naive to believe that it is impossible for us to proceed to substantial actions for amending the Constitution, as a first step towards our more general Plan as described above, without expecting the Turks to create or stage incidents and clashes. For this reason, the existence and the strengthening of our Organization is imperative because:

(a) if, in case of spontaneous resistance by the Turks, our counter attack is not immediate, we run the risk of having a panic created among the Greeks, in towns particular. We will then be in danger of losing vast areas of vital importance to the Turks, while if we show our strength to the Turks immediately and forcefully, then they will probably be brought to their senses and restrict their activities to insignificant, isolated incidents.

(b) In case of a planned or unplanned attack by the Turks, whether this be staged or not it is necessary to suppress this forcefully in the shortest

RESHAPING OF CYPRUS: A TWO-STATE SOLUTION

possible time, since, if we manage to become masters of the situation within a day or two, outside intervention would not be possible, probable or justifiable.

(c) The forceful and decisive suppressing of any Turkish effort will greatly facilitate our subsequent actions for further Constitutional amendments, and it should then be possible to apply these without the Turks being able to show any reaction. Because they will learn that it is impossible for them to show any reaction without serious consequences for their Community.

(d) In case of the clashes becoming widespread, we must be ready to proceed immediately through actions (a) to (d), including the immediate declaration of ENOSIS, because, then, there will be no need to wait or to engage in diplomatic activity.

5. In all these stages we must not overlook the factor of enlightening, and of facing the propaganda of those who do not know or cannot be expected to know our plans, as well as of the reactionary elements. It has been shown that our struggle must go through at least four stages and that we are obliged not to reveal our plans and intentions prematurely. It is therefore more than a national duty for everyone to observe full secrecy in the matter. Secrecy is vitally essential for our success and survival. This, however, does not prevent the reactionaries and irresponsible demagogues from indulging in false patriotic manifestations and provocations. Our Plan would provide them with the possibility of putting forward accusations to the effect that the aims of our leadership are not national and that only the amendment of the Constitution is envisaged. The need for carrying out Constitutional amendments in stages and in accordance with the prevailing conditions, makes our job even more difficult. All this must no however, be allowed to drag us to irresponsible demagogy, street politics and a race of nationalism. Our deeds will be our undeniable justification. In any case owing to the fact that, for well-known reasons, the above Plan must have been carried out and borne fruit long before the next elections, we must distinguish ourselves with self-restraint and moderation in the short time that we have. Parallel with this, we should not only maintain but reinforce the present unity and discipline of our patriotic forces. We can succeed in this only by properly enlightening our members so that they in turn enlighten the public. Before anything else we must expose the true identity of the reactionaries. These are petty and

irresponsible demagogues and opportunists. Their recent history shows this. They are unsuccessful, negative and antiprogressive elements who attack our leadership like mad dogs but who are unable to put forward any substantive and practical solution of their own. In order to succeed in all our activities we need a strong and stable government, up to the last minute. They are known as clamorous slogan-creators who are good for nothing but speech-making. When it comes to taking definite actions or making sacrifices they are soon shown to be unwilling weaklings. A typical example of this is that even at the present stage they have no better proposal to make than to suggest that we should have recourse to the United Nations. It is therefore necessary that they should be isolated and kept at a distance. We must enlighten our members about our plans and objectives ONLY VERBALLY. Meetings must be held at the sub-headquarters of the Organization to enlighten leaders and members so that they are properly equipped to enlighten others. NO WRITTEN EXPLANATION OF ANY SORT IS ALLOWED. LOSS OR LEAKAGE OF ANY DOCUMENT PERTAINING TO THE ABOVE IS EQUIVALENT TO HIGH TREASON. There can be no action that would inflict a heavier blow to our struggle than any revealing of the contents of the present document or the publication of this by the opposition. Outside the verbal enlightenment of our members, all our activities, and our publications in the press in particular, must be most restrained and must not divulge any of the above. Only responsible persons will be allowed to make public speeches and statements and will refer to this Plan only generally under their personal responsibility and under the personal responsibility of the Chief of sub-headquarters concerned. Also, any reference to the written Plan should be done only after the formal approval of the Chief of the sub-headquarters who will control the speech or statement. But in any case such speech or statement MUST NEVER BE ALLOWED TO APPEAR IN THE PRESS OR ANY OTHER PUBLICATION. The tactic to be followed: Great effort must be made to enlighten our members and the public VERBALLY. Every effort must be made to show ourselves as moderates. Any reference to our plans in writing, or any reference in the press or in any document is strictly prohibited. Responsible officials and other responsible persons will continue to enlighten the public and to increase its morale and fighting spirit without ever divulging any of our plans through the press or otherwise.

NOTE: The present document should be destroyed by burning under the personal responsibilities of the Chief of the sub-headquarters and in the presence of all members of the staff within 10 days of its being received. It is strictly prohibited to make copies of the whole or any part of this document. Staff members of sub-headquarters may have it in their possession only under the personal responsibility of the Chief of sub-headquarters, but in no case is anyone allowed to take it out of the office of sub-headquarters.

The Chief
AKRITAS

APPENDIX C

THE CONSTITUTION OF THE TURKISH REPUBLIC OF NORTHERN CYPRUS

PREAMBLE

Whereas the Turkish Cypriot People is an inseparable part of the great Turkish Nation which lived independent and fought for its rights and liberties all along its history; and

Whereas the Turkish Cypriot People, in the face of events directed against its national existence and right to life, since 1878 when it was broken away from its motherland, which were intensified especially after 1955 and took the form of armed terrorism, aggression and suppression, has organised its resistance as a mature community in unity and integrity; and

Whereas the Turkish Cypriot People has established that there cannot be individual rights and liberties without the acquisition of communal rights and Liberties, through the bitter experiences it had undergone until the year 1974 when the Peace Operation, which was carried out by the Heroic Turkish Armed Forces by virtue of the Motherland's natural, historical and legal right of guarantorship emanating from Agreements, provided to the Turkish Cypriots the means of living in peace, security and liberty; and

Whereas, in the face of attempts made to deprive it of all its rights emanating from history, international agreements and from human rights declarations and covenants and to destroy completely its existence in Cyprus; and in the face of a Republic of Cyprus which has, since 21 December 1963. Come under the monopoly of the Greek Cypriots through unlawful means, which has been transformed into a Greek Cypriot State not only from the point of view of its composition but also from the point of view of the policy it followed, and Which has, as a result of its racist and discriminatory policy and actions serving Pan-Hellenist expansionism, departed from the Agreements and the principles embodied in the Constitution and thus lost its legitimacy, the Turkish Cypriot People has, in exercise of its right of self-determination, proclaimed before the world and history the establishment of the Turkish Republic of Northern Cyprus; Now, therefore,

For the purposes of:

Giving life to the Proclamation of Independence which was accepted unanimously and with great enthusiasm on 15th November 1983

Continuing its existence in its own homeland in full security and humane order;

Establishing a democratic and secular State with a plural party system based on social justice aiming to protect human rights and liberties, the rule of law and the peace and welfare of the individual and Community; and

Being faithful to the Principles of Atatürk and in particular for spreading His-principle of " Peace in the Homeland, Peace in the World ";

THE TURKISH CYPRIOT PEOPLE with whom the absolute right to sovereignty rests;

Approves and proclaims this Constitution passed by the Constituent Assembly of the Turkish Republic of Northern Cyprus as the Constitution of the Turkish Republic of Northern Cyprus established on 15th November 1983;

Entrusts it to the vigilant guarding of its children who are devoted to freedom, justice and virtue, with the belief that the real guarantee lies in the hearts and the will of the citizens.

PART I. - GENERAL PROVISIONS

The Form and Characteristics of the State:
Article 1

The Turkish Republic of Northern Cyprus is a secular republic based on the principles of supremacy of democracy, social justice and law.

The Integrity, Official Language, Flag, National Anthem and Capital of the State:
Article 2

1. The State of the Turkish Republic of Northern Cyprus is an indivisible whole with its territory and people.
2. The official language is Turkish.
3. The Flag and the National Anthem of the Turkish Republic of Northern Cyprus are prescribed by law.
4. The capital of the Republic is Nicosia (Lefkosha).

Sovereignty:
Article 3

1. Sovereignty shall vest in the people comprising the citizens of the Turkish Republic of Northern Cyprus, without condition or reservation.
2. The people shall exercise its sovereignty, within the framework of the principles laid down by the Constitution, through its competent organs.
3. No group, class or person can claim sovereignty to itself.
4. No organ office or authority can exercise any power which does not emanate from this Constitution.

The Legislative Power:
Article 4

Legislative power shall vest in the Assembly of the Republic on behalf of the people of the Turkish Republic of Northern Cyprus.

The Duties and Powers of the Executive:
Article 5

The executive duties and powers shall be carried out and exercised by the President of the Republic and the Council of Ministers in accordance with the Constitution and laws.

Judicial Powers:
Article 6

The judicial powers shall be exercised on behalf of the people of the Turkish Republic of Northern Cyprus by independent courts.

Supremacy and Binding Force of the Constitution:
Article 7

1. Laws shall not be contrary to or inconsistent with the Constitution.
2. The provisions of the Constitution shall be the fundamental legal principles binding the legislative, executive and judicial organs, the administrative authorities of the State and individuals.

Equality:
Article 8

1. Every person shall be equal before the Constitution and the law without any discrimination. No privileges shall be granted to any individual, family, group or class.
2. The organs and the administrative authorities of the State are under an obligation to act in conformity with the principle of equality before the law and not to make any discrimination in their actions.
3. The benefits acquired or to be acquired by persons, who are economically weak, by virtue of the Constitution and the laws, cannot be eliminated by putting forward this Article.

Provisions that cannot be changed:
Article 9

The provisions embodied in Article I, in paragraphs (I) and (2) of Article 2 and

In Article 3 of this Constitution cannot be changed; nor can any proposal be made for changing them.

PART II. - FUNDAMENTAL RIGHTS, LIBERTIES AND DUTIES
Chapter I
GENERAL PROVISIONS

The Nature of Fundamental Rights and their Protection:
Article 10

1. Every person has, by virtue of his existence as an individual, personal fundamental rights and liberties which cannot be usurped, transferred or renounced.
2. The state shall remove all political, economic and social obstacles which restrict t u fundamental rights and liberties of the individual in a manner incompatible with the individual's well-being; social justice and the principles of a state under the rule of law; it shall prepare the necessary conditions for the development of the individual's material and moral existence.
3. The legislative, executive and judicial organs of the State, within the spheres of their authority, shall be responsible for ensuring that the provisions of this Part are wholly implemented.

The Essence and Restriction of Fundamental Rights and Liberties:
Article 11

Fundamental rights and liberties can only be restricted by law, without affecting their essence, for reasons such as public Interest, public order, public morals, social justice, national security, public health and for ensuring the security of life and property of persons.

Fundamental Rights and Liberties and Powers not to be Misused:
Article 12

No provision of this Constitution shall be construed or interpreted as to give any real or legal person, group or class of persons the right and authority to commit acts or to engage in activities aimed at changing the rights and status of the Turkish Republic of Northern Cyprus and of the Turkish Cypriot people guaranteed by this Constitution or at destroying the order established by this

---

Constitution or at removing the fundamental rights and liberties recognised by this Constitution.

The Status of Aliens:
Article 13

The rights and liberties referred to in this Constitution may be restricted by law in respect of aliens, in accordance with international law.

BIBLIOGRAPHY

ADAMS, T. W. *Cyprus: A Possible Prototype for Terminating the Colonial Status of a Strategically Located Territory.* Unpublished Ph.D. dissertation, University of Oklahoma, 1962.

———. *US Army Area Handbook for Cyprus.* Washington, D.C.: Government Printing Office, 1964.

———. *AKEL: The Communist Party of Cyprus.* Stanford: Hoover Institution Press, 1971.

ADAMS, T. W. and A. J. COTTRELL. *Cyprus between East and West.* Baltimore: John Hopkins University Press, 1968.

AIMILIANIDES, A. K. *Hellenic Cyprus.* Nicosia: Ethnarchic Council of Cyprus, 1946.

ALASTOS, D. *Cyprus Guerrilla: Grivas, Makarios and the British.* London: Heinemann, 1960.

———. *Cyprus in History: A Survey of Five Thousand Years.* 2nd ed. London: Zeno Publishers, 1976.

———. *Cyprus: Past and Future.* London: Committee for Cyprus Affairs, 1943.

ALASYA, H. F. *History of Cyprus and the Island's Principle Antiquities.* Nicosia: M. Fikri Printing Office, 1939.

ANASTASIOU, HARRY. *The Broken Olive Branch: Nationalism Ethnic Conflict, and the Quest for Peace in Cyprus.* Vol. I and Vol. II. New York: Syracuse University Press, 2008.

ANDRIOPOULOS, A. "The United Nations Peacekeeping Force in Cyprus and the Changing Greek Regimes." Ph.D. dissertation, Fordham University, 1970. (Microfilm).

ANTHEM, T. *The Greeks Have a Word for It: Enosis.* London: St. Clemens Press, [n.d.].

ARMAOGLU, F.H. *Kibris Meselesi, 1954–1959: Turk Hukumeti ve Kamu Oyunun Davranislari.* Ankara: Sevin Matbassi, 1963.

ARNOLD, P. *Cyprus Challenge.* London: Hogarth Press, 1956.

ASMUSSEN, JAN. *Cyprus at War: Diplomacy and Conflict During the 1974 Crisis.* New York: I. B. Tauris and Co. Ltd., 2008.

ATTALIDES, Michael. *Cyprus: Nationalism and International Politics.* New York: St. Martin's Press, 1979.

AVEROFF-TOSSIZZA, E. *Lost Opportunities: The Cyprus Question, 1950–1963.* New York: New Rochelle, 1986.

BAHCHELI, T. *Greek-Turkish Relations Since 1955.* Boulder, CO: Westview Press, 1989.

BALL, G. W. *The Past Has Another Pattern.* New York: W. W. Norton and Col, 1982.

BARKER, D. *Grivas: Portrait of a Terrorist.* London: Camelot Press, 1959.

BARTH, F. (ed.) *Ethnic Groups and Boundaries: The Social Organization of Cultural Difference.* Boston: Little, Brown 1969.

BARTLETT, C and E. WEINTAL. *Facing the Brink.* New York: Scribners, 1967.

BEDEVI, V. H. *Cyprus Has Never Been a Greek Island.* 3rd ed. Nicosia: Halkin Sesi Press, 1964.

BEER, F. A. *Integration and Disintegration in NATO.* Columbus: Ohio State University Press, 1969.

BELL, W. and W. FREEMAN. (eds.) *Ethnicity and Nation Building.* Beverly Hills: Sage, 1974.

BILGI, A. S. *Le conflict De Chypre et Les Cypriotes Turcs.* Ankara: Ajans-Turk Matbaasi, 1961.

BILGI, A. S., et al. *Cyprus: Past/Present/Future.* Ankara: Ajans-Turk Matbaasi, [n.d.].

BOLUKBASI, S. *The Superpowers and the Third World: Turkish American Relations and Cyprus.* Lanham, MD: University Press of America, 1988.

BOROWIEC, A. *The Mediterranean Feud.* New York: Praeger, 1983.

————. *Cyprus: A Troubled Island.* Westport, CT: Praeger, 2000.

BOYD, J. M. *United Nations Peace-Keeping Operations: A Military and Political Appraisal.* New York: Praeger, 1971.

BRASS, P. R. (ed.) *Ethnic Groups and the State.* Totowa, NJ: Barnes and Noble, 1985.

BRIERLY, J. L. *The Law of Nations.* New York: Oxford University Press, 1963.

BROWN, N. *Strategic Mobility.* New York: Praeger, 1964.

BROWN, L. R. *World Without Borders: The Interdependence of Nations.* New York: Foreign Policy Association, 1972.

BRYANT, R. *Imagining the Modern: The Cultures of Nationalism in Cyprus.* London: I. B. Tauris, 2004.

————. *The Past in Pieces Belonging in the New Cyprus*. Philadelphia: University of Pennsylvania Press, 2010.

BUNGE, F. M. *Cyprus: A Country Study*. Washington, D.C.: The American University, 1980.

BYFORD, J. W. *Grivas and the Story of EOKA*. London: Hale, 1959.

CALOTYCHOS, V. (ed.) *Cyprus and Its People: Nation, Identity, and Experience in an Unimaginable Community, 1955–1997*. Boulder, Colorado: Westview Press, 1998.

CHACALLI, G. *Cyprus Under British Rule*. Nicosia: Phoni Tis Kyprou, 1902.

CHRISTODOULOU, D. *Cyprus Certificate Geographies*. London: Longmans, Green 1954.

CHRYSOSTOMIDES, K. *The Republic of Cyprus: A Study in International Law*. The Hague, Netherlands: Martinus Nijhoff Publishers, 2000.

CLERIDES, G. *Cyprus: My Deposition*. 4 vols. Nicosia: Alithia Publishing, 1989–92.

CLOGG, R. A. *A Short History of Modern Greece*. Cambridge: Cambridge University Press, 1979.

CLOGG, R. A. and G. YANNOPOULOS. (eds.) *Greece under Military Rule*. New York: Basic Books, 1972.

Communism in Cyprus. Nicosia: Government Printing Office, [n.d.].

CONSTAS, D. (ed.) *The Greek-Turkish Conflict in the 1990s: Domestic and External Influences*. London: Macmillan Press, 1991.

CONSTAS, D. and T. STAVROU. (eds.) *Greece Prepares for the Twenty-First Century*. Washington, D.C: Woodrow Wilson Center Press, 1995.

COTTRELL, A. J. and J. E. Dougherty. *The Politics of the Atlantic Alliance*. New York: Praeger, 1964.

COUFOUDAKIS, V. (ed.) *Essays on the Cyprus Conflict*. New York: Pella, 1976.

———. *Cyprus: A Contemporary Problem in Historical* Perspective. Minneapolis, MN: University of Minnesota, 2006.

COULOUMBIS, T. A. *Greek Political Reaction to American and NATO Influences*. New Haven: Yale University Press, 1966.

———. *The United States, Greece, and Turkey: The Troubled Triangle*. New York: Praeger, 1983.

COYLE, D. J. *Minorities in Revolt: Political Violence in Ireland, Italy, and Cyprus*. New Jersey: Fairleigh Dickinson University Press, 1983.

CRASHAW, N. *The Cyprus Revolt: An Account of the Struggle for Union with Greece*. London: Allen and Unwin, 1978.

CRAWFORD, J. *The Creation of States in International Law*. Oxford: Clarendon Press, 1979.

Crisis on Cyprus. Washington: United States Government Printing Office, 1974.

Cyprus Demands Self-Determination. Washington, D.C.: Royal Greek Embassy Information Service, 1954.

Cyprus Treaty Guarantee. London: H. M. Stationery Office, 1959.

Cyprus: The Background. London: Royal Institute of International Affairs, 1959. (Chatham House Memoranda.)

Cyprus: The Dispute and the Settlement. London: Oxford University Press, 1969. (Chatham House Memoranda.)

Cyprus Problem Before the United Nations, The. Nicosia: Public Information Office, 1965.

Cyprus: Touchstone for Democracy. Athens: Constantinidis and Michalas, 1958.

Cyprus: Turkish Reply to Archbishop Makarios' Proposals. [n.p.] Turkish Aid Society of New York, Inc., [n.d.].

DENKTASH, R. *The Cyprus Triangle.* Winchester: Allen and Unwin, 1982.

DEITZ, THOMAS. (ed.) *The European Union and the Cyprus Conflict: Modern Conflict, Postmodern Union.* Manchester: Manchester University Press, 2002.

DIMITRAS, P. E. *The Greek-Turkish Conflict in the 1990s: Domestic and External Influences.* New York: St. Martin's Press, 1991.

DODD, C. H. *The Political Social and Economic Development of Northern Cyprus.* Cambridgeshire, England: Eothan Press, 1993.

DROUSIOTIS, M. *Cyprus 1974: Greek Coup and Turkish Invasion.* Berlin: Mannheim and Monhesee, 2006.

DURRELL, L. *Bitter Lemons.* London: Faber and Faber, 1957.

EDEN, A. *Full Circle.* Boston: Houghton, Mifflin, 1960.

EHRLICH, T. *Cyprus, 1958–1967: International Crises and the Role of Law.* New York: Oxford University Press, 1974.

EVRON, Y. *The Middle East: Nations, Superpowers, and Wars.* New York: Praeger, 1973.

Facts about Cyprus. Nicosia: The Cyprus Chamber of Commerce and Industry, January 10, 1964.

FAUSTMANN, H. and N. PERISTIANIS (ed.), *Britain in Cyprus: Colonialism and Post-Colonialism 1878–2006.* Berlin, Germany: Mannheim und Mohnesee, 2006.

FENWICK, C. G. *International Law.* New York: Appleton-Century-Crofts, 1962.

FLINN, H. W. *Cyprus: A Brief Survey of its History and Development*. Nicosia: W. J. Archer, 1924.

FOLEY, C. *Legacy of Strife: Cyprus from Rebellion to Civil War*. 2nd ed. Baltimore: Penguin Books, 1964.

———. (ed.) *The Memoirs of General Grivas*. London: Longmans, Green, 1964.

FOLEY, C. and W. I. SCOBIE. *The Struggle for Cyprus*. Stanford: Hoover Institution Press, 1975.

FOOT, H. *A Start in Freedom*. New York: Harper and Row, 1964.

FOOT, S. *Emergency Exit*. London: Chatto and Windus, 1960.

FREY, F. *The Turkish Political Elite*. Cambridge: Massachusetts Institute of Technology Press, 1965.

GAZIOGLU, A. *Ingiliz Idaresinde Kibris*. Istanbul: Erkin Basmevi, 1960.

GELLNER, E. *Nations and Nationalism*. Ithaca, NY: Cornell University Press, 1983.

GIBBONS, H. S. *Peace Without Honour*. Ankara: ADA Publishing House, 1969.

GLAHN, G. VON. *Law among Nations*. New York: Macmillan, 1965.

GOBBI, H. J. *Rethinking Cyprus*. Tel Aviv: Aurora, 1993.

GOTTLIEB, G. *Nation against State: A New Approach to Ethnic Conflicts, the Decline of Sovereignty, and the Dilemmas of Collective Security*. New York: Council on Foreign Relations, 1993.

Great Britain. Colonial Office. *Conference on Cyprus: Documents Signed and Initialed at Lancaster House on February 19, 1959*. Cmnd, 679. London: Her Majesty's Stationery Office, 1959.

—————. Constitutional Proposals for Cyprus: Report Submitted to the Secretary of State for the Colonies by the Right Hon. Lord Radcliffe, C.B.E. Cmnd, 42. London: Her Majesty's Stationery Office, 1956.

—————. Cyprus. Cmnd, 1093. London: Her Majesty's Stationery Office, 1960.

—————. Cyprus: Statement of Policy. Cmnd, 455. London: Her Majesty's Stationery Office, 1956.

—————. Terrorism in Cyprus: The Captured Documents. London: Her Majesty's Stationery Office, 1956.

—————. The Tripartite Conference on the Eastern Mediterranean. Cmnd, 9594. London: Her Majesty's Stationery Office, 1955.

GRIVAS, G. The Memoirs of General Grivas, ed. C. Foley. New York: Praeger, 1965.

GUDEK, B., et al. Kibris. Ankara: Ajans-Turk Matbaasi, 1964.

GUNNIS, R. Historic Cyprus: A Guide to its Towns and Villages Monasteries and Castles. 2nd ed. London: Methuen, 1956.

GURR, T. R. and B. HARFF. Ethnic Conflict in World Politics. Boulder, CO: Westview Press, 1994.

GURSOY, C., et al. Kibris ve Turkler. Ankara: Ayyilidiz Matbaasi, 1964.

HANNAY, LORD. Cyprus: The Search for a Solution. London: IB Tauris, 2005.

HARBOTTLE, M. The Impartial Soldier. London: Oxford University Press, 1970.

HARRIS, G. S. Troubled Alliance: Turkish-American Problems in Historical Perspective, 1945–1971. Washington, D.C.: American Enterprise Institute, 1972.

HART, P. T. Two NATO Allies at the Threshold of War, Cyprus: A Firsthand

Account of Crisis Management, 1965–1968. Durham: Duke University Press, 1990.

HERACLIDES, A. *The Self-Determination of Minorities in International Politics.* London: Frank Cass, 1991.

HILL, G. (Sir). *A History of Cyprus.* 4 vols. Cambridge: Cambridge University Press, 1940–52.

History Speaks: A Documentary Survey. Nicosia: Turkish Communal Chamber, 1964.

HITCHENS, C. *Hostage to History: Cyprus from the Ottomans to Kissinger.* New York: Noonday Press, 1989.

HOME, G. C. *Cyprus then and Now.* London: Dent, 1960.

HOROWITZ, D. L. *Ethnic Groups in Conflict.* Berkeley: University of California Press, 1985.

HOWARD, H. N. *Turkey, the Straits, and US Foreign Policy.* Baltimore: Johns Hopkins University Press, 1975.

IATRIDES, J. O. *Balkan Triangle: Birth and Decline of an Alliance across Ideological Boundaries.* The Hague: Mouton, 1978.

IERODIAKONOU, L. *The Cyprus Question.* Stockholm: Almquist and Wiksell, 1971.

ILGAZ, H. *Kibris Notlari.* Istanbul: Dogan Kardes yayinlari, 1949.

Information Services. *Cyprus Today.* London: Her Majesty's Stationery Office, 1955.

IOANNIDES, C. P. *In Turkey's Image: The Transformation of Occupied Cyprus into a Turkish Province.* New York: Caratzas, 1991.

———. (ed.) *Cyprus: Domestic Dynamics, External Constraints.* New Rochelle, NY: Caratzas, 1992.

———. *Realpolitik in the Eastern Mediterranean: From Kissinger and the Cyprus Crisis to Carter and the Lifting of the Turkish Arms Embargo*. New York: Pella Publishing Company, 2001.

ISACHENKO, D. *The Making of Informal States: Statebuilding in Northern Cyprus and Transdniestria*. New York, NY: Palgrave Macmillan, 2012.

JAMES, A. *The Politics of Peace-keeping*. London: Praeger, 1969.

———. *Peacekeeping in International Politics*. New York: St. Martin's Press, 1990.

JEFFERY, G. *A Description of the Historic Monuments of Cyprus*. Nicosia: William James Archer, 1918.

JONES, W. B. *Grivas and the Story of EOKA*. London: Robert Hale, 1959.

JOSEPH, J. S. *Cyprus: Ethnic Conflict and International Politics*. New York: St. Martin's Press, 1997.

KALOUDIS, G. S. *The Role of the UN in Cyprus from 1964 to 1979*. New York: Peter Lang, 1991.

KARAGIL, N., comp. *Kibris Meselesi Uzerinde Son Konusmalar Ve Yazilar*. Istanbul: Anil Matbaasi, 1964.

KARAYIANNIS, G. *The Cyprus Problem, December 1963–August 1964*. Nicosia: Pan Publishing House, 1967.

KARPAT, K. H. (ed.) *Political and Social Thought in the Contemporary Middle East*. New York: Praeger, 1970.

KAYE, M. M. *Death Walked in Cyprus*. London: Staples Press, 1956.

KEEFE, E. K., et al. *Area Handbook for Cyprus*. Washington, D.C.: Government Printing Office, 1971.

KELLING, G. H. *Countdown to Rebellion. British Policy in Cyprus, 1939–1955*. Westport, Connecticut: Greenwood Press, 1990.

KESHISHIAN, K. K. *Romantic Cyprus*. London: Mark and Moody, 1960.

KITROMILIDES, P. M. and T. A. COULOUMBIS. "Ethnic Conflict in a Strategic Area: The Case of Cyprus," in A. Said and L.R. Simmons (eds.) *Ethnicity in an International Context*. New Brunswick: Transaction Books, 1976.

KITROMILIDES, P. M. and M. EVRIVIADES. *Cyprus*, rev. edn. Oxford: Clio Press, 1995.

KIZILYUREK, N. *Milliyetcilik Kiskacinda Kibris* (Cyprus in the Throes of Nationalism). Istanbul: Iletisim, 2002.

KOCAGUNEY, B. *Elli Bin Turk Sehidinin Yatagi Kibris*. Istanbul: Ulku Kitap Yurdu, 1953.

KOKDEMIRE, N. *Kibris: Dunku-Bugunku*. Ankara: Istiklal Matbaasi, 1956.

KOSLIN, A. P. *The Megali Idea: A Study of Greek Nationalism*. Ph.D. Dissertation. Johns Hopkins University, Baltimore, 1958.

KOUCHOUK, M. F. *The Cyprus Question: A Permanent Solution*. Nicosia: Halkin Sesi Press, 1957.

———. *The Voice of Cyprus*. Nicosia: Bozkurt Press, 1956.

KOUMOULIDES, J. T. A. (ed.) *Cyprus in Transition 1960–1985*. London: Tigraph, 1986.

KOUSOULAS, D. G. *Modern Greece: Profile of a Nation*. New York: Scribner's Sons, 1974.

KRAMER, H. *A Changing Turkey: The Challenge to Europe and the United States*. Washington, D.C.: Brookings Institution Press, 2000.

KUNIHOLM, B. R. *The Origins of the Cold War in the Near East: Great Power Conflict and Diplomacy in Iran, Turkey, and Greece*. Princeton: Princeton University Press, 1980.

KYRIAKIDES, S. *Cyprus: Constitutionalism and Crisis Government.* Philadelphia: University of Pennsylvania Press, 1968.

KYROU, A. A. *Elliniki Exteriki Politic.* Athens: Zombola Press, 1955.

LANDAU, J. M. *Radical Politics in Turkey.* Leiden: Brill, 1974.

LEE, D. E. *Great Britain and the Cyprus Convention Policy of 1878.* Cambridge: Harvard University Press, 1934.

LENCZOWSKI, G. (ed.) *United States Interests in the Middle East.* Washington, D.C.: American Enterprise Institute, 1968.

LINDNER, E. *Making Enemies: Humiliation and International Conflict.* Westport, CT: Preager Security International, 2006.

KIJPHART, A. *Democracy in Plural Societies.* New Haven: Yale University Press, 1977.

LOHER, F. V. and A. B. JOYNER. *Cyprus: Historical and Descriptive.* New York: J. J. Little, 1878.

LOIZOS, P. *The Greek Gift: Politics in a Cypriot Village.* New York: St. Martin's Press, 1975 and Oxford: Blackwell, 1975.

LUARD, E. (ed.) *The International Regulation of Civil Wars.* New York: New York University Press, 1972.

LUKE, H. (Sir) *Cyprus Under the Turks, 1571–1878.* London: Oxford University Press, 1921.

———. *Cyprus: A Portrait and an Appreciation.* London: Harrap, 1957.

MAIER, F. *Cyprus: From Earliest Time to Present Day.* London: Eleck Books, 1968.

MAKOVSKY, A. and S. SAYARI (ed.) *Turkey's New World: Changing Dynamics in Turkish Foreign Policy.* Washington, D.C.: The Washington Institute for Near East Policy, 2000.

MARKIDES, K. *The Rise and Fall of the Cyprus Republic*. New Haven: Yale University Press, 1977.

MAYES, S. *Cyprus and Makarios*. London: Putman, 1960.

———. *Makarios: A Biography*. New York: St. Martin's Press, 1981.

MCKINNON, C. *Turkey and Greece: Closer Unity—Now!* New York: Vantage Press, 1968.

MCNAIR, A. D. *The Law of Treaties: British Practice and Opinions*. Oxford: Clarendon Press, 1961.

METIN, H. *Kibris Tarihine Toplu Bir Bakis*. Nicosia. Halkin Sesi Basimevi, 1959.

MEYER, A. J. and S. VASSILIOU. *The Economy of Cyprus*. Cambridge: Harvard University Press, 1962.

MICHALIS, M. S. *Resolving the Cyprus Conflict: Negotiating History*. London: Palgrave. Macmillan, 2009.

MILL, J. S. *Consideration on Representative Government*. New York: Dutton, 1951.

MILLER, L. B. *Cyprus: The Law and Politics of Civil Strife*. Cambridge, Mass.: Harvard University Press, Center for International Affairs, 1968.

MOSKOS, C. C., Jr. *Greek-Americans: Struggle for Success*. Englewood Cliffs: Prentice Hall, 1980.

NEDJATIGIL, Z. M. *The Cyprus Question and the Turkish Position in International Law*. Oxford: Oxford University Press, 1989.

NEWMAN, P. *A Short History of Cyprus*. London: Green, 1953.

NURI, E. *Turkey: A Country Study*. Washington, D.C.: The American University, Foreign Area Studies.

OBERLING, P. *The Road to Bellapais: The Turkish Cypriot Exodus to Northern Cyprus*. New York: Columbia University Press, 1982.

O'MALLEY, B. and I. CRAIG. *The Cyprus Conspiracy*. New York: I. B. Tauris Publishers, 1999.

ORR, C. W. J. *Cyprus Under British Rule*. London: Robert Scott, 1918.

OZKIRIMLI, U. and S. A. SOFOS. *Tormented by History: Nationalism in Greece and Turkey*. New York: Columbia University Press, 2008.

PANTELI, S. *A New History of Cyprus: From the Earliest Times to the Present Day*. London: East-West Publication, 1984.

PAPADKIS, Y. *Echoes from the Dead Zone: Across the Cyprus Divide*. London: IB Tauris, 2005.

PAPADKIS, Y., N. PERISTIANIS, and G. WELZ. *Divided Cyprus: Modernity, History, and an Island in Conflict*. Bloomington, IN: University Press of Indiana, 2006.

PAPANDREOU, A. *Democracy at Gunpoint: The Greek Front*. New York: Doubleday, 1970.

PARIS, P. *The Impartial Knife*. New York: David McKay, 1962.

PATRICK, R. *Political Geography and The Cyprus Conflict, 1963–1971*. Waterloo, Iowa: University of Waterloo Press, 1976.

PERICLEOUS, C. *The Cyprus Referendum: A Divided Island and the Challenge of the Annan Plan*. London: I. B. Tauris, 2009.

Planned Massacre of Turks in Cyprus. Ankara: Turkey at Ajans-Turk Press, [n.d.].

POLYVIOU, P. G. *Cyprus: Conflict and Negotiation, 1960–1980*. London: Holmes and Meier, 1980.

POTIER, T. *Cyprus: Entering Another Stalemate.* London: Chatham House, 2005.

PURCELL, H. D. *Cyprus.* New York: Praeger, 1968.

RICHMOND, O. P. *Mediating in Cyprus: The Cypriot Communities and the United Nations.* Portland, OR: Frank Cass Publishers, 1998.

RIGGS, R. E. *Foreign Policy and US/UN International Organization.* New York: Appleton-Century-Crofts, 1971.

RINGER, B. R. and E. R. LAWLESS. *Race-Ethnicity and Society.* New York: Routledge, 1989.

RIZA, H. A. *The House of Representatives—The Separate Majority Right.* Nicosia: Halkin Sesi Press, 1963.

ROSSIDIS, Z. G. *The Island of Cyprus and Union with Greece.* 3rd ed. Athens: [n.p.], 1954.

ROTHSCHILD, J. *Ethnopolitics: A Conceptual Framework.* New York: Columbia University Press, 1981.

ROUSSEAU, J. J. *The Social Contract.* London: J.M. Dent, 1913.

Royal Institute for International Affairs. *Cyprus: The Dispute and the Settlement.* London: Chatham House Memoranda, 1959.

RUBINSTEIN, A. Z. *Soviet Policy toward Turkey, Iran, and Afghanistan: The Dynamics of Influence.* New York: Praeger, 1982.

SAID, A. (ed.) *Cyprus: A Regional Conflict and Its Resolution.* London: Macmillan, 1992.

SAID, A. and L. R. SIMMONS (eds.) *Ethnicity in an International Context.* New Brunswick, NJ: Transaction Books, 1976.

SALEM, N. (ed.) *Cyprus: A Regional Conflict and Its Resolution.* London: Macmillan, 1992.

SALIH, H. I. *Cyprus: An Analysis of Cypriot Political Discord.* New York: Theo. Gaus, Sons, 1968.

―――. *Impact of Diverse Nationalism on a State.* Alabama: University of Alabama Press, 1978.

―――. *Cyprus: Ethnic Political Counterpoints.* Lonham, MD; University Press of America, 2004.

SCOTT, A. M. *The Dynamics of Interdependence.* Chapel Hill: University of North Carolina Press, 1982.

SELIGMAN, A. *The Turkish People of Cyprus.* London: Press Attache's Office, Turkish Embassy, 1956.

Soviet Union and the Middle East: A Summary Record. The 23rd Annual Conference of the Middle East Institute, Washington, D.C., October 10–11, 1969.

SPEARS, E. (Sir). *The Orthodox Church in Cyprus.* London: Turkish Press Attache's Office, [n.d.].

SPYRIDAKIS, C. A. *A Brief History of Cyprus.* 3rd ed. Nicosia: Zavallis, 1964.

―――. *A Brief History of the Cyprus Question.* Nicosia: Cyprus Ethnarchy Office, 1954.

STAVROU, N. A. *Allied Politics and Military Interventions: The Political Role of the Greek Military.* Athens: Papazeses, 1977.

STEARNS, M. *Entangled Allies: US Policy Toward Greece, Turkey, and Cyprus.* New York: Council of Foreign Relations Press, 1992.

STEFANIDIS, I. D., *Isle of Discord: Nationalism, Imperialism, and the Making of the Cyprus Problem.* New York: New York University Press, 1999.

STEGENGA, J. *The United Nations Force in Cyprus.* Columbus: Ohio State University Press, 1968.

STEPHENS, R. *Cyprus, A Place of Arms: Power Politics and Ethnic Conflict in the Eastern Mediterranean.* London: Pall Mall, 1966.

ST. JOHN-JONES, L. W. *The Population of Cyprus.* London: Maurice Temple Smith, 1983.

STORRS, R. (Sir). *A Chronology of Cyprus.* Nicosia: Government Printing Office, 1930.

———. *The Memoirs of Sir Ronald Storrs.* New York: G. P. Putnam's Sons, 1937.

———. *Orientation.* London: Nicholson and Watson, 1943.

STORRS, R. (Sir) and B. J. O'BRIEN. *The Handbook of Cyprus.* 9th ed. London: Christophers, 1930.

SUHRKE, A. and L. G. NOBLE. (eds.) *Ethnic Conflict in International Relations.* New York: Praeger, 1977.

TEVETOGLU, F. *Kibris ve Kommunism.* Ankara: Ajans-Turk Matbaasi, 1966.

THEOPHANOUS, A. *The Political Economy of a Federal Cyprus.* Nicosia: Intercollege Press, 1996.

THEOPHYLACTOU, D. A. *Security, Identity and Nation Building.* Aldershot: Avebury, 1995.

THORP, W. L. *Cyprus: Suggestions for a Development Programme: Prepared for the Government of the Republic of Cyprus.* New York: United Nations, 1961.

TOCCI, N. *EU Accession Dynamics and Conflict Resolution: Catalyzing Peace or Consolidating Partition in Cyprus.* Aldershot: Ashgate Publishing, 2004.

TORNARITIS, C. G. *The Treaty of Alliance.* Nicosia: Printing Office of the Republic of Cyprus [n.d.].

TORUN, S. *Tukiye, Ingiltere ve Yunanistan Arasinda Kibrisin Politik Durumu.* Istanbul: Gazateciler Matbaasi, 1956.

TREMAYNE, P. *Below the Tide*. London: Hutchinson of London, 1958.

Turkey and Cyprus: A Survey of the Cyprus Question with Official Statements of the Turkish Viewpoint. London: Press Attache's Office, Turkish Embassy, 1956.

Turkiye Milli Genclik Teskilati. *Kibris Meselesi ve Turkiye*. Istanbul: Anil Matbaasi, 1954.

VALI, F. *Bridge across the Bosporus: The Foreign Policy of Turkey*. Baltimore: Johns Hopkins University Press, 1971.

———. *The Turkish Straits and NATO*. Stanford: Hoover Institution Press, 1972.

VANEZIS, P. N. *Makarios: Faith and Power*. London: Abelard-Schuman, 1971.

———. *Makarios: Pragmatism and Idealism*. London: Abelard-Schuman, 1974.

———. *Cyprus: The Unfinished Agony*. London: Abelard-Schuman, 1977.

VOLKAN, V. D. *Cyprus, War and Adaptation: A Psychoanalytic History of the Two Ethnic Groups in Conflict*. Charlottesville: University Press of Virginia, 1979.

———. *Blind Trust: Large Groups and Their Leaders in Times of Crisis and Terror*. Charlottesville, VA: Pitchston Publishing, 2004.

VOLKAN, V. D. and N. ITSKOWITZ. *Turks and Greeks: Neighbors in Conflict*. Huntington Combs: Eothen Press, 1994.

WAINHOUSE, D. W. *International Peacekeeping at the Crossroads: National Support, Experience and Prospects*. Baltimore: Johns Hopkins University Press, 1973.

WALLERSTEIN, I. *The Modern World System*. New York: Academic Press, 1974.

WEINTEL, E. and C. BARTLETT. *Facing the Brink: An Intimate Study of Crisis Diplomacy.* New York: Scribner's Sons, 1967.

WEIR, W. W. *Education in Cyprus.* Larnaca: American Academy, 1952.

WINDSOR, P. "NATO and the Cyprus Crisis." Adelphi Paper no. 14. London: Institute for Strategic Studies, 1964.

WOODHOUSE, C. M. *Apple of Discord: A Survey of Recent Greek Politics in their International Setting.* London: Hutchison, 1948.

———. *The Struggle for Greece, 1941–49.* London: Hart-Davis, MacGibbon, 1976.

———. *Karamanlis: The Restorer of Greek Democracy.* Oxford: Clarendon, 1982.

XYDIS, S. G. *Greece and the Great Powers, 1944–47: prelude to the Truman Doctrine.* Thessaloniki: Institute for Balkan Studies, 1963.

———. *Cyprus: Conflict and Conciliation, 1954–58.* Columbus: Ohio State University Press, 1967.

———. *Cyprus: Reluctant Republic.* The Hague: Mouton, 1973.

YANACOPOULOU, E. A. *The Cypriot Nationalist Movement.* MA Thesis, Georgetown University, 1958.

YASIN, O. *Kanli Kibris; Bir Sahlanisin Destani.* Istanbul: Barlik Yayinevi, 1954.

YENNARIS, C. *From the East: Conflict and Partition in Cyprus.* London: Elliot and Thompson, 2003.

CONCLUSION

All nationalists have the power of not seeing
resemblances between similar sets of facts. . . .
The nationalists not only does not disapprove of
atrocities committed by his own side, but he has
a remarkable capacity of not even hearing about
them. . . . In nationalist thought there are facts
which are both true and untrue, known.

—Orwell (2000, 307–308)

The two Cypriot community's primary allegiance has not been directed to achieve a common national identity. Affirmations of Greek and Turkish patriotism and pride in the achievements of the motherlands continue to nurture more ambivalent attitudes toward the emergence of a Cypriot society. The inability of the two ethnic communities to transcend the entrenched nationalistic sentiments eroded the desired common attitudes on the island. The promotion of Hellenism and Kemalism pose a challenge to Cypriots to define as to their own identity and allegiance. Ethnic, cultural, and religious differentiation emerges as a central fault line; natural consequences would be a decline in Cypriot identity. The source of group identity is the nation-state, but the trend toward globalization is changing this focus based primarily on ethnicity and religion. The search for group identity reinforces an us-versus-them response to perceiving a common enemy.

The Zurich-London Agreements of 1959 were a compromise between Great Britain, Greece, Turkey, and the two Cypriot community leaders that satisfied the signatories' national and strategic interests. The Greek Cypriots attempt to modify the 1960 constitution by armed coercion would have eroded the Turkish constitutional rights, but it was a premeditated strategic step to *enosis*.

After the communal crisis of 1963 to 64, the Greek Cypriots clung to all the political, economic, and financial advantages over the Turkish Cypriots, and the successive presidents, during their tenure, tightened the grip to promote and harness the growing disparity. The political repression and destruction of the constitution contributed to the loss of faith in a future peace and reconciliation. From 1964 to 1974, ethnic friction was intensified by the restrictive aggressive economic blockade. The Greeks regarded the Turkish Cypriot state as illegitimate and isolated it internationally hoping for its demise. Ankara's immediate task was to stop the Greek bid to dominate Cyprus, so Turkey responded with financial assistance and the Turkish military made Northern Cyprus a safe haven for the Turkish Cypriots. The growing dominance and influence of Turkey in Northern Cyprus after the invasion in 1974 accentuated the Greco-Turkish rivalry, causing resentment and a suspicion of territorial expansion. It was the Greek's aggressive assertion of its dominance over the Turks, and incorporation of Cyprus to Greece by force of arms, that were the compelling reasons for the Turkish action in 1974. The geopolitical geostrategic location of Cyprus and its emerging Greek territorial designs near Turkey's soft underbelly in the eastern Mediterranean were also factors that gripped the Turks with a sense of insecurity and vulnerability. The Greeks reluctantly bowed to a *fait accompli* following their humiliating defeat in 1974, but the prospects for accommodation with the Turks for a unified Cyprus look steadily dimmer; *de facto* partition seems ever more permanent.

A common syndrome of "us-and-them" ethnic consciousness is denial of recognition of equality in order to keep the Turkish Cypriots at bay and sustain the Greek Cypriots' sense of superiority and tight control of the state bureaucracy. The orientation that made the Cypriot Greeks feel powerful is their total grip on control of the state system since 1964. The result has been the manipulation of the state system to maximize Cypriot Greeks' economic and financial control as well as security and political interests. There exists a pull and tug between south and north as rival claimants to political legitimacy struggle at the price of disunity. The UN peacekeeping force on Cyprus (UNFICYP) was dispatched to the island in April 1964, but in addition to maintaining some stability along the "Green Line" (the Turks call it the Attila line) buffer zone, it has diminished the ethnic urgency for a comprehensive settlement. UNFICYP's mandate has preserved the relative stability and the status quo, but without the presence of thirty thousand Turkish troops on the island, the Greeks would not have been deterred in their war campaign to neutralize the Turks. UN attempts to broker a settlement or narrow the Greek-Turkish differences on the Cyprus issue have been unsuccessful. The two ethnic groups have been unable to reconcile their constitutional, security, and territorial issues. The Greeks are receptive to a settlement to reduce the Turkish territorial expansion or military presence on the island, but to Ankara, the Cyprus issue is not a high priority nor will it be receptive to any new initiative based on territorial concessions to achieve a Cyprus settlement. The Turkish military and the public are very skeptical of the Greek political designs and the government in Ankara is responsive to their opinion. Both dislike the status quo but with great passion would stir ethnic nationalism to tear down the state system built in 1960 and replaced it with a new one compatible with their interests. The result has been the aspiration to pursue a different vision of Cyprus's future. Makarios Drousiotis, in an editorial in *Cyprus Mail* on May 11, 2008, charged that the Greek Cypriot mass media continues to refuse to accept the realities in Cyprus.

> At least until the year 2000, I have never located a single article in any [Greek] Cypriot newspaper, dealing with any minor issue, in which the other side was acknowledged to be in the right even in the slightest way. This phenomenon is not confined to the past-1974 era, when grief over the disaster did not leave any margin for self-criticism, but it also extends back to the first years of the Republic, when we Greek Cypriots had the upper hand.[554]

The basis of a settlement must have as its principle the recognition that it must transcend ethnocentric interests in order to achieve an equitable settlement.

The Cypriot political system is plagued by a continued response to competitive ethnocentric nationalistic agenda instead of championing for the common benefits of all the citizens. The contending camps have proved unwilling or unable to prod one another to play their respective roles to do something constructive with plentiful meaningful opportunities to act in the public interest. The prospect for a Cyprus settlement diminishes with reluctance to accept broader ideas for collective interest or seek agreements acceptable by both communities. The Greco-Turkish relations are also plagued by the demarcation of the Aegean Sea involving the continental shelf, the territorial sea, and the sovereign airspace. Their differences on theses issues in 1976, 1987, and 1996 brought the two countries to the brink of war.[555] To prevent a military confrontation, Greece and Turkey had summit meetings in 1988 to calm the tensions and resolve the disputes in an atmosphere of mutual trust by a process of conflict resolution. Turkish Prime Minister Turgut Ozal visited Greece, in May 1988, the first Turkish leader in thirty-five years, and in a speech, said the following:

> Both nations have millennium-long common history. We have had good and bad times. Alongside our cultural differences have emerged profound common characteristics rising out of a long interactive process. Our relationship has been passionate and volatile, and this has had as much to do with the founding of lasting friendship on the grounds of common cultural aspects and common memories of peaceful times as with hostile relations based on cultural differences and dark periods. Our disappointments can be as influential as our mutual affection, and can lead our two countries to extreme reactions. The mutual sympathy we feel in times of peace can become enmity because of some insignificant incident. We can fly over the peak of euphoria out of the abyss of struggle. It is not very easy to establish stable relationships on this story of historical past.[556]

The Davos process achieved some success but failed to resolve the major issue. To soothe Greece's humiliation in the 1974 war on the island, significant progress in the Aegean Sea dispute would be relative to the progress on the Cyprus issue. Prime Minister of Greece Constantine Mitsotakis in a speech in 1988 said the following:

> The Turks must be made to understand that it will be impossible to make progress in Greek-Turkish relations, as well as in Turkey's attachment to the European Community if they do not solve the Cyprus issues first, and then address the Greek-Turkish differences.[557]

Despite the sharply contending views, with determination to address the problems in good-faith effort, they will manage to reach a settlement but continue to fall short of an agreement. The challenge is to make all the necessary decisions and painful trade-offs and success in such an endeavor will amply reward both ethnic groups and lead to broader ends. For the emergence of a new political mind-set, both community leaders must stop demonizing the other in order to give rise to reunification. Ethnic nationalism and emotional connections consumed by constituencies shape group behavior. Competing interests instead of addressing Cypriots' collective needs drive these two ethnic groups. Since 1960, the absence of a collective common identity has failed to promote the emotional forces, which are a bonding agent and psychological stimulus for reunification. The fading Cypriot identity will have profound implications for Cyprus' future. A new Cypriot identity needs a sharp break from the past in order to unite the two Cypriot communities. Without abandoning their identity as Greeks and Turks defined by their indigenous culture, ethnicity, language, and religion, the two communities can concentrate on promoting psychological security in order to create a permanent *modus vivendi*, which is necessary for communal harmony.[558]

As we have witnessed, the intense opposition to the Annan Plan saw the emergence of rising expectations by the Greek Cypriots, and the underlying contrast egress as to the political and nationalism agenda of the two communities. A fundamental requirement in diplomacy is that all the parties must compromise to reach the desired outcomes without sacrificing the national interest of the nation. The challenges the Cypriots are confronting must be overcome in a spirit of partnership. A partisan agenda polarizes the Cypriots and erodes the cultivated trust by the international community. In making painful choices, Cypriot leaders must demonstrate judgment and strength, which are vital in the search for an amicable settlement. An envisioned direction with a new agenda can emerge for common values, security, political and social justice to close the deep fissures caused by the ethnic crisis on the island. The political deadlock will have adverse consequences as to the reunification and the *de facto* partition of the island undoubtedly will continue and likely be permanent.

The Greek Cypriots use of armed coercion against the Turkish Cypriots failed to achieve the expected result—*Enosis*. The *enosists* decided to reduce the level of violence against the Turkish Cypriots and placed more emphasis on economic embargo, the backing of the European Union and the international community for the achievement of their goal. The economic sanctions against the Turkish Cypriots failed to sap their will to resist the Greek Cypriot attempt to implement the formulation of *enosis*. The Turkish Cypriots were willing to negotiate an agreement for the formation of a federal constitutional political system for an independent Cyprus, but are gradually opting for a two-state system.

The result of empirical studies support the continuing deadlock in the Cyprus negotiations appears to be likely for the permanent division of the island. A survey by KADEM (Cyprus Social and Economic Research Centre) research group headed by a Turkish Cypriot sociologist Muharrem Feiz was widely publicized by the media on Cyprus on January 29, 2007. The survey revealed that 65 percent of the Turkish Cypriots supported the permanent division of Cyprus into two ethnic separate states. The UN-commissioned survey conducted between January 26 and February 19, 2007, published on April 24 supports these numbers. It found that 57 percent of Greek Cypriots and 70 percent of Turkish Cypriots do not foresee a settlement in the near future. Ninety percent of Turkish Cypriots and 87 percent of Greek Cypriots haven't had any substantial personal or professional contact with each other. The survey found that 39 percent of Greek Cypriots have never crossed to the north since the first crossing point opened in 2003 while 28 percent of Turkish Cypriots haven't visited the south.[559] During an additional study, two polls were carried out by KADEM in July 2008 for the Turkish Cypriot National Unity Party (UBP), and one for the Greek Cypriot newspaper *Simerini* with a sample of 875 Turkish Cypriots, and the results were as follows: 62 percent supported a solution to the Cyprus problem based on two independent equal states; 7 percent supported the continuation of the current situation; 14 percent supported a strong federal state system; 10 percent supported a confederal state based on two independent states system; 71 percent postulate that the new negotiations for a comprehensive settlement as to the Cyprus problem will fail; 67 percent would vote against the 2004 Annan Plan if the referendum was repeated; 80.6 percent had trust in Turkey, but only 6.7 percent in the Republic of Cyprus; 82 percent did not want to live under a Greek Cypriot administration; 46 percent did not want to return any territory to the Republic of Cyprus; 50 percent agreed the return of some territory varying from 5 percent to 15 percent; and 43.5 percent felt favorable toward President Demetris Christofias.[560] According to polls, "65 percent of Greek Cypriots between the ages of 18 and 34 do not want to live together with Turkish Cypriots."[561] KADEM surveyed 1,387 Turkish Cypriots and the results were reported in *Kibris* newspaper on March 4, 2009. The survey results revealed that 53.8 percent would vote "no" to the same Annan Plan submitted to the communities in 2004; 62.6 percent wanted two completely separate independent states; 55.9 percent did not believe that a negotiated solution would be reached between Christofias and Talat; 15.6 percent supported Talat's policy on the Cyprus problem; 38 percent partly supported Talat's policy; 27.6 percent did not support Talat's policy at all; and 15.1 percent did not support Talat.[562]

A true measure of national solidarity is the ability of a society to influence the fate of a state. Cyprus was unable to construct a viably integrated society due in large part to a complex constitutional power structure. Some of the more problematic issues relate to the absence of collective action; solidarity; security; equal economic, educational, and business opportunities; religious tolerance; and a real sense of Cypriot identity. As a result, a consensus for a collective action could never have emerged with such a complicated power structure in place. There is and has always been an inherent bad faith relationship between the two communities. Both sides shared equally strong levels of hostility, and distrust, undeniably solidified a belief that partition is inevitable. Following the events in 1964 to present, the change in the political culture and the absence of common goals has not produced a viable political system. The shift in public loyalties undermined the foundation and acceptance as to the legitimacy of the political system established on August 16, 1960. Turkish public does not identify themselves with the political system in the south, and the public opinion surveys show skepticism and lack of popular support for a federal solution and a preference to a permanent division.

A major shift from a federal solution to a permanent division was the result of the Greek Cypriot rejection of the Annan Plan, the negative portrayal of the Greek Cypriots in the Turkish Cypriots press, the nationalistic rhetoric, and the growing polarization of the two communities on the island. The major argument that led the Greek Cypriot to vote against the Annan Plan by 76 percent on April 24, 2004, was the failure to call for the complete demilitarization of the island and the abolishment of any country's right to unilaterally intervene in Cyprus. Even if the security issue was to be resolved, the prospect for the success of a federal system is in doubt. Ronald L. Watts, relative to federal solution, identifies issues of concern.

> The problem within two-unit federations generally has been that insistence upon parity in all matters between the two units has usually tended to produce impasses and deadlocks. This is because there is no opportunity for shifting alliances and coalitions among the constituent units, which is one of the ways in which multi-unit federations are able to resolve issues. Furthermore, since invariable one of the two units is less populous than the other . . . that unit has usually been particularly conscious of the continuous need to insist upon equality of influence in federal policy making, while the larger unit . . . has developed a sense of grievance over the constraints imposed upon it to accommodate the smaller unit.[563]

The survey clearly identified a trend toward nationalism on both sides and a hardening of the Turkish Cypriots' attitude toward the Greek Cypriots. Politicians and ordinary ethnic citizens have not socialized since 1964 to accept the established institutional arrangements or consociationalism to bring a pragmatic government that works and appeal to voters. The ethnic leader's power struggle created contest to assert unprecedented political power to frustrate their opponent. The ethnic difference between the Greek and Turkish Cypriots about national identity dominates Cypriot politics. Armed violence, discrimination as to a political power-sharing, the lack of economic and business opportunities to the Turkish Cypriots have questioned the Greek Cypriots commitment to the resolution of the Cyprus crisis since 1964.

The ethnic conflict of 1960s and 1970s has intensified the political, cultural, and social tensions, and has shaped the present political attitudes of the two communities. Many Greeks consider Turkey as Greece's most important threat and that Cyprus is Greek and the Turkish Cypriots should acquiesce to Greek Cypriot rule, or leave the island. Looking back, because the numerous opportunities that presented themselves were not exploited; therefore, no breakthrough was achieved. This resulted in hostilities and animosities which have continued to simmer for over forty years. UN capacity to mediate rapidly diminished due to the ongoing bickering over the proposed plans for a settlement; therefore, a genuine partnership was never nurtured. Papadopoulos' shabby treatment of the Turkish leaders was clearly irresponsible and contributed to growing skepticism as to political equality and partnership in a state system. Political integration waned, trust and security were never promoted, growing awareness of separate political identity betrayed compromise, and nationalist conspiracy for *enosis* represented the reaffirmation of the *Megali Idea*. Greece and Turkey were at virtual war over the continental shelf in the Aegean, and continued stalemate has narrowed options causing the promotion of a two-state solution. The political and economic isolation of the Turkish Cypriots set the stage for the *de facto* partition of Cyprus and snuffed out any lingering hope of a settlement. The Greek Cypriot argument that the Cyprus government is the only legitimate authority on the island has been eroding, clearing the way for two self-governance sovereign states. Tim Potier maintains that "Too many Greek Cypriots continue to view Cyprus as a 'Greek state.' . . . Recent events only encourage the view that they never intended to share power with the Turkish Cypriots."[564] Any discussion of Cyprus's future must proceed from the realities that stem from the events of 1964, 1967, and 1974. During this time, the Greek Cypriots forced the Turkish Cypriots to flee their homes. Many were killed, traumatized, humiliated, and deprived of their constitutional rights and economic well-being. They suffered a collective punishment. To avoid a confrontation with the Turks, *enosis* has been abandoned for now, but it continues to have broad appeal to die-hard Greek nationalists. Makarios, as the embodiment of Greek national identity, consistently promoted a vision of Cyprus destined to be part of Greece. With all the passions of his life, Makarios was preoccupied throughout his leadership with a mission to secure *enosis*. In a speech in March 1971, Makarios expressed the Greek Cypriot ethos as to *enosis*.

> Cyprus is a Greek island. It was Greek from the dawn of history and it shall remain Greek forever. We have taken it over as a wholly Greek island and shall preserve it as an undivided Greek island until we hand it over to mother Greece.[565]

The fundamental notions of compromise and good-faith negotiations that should determine the nature of a negotiated settlement ceased to exist. Acquiescence to an eventual two-state solution will eventually be an attractive option dictated by reality and undoubtedly redefine prevailing Greco-Turkish long-term national interests in region.

Since 1974, a distinct administrative institution exists in northern and southern parts of Cyprus, and each entity's political legitimacy is advanced by the popularly elected assemblies. The Turkish Cypriots are unresponsive to Greek Cypriot parliamentary rules and are bound only by TRNC assembly rules whose legitimacy is accorded as a result of popularly elected government, with law enforcement authority in Northern Cyprus. The separateness of the two ethnic communities has pushed the two communities to resist efforts in keeping the process of reconciliation moving. Each developed a separate national, institutional, and political identity. The existence of separate autonomous political entities has been the driving force in shaping the permanency of future Cypriot relationship. A federal solution emerged as a counter-proposal to *Enosis/Taksim*, but the idea was stillborn. The agenda of the radical nationalists divides and blocks reconciliation despite a great deal of public consensus for a negotiated compromise. In addition, the political leaders have not engaged in a sustained negotiation, and consequently, public opinion in recent years has become ambivalent and skeptical of a settlement. The rejection of a federal solution makes the creation of two-state systems a much more viable alternative arrangement.

The shared common sovereignty under the Zurich-London Accords of 1959 failed due to continuous conflict over the "impositions" of constitutional restraints on the Greek Cypriot majority. Refusal to obey limitations bound by the constitution, and without securing the consent of all the signatories to the Zurich-London Accords for change, President Makarios's unilateral reliance on the ultimate right of the majority attempted to alter the constitution under the 13-amendments. Promotion of Greek Cypriot political interests contributed

---

to the chronic communal strife from 1963 to 1974, and put to risk the claim of shared common sovereign-political equality of the two communities.

The administrative authorities in the north and south exercise the sovereign powers to enact and enforce laws, but there are competing laws laid down by two competing authorities. The two states are enforcing their dictates and power in a political environment that has poisoned relationships and the lack of concessions or accommodations do not offer much hope of finding a settlement. In this setting, there are two distinct nation-states with defined boundaries and political-administrative institutions with ultimate authority to assert their sovereignty. David Miller, in his book *On Nationality*, wrote that a nation is a self-conscious social unit characterized as a community with an aspiration to be politically entitled to self-determination with a qualified right to establish an independent state.[566] The Turkish Cypriot state was established as a response to the political crisis, diversity, differences as to national identity, and the will of the people to escape from the Greek Cypriot oppression. In Northern Cyprus, the Turkish Cypriots have succeeded in establishing a common law backed by authority over its territorial claims. Charles McIlwain put it this way: "The chief historical prerequisite to the growth of a conception of sovereignty is the existence of a 'nation,' with a governmental organ competent to make true law."[567] As Andrew Vincent put it, "the concept of sovereignty formally implies a power that is absolute, perpetual, indivisible, imprescriptible and inalienable.... Sovereignty embodies the entire body of authority necessary to bring the state into existence."[568] The impulse to independence by the Turkish Cypriots is the urge to dissociate themselves from the Greek Cypriots so that ultimate authority can be exercised over its sovereign-independent state.

Turkish Cypriots are driven to retain the powers necessary to administer the affairs of their sovereign state to which they feel entitled. According to a poll conducted by TRNC in 2007, 60 percent of the Turkish Cypriots favor two-state solution.[569] KADEM research company survey in TRNC in November 2009 showed that 77.9 percent of the Turkish Cypriots favored two-state solution and 63 percent did not believe that the Christofias-Talat peace talks would be concluded successfully.[570] The Elite Research Agency, located in Turkey, conducted a survey between February 13 and 21, 2010. A face-to-face interview was conducted with 800 people in Northern Cyprus. Thirty-four percent supported the two-state system, 30 percent endorsed the federal system, 21 percent had no opinion, 9 percent wanted a single state, and 6 percent favored the integration of TRNC with Turkey.[571] To sustain the independence, it is essential for the Turkish Cypriots to secure international acceptance to assert their own rightful sovereign powers. Their claim to independence and sovereignty will yield the Turkish Cypriots an equal treatment in relation to other governments, including the Greek Cypriot state. They aspire to have access to other states to foster commercial relations, international institutions, *de jure* recognition of the government, and as *bona fide* democratic government that it hopes of joining the European Union. This outlook is the outcome of pattern of thought that the Cypriot dispute could be settled by embracing the two-state system.

Ethnic nationalism preceded both statehood and independence, and the formation of a state did not create a nation. An independent state formed in 1960 did not forge a new national identity or homogenization of cultures to replace Greekness or Turkishness. Instead, Greekness and Turkishness identity emergence gained ascendance in propagating ethnic national awakening to achieve two separate sovereign independent states. Peoples and nations have the right to exist under international law, and the right of self-determination and equal rights are specifically protected under article 1, 55, chapters 11 and 12, of the United Nations Charter. Finally, states parties of the International Covenant of Civil and Political Rights adopted by the UN General Assembly in 1976 imposes obligations on states to promote the right of self-determination that allows the people to determine their own political, economic, cultural, and social institutions, and enforce the law. Furthermore, a nation must have *de facto* control over its territory in order for the world states to consider it as a state with legal personality before the community of states. *De jure* recognition acknowledges the legal authority of the government to speak and act for the state, meaning full recognition that allows full diplomatic relations with other states. Peoples or nations create their own state that becomes the vehicle to pursue self-determination in order to exercise its own autonomy.[572] The politicalization of ethnicity promoted the recognition that Greek and Turks constituted a separate cultural community and each were entitled to have state of their own. The threat of nonrecognition of TRNC has not reversed *de facto* independence and had little effect on reversing the course in the declaration of statehood in 1983. The international community is withholding diplomatic recognition (expect Turkey) of TRNC until it legitimated its sovereign statehood. The process toward permanent separation of the two states will ultimately be recognized as the best alternative to the ongoing political saga over the allocation of constitutional powers to ethnic representatives.

The buffer zone opening failed to forge a genuine interest for the reunification of the island, nor did it build the expected confidence by engaging in a constructive dialogue, because a deep skepticism remained as to the communal's true intentions. President Christofias's aim has been to find a solution consistent in the commitment assumed by President Makarios and all the presidents of

Cyprus—a bizonal, bicommunal federation with a single sovereignty and nationality and one international personality. This solution will terminate the stationing of Turkish troops and settlements, and the return of the Greek Cypriots to their property in TRNC. The Turks are ideologically committed to a two-state solution within the boundaries of 1974, which provoked serious friction with the Greek Cypriots. An honest attempt and acknowledgement as to existing realities were needed to reach a common ground of true dialogue, to deal with the challenges, and to make the necessary concessions for the Cyprus settlement, but instead, the talks were overshadowed with the ethnocentric national interests.

These agonizing competitive interests have paralyzed the advocates of shared "governance" compromise, and the unresolved conflict has allowed the two ethnic groups in Cyprus to go their separate ways. The security dilemma, the failure in power-sharing arrangements, and a strong resistance by the majority for the minority to pursue its interest made it difficult to bridge the ethnic divide.[573] The Turkish Cypriots are driven by the need for security, trust, and governance that the Greek Cypriots have been incapable of satisfying. The Greek Cypriots' insatiable appetite for power and domineering is the underlying cause of concerns for the Turkish Cypriots. How could the Turkish Cypriots trust in the good intentions of the Greek Cypriots and overcome the security and trust dilemma? Unfortunately, the contesting adversaries' motives and intentions in past and present conflict seems to be interests based upon fear. The power of fear undermines the prospects of trust-building and the two adversaries continue to be haunted by the horrific violence and brutality of the past. The absence of mutual trust-affirming commitments represents a great obstacle in constructing a cooperative effort essential for the realization of common goals. Both sides' inability to moderate their political posture to accommodate the interests of the other masked a sinister intention to achieve certain ends. One's suspicion about the intentions of the other provoked fear and uncertainty rather than trust to peaceful intent for the welfare of both. In the absence of trust, both sides' peaceful intentions evaporated severely limiting the prospects of reconciling the security dilemma. The inability of both sides to signal sufficient reassurances resulted in seeking advantages characterized as security competition and political power. Their inability to signal positive intentions to each other reduced incentives for a negotiated settlement escalating the spiral of mistrust and insecurity. Consequently, each side was on their guard to respond to strategic political gains perceived as a threat to their security or the status quo in the region. Above all, the suspicion and fear has driven the two adversaries so far apart that they prevent the growth of understanding and cooperation, which, in turn, diminished the possibility of reunification. President Christofias at the EU Summit in Brussels on October 29, 2009, expressed his pessimism as to the reunification of the island.[574] The next day, in a crude historical analogy, Christofias compared the EU's concessions to Turkey to the appeasement of Adolf Hitler applied to the foreign policy of British Prime Minister Neville Chamberlain between 1937 and 1939.[575] Not surprisingly, any hope of real cooperation, as opposed to rivalry, has proved to be a vicious circle of power and security competition.

The politicization of ethnic identity, grievances, led to the awakening of national identity paving the way to the conscious creation of nation-state. Both communities are entitled to pursue a diverse range of interests, as transpired in former Yugoslavia, and make separate decisions to their independence. The Serbian province of Kosovo, which is mainly populated by ethnic Albanians, declared its independence on February 17, 2008, despite the fierce opposition from Greece, Cyprus, Romania, Slovakia, and Spain. Russian President Vladimir Putin on February 14, 2008, drew parallels between Kosovo independence and TRNC, and admonished Europe of double standards. Putin said the following:

> I don't want to say anything that would offend you, but for 40 years northern Cyprus has practically had independence. . . . Why aren't you recognizing that? Aren't you ashamed, Europeans, for having double standards?[576]

Russia's first deputy prime minister Sergei Ivanov expressed a similar opinion. "If NATO and the EU countries recognize Kosovo's independence, they will have to recognize north Cyprus."[577]

Cyprus vehemently opposed Kosovo's unilateral declaration of independence, because it would set a precedent for TRNC, which declared it a state in 1983. A different approach to the resolution of conflicts might suppress recurring constitutional crisis. The Greek Cypriots have been emphatic in rejecting and openly rebuking any further prospect of "shared constitutional governance" with the Turkish Cypriots. The Turkish Cypriots take pride in being successful in administering the political, economic, legal, and social affairs of their community in Northern Cyprus since 1974. Neither ethnic community is willing to make great sacrifices or compromises to hold the Republic of Cyprus together. Any formula that will diminish their cause or weight in "share constitutional powers" will continue to drive a wedge that will motivate them to consider the two-state system as the best alternative.

INDEX

leaders, x, 26, 50, 61–62, 64, 78, 81, 84, 99, 101, 106–10, 112–13, 115–16, 118, 127, 132, 135, 137, 139, 143, 150, 159

leadership, xii, 63, 90, 98, 118, 176, 181–82, 219

Lebanon, 4, 93, 95

Ledra Street, 108

legislation, 52, 164–65, 170

Legislative Power, 187

legitimacy, x, 25, 60, 145, 186, 217, 219

liberties, 7, 9, 25, 48, 52, 185–86, 189–90

Limnitis, 115, 129

London, 3, 9, 67, 111, 144, 160

loyalty, 5–7, 15, 29–30

M

majorities, separate, 158, 163–65

Makarios, x–xi, 2–4, 9, 18–21, 140, 144–48, 153, 157–58, 174–75, 218–19, 221

Mediterranean, Eastern, xiii, 94–95, 97, 212

Megali Idea, xii–xiii, 13, 19, 218

members, xii, 8, 12–13, 16, 36, 40, 43, 46, 49, 55–56, 60, 72, 82, 101, 117, 119–20, 123–25, 146, 151–52, 158–59, 162, 164–66, 172–74, 179, 181–82

membership, 53, 56–57, 66, 70–71, 73–75, 83, 88, 91–92

member states, 47, 54, 61, 67–68, 74, 90, 121

memorandum, 111, 157

military, 10, 48, 57, 97–98, 213

Milliyet, 58

Municipalities, 158, 163, 165–67

Muslim nation, 72, 86, 88, 92

Muslims, 22, 56, 73, 86, 88, 91, 98–99

N

national identity, 10, 20, 29, 218, 220

national interest, xi–xiii, 31, 34, 59, 63, 87, 125, 136–37, 143, 145, 215, 222

nationalism, ix–x, 3, 5–7, 10, 14–16, 18–20, 23, 49, 181, 217

nationalist, 10, 60, 62, 69, 86, 97, 120, 128, 211

nationality, 5, 49, 220, 222

national problem, 175

National Unity Party (NUP), 30, 50, 62

nations, xvii, 5–7, 18, 20, 92, 95, 127, 143, 214–15, 220–21

nation-state, xii, 4, 6–7, 10–11, 15, 17, 132, 211, 223

NATO (North Atlantic Treaty Organization), 4, 18, 71–72, 102, 120, 223

negotiated settlement, xiii, 55, 60, 82, 110, 124–25, 143, 219, 222

negotiation process, 37, 67, 108–9

negotiations, x, xii, xiv, 20–21, 24–25, 30–34, 37, 39, 43, 47–48, 51–52, 54–57, 59, 63–68, 74, 78, 81–83, 87, 93–95, 100, 102, 106–11, 113–19, 121, 123, 125–27, 129, 132, 134–39, 143, 145, 147–48, 153, 165, 179

negotiators, 109, 111, 139

Netherlands, 66, 71–72

New York Times, 89

Nicosia, 3, 10, 21, 30, 44, 54, 56, 65–66, 68, 75, 112, 114–16, 121, 144, 148–49, 187

1979 Ten-Point Agreement, 110, 148

1960 Treaty of Guarantee, 3, 144, 153, 177–79

numerical strength, 159, 169–70

NUP (National Unity Party), 30, 50, 62

O

officers, 169, 173

OIC (Organization of the Islamic Conference), 44, 46

oil explorations, 93–94, 149

opposition, 10, 34, 37–38, 66–67, 72–74, 84, 89, 98, 115, 135, 144, 182, 223

Organization for Security and Cooperation in Europe (OSCE), 54

Organization of Greek Cypriot Patriots, 2

P

Papadakis, Yiannis, 13
Papadopoulos, Tassos, 2, 9–10, 23, 30–34,
    37–39, 42–43, 46, 50–51, 55–60,
    62–63, 65–67, 69, 74–75, 77–78,
    82–84, 87, 90, 99–100, 110, 125,
    152–54, 218
parliament, 9, 23, 30, 32, 36, 38, 50, 69–70,
    75, 90, 97, 101, 124, 126, 131,
    151–52
participation, ratio of, 171–72
participation of Greek and Turkish
    Cypriots, 159, 170
parties, x, xiv, 30, 33, 35, 37, 40, 50, 65,
    87–88, 100, 102, 106–7, 109, 111,
    113, 135, 137, 144, 150, 153, 167–
    68, 215
partnership, x, 17–18, 21, 24–25, 59, 87, 94,
    96, 112, 114, 116, 215, 218
patriotism, 5–6, 11, 115, 132, 211
peace, x–xi, 15, 22–23, 33–34, 38, 56, 62,
    65, 69, 94, 96–97, 106, 117, 120,
    123, 125, 128–30, 132–33, 135,
    138, 143–46, 151, 154, 185–86,
    212, 214
peacemaking, 25, 143
personnel, 168
Police, 159, 169
political institutions, 6, 8, 16–17, 100, 113
political leaders, ix, 58, 118, 219
political settlement, 18, 24, 30, 58, 67, 74,
    146
population, 6, 13, 17, 35, 61, 82, 132, 151–
    52, 171–72
power, 3–5, 9, 11, 14, 16, 18, 33, 59, 61, 63–
    64, 83, 88, 98, 117, 123, 128, 131,
    140, 148, 160–61, 173, 179, 187–89,
    211, 218, 220, 222–23
    judicial, 188
presidency, 3, 9, 50, 62–63, 97–98, 101,
    119, 147

president, 4, 36, 38–39, 50, 53, 63, 92, 98,
    100, 118–19, 124, 128, 130–31, 136,
    152, 154, 158–63, 166, 169, 173–74,
    188, 212, 221
presides, 162–63
provisions, 2, 24, 32, 35, 37, 45, 69–70,
    102, 158–66, 168, 170–74, 177–78,
    187–89
public servants, 171–73
Public Service, 159, 170–73
Public Service Commission, 159, 172–73

R

reconsideration, 160–61
referendum, 31–33, 36, 38–41, 44, 56, 58,
    64, 66, 86, 107, 125, 127, 153, 176,
    216
resolution, x, xvii, 8, 22, 24–25, 33, 40–41,
    43–46, 55, 58, 62–63, 69, 74, 84,
    90, 96, 99–101, 109, 112, 117, 125,
    128, 134, 136–37, 139–40, 145,
    154, 218
reunification, ix–x, 10, 25, 29, 33, 42–43,
    62, 89, 94, 101, 113, 125–26, 134,
    138, 153, 214–15, 221, 223
ruling, 121–22
Russia, xiii, 40–41, 76, 96, 120, 179, 223

S

safeguards, 139–40, 165, 167, 174, 177
Sampson, Nikos G., 3, 12, 140, 147
security, xii, 24–25, 33, 36–37, 43, 48,
    50, 62, 65, 87, 100, 107–8, 114–15,
    124–25, 129, 133, 138, 143–44,
    146–47, 150, 160–61, 169, 185, 189,
    212–13, 215–16, 218, 222
self-determination, 6–7, 146, 175–78, 186,
    220–21
senate, 36, 124, 131, 151–52
separation, xi, 6, 29, 84, 105, 128, 160,
    166–68
settlement, x–xi, xiii, xvii, 15, 18, 25–26,
    31–32, 34, 37, 40, 43, 53, 55, 57–59,
    62, 64, 69, 76–77, 82–84, 87, 89, 98,

ENDNOTES

1. I have chosen to use the translation of Greek and Turkish words and names one finds in the leading American and European news media.
2. *Today's Zaman, New York Times*, online, August 6, 7, 2009; "Turkey and Russia: Old rivals, new partners," *The Economist*, vol. 392, no. 8644, August 15, 2009, pp. 47–48.
3. *Hurriyet*, online, August 16, 2009.
4. Polykarpos Yorgadjis was implicated in the assignation plot against President Makarios on March 8, 1970, when his helicopter was shot down. On March 15, 1970, Yorgadjis was killed, and on May 13, six men were charged with attempted murder of Makarios. In November 1970, four were sentenced to fourteen years of imprisonment and two were acquitted.
5. Michael A. Attalides, *Cyprus: Nationalism and international politics* (New York: St. Martin's Press, 1979), p. 56.
6. Ibid., p. 182.
7. From March 1978 to September 1983, Rolandis was the minister of foreign affairs and minister of commerce, industry and tourism from February 28, 1998, until February 28, 2003, of the Republic of Cyprus. From May 1991 until May 1996, he was a member of the House of Representatives. In 1976, he was one of the founding members of the Democratic Movement that later on was renamed as Democratic Party.
8. *Cyprus Mail*, online, June 8, 2008.
9. Richard A. Patrick, edited by James H. Bater and Richard Preston, *Political Geography and the Cyprus Conflict: 1963–1971* (Waterloo, Iowa: University of Waterloo, 1976), p. 21.
10. Van Coufoudakis, *Cyprus: A Contemporary Problem in Historical Perspective* (Minneapolis, MN: University of Minnesota, 2006), p. 83.
11. See Salih, H. I., *Cyprus: The Impact of Diverse Nationalism on a State* (Alabama: The University of Alabama Press, 1978), p. 47–50. The Cyprus issue and the Geneva conference were summarized in a speech, "Cyprus: The Anatomy of the Problem," delivered by Dean Acheson before the Chicago Bar Association, March 24, 1965.
12. Georgios Grivas Digenis was born in Cyprus on June 6, 1897, in Chrysaliniotissa, Nicosia, and grew up at Tricomo, in the District of Famagusta. After his studies at

Pancyprian Gymnasium in Nicosia, he attended the Athens Military Academy in 1916. Grivas served in the Greek army and fought the Turks in Asia Minor until the defeat of the Greek army by the forces of Mustafa Kemal in 1922. In 1946, he retired from the Greek army. He collaborated with Makarios for Enosis from 1954 to 1959. He adopted the name Digenis as the leader of the EOKA guerilla organization in the struggle against the British rule in Cyprus. He returned to Cyprus in 1964 from Greece to take over the Supreme Command of the Greek Cypriot forces against the Turkish Cypriots. After the November 1967 clashes with the Turkish Cypriots and Turkey's intervention in the war, Athens recalled Grivas back to Athens. He secretly returned to Cyprus and formed EOKA B to oust Makarios to change his policy and adopt the line of Enosis. He died on January 27, 1974, in Limassol of heart failure.

13. Makarios Drousiotis, *Cyprus 1974: Greek Coup and Turkish Invasion* (Berlin: Mannheim and Mohnesse, 2006), p. 191.
14. Michael Attalides, *Cyprus: Nationalism and Internation Politics* (New York: St. Martin's Press, 1986), p. 183.
15. Ibid., p. 66.
16. Rothman, Jay, Conflict Research and Resolution. Cyprus, Annals of AAPSS (1991), 518:95–108. See also Bose, Sumantra, *Contested Lands: Israel-Palestine, Kashmir, Bosnia, Cyprus, and Sri Lanka* (Cambridge, Massachusetts: Harvard University Press, 2007).
17. Evelin Lindner, *Making Enemies: Humiliation and International Conflict* (Wesport, CT: Praeger Security International, 2006), p.121.
18. Hans Kohn, *The Idea of Nationalism: A study of Its Origin and Backgrounds*. 2nd ed. (New York: Macmillan, 1961), p.16. Hans Kohn states that Nationalism "is first and foremost a state of mind, an act of consciousness." See also Hans Kohn, *Nationalism: Its Meaning and History* (Princeton, NJ: Van Nostrand, 1955), p. 9, and John Hutchinson and Anthony D. Smith, (eds.) *Nationalism* (New York: Oxford University Press, 1994), pp. 36–46. Ernest Gellner, *Nations and Nationalism* (Ithaca, N.Y.: Cornell University Press, 1983).
19. Hans Kohn, *The Idea of Nationalism.* 2nd ed. (New York: Collier-Macmillan, 1967), ch. 5, and Anthony D. Smith, *The Ethnic Origins of Nations* (Oxford: Blackwell Publishing, 1988), ch. 6.
20. William Bloom, *Personal Identity, National Identity* and *International Relations* (Cambridge University Press, 1990), pp. 52–53.
21. Walker Conner, *A Few Cautionary Notes On the History and Future of Ehnonational Conflicts* in Andreas Wimmer, Richard J. Goldstone, Donald L. Horowitz, Ulrike Joras, and Conrad Schetter (eds.), *Facing Ethnic Conflicts: Toward a New Realism* (Lanham, MD: Rowman and Littlefield Publishers, 2004), p. 23.
22. David Miller, *On Nationality* (Oxford: Clarendon Press, 1995), p. 70, 129, 163–4. See also David Miller, "The Ethical Significance of Nationality." *Ethics*, vol. 98, no. 4 (July 1998), pp. 647–662. See also Anthony D. Smith, *Theories of Nationalism*. 2nd ed. (New York: Harper and Row, 1971).
23. Charles A. Kupchan, *The End of the American Era* (New York: Alfred A. Knopf, 2003), p. 116.
24. Ibid.

25. Maurizio Viroli, *For Love of Country: An Essay on Patriotism* (Oxford: Clarendon Press, 1995), p. 1, 12.

26. Philip G. Roeder, *Where Nation-States Come From: Institutional Change in the Age of Nationalism* (Princeton, NJ: Princeton University Press, 2007), p. 22.

27. See Ernest Gellner, *Nations and Nationalism* (Ithaca, NY: Cornell University Press, 1983).

28. John Locke, *Two Treatises of Government* (London: A&J Churchill, 1960).

29. Roger Scruton, *A Dictionary of Political Thought* (New York: Harper and Row, 1982); See also George DeVos, *Ethnic pluralism: Conflict and Accommodation* in George DeVos and L. Komanucci-Ross (eds.), *Ethnic Identity: Cultural Continuities and Change* (Palo Alto, CA: Mayfield, 1975), pp. 5–41; Vamik Volkan, *Blind Trust: Large Groups and Their Leaders in Times of Crisis and Terror* (Charlottesville, Virginia: Pitchstone Publishing, 2004), pp. 23–55.

30. Ernest Baker, *National Character and the Factors in its Formation* (London, 1927), p. 17. Quoted in Norman D. Palmer and Howard C. Perkins, *International Relations: The World Community in Transition*, 3rd ed. (New Delhi: CBS Publishers, 1985), p. 19.

31. Marc Howard Ross, *Cultural Contestation in Ethnic Conflict* (Cambridge: Cambridge University Press, 2007), p. 22.

32. Samuel P. Huntington, "The Clash of Civilizations?" *Foreign Affairs,* vol. 72, no. 3 (Summer 1973), pp. 22–49, at 27.

33. Joseph Rothschild, *Ethnopolitics: A Conceptual Framework* (New York: Columbia University Press, 1981), p. 96, 99.

34. Anthony D. Smith, *The Ethnic Origins of Nations* (Oxford: Blackwell Publishing, 1988), p. 32.

35. Peter Turchin, *War and Peace and War: The Rise and Fall of Empires* (New York: Penguin, 2006) p. 5.

36. *Cyprus Mail,* July 29, 2007. Tassos Mikolaou Papadopoulos was born on January 7, 1934, in Nicosia. He was educated at the Pancyprian Gymnasium in Nicosia and studied law in London. In the 1950s, he was active in PEKA, the political section of EOKA. He was against the signing of the Zurich-London Agreements. He served as minister of the interior, minister of finance, minister of labor and social insurance, minister of health, and minister of agriculture and natural resources. He served as advisor to Galfkos Clerides in the intercommunal talks until 1976. He was elected to parliament in 1970 until 2000. He assumed the presidency on February 28, 2003, to February 28, 2008, with the support of Diko, Kisos, and AKEL. Papadopoulos died from lung cancer in Nicosia on December 12, 2008. He was seventy-four. Grave robbers stole the corpse of Papadopoulos by digging up his coffin at the Deftera Village cemetery on December 11 or 12, 2009, just before the first anniversary of his death. *New York Daily,* online, December 11, 2009, and *Cyprus Weekly,* online, December 15, 2009. His body was found on March 8, 2010, at Strovolos cemetery in the Nicosia district. Two Greek Cypriots and an Indian were asking for 200,000 euros from Papadopoulos's family to reveal where the corpse was hidden. *Cyprus Mail, New York Times,* online, March 9, 11, 2010. Police spokesman Michalis Katsounotos told the media that Papadopoulos's "body was found inside another grave and covered with a thin layer of soil." BBC News, online, march 10, 2010.

---

37. *Cyprus Mail*, online, February 1, 2009.
38. Humiliation is addressed in Evelin Lindner's book. The psycho-political analysis of intergroup conflict, see Vamik D. Volkan and Joseph Montville, *Blind Trust: Large Groups and Their Leaders in Times of Crisis and Terror* (Charlottesville, VA: Pitchstone Publishing, 2004); V. D. Volkan, D. A. Julius, and J. V. Montville, eds. *The Psychodynamics of International Relationships*, vol. 1: *Concepts and Theories*; vol. 2: *Unofficial Diplomacy at Work* (Lexington, MA: Lexington Books, 1990–1991).
39. Evelin Linder, pp.128–129.
40. *Cyprus Mail*, online, November 11, 2007.
41. *The Cyprus Weekly*, online, December 24, 2009.
42. *Cyprus Mail*, online, November 9, 2007, and *Halkin Sesi*, online, November 13, 2007.
43. Bogdam Denitch, *Ethnic Nationalism: The Tragic Death of Yugoslavia* (Minneapolis: University of Minnesota Press, 1994), p. 143.
44. See J. H. Hertz, "Idealist Internationalism and Secuirty Dilemma," *World Politics II* (1950), pp. 157–180.
45. Vamik D. Volkan, *Cyprus: War and Adaptation, A Psychoanalytic History of Two Ethnic Groups in Conflict* (Charlottesville, Virginia: University Press of Virginia, 1979), p. 118.
46. V. P. Gagnon Jr., "Ethnic Nationalism and International Conflict: The Case of Serbia," *International Security*, vol. 19, no. 3, Winter 1994/95, p. 132.
47. Ibid.
48. For an in-depth study of the Greek independence movement (1821–1829) from the Ottoman rule, and its realization of the Megali Idea to form a Greater Greece in the image of Byzantium, see Douglas Dakin, *The Unification of Greece, 1770–1923* (London: Ernest Benn, 1972), and John Campbell and Philip Sherrard, *Modern Greece* (London: Ernest Benn, 1968), chs. 1, 4–5.
49. Yiannis Papadakis, *Echoes from the Dead Zone: Across the Cyprus Divide* (London: I. B. Tauris and Co., 2005), p. 8.
50. Harry Anastasiou, *The Broken Olive Branch: Nationalism, Ethnic Conflict, and the Quest for Peace in Cyprus*, vol. 1 (Syracuse, New York: Syracuse University Press, 2008), p. 32.
51. Ibid., p. 76.
52. *Cyprus Mail*, online, September 6, 2008.
53. *Cyprus Mail*, online, September 6, 2008.
54. (Ibid.) In an editorial, *Cyprus Mail*, online, on September 6, 2008, writes, "If we think this is the kind of history that we ought to be teaching our children, then we should forget about reunification. If we think that an education that encourages children to drape themselves in the Greek flag and go out on nationalist political demonstrations during school hours is not chauvinist, then what are we doing even talking to the Turkish Cypriots?"
55. *Cyprus Main*, online, September 9, 2008; *Cyprus Weekly*, online, September 12, 2008.
56. *Cyprus Weekly*, online, November 7, 2008.
57. Timothy Garton Ash, *Free World: America, Europe, and the Surprising Future of the West* (New York: Random House, 2004), p. 197.

58. Ted Robert Gurr and Barbara Harff, *Ethnic Conflict in World Politics* (Boulder, CO: Westview Press, 1994), p. 42.
59. Obelisk International, *Yahoo! News*, online, August 9, 2007.
60. Todd Gitlin, *The Twilight of Common Dreams* (New York: Metropolitan Books, 1995), p. 225.
61. Antonia Darder and Rodolfo D. Torres, *After Race: Racism after Multiculturalism* (New York: New York University Press, 2004), p. 5.
62. Edward Azar, *The Management of Protracted Social Conflict: Theory and Cases* (Hampshire, England: Dartmouth Publishing Co., 1990), p. 16.
63. Glen D. Camp, "Greek-Turkish Conflict over Cyprus," *Political Science Quarterly* (1980), 95: 43–60.
64. Nicos Peristianis, "Cypriot Nationalism, Dual Identity, and Politics," p. 103 in *Divided Cyprus: Modernity, History, and An Island In Conflict*, edited by Yiannis Papadakis, Nicos Peristianis, and Gisela Welz (Bloomington, IN: Indiana University Press, 2006).
65. Ibid., p. 102.
66. Kyriacos C. Markides, *The Rise and Fall of the Cyprus Republic* (New Haven: Yale University Press, 1977), p. 11.
67. In the late 1950s, EOKA leaflets for Karavas and Lapithos villages in Kyrenia district, Cyprus, were printed on mimeograph machine by the Greek Cypriot nationalists employed by the Foreign Broadcast Information Service (FBIS). FBIS has been the preeminent collector of open source information by monitoring shortwave radio programs for the Central Intelligence Agency (CIA). Under the National Security Act of 1947, Foreign Broadcast Monitoring Service (FBMS) was created and later it was renamed FBIS as a part of the CIA. Since 1974, FBIS in Karavas remains closed, and it continues to operate in Vienna, Austria, and in London, England.
68. Rebecca Bryant, "An Education in Honor: Patriotism and Rebellion in Greek Cypriot Schools," p. 59 and 65, in *Cyprus and Its People: Nation, Identity, and Experience in an Unimaginable Community, 1955–1997*, edited by Vangelis Calotychos (Boulder, Colorado: Westview Press, 1998).
69. Spyros Spyrou, "Children Constructing Ethnic Identities in Cyprus," in Yiannis Papadakis, Nicos Preistianis, and Gisela Welz, *Divided Cyprus*, op. cit., pp. 127–136.
70. *Cyprus Mail*, ABC News, online, September 26, 2007. See also Umut Ozkirimli and Spyros A. Sofos, *Tormented by History: Nationalism in Greece and Turkey* (New York: Columbia University Press, 2008), pp. 179–180.
71. Attalides, op. cit., p. 35.
72. As quoted by Richard A. Patrick, op. cit., pp. 175–176.
73. Volkan, *Cyprus: War and Adaptation*, op. cit., pp. 33–34.
74. Ibid.
75. For an in-depth analysis of the Cypriot crisis, see H. Ibrahim Salih, *Cyprus: Ethnic Political Counterpoints* (Lanham, MD: University Press of America, 2004).
76. *Cyprus Mail*, online, January 18, 2008.
77. *Cyprus Mail*, *Hurriyet*, online, July 25, 2009.
78. *Cyprus Mail*, online, July 30, 2009.

---

79. *New York Times,* January 23, 1991. About 40,000 Russian settlers are residing in Limassol in the south of the island. *Today's Zaman,* online, June 24, 2012.

80. Vamik D. Volkan, "Turks and Greeks of Cyprus: Psychopolitical Considerations," p. 279, in Ibid. *Cyprus and Its People,* edited by Vangelis Calotychos. See also Vamik D. Volkan and N. Itskowitz, *Turks and Greeks: Neighbours in Conflict* (Huntington, Cambs.: Eothen Press, 1994), Vamik D. Volkan, *Cyprus: Wars and Adaptation* (Charlottesville: University Press of Virginia, 1979).

81. Glen D. Camp, "Greek-Turkish Conflict Over Cyprus," *Political Science Quarterly,* 95:1. Spring, p. 69.

82. *Turkiye,* March 5, 2004.

83. *Cumhuriyet,* March 5, 2004.

84. The Athens News Agency at http://www.ana.gr/, March 5, 2004.

85. Ibid.

86. Costas Karamanlis was born in 1956, studied law at Athens University and economics at Deree College. He completed his postgraduate studies at the Fletcher School of Law and Diplomacy at Tufts University in Boston, with a master's degree in political and financial science, and received his PhD in diplomatic history. He served in the navy from 1977 to 1979. He is a prolific writer and founding member and president of the KIPAEA.

87. President Papadopoulos had a series of meetings with Serdar Denktash in Switzerland prior to April 24 referenda on the Annan Plan. The purpose of the meetings was to come to an amicable Cyprus settlement and make the necessary changes to be incorporated to the UN plan. The Cyprus News Agency at http://www.cyna.org. cy, September 13, 2004. *Kibris,* September 15, 2004. The Athens News Agency at http://www.ana.gr/, September 18, 2004. The Greek government was informed as to the Greek and Turkish Cypriot meetings to discuss the possibility of postponing the referendums on the Annan Plan.

88. *New York Times,* online, March 26, 2004.

89. The Cyprus News Agency at http://www.cyna.org.cy, March 29, 2004.

90. Ibid.

91. Thucydides (translated by Rex Warner) in his *History of the Peloponnesian War* (New York, NY: Penquin Books, 1954), p.242, remarks that patriotic slogans silenced the dissenters in Athens prior to that city's invasion of Sicily in 415 BC "to think of the future and wait was merely another way of saying one was a coward; any idea of moderation was just an attempt to disguise one's unmanly character; ability to understand a question from all sides meant that one was totally unfitted for action. Fanatical enthusiasm was the mark of a real man, and to plot against an enemy behind his back was perfectly legitimate self-defense. Anyone who held violent opinions could always be trusted, and anyone who objected to them became a suspect."

92. Disy MP Kate Clerides, daughter of former president Glafcos Clerides, in an interview with *Kibris,* said that President Papadopolous did not want a Cyprus solution and that's why he sets "unattainable goals," and the Turkish settlers in the north had a right to stay on the island. "Akel acts if it doesn't understand what's going on, as if it can't see that we are heading towards a permanent division with our own stamp and approval," she said. *Cyprus Weekly,* August 31, 2004.

93. The Cyprus News Agency at http:/www.cyna.org.cy April 1, 2004.
94. A proponent point of view of Annan Plan. See *Politis* (Greek Cypriot newspaper), an interview of Nicos Fieros "Diastasis" August 15, 2004.
95. BBC News, online, April 7, 2004.
96. *Sabah*, April 13, 2004.
97. *Turkiye*, April 13, 2004.
98. *Milliyet*, April 16, 2004; *Turkish Daily*, April 19, 2004. Chief of Turkish General Staff of the Turkish Armed Forces, General Yasar Buyukanit, on March 16, 2007, in his address at the War Academy in Istanbul declared his opposition to Annan Plan because the plan included derogations to satisfy both sides. *Milliyet*, March 29, 2007.
99. For the full text of the address of President Papadopoulos, see the Cyprus News Agency at http://www.cyna.org.cy, April 8, 2004; *New York Times*, online, April 8, 2004.
100. The Cyprus News Agency at http://www.cyna.org.cy, April 12, 2004.
101. BBC News, online, April 21 and 22, 2004; The Athens News Agency at http://www.ana.gr, April 22, 2004.
102. Ibid.
103. BBC News, online, April 19, 2004; The Athens News Agency, http://www.ana.gr, April 22, 2004.
104. The Cyprus News Agency, http://www.cyna.org.cy, April 19, 2004. For the full text of Annan's Cyprus report, see Ibid. April 20, 2004.
105. *Cyprus Mail*, January 12, 2005; www.dailypioneer.com, January 12, 2005.
106. The Cyprus News Agency, online, January 12, 2005. The Annan Plan of May 2004 was not endorsed by the UN Security Council. On June 10, Annan asked the UN Security Council to reconsider it. The Cyprus News Agency, online, June 10, 2005; *Cyprus Mail*, online, June 11, 2005.
107. The Athens New Agency, http://www.ana.gr, April 22, 2004.
108. *Aksam*, April 22, 2004.
109. For the full text of the resolution, see the Athens News Agency, http://www.ana.gr, April 22, 2004.
110. *Cyprus Weekly*, online April 21, 2004, pp.1–20.
111. Amnesty International Report 2005, http://web.amnesty.org/report2005/index.eng, May 31, 2005; *Cyprus Mail*, May 28, 2005.
112. The Cyprus News Agency, http://www.cyna.org.cy April 24, 2004. President of the European Parliament Josephy Borrel on September 28 during his visit to Cyprus seemed to declare that he was sympathetic to the Cypriot Greeks rationale for rejecting the UN Plan. The Athens News Agency, http://www.ana.gr, September 29, 2004. On October 15, Papadopoulos claimed that the UN had given money to Greek Cypriots in return for endorsing the Annan Plan. Turkishpress.com, online, October 16, 2004. The U.S. dismissed the press allegations that both Washington or UN were involved in bribing the Greek Cypriots to endorse the Annan Plan. The Cyprus News Agency, the Athens News Agency, online, October 21, 2004; *Cyprus Weekly*, online, October 31, 2004.
113. *Kibris, Hurriyet*, online July 8, 2004. Despite the efforts of EU Enlargement Commissioner Guenter Verheugen and Great Britain, Greece and the Republic of Cyprus objected to the EU plan to lift the trade restrictions and aid to TRNC. The

Greeks base their legal arguments on article 133 of the EU, which governs the EU's relations with other countries. *Kathimerini*, September 3, 2004. On September 17, 2004, EU failed to forge a consensus on direct trade and 259 million euros financial aid package for the Turkish Cypriots due to Greek Cypriot objections. *Cyprus Weekly*, September 20, 2004. On October 18, EU deferred discussion to 2005 for direct trade between member states and TRNC. The Cyprus News Agency, online, October 18, 2004. The European Parliament's plenary session on November 17 voted in favor of providing 259 euros in financial support to Turkish Cypriots over a two-year period, 2004–2006. The purpose of the financial aid was to facilitate the reuniting of Cyprus. The Athens News Agency, online, November 18, 2004. EU Commissioner for Enlargement Olli Rehn and Luxemburg Foreign Minister Nicolas Schmit during their contracts with the two community leaders in Nicosia on May 12 said, "We cannot just leave these commitments which were taken by the Council of the EU to support financially the Turkish Cypriot community in terms of financial aid, and also in terms of breaking the economic isolation of this part of the country." *Cyprus Mail, Cyprus Weekly*, online, May 13, 2005. On September 18, 2007, the European Commission published its annual report for 2006–2007 on the implementation of a 259 euros aid package for the Turkish Cypriot community. United Nation, S/2007/699, December 3, 2007, p. 2. Despite all the EU promises as to 259 million euros as financial aid to northern Cyprus, as of January 4, 2008, only 30 million euros has been delivered. *Turkish Daily News*, online, January 3, 2008. According to a report in *Cyprus Mail* on March 7, 2008, Republic of Cyprus filed six cases with the Court of First Instance at the European Court of Justice to stop the aid package, because TRNC bodies were involved in the EU aid projects and "allowing this constitutes an upgrade of the breakaway Turkish Cypriot state." The paper also reported that "at the end of last month, 83 million euro, or 32% of the money had been allocated to tendered projects and 38 million euro, or 15%, has already been contracted out." The projects in TRNC include a waste management, the rehabilitation of the Lefka copper mine, financial support for the Committee of Missing Persons, traffic safety management, and the deming in the buffer zone. A deadline for using the 259 euros promised to the Turkish Cypriots in 2004 by the EU is drawing near, "yet by March 2008 only 5% of it had been spent." "No Love Lost," *The Economist*, vol. 387, no. 8582, May 31–June 6, 2008, pp. 8–9. On June 3, 2008, Cyprus withdrew eight tenders to the European Court of Justice against the ten-million-euro financial aid package taken from a 259-million-euro package promised to the Turkish Cypriots by the EU. The dispute was settled after the European Commission agreed to revise the wording that the Greek Cypriots feared that it would "constitute recognition of a separate state entity on the island." The financial aid package would have been jeopardized because the tenders would have had to be cancelled. The financial aid projects included a waste management project, the rehabilitation of the Lefka copper mine, financial support for the Committee for Missing Persons, traffic safety management, and demining in the buffer zone. *Cyprus Mail, Kibris*, online, June 4, 2008. "More than 100 million euros [$155 million has already been tendered—without objection from the Greek Cypriot government]." *Today's Zaman*, online, June 4, 2008. The European Commission report says, "In the Second Annual Report 2007 on the implementation of Community assistance under Council Regulation [EC] No. 389/2006 of 27 February 2006 establishing an instrument of financial support for encouraging the economic development of the Turkish Cypriot community, covering the period from 1 March until 31 December 2007, the Commission says that, out of the overall allocation of 259 million euros, 240.15 million euros was allocated to the operational part of the aid programme." The Athens News Agency, http://222.ana.gr/, September 16, 2008. The European Commission on July 8, 2009, approved just under 260 euros to facilitate reunification of Cyprus by encouraging economic development of the Turkish Cypriot community. Funds were to be used for water supply, waste water treatment, solid waste management, energy supply and telecommunications. Students and teachers, NGOs, farmers, small businesses, schools, villages, civic society organizations, and small- and medium-size enterprises were also to be provided financial assistance. By the end of May 2009, 84.5 million euros were contracted and the remaining funds were to be contracted before the end of 2009 *Cyprus Mail*, online, July 9, 2009.

114. The Cyprus News Agency, http://www.cyna.org.cy, July 10, 2004. "The $30.5 million dollars pledged by the US Congress have also been held up with technical difficulties." (Amanda Akcakoca, "Cyprus Looking to a Future Beyond the Pasts," *European Policy Centre*, issue paper no. 32, May 12, 2005. p. 8.)

115. The Cyprus News Agency, http://www.cyna.org.cy, June 2, 2004. In his address to the 59th session of the UN General Assembly on September 23, 2004, President Papadopoulos reiterated that a Cyprus settlement should be dependant upon "the withdrawal of [Turkish] troops and [Turkish] settlers . . . the just resolution of land and property . . . and the respect of the right of return of refugees." For the full text of the speech, see H. E. Mr.Tassos Papadopoulos, President of the Republic of Cyprus, United Nations online, September 23, 2004. http://www.UN.org/, p. 3. *Cyprus Weekly*, September 24, 2004. Determined to maintain the grip on the political power, Papadopoulos's effort was to promote changes in the Annan Plan advantageous to Greek Cypriot interest. Due to the prevailing mistrust of the Greek Cypriots, the Cypriot Turks claim that Turkey can only guarantee their survival. The Turks do not put too much faith in EU to safeguard their safety because of its poor record in failing to prevent the Serb slaughter of Muslims in Bosnia. Any satisfactory solution on Cyprus will either include the physical presence of Turkish troops on Cyprus or some other arrangement that will guarantee the Turkish Cypriot's safety. As to Turkey's Cyprus policy, see Ersin Kalaycioglu, "Troubled Waters: Cyprus and Turkish Foreign Policy," Istanbul, Bogazici University, undated, mimeography, p. 13.

116. Ibid. On September 15, Mehmet Ali Talat, prime minister of TRNC, maintained that when appropriate conditions prevail, UN Secretary-General Kofi Annan would undertake a new initiative in Cyprus. Turkiskpress.com, online, September 15, 2004. Annan will likely resume his good offices in Cyprus when the Greek Cypriots "will reflect on their position so that future efforts can have a chance to succeed." The Athens News Agency, http://www.ana.gr, September 15, 2004. For the full text of the report, see United Nations Report of the Secretary-General on the Work of the Organization, General Assembly, Official Records, 59th session, supplement no.1. (A/59/1), August 20, 2004, pp. 5–6.

117. Ibid.

118. The Cyprus Broadcasting Corporation, http://www.cybe.com.cy/, June 3, 2004; *New York Times*, online, June 2, 2004.

119. The Cyprus News Agency, http://www.cyna.org.cy, June 4, 2004. The UK's Minister for Europe Denis MacShane, during his visit to Cyprus, told the Cypriots on October 22 that the international community failed to facilitate the island's reunification, and the "next step has to be on the island." BBC News, online, October 22, 2004.

120. United Nations. Report of Secretary-General on his mission of good offices in Cyprus, May 28, 2004 /S/2004/437/.

121. Ibid.

122. For the full text of Cyprus President's letter to Annan, see the Cyprus News Agency, http://www,cyna.org.cy, June 8, 2004. AKEL accused President Papadopoulos that in April 2005 EOKA B was invited to the Presidential Palace to plan the campaign against the return of the Annan plan. EOKA B was a pro-enosis paramilitary organization formed in 1970 under General Grivas with the support of the military *Junta* in Athens. On July 15, 1974, EOKA B and the National Guard launched a coup against President Makarios and installed Nicos Sampson as president. *Cyprus Mail*, October 24, 2007.

123. The Cyprus News Agency, http://www.cyna.org.cy, June 17, 2004. On September 17, Nikos Katsourides of AKEL during his meeting with the Turkish Cypriot party leaders in TRNC stated that it was possible to make changes on the Annan Plan without affecting its philosophy. The Athens News Agency, online, September 17, 2004.

124. **Resolution 1548 (2004)**
Adopted by the Security Council at its 4989th meeting, on 11 June 2004
The Security Council,

Welcoming the report of the Secretary-General of 26 May 2004 (S/2004/427)

On the United Nations operation in Cyprus, and in particular the call to the parties to assess and address the humanitarian issue of missing persons with due urgency and seriousness,

Noting that the Government of Cyprus is agreed that in view of the prevailing conditions in the island it is necessary to keep the United Nations peacekeeping force in Cyprus (UNFICYP) beyond 15 June 2004,

Welcoming the Secretary-General's intention to conduct a review, to be completed within three months, on UNFICYP's mandate, force levels and concept of operation, in view of the 24 April 2004 referenda and taking into account developments on the ground, and the views of the parties,

Welcoming and encouraging efforts by the United Nations to sensitize peacekeeping personnel in the prevention and control of HIV/AIDS and other communicable diseases in all its peacekeeping operations,

1. *Reaffirms* all its relevant resolutions on Cyprus, in particular resolution 1251 (1999) of 29 June 1999 and subsequent resolutions;

2. *Decides* to extend the mandate of UNFICYP for a further period ending 15 December 2004 and to consider the recommendations of the Secretary-General in his review of UNFICYP and to act upon them within one month of receiving them;

3. *Urges* the Turkish Cypriot side and the Turkish forces to rescind without

delay all remaining restrictions on UNFICYP, and calls on them restore in Strovilia the military status quo which existed there prior to 30 June 2000;

    4.   *Requests* the Secretary-General to submit a report on the implementation of this resolution concurrent with the report provided for above;

    5.   *Decides* to remain seized of the matter.

125. The Athens News Agency at http://www.ana.gr/, June 14, 2004.

126. *New York Times*, online, May 4, 2004. An American consulting firm Bearing Point was in TRNC on September 27 to make recommendations as to $30.5 million U.S. financial aid package approved for the economic development and spur unification of the island. *Turkiye*, September 28, 2004.

127. *Halkin Sesi, Kibris*, June 29, 2005.

128. *Turkish Daily News*, July 17, 2004; BBC News, online, July 16, 2004; The Athens News Agency, http://www.ana.gr/, July 16, 2004. For the full text of "Confidence Building Measures," see the Cyprus News Agency, http://www.cyna.cy, July 22, 2004.

129. *Kathimerini*, July 31, August 1, 2004. For the full text of the measures of public use vehicles for Turkish Cypriots, see the Cyprus News Agency, http://www.cyna.org.cy, July 30, 2004.

130. On August 8, 2004, France blocked the UN Security Council from announcing a resolution lifting the isolation of TRNC.

131. BBC News, online; Turkishpress.com, August 23, 2004. At a seminar in Nicosia, the American ambassador Michael Klosson on November 9 said that the U.S. was ready to open trade with Turkish Cypriot businessmen. *Kibris*, November 10, 2004; *Cyprus Mail*, January 16, 2005.

132. To frustrate the improving political landscape across the Greek Line, the radical elements in the north bombed a church but failed to achieve the desired results. On August 27, 2004, a bomb exploded at the entrance of the Greek Orthodox Cathedral of Agios Mamas in Morfou, Turks call it Guzelyurt, causing damage to windows and the church's entrance. Morphou Bishop Neofytos conducted the ceremonies at the church in celebration of the saints' name day on September 1–2 after thirty years. Mehmet Ali Talat, the premier of TRNC said that "measures have been taken so that service could be held in quiet, peaceful way and they will continue to be taken. . . . No one has the right to upset our internal peace." Associated Press, online, August 27, 2004. President Papadopoulos was critical of Bishop Neofytos in making arrangements for the ceremonies with TRNC without consulting the government and the refugee municipality council. *Cyprus Weekly*, August 29, 2004.

133. *Kibris*, August 25, 2004. Under the Green Line regulations, twelve tons of watermelons were transported from the north to the south of the island, but one hundred kilograms of fish were denied entry by the Republic of Cyprus. The EU Commission in 2006 reported the under the Green Line trade goods from north to south almost doubled to 3,380,850 compared to 1,734,770 Cyprus pounds and trade from south to north was 1,027,688 compared to 442,408 Cyprus pounds. *Cyprus Mail*, September 25, 2007.

134. Turkishpress.com, online, September 28, 2004; *Cyprus Mail*, January 15, 2005.

135. *Kibris*, September 29, 2004.

136. *Phileleftheros*, September 28, 2004; *Cyprus Weekly*, September 30, 2004. For the full

text, see United Nations, *Security Council* "Report of the Secretary-General on the United Nations Operation in Cyprus," (S/2004/756) September 24, 2004.

137. United Nations, *Security Council*, S/Res/1568 (2004), October 22, 2004.

Resolution 1568 (2004)

Adopted by the Security Council at its 5061st meeting, on October 22, 2004

The Security Council,

Welcoming the report of the Secretary-General of 24 September 2004 (S/2004/756) on the United Nations operation in Cyprus,

Reiterating its call to the parties to assess and address the humanitarian issue of missing persons with due urgency and seriousness, and welcoming in this regard the resumption of the activities of the Committee on Missing Persons since August 2004,

Welcoming the Secretary-General's review of the United Nations peacekeeping operation in Cyprus (UNFICYP), pursuant to resolution 1548 (2004) of 11 June 2004,

Noting that the government of Cyprus is agreed that in view of the prevailing conditions in the island it is necessary to keep UNFICYP beyond 15 December 2004,

Taking note of the assessment of the Secretary-General that the security situation on the island has become increasingly benign over the last few years and that a recurrence of fighting in Cyprus is increasingly unlikely,

Welcoming the Secretary-General's intention to conduct a further review on UNFICYP's mandate, force levels and concept of operation in advance of the next renewal of UNFICYP's mandate, continuing to take into account developments on the ground and the views of the parties,

Echoing the Secretary-General's gratitude to the Government of Cyprus and the Government of Greece for their voluntary contributions to the funding of UNFICYP, and his request for further voluntary contributions from other countries and organizations,

Welcoming and encouraging efforts by the United Nations to sensitize peacekeeping personnel in the prevention and control of HIV/AIDS and other communicable diseases in all its peacekeeping operations,

1. *Reaffirms* all its relevant resolutions on Cyprus, in particular resolution 1251 (1999) of 29 June 1999 and subsequent resolutions;

2. *Endorses* the Secretary-General's recommendations for the amendment of the concept of operations and force level of UNFICYP, as outlined in his report of 24 September 2004;

3. *Decides* to extend the mandate of UNFICYP for a further period ending 15 June 2005;

4. *Urges* the Turkish Cypriot side and Turkish forces to rescind without delay all remaining restrictions on UNFICYP, and calls on them to restore in Strovilia the military status quo which existed there prior to 30 June 2000;

5. *Requests* the Secretary-General to submit a report on implementation of this resolution concurrent with the review provided for above;

6. *Decides* to remain seized of the matter.

138. *Halkin Sesi*, October 24, 2004.
139. *Daily Star*, October 1, 2004. U.S. Ambassador to Cyprus Michael Klosson in his address to the Cyprus-American Business Association on October 13 said, "Continued Turkish Cypriot acceptance of painful compromises incorporated in the Annan Plan should not be taken for granted." The Cyprus News Agency at http://www.cyna.org.cy, October 14, 2004.
140. *Turkiye*, October 5, 2004. The Cyprus government offered to allow the release of 259 million euros of EU aid to Turkish Cypriots in return for Varosha. *Cyprus Mail*, November 10, 2005.
141. *Kibris*, October 5, 2004. SETimes.com, November 19, 2009. "The survey of 5,000 people in Germany, France, the UK, Spain and Poland showed that 68.5% have positive opinions about Turkey, as opposed to the 25% with negative opinions."
142. *Milliyet, Cyprus Weekly*, online, December 8, 2005. *Cyprus Mail*, online, December 8, 28, 2005. Almost half of the 259 million euro grant extended to the Turkish Cypriots was withdrawn by the EU because the Turks insisted that the aid package should not be linked to the concession demands on Varosha, directed trade through the Famagusta Port, and established a moratorium on the sale of Greek properties in TRNC. *Cyprus Mail*, online, December 29, 2005. On October 27, 2006, EU released a first credit tranche of 38.1 million euros for TRNC. *Turkey's*, October 27, 2006.
143. *Milliyet*, online, December 9, 2005.
144. *Cyprus Mail, Cyprus Weekly*, February 4, 5, 2005.
145. *Financial Mirror* (Cyprus) reported on February 27, 2006, that as part of the direct trade agreement changes to Protocol 10 of Accession Treaty would have to be passed unanimity. The direct trade regulation before covered "other countries and territories" outside the EU customs union. The legal basis needed only a qualified majority to pass (under Article 133 [4]), common commercial Policy, EC Treaty.
146. Turkey signed an Association Agreement with the European Community in 1963, applied for EU Membership in 1987, became a candidate in 1999, and in 2002 EU set out all requirements Turkey had to meet before membership.
147. *Washington Post*, October 7, 2004.
148. "Why Europe Must Say Yes to Turkey," *The Economist*, vol. 372, no. 8393, September 18–24, 2004, p. 14. Republic of Cyprus would lobby EU member states ahead of EU summit on December 17, 2004, to link Turkey's accession bet to progress on Cyprus settlement. *Daily Times*, October 9, 2004. On October 10, Papadopoulos said, "We will decide at the December EU summit whether or not to veto Turkey beginning its accession talks." Greek President Kostis Stefanopolous echoed Papadopoulos in regard to veto and said, "Athens will help Turkey gain full membership; however, Ankara has international obligations to fulfill." *Cumhuriyet*, October 11, 2004; *Cyprus Weekly*, online; *Financial Times*, online, October 11, 2004. At the EU Trokia, Ireland, Netherlands, and Luxemburg meeting at The Hague on November 24, Turkey's shortcomings on the Copenhagen Criteria were noticeably the Turkish Penal Code and the failure to extend the customs union protocol's implementation to Cyprus. *Turkiye*, November 25, 2004, *Cyprus Weekly, Star*, November 29, 2004.
149. M. Hakan Yavuz and Mujeeb R. Khan, "Turkey and Europe: Will East Meet West?" *The Current History*, vol. 103, no. 676, November 2004, p. 393.

150. The European Commission pressured Turkey not to adopt a penal code making adultery a criminal offense. Turkish parliament in order not to risk jeopardizing Turkey's EU bid, on September 26 overwhelmingly approved penal code reforms. BBC News, online, September 21, 26, 2004; *Washington Post*, online, September 26, 2004.
151. Commission of the European Communities. "Recommendation of the European Commission on Turkey's Progress Towards Accession," Brussels, 6.10.2004. COM (2004) 656 final. http://europa.eu.int/index_on.htm, p. 3.
152. Ibid., p. 5. Olli Rehn, the EU's commissioner of enlargement, has suggested giving members the power to close their borders to Turkish migrants if admission leads to a flood of poor Turks seeking work. About 4 million Turks are cheap labor for EU states but are not assimilated into the indigenous population. Turkey has rejected the proposal. *Washington Post*, online, October 7, 2004.
153. Ibid., p. 6.
154. Ibid., p. 8.
155. Ibid., p. 10.
156. Ibid., p. 11, 13.
157. Ibid., p. 13.
158. *The Financial Times*, September 10, 2004.
159. Ibid.
160. The Athens Agency, online, October 12, 2004.
161. Samuel P. Huntington, *The Clash of Civilizations and the Remaking of World Order* (London: Touchstone Books, 1997), p. 162.
162. BBC News, http://www.news.bbc.co.uk, October 20, 2004. The legal writers until 1856 held the view that laws of nations applied only to the community of Christian nations. The Treaty of Paris on March 30, 1856, admitted the Ottoman Empire "to participate in the public law and system of Europe." Michael Hurst (ed.), *Key Treaties for the Great Powers 1814–1914*, vol. 1 (New York: St. Martin's Press, 1972), pp. 317–327.
163. *New York Times*, October 7, 2004. "To Brussels, on a Wind and a Prayer," *The Economist*, vol. 373, no. 8396, October 9, 2004. pp. 45–46.
164. *Hurriyet*, November 11, 2004.
165. *Turkiye, Kibris, Halkin Sesi*, October 21, 22, 2004; *Kathimerini; Cyprus Weekly*, October 21, 2004. *Turkiye*, November 11, 2004.
166. *Yeni Safak*, October 21, 2004.
167. *Ortam*, November 1, 2004.
168. *Aksam*, November 23, 2004.
169. The treaty establishing the EU constitution, which will go into effect in 2009, was signed in Rome on October 29 by the leaders of the twenty-five member states, including the leaders of Bulgaria, Croatia, Romania, and Turkey who are moving toward EU accession. *New York Times*, online, October 29, 2004. The treaty was the result of twenty-eight months of debate and it may take effect until 2007. *Washington Post*, online, October 2004, Turkishpress.com. November 18, 2004. *Zaman*, November 18, 2004.
170. Foreign Minister Gul in his address to Turkish parliament on November 9 said that recognizing the Greek Cypriot administration was out of the question. *Aksam*, November 11, 2004; *Zaman*, November 18, 2004.

171. *Zaman*, November 2, 2004, in an interview, Gul said, "As far as we are concerned the Annan Plan is finished." *Hurriyet*, November 23, 2004.

172. *Cumhuriyet*, November 3, 2004.

173. The Cyprus News Agency, online, BBC News, online, November 12, 2004, *Cyprus Weekly*, November 19 and December 10, 2004; General Yasar Buyukanit, commander of the land forces of the Turkish army, on his visit to inspect the Turkish armed units on Cyprus on January 25 said, "We, as an army, are having our armed forces on the island of Cyprus for the security of the Turkish Cypriots, taking strength by the agreements. Before a final and lasting agreement, not even a single soldier will go from here." Turkishpress.com, January 25, 2005; *Milliyet*; *Kibris*, online, January 26, 2005.

174. EU was reluctant to back the demands of the Greek Cypriots. *Kathimerini*, online, December 10, 2004, AKEL, Disy, and the united Democrats were opposed to veto Turkey's accession. The Greek government had made it "crystal clear" to Papadopoulos that veto was out of the question. *Cyprus Weekly*, December 11, 2004. Cypriot Foreign Minister George Iacovou on December 13 told the reporters in Brussels, "We have not asked for legally defined recognition but normalization of relations in general and in particular, in the bilateral field." Turkishpress.com, December 13, 2004.

175. The Macedonian Press Agency at http://www.mpa.gr, November 11, 2004; *Cyprus Weekly*, November 15, 2004.

176. *Kathimerini*, December 1, 2004.

177. Turkey and Armenia signed two landmark protocols outlining the restoration of bilateral ties and opening their shared border in Zurich on October 10, 2009. The two protocols will be submitted to the respective parliaments for ratification on each side. President of Armenia, Serge Sarlisian, before the signing ceremony said that the restoration of diplomatic relations and open mutual borders was based on "proginatism and forward-looking sustained work." *Today's Zaman*, online, October 12, 2009. On October 12, President Sarkisean said that he will go to Bursa, Turkey, on October 14 to a football World Cup qualifier between the two national teams, returning the gesture by Turkey's president in 2009. *New York Times*, online, October 12, 2009.

178. European Parliament Committee on Foreign Affairs, *Draft Report* on the 2004 regular report and the recommendation of the European Commission on Turkey's progress toward accession (COM[2004]0656-C6-0148/2004-2004/2182[INI], PR/545203EN.doc., Rapporteur: Camiel Eurlings; See also Communication from the Commission to the Council and the European Parliament, Brussels, 6.10.2004, COM[2004]656 final).

179. *Kathimerini*, December 1, 2004.

180. *Milliyet*, November 30, 2004; *Cumhuriyet*, December 2, 2004; *Washington Post*, December 10, 2004.

181. European Parliament, Committee on Foreign Affairs, *Amendments* 1-426, PE349, 948/1-426, (COM[2004]0656-C6-0148/2004-2004/2182[INI], Draft report Camiel Eurlings. 126pp.).

182. World–AFP, http://news.yahoo.com, December 3, 2004.

183. Ibid.

184. The Athens News Agency, online, December 7, 2004.

185. *Milliyet, Dunya*, December 5, 2004.

---

186. Russian President Vladimir Putin's visit to Turkey from December 5 to 7 further strengthened EU accession negotiations and bilateral relations between the two countries. *Milliyet*, December 7, 2004.
187. European Parliament on Foreign Affairs, *Final Report*, on the 2004 regular report and the recommendation of the EC on Turkey (COM[2004]0656-C6-0148/2004–2004/2182[INI]), RR/34731OEN.doc., Rinal A6-0063/2004, Rapporteur: Camiel Eurlings, 3.12.2004, pp.20.
188. According to Greek Cypriot media, the United States had cautioned Cyprus not to use its veto against Turkey in the upcoming summit and it was threatened with the dire repercussions. The Athens News Agency, online, December 8, 2004, BBC News, online, December 10, 2004, French Foreign Minister Michel Barnier on December 13 said that he will ask Turkey to acknowledge the 1.5 million killing of Armenians in 1915 when it begins EU accession talks under the pressure of the 300,000 Armenians living in France the government was forced to pass a law recognizing the Armenian genocide in 2001. BBC News, online, December 13, 2004.
189. *New York Times*, December 14, 2004; *Financial Times, Milliyet, Star*, December 15, 2004; *Hurriyet, Yeni Duzen, Kibris, Halkin Sesi*, December 16, 2004.
190. Ibid.
191. "The Unwelcome Guests," *The Economist*, vol. 373, no. 8405, December 11–17, 2004. pp. 48–49.
192. The Macedonian Press Agency, December 17, 2004. See also European Parliament resolution on the 2004 regular report and the recommendation of the European Commission on Turkey's progress toward accession (COM[2004]0656-C6-0148/2004–2004/2182 [INI]) Provisional Edition, P6-TA-PROV(2004)0096, A6-0063/2004, December 15, 2004, pp.1–12.
193. Washington Post.com, December 17, 2004. The U.S. State Department spokesman Richard Boucher said that the accord agreed to in Brussels did not involve "questions of a settlement [of the Cyprus issue] or even questions of recognition, just some questions about how it's handled in the [EU] accession process." http://news.yahoo.com, Turkishpress.com, December 17, 2004. A de facto recognition is a provisional recognition that the government is in actual control of the political system of the state. By extending a de facto recognition to a state, the recognizing government sets conditions that must be met before a de jure recognition is extended. When doubts exist as to the legality of a state, the objectionable conditions must be removed for a de jure recognition. This implies that a de facto recognition is temporary and could be withdrawn if the set conditions by the recognizing state are not fulfilled. De facto recognition issue arises when the political legitimacy of a government, which may have come to power outside of the constitutional process, is in question. The existence of an internationally unrecognized TRNC in northern Cyprus, except by Turkey, cannot be denied because it continues to have absolute and exclusive control of the political and military power over northern Cyprus since 1974. Implicit recognition (also known as implied or tacit recognition) can result in the conclusion of a bilateral treaty with the unrecognized state. The Cyprus government is a party to a multipartite agreement (the Customs Union) to which Turkey is a party, but it does not imply or compel any of the signatories to extend or imply a de facto recognition under international law.

Gerhard von Glahn, *Law Among Nations* (7th ed. Boston: Allyn and Bacon, 1996), pp. 70, 79, 86. *Cyprus Mail*, March 30, 2005. Heather Grabbe, "When Negotiations Begin: The Next Phase in EU-Turkey relations," Center for European Reform, London, November 2004, info@cer.org.uk/www.cer.org.uk, p. 3. The author is of the opinion that "Turkey will have to recognize Cyprus before it will be able to join the EU, and to remove Turkish troops from the island."

194. The Athens News Agency, online, June 22, 2005.
195. Turkishpress.com, December 17, 2004.
196. *Washington Post*, online, December 17, 2004.
197. *New York Times*, online, December 17, 2004.
198. *Cyprus Weekly*, December 23, 2004.
199. *Hurriyet*, December 24, 2004; *Milliyet*, December 27, 2004; *Radical*, December 28, 2004. *Kibris*, January 22, 2005. The Turkish Resistance Organization (TMT) was reconstituted in Britain with twenty-one agenda items as to "The Real Solution in Cyprus."
200. *Cumhuriyet*, December 28, 2004; *Milliyet*, Ankara Anatolia News Agency, December 30, 2004.
201. Ibid.
202. *Star*, December 24, 2004; *Cyprus Weekly*, December 23, 2004.
203. *Haravghi*, December 27, 2004; *Cyprus Mail*, December 23, 28, 2004.
204. *Cyprus Mail, Hurriyet*, January 19, 2005.
205. *Cyprus Mail, Cyprus Weekly, Star*, February 10, 2005.
206. *Cyprus Weekly, Cyprus Mail, Cumhuriyet*, February 11, 2005.
207. *Hurriyet*, February 14, 2005.
208. *Aksam, Kibris*, June 15, 2005.
209. *Cyprus Mail*, January 16, 2005.
210. *Cyprus Mail*, March 22, 2005.
211. In an article in *Ta Nea* (Athens), Alexis Heraclides, a lecturer at Greece's Pantion University, writes the following:

> The Cyprus problem cannot be solved—and will not be solved—as long as the majority of Greek Cypriots are not in a position to comprehend the level of their responsibility for the situation in Cyprus up to the fait accompli of 1974. And this is, I would say, the deeper meaning of the "resounding no" of April 24, 2004—they said no because they cannot yet face up to their guilt for that period.

Heraclides clearly blames the Greek Cypriot leaders for the horrific mistakes committed starting with the bloody events of 1963, and the fait accompli in Cyprus following 1974. *Cyprus Mail*, January 30, 2005. At a gathering in Nicosia on May 16, 2005, the eighty-six-year-old former president of Cyprus Glafcos Clerides, who served two consecutive terms in office from 1993 to 2003, remarked that every time a proposal for a Cyprus settlement was rejected, the next proposal was worse that the previous one. *Cyprus Mail*, May 18, 2005; *Cyprus Weekly*, May 20, 2005.

———

212. *Cyprus Mail*, February 13, 2005; *Financial Times*, February 16, 2005; *Turkiye, Milliyet*, February 17, 2005.
213. *Financial Times*, February 17, 2005; *Kibris, Hurriyet*, February 18, 2005.
214. *Cyprus Mail*, May 26, 31, 2005; *Kibris, Halkin, Sesi, Cumhuriyet*, May 31, 2005.
215. The Cyprus News Agency, online, Turkishpress.com, online, May 19, 2005; *Cyprus Weekly*, May 20, 2005.
216. *International Herald Tribune, Kibrisli*, online, July 1, 2005.
217. *Cumhuriyet, Star, Turkiye*, online, July 18, 2005.
218. *Kibris, Cyprus Mail*, July 28, 2005.
219. Corey Robin, *Fear: The History of a Political Idea* (New York: Oxford University Press, 2004), p. 252.
220. "Cyprus: Shadowed Northern Lights," *The Economist*, vol. 374, no. 8315, February 26–March 4, 2005, p. 53. The Interior Minister of Cyprus Andreas Christou, on May 24, said that since restrictions on movement were lifted in April 2003, his government had issued 32,000 passports, 63,600 birth certificates, and 57,300 identity cards to Turkish Cypriots. *Cyprus Mail*, May 25, 2005.
221. *Cyprus Mail*, April 30, 2005.
222. Ibid.
223. *Cyprus Weekly*, May 6, 2005.
224. Chief of General Staff General Hilmi Ozkok in a speech at the War Academies Command in Istanbul on April 20, 2005, said that the army would not pull back forces from Cyprus and removing troops without a settlement on the island will undermine Turkey's national security. He endorsed Turkey's EU membership, but not at any price. "It is Turkey's fundamental interests to be a member of the EU. But it is very wrong for the EU to see this as a favor to us. . . . If there is no agreement, if Turkey does not enter the EU, it does not mean the end of the world." *Cyprus Mail, Cumhuriyet, Aksam*, April 21, 2005. For the full text of Ozkok's speech at the staff college in Turkish, go to www.tsk.mil.tr., April 21, 2005.
225. The Greco-Turkish Cypriot "secret talks" in Brussels, organized by Luxemburg's EU presidency and the European Commission, collapsed on June 16, 2005. The negotiations centered on EU aid and direct trade with TRNC, the return of Varosha to the Greek Cypriots, and the property in the north. *Cyprus Times*, June 16, 2005; *Cyprus Mail, Kibris, Cumhuriyet*, online, June 17, 2005.
226. *Kibris, Yeni Duzen, Hurriyet*, February 21, 2005; *Cyprus Mail*, February 22, 2005. "Cyprus and Turkey: Talat ho!" *The Economist*, vol. 375, no. 8423, April 23–29, 2005, pp. 51–52.
227. *Milliyet*, May 5, 2005.
228. The Athens News Agency at http://www.ana.gr., April 19, 2005.
229. Mehmet Ali Talat was born in upper Kyrenia in 1952. After completing high school, he continued his studies at Ankara University in electrical engineering. While in Turkey, he was active in left-wing politics. He joined the center-left Republican Turkish Party (CTP) and became an active player in Turkish Cypriot politics. He repaired refrigerators and air conditioners before becoming a full-time politician.
230. *Kibris*, April 19, 2005; *New York Times*, online, June 8, 2005.

231. *Cyprus Mail*, May 10–11, 2005; *Hurriyet*, May 10, 2005; *New York Times*, online, June 8, 2005.

232. United Nations, *Security Council*, "Report of the Secretary-General on the United Nations operation in Cyprus," S/2005/353, May 27, 2005, p. 10.

Resolution 1604 (2005)

Adopted by the Security Council at its 5200th meeting, on 15 June 2005

The Security Council,

Welcoming the report of the Secretary-General of 27 May 2005 (S/2005/353) on the United Nations operation in Cyprus,

Reiterating its call to the parties to assess and address the humanitarian issue of missing persons with due urgency and seriousness, and welcoming in this regard the resumption of the activities of the Committee on Missing Persons since August 2004,

Welcoming the Secretary-General's review of the United Nations peacekeeping operation in Cyprus (UNFICYP), pursuant to resolution 1568 (2004) of 22 October 2004,

Noting that the Government of Cyprus is agreed that in view of the prevailing conditions in the island it is necessary to keep UNFICYP beyond 15 June 2005,

Taking note of the assessment of the Secretary –General that the security situation on the island continues to be stable and that the situation along Green Line remains calm, and, nonetheless, that there were no problems in few sensitive areas, and welcoming in this context the further decrease in the overall number of incidents involving the two sides,

Welcoming the Secretary-General's intention to keep the operations of UNFICYP under close review, continuing to take into account developments on the ground and the views of the parties, and to revert to the Council with recommendations for further adjustments as appropriate to UNFICYP's mandate, force levels and concept of operation once he judges that sufficient time has passed since the implementation of UNFICYP's new concept of operations to make this assessment,

Taking note with satisfaction of the lifting of restrictions of movement of UNFICYP by the Turkish Cypriot side and the Turkish forces, and taking note in this connection that UNFICYP enjoys good cooperation from both sides,

Welcoming the fact that over seven million grossing by Greek Cypriots to the north and Turkish Cypriots to the south have taken place, and encouraging the opening of additional crossing points,

Expressing concern at the increase in crime across the ceasefire line and urging both sides to increase cooperation in order to address this issue,

Welcoming all efforts to promote bicommunal contacts and events, including, inter alia, on the part of the United Nations, and urging the two sides to promote further bicommunal contacts and to remove any obstacles to such contacts,

Echoing the Secretary-General's gratitude to the Government of Cyprus and the Government of Greece for their voluntary contributions to the funding of UNFICYP, and his request for further voluntary contributions from other countries and organizations,

Welcoming and encouraging efforts by the United Nations to sensitize peacekeeping personnel in the prevention and control of HIV/AIDS and other communicable diseases in all its peacekeeping operations,

1. *Reaffirms* all its relevant resolutions on Cyprus, in particular resolution 1251 (1999) of 29 June 1999 and subsequent resolutions;

2. *Decides* to extend the mandate of UNFICYP for a further period ending 15 December 2005;

3. *Calls* on the Turkish Cypriot side Turkish forces to restore in Strovilia the military status quo which existed there prior to 30 June 2000;

4. *Requests* the Secretary-General to submit a report on implementation of this resolution by 1 December 2005;

5. *Welcomes* the efforts being undertaken by UNFICYP to implement the Secretary-General's zero tolerance policy on sexual exploitation and abuse and to ensure full compliance of its personnel with the United Nations code of conduct, requests the Secretary-General to continue to take all necessary action in this regard and to keep the Security Council informed, and urges troop-contributing countries to take appropriate preventive action including the conduct of pre-deployment awareness training, and to take disciplinary action and other action to ensure full accountability in cases of such conduct involving their personnel;

6. *Decides* to remain seized of the matter.

United Nations, *Security Council*, S/RES/1604(2005), June 15, 2005.

233. On October 18, 2005, Cyprus government, after four years, launched its first six-day major military exercises "Nikiforos" by the National Guard without Greece. Papadopoulor defended the decision as to the military exercises due to the continued preserve of Turkish military on the island. *Cyprus Mail*, online, October 18, 2005. The "toros-2005" military exercises were performed by the Turkish forces in Cyprus from November 23 to 25. Turkishpress.com, November 22, 2005.

234. Papadopoulos handed Sir Kieran Prendergast a proposal for the resolution of Cyprus crisis: (1) The removal of all foreign troops, Greek and Turkish, and the demilitarization of the island; (2) The guarantor powers rights, Greece, Turkey, and Great Britain, shall be null and void; (3) The UN Security Council shall be the guarantor power; (4) The return of immovable property in the north to their rightful owners (Greek Cypriots); (5) A 30,000 limitation on settlers from Turkey; (6) Power in the central government shall be determined by the rules based on proportional representation; (7) The UN secretary-general shall have no role in arbitration; (8) An open-ended negotiations; and (9) No linkage of Cyprus issue with Turkey's EU accession negotiations. NTV (Turkish television network) broadcast on June 2, 2005; *Cyprus Mail*, June 3, 2005.

235. For the full text of Sir Kieran Prendergast's report to the UN Security Council on June 22, 2005, see United Nations, *Security Council*, 5211th Meeting (AM), Press Release SC/8422, June 22, 2005. See also the Cyprus News Agency at http://www.cyna.org.cy, June 22, 2005, *Cyprus Weekly*, June 23, 2005, *Cyprus Mail*, June 23, 24, 2005.

236. *Cyprus Mail*, May 19, 2005.

237. The Athens News Agency, online, May 17, 2005.

238. **Resolution 1642 (2005)**

Adopted by the Security Council at its 5324th meeting, on 14 December 2005

The Security Council

Welcoming the report of the Secretary-General of 29 November 2005 (S/2005/743) on the United Nations operation in Cyprus,

Reiterating its call to the parties to assess and address the humanitarian issue of missing persons with due urgency and seriousness, and welcoming in this regard the resumption of the activities of the Committee on Missing Persons since August 2004, as well as the Secretary-General's intention to appoint the Third Member as of January 2006 and to reinforce his office,

Noting that the Government of Cyprus is agreed that in view of the prevailing conditions in the island it is necessary to keep UNFICYP beyond 15 December 2005,

Taking note of the assessment of the Secretary-General that the security situation on the island continues to be stable and that the situation along the Green Line remains calm, welcoming in this context the further decrease in the overall number of incidents involving the two sides, while noting nonetheless that there were incidents of significant concern,

Urging both sides to avoid any action which could lead to an increase in tensions and taking note with concern, in this context, of the conduct, for the first time since 2001, of the "Nikiforos" military exercise, and afterwards, the "toros" military exercise,

Regretting that progress towards a political solution has been negligible at best and urging both sides to work towards the resumption of negotiations for a comprehensive settlement,

Welcoming the Secretary-General's continuous engagement in the search for a comprehensive settlement of the Cyprus problem,

Welcoming all demining activity in the buffer zone, including the agreement to begin the clearing of Turkish Forces minefields in Nicosia and surrounding areas within the buffer zone,

Expressing concern that, since the release of the Secretary-General's report, differences have arisen over construction activity related to the proposed additional crossing point at Ledra Street and urging both sides to cooperate with UNFICYP to resolve this issue,

Welcoming the Secretary-General's intention to keep the operations of UNFICYP under close review continuing to take into account developments on the ground and the views of the parties, and to revert to the Council with recommendations as appropriate for further adjustments to UNFICYP's mandate, force levels and concept of operation as soon as warranted,

Welcoming the fact that over nine million crossings by Greek Cypriots to the north and Turkish Cypriots to the south have taken place, and encouraging the opening of additional crossing points,

Welcoming all efforts to promote bicommunal contacts and events, including, inter alia, on the part of the United Nations, and urging the two sides to promote further bicommunal contacts and to remove any obstacle to such contacts,

Echoing the Secretary-General's gratitude to the Government of Cyprus and the Government of Greece for their voluntary contributions to the funding of

UNFICYP, and his request for further voluntary contributions from other countries and organizations,

Welcoming and encouraging efforts by the United Nations to sensitize peacekeeping personnel in the prevention and control of HIV/AIDS and other communicable diseases in all its peacekeeping operations,

1. *Reaffirms* all its relevant resolutions on Cyprus, in particular resolution 1251 (1999) of 29 June 1999 and subsequent resolutions;

2. *Expresses* its full support for UNFICYP and decides to extend its mandate for a further period ending 15 June 2006;

3. *Calls on* the Turkish Cypriot side and Turkish forces to restore in Strovilia the military status quo which existed their prior to 30 June 2000;

4. *Requests* the Secretary-General to submit a report on implementation of this resolution by 1 June 2006;

5. *Welcomes* the efforts being undertaken by UNFICYP to implement the Secretary-General's zero tolerance policy on sexual exploitation and abuse and to ensure full compliance of its personnel with the United Nations code of conduct, requests the Secretary-General to continue to take all necessary action in this regard and to keep the security Council informed, and urges troop-contributing countries to take appropriate preventive action including the conduct of pre-deployment awareness training, and to take disciplinary action and other action to ensure full accountability in cases of such conduct involving their personnel;

6. *Decides* to remain seized of the matter.

239. *Kibris*, May 26, 2005; *Cyprus Mail*, May 27, 2005.

240. George Will, "The European State of Mind," *Fort Worth Star Telegram*, May 29, 2005, p. 3E. See also BBC News, online, May 29, 2005; *International Herald Tribune*, online, May 31, 2005.

241. "Turkey and the European Union: Mountains Still to Climb," *The Economist*, Vol. 375, No. 8426, May 14–20, 2005, p. 53; *New York Times*, online, June 3, 20, 2005; *Financial Times*, June 20, 2005.

242. *New York Times*, online, June 15, 2005.

243. "Turkey and the EU: Reason to Worry," *The Economist*, vol. 375, no. 8429, June 4–10, 2005, p. 50.

244. *Christian Science Monitor*, online, June 14, 2005.

245. "Divided Cyprus: Leaps of Doubt," *The Economist*, vol. 375, no. 8426, May 14–20, 2005, p. 54.

246. *Cyprus Mail*, August 15, 2005.

247. See also "Greece and Turkey: Mission to Ankara," *The Economist*, vol. 376, no. 8439, August 13–19, 2005, p. 43.

248. *Financial Times*, August 8, 9, 2005.

249. *New York Times*, online, September 7, 2005.

250. *Financial Times*, online, September 2, 2005.

251. The Cyprus Broadcasting Corporation, online, September 2, 2005.

252. BBC news, online, *Cyprus Mail*, September 3, 2005; "Turkey and the EU: Bazaar

Bargaining," *The Economist*, vol. 376, no. 8442, September 3–9, 2005, pp. 46–47; *Times*, online, September 6, 2005.

253. *Cyprus Mail*, September 7, 2005.

254. Ibid.

255. *International Herald Tribune*, online, September 8.

256. *Cyprus Mail*, online, September 13, 2005.

257. Tehrantimes.com, *Cyprus Mail*, September 14, 2005; *International Herald Tribune*, online, September 15, 2005. Erdogan and Papadopoulos had "an unofficial meeting" on September 15 at the UN headquarters in New York. The Cyprus News Agency, online, September 15, 2005. According to news reports, the two leaders discussed the creation of two-state entities under a confederal system. Papadopoulos described Erdogan's proposition as unacceptable. *Cyprus Mail*, online, September 18, 2005.

258. *Cyprus Mail*, September 20, 2005.

259. BBC News, online, September 20, 2005.

260. In an interview with *Phileleftheros* on November 13, 2055, Tasos Tzionis, the head of the president's diplomatic office, said that the Annah Plan could not be accepted as a basis for negotiations and it would show "disrespect to the will and judgment of the people" and would be "a doomed procedure from the start."

261. The Athens News Agency, BBC News, online, September 21, 2005.

262. BBC News, online, September 22, 2005.

263. "Turkey and Europe: Too Soon for Turkish Delight," *The Economist*, vol. 377, no. 8446, October 1–7, 2005, pp. 45–46. On October 25, 2005, EU approved the counterstatement to the Turkish unilateral declaration not recognizing the Republic of Cyprus. Turkey is expected to fully implement the customs union protocol for Cyprus, and failure to implement its obligations in full will affect its accession negotiations. On October 27, Erdogan, at the European summit in London, said that unless the economic blockade imposed on TRNC were lifted "whatever the consequences, the [Turkish] ports won't be opened" to Republic of Cyprus. *Zaman*, online, October 28, 2005.

264. *New York Times*, online, *Cyprus Weekly*, online, September 30, 2005.

265. In the commentary "No to Islamist Turkey," Frank J. Gaffney Jr. writes, "Prime Minister Erdogan is systematically turning his country from a Muslim secular democracy into an Islamofacist state governed by an ideology anathema to European values and freedoms." *Washington Times*, September 27, 2005. Turkey is oppose to NATO security arrangement with Cyprus, because Greece and the Greek Cypriot administration block its own security arrangement with EU military planning. "Turkey, Cyprus, and NATO: Fogh in the Agean," *The Economist*, Vol. 392, No. 8648, September 12–18, 2009, p. 57.

266. *Times*, online, September 29, 2005.

267. *Cyprus Mail*, September 29, 2005.

268. *The Times*, online, September 29, 2009.

269. *Milliyet*, online, September 30, 2005.

270. *Times*, online, Turkishpress.com, October 3, 2005.

271. French President Jacques Chirac remarked to the media that Turkey would need a "major Cultural Revolution before joining the EU and reiterated that France would hold a referendum on admitting Ankara to the bloc." Austria also plans to such a vote,

and other bloc members may also hold one. *New York Times, Times,* online, October 4, 2005. Erdogan responded to Chirac's remarks by saying, "We respect the culture of EU countries, but we have our own culture and civilization and they should be respected in the same way.... The basic creeds of the EU include enrichment by bringing together different cultures." Turkishpress.com, October 6, 2005.

272. The Hellenic Radio (ERA), www.ert.gr/, October 3, 2005.

273. For the full text of the EU negotiating framework with Turkey, see http://www. europa.EU.int. The EU's relations with Turkey, October 11, 2005. For the full text, see European Commissions, "Turkey: 2005 Progress Report," Brussels, 9 November 2005, Sec. (2005) 1426 pp. http://europe.eu.int/comm/enlargement/report_2005/. Turkey must recognize and fully implement the customs union protocol with Cyprus in 2006. If Turkey refuses to comply with the EU demands, then its accession negotiations may stop. Turkey is also expected to comply with the judgment of the European Court of Human Rights ruling with the property rights of the Greek Cypriots.

274. *New York Times,* online, June 29, 2005.

275. *New York Times, Today's Zaman,* online, April 5, 2009.

276. BBC News, online, April 6, 2009.

277. "Turkey and Barack Obama: Friends by the Bosporus," *The Economist,* Vol. 391, No. 8626, April 11, 2009, p. 50.

278. *Today's Zaman,* online, June 1, 2009; "Cyprus, Turkey and the European Union: A Mediterranean Maelstrom," *The Economist,* vol. 393, no. 8661, December 12–18, 2009, pp. 56–58. "Turkish support for EU accession fell from 70% in 2004 to 42% in 2008." *Hurriyet,* online, December 15, 2009. In a Eurobarometer survey conducted by the European Commission, 45 percent of the Turks believe that Turkey's membership in the EU is "a good thing," but 50 percent said that it will benefit Turkey as a member—a seven percentage point drop from the previous study.

279. For an in-depth study as to Turkey's EU accession progress, see Ioannis N. Grigoriadis, *Trials of Europeanization: Turkish Political Culture and the European Union* (New York: Palgrave MacMillan, 2009).

280. *Financial Times, Telegraph, New York Times, Today's Zaman,* online, November 21, 2009.

281. Sahin Alpay, "Turkey and the EU: Still Relevant for Each Other," *Today's Zaman,* online, April 30, 2012.

282. *Ankara Anatolia News Agency,* online, July 5, 2009.

283. *Washington Times,* October 29, 2005; *Cyprus Mail,* online, October 30, 2005. See James E. Kapsis, "From Desert Storm to Metal Storm: How Iraq Has Spoiled U.S.-Turkish Relations," *Current History,* vol. 104, no. 685, November 2005, pp. 380–389.

284. *Cyprus Mail,* online, CNN.com, January 25, 2006.

285. *Cyprus Mail,* online, February 9, 2006.

286. *Kathimerini,* online, February 10, 2006. See also "Turkey and Cyprus: Island Trouble," *The Economist,* vol. 378, no. 8462, January 28, 2006, pp. 49–50.

287. The Republic of Cyprus Press and Information Office Server at http://www.pio.gov. cy/, January 26, 2006. Annan offered his support for Turkey's action plan for Cyprus. *Today's Zaman,* online, July 7, 2006.

288. *Cyprus Mail,* online, January 31, 2006.

289. *Cyprus Mail*, online, January 26, 2006.
290. *Cyprus Mail*, online, February 2, 2006.
291. *Cyprus Mail*, online, March 2, 2006.
292. Ibid.
293. *Cyprus Mail*, online, March 7, 2006.
294. *Cyprus Mail*, online, March 25, 2006.
295. Ibid.
296. On March 28, Papadopoulos said, "They are not technical committees but committees on matters of a technical nature." *Cyprus Mail*, online, March 29, 2006.
297. *Cyprus Mail*, online, March 25, 2006.
298. Ibid.
299. **Resolution 1687 (2006)**
    Adopted by the Security Council at its 5465th meeting, on 15 June 2006
    The Security Council,

    Welcoming the report of the Secretary-General of 23 May 2006 (S/2006/315) on the United Nations operation in Cyprus,

    Reiterating its call to the parties to assess and address the humanitarian issue of missing persons with due urgency and seriousness, and welcoming in this regard the resumption of the activities of the Committee on Missing Persons since August 2004, as well as the appointment by the Secretary-General of a Third Member who will assume his duties in July 2006,

    Noting that the Government of Cyprus is agreed that in view of the prevailing conditions in the island it is necessary to keep UNFICYP beyond 15 June 2006,

    Taking note of the assessment of the Secretary-General that the security situation on the island continues to be stable and that the situation along the Green Line remains calm, and expressing the hope that there will be a decrease in the overall number of incidents involving the two sides,

    Urging both sides to avoid any action which could lead to an increase in tension and , in this context, noting with concern sequential developments in the vicinity of Dherinia, the increase in unauthorized construction of building for personal and commercial use in the buffer zone, and developments at certain checkpoints in sector four, including new restriction on UNFICYP's freedom of movement, and encouraging both sides to engage in consultations with UNFICYP on the demarcation of the buffer zone, and to respect UNFICYP's mandate and operation in the buffer zone,

    Regretting that the gap between words and deeds remains too great for the Secretary-General to resume fully his good offices mission and urging progress towards the resumption of negotiations for a comprehensive settlement. In this context welcoming the Secretary-General's efforts to encourage renewed bicommunal contacts, and the agreement to a proposal to establish a mechanism for bicommunal discussions at the technical level, as well as the agreement of both leaders to meet on the occasion of the installation of the Third Member of the Committee on Missing Persons on Cyprus,

    Welcoming progress in demining, particularly in the Nicosia area, and expressing strong support for UNFICYP's efforts to extend demining operations to Turkish Forces minefields in the rest of the buffer zone,

    Welcoming the fact that over 10 million crossings by Greek Cypriots to the north and Turkish Cypriots to the south have taken place peacefully, and encouraging the opening of additional crossing points,

Expressing concern at continued disagreement over construction activity relating to the proposed additional crossing point at Ledra Street and urging both sides to cooperate with UNFICYP to resolve this issue,

Welcoming the emphasis of the Special Representative of the Secretary-General on greater cohesiveness in the efforts of the United Nations family in Cyprus, as well as the Secretary-General's intention to keep the operations of UNFICYP under close review while continuing to take into account development on the ground and the views of the parties, and to revert to the Council with recommendations as appropriate for further adjustments to UNFICYP's mandate, force levels and concept of operation as soon as warranted,

Welcoming all efforts to promote bicommunal contacts and events, including inter alia, on the part of the United Nations, and urging the two sides to promote further bicommunal contacts and to remove any obstacles to such contacts,

Echoing the Secretary-General's gratitude to the Government of Cyprus and the Government of Greece for their voluntary contributions to the funding of UNFICYP, and his request for further voluntary contributions from other countries and organization,

Welcoming and encouraging efforts by the United Nations to sensitize peacekeeping personnel in the prevention and control of HIV/AIDS and other communicable diseases in all its peacekeeping operations,

1. *Reaffirms* all its relevant resolutions on Cyprus, in particular resolution 1251 (1999) of 29 June 1999 and subsequent resolutions;

2. *Expresses* its full support for UNFICYP, including its mandate in the buffer zone, and decides to extend its mandate for a further period ending 15 December 2006;

3. *Calls on* the Turkish Cypriot side and Turkish forces to restore in Strovilia the military status quo which existed there prior to 30 June 2000;

4. *Encourages* active participation in bicommunal discussions at the technical level, under the leadership of the SRSG, and expresses its full support for the latter;

5. *Requests* the Secretary-General to submit a report on implementation of this resolution by 1 December 2006;

6. *Welcomes* the efforts being undertaken by UNFICYP to implement the Secretary-General's zero tolerance policy on sexual exploitation and abuse and to ensure full compliance of its personnel with the United Nations code of conduct, requests the Secretary-General to continue to take all necessary actions in this regard and to keep the Security Council informed, and urges troop-contributing countries to take appropriate preventive action including the conduct of pre-deployment awareness training, and to take disciplinary action and other action to ensure full accountability in cases of such involving their personnel;

7. *Decides* to remain seized of the matter.

300. *Milliyet, Kibris,* online, April 14, 2006.

---

301. *Cyprus Mail, New York Times,* online, April 26, 2006.

302. *Cyprus Mail, Volkan, Kibris,* online May 6, 2006.

303. On May 28, former president Glafaces Clerides, accompanied by his daughter, crossed north for the first time in five years for a dinner with Mehmet Ali Talat in the presidential palace. Clerides's intention was to break the ice and lay the groundwork for a face-to-face talk between Papadopoulos and Talat. *Cyprus Weekly,* online, May 29, 2006.

304. *Kibris,* online, June 9, 2006.

305. BBC news, online, CNN.com, online, June 12, 2006.

306. Reuters. Yahoonews.com, June 13, 2006.

307. Ibid.

308. AFP.Yahoonews.com, June 13, 2006.

309. *Cyprus Mail,* online, June 16, 2006.

310. *Today's Zaman,* online, January 28, 2009.

311. BBC News, online, June 16, 2006.

312. *Cyprus Mail,* online, June 18, 21, 2006.

313. *Kathimerini,* online, June 19, 2006.

314. *Zaman,* online, June 19, 2006.

315. BBC News, *Times,* online, July 3, 2006; *Cyprus Mail,* online, July 5, 2006.

316. A panel of scholars led by Andreas Auer, professor of constitutional law at the University of Geneva, in June 2006 organized a workshop on Cyprus conflict. In early April 2007, the panel met in Nicosia and advocated the establishment of constitutional convention composed of eighty to one hundred members to draft a new constitution for Cyprus to be approved by the Greek and Turkish Cypriot communities. The constitutional convention was to be under the auspices of the European Union and the United Nations. The 1960 Treaty of Establishment giving United Kingdom, Greece, and Turkey the right to maintain forces on the island were to be mollified. *Cyprus Weekly,* April 9, 2007.

Implementing power-sharing agreement may be a strong incentive, but the historical evidence suggests that without effective security, trust, and a willingness to live together, it is unlikely that this government can survive without checks from and outside power. Power-sharing came to an end with a civil war that started in December 1963 and concluded with the Turkish invasion in 1974. The two ethnic combatants partitioned the island *as a result* of the failure of power-sharing deals, and since then, each side has consolidated military power to maintain its own security and reaffirm more leverage for its own benefit. It is not difficult to imagine that Cyprus could be the *casus belli* that ignites a major confrontation between Greece and Turkey. Conflict is not inevitable but peace is a fragile edifice that can easily collapse in the face of self-interest. It should be borne in mind that conceptual as well as empirical studies show definitively large portions of both ethnic groups have already acquiesced to the permanency of a divided island.

317. **Resolution 1728 (2006)**
Adopted by the Security Council at its 5593rd meeting, on 15 December 2006
The Security Council,

Welcoming the report of the Secretary-General of 1 December 2006 (S/2006/931) on the United Nations operation in Cyprus,

Noting that the Government of Cyprus is agreed that in view of prevailing conditions in the island it is necessary to keep UNFICYP beyond 15 December 2006,

Taking note of the assessment of the Secretary-General that the security situation on the island continues to be generally stable and that the situation along the Green Line remains calm, and welcoming the decrease in the overall number of incidents involving the two sides,

Urging both sides to avoid any action which could lead to an increase in tension such as military exercises and, in this context, noting with concern that disagreements have arisen over civilian activities in the buffer zone, including farming and construction, and encouraging both sides to engage in consultations with UNFICYP on the demarcation of the buffer zone, respecting UNFICYP's mandate, and to reach an agreed approach to UNIFCYP's operations in the buffer zone on the basis of the United Nations 1989 aide-memoire,

Expressing its strong appreciation for the work of Under-Secretary-General Gambari in achieving the 8 July agreement and welcoming the principles and decisions enshrined therein, including recognition that status quo is unacceptable and that a comprehensive settlement based on a bicommunal, bizonal federation and political equality, as set out in the relevant Security Council resolutions, is both desirable and possible and should not be further delayed, but noting, with regret, the Secretary-General's assessment that continued lack of trust between the parties has so far prevented the implementation of any of those decisions, underlining the need to implement the 8 July agreement without further delay, and expressing the hope that the recent positive reaction of the leaders of both communities to suggestions by the United Nations will result in the finalization of the preparatory phase as soon as possible in order to prepare the ground for fully-fledged negotiations leading to a comprehensive and durable settlement,

Welcoming continued progress in demining, expressing strong support for UNFICYP's efforts to extend demining operations to Turkish Forces minefields in the rest of the buffer zone, and welcoming the prospect that it could be declared free of mines within two years,

Reiterating its call to the parties to assess and address the humanitarian issue of missing persons with due urgency and seriousness, and welcoming in this regard the resumption of the activities of the committee on Missing Persons since August 2004, and the progress which has since been made, as well as the appointment by the Secretary-General of a third member,

Welcoming the continuing crossings by Greek Cypriots to the north and Turkish Cypriots to the south which have taken place peacefully, and encouraging early progress on other confidence-building measures, such as the opening of additional crossing points, including at Ledra Street,

Welcoming all efforts to promote bicommunal contacts and events, including, inter alia, on the part of the United Nations, and urging the two sides to promote further bicommunal contacts and to remove any obstacles to such contacts,

Expressing concern, in this respect, that opportunities for constructive public debate about the future of the island, within and between the communities, are becoming fewer, and that this atmosphere is hampering, in particular, efforts to foster bicommunal activities intended to benefit Greek Cypriots and Turkish Cypriots, and to promote reconciliation and build trust in order to facilitate a comprehensive settlement,

Noting the primary role of the United Nations in assisting the parties to bring the Cyprus conflict and division of the island to a comprehensive and durable settlement,

Reaffirming the importance of the Secretary-General continuing to keep the operations of UNFICYP under close review while continuing to take into account developments on the ground and the views of the parties, and reverting to the Council with recommendations as appropriate for further adjustments to UNFICYP's mandate, force levels and concept of operation as soon as warranted,

Echoing tithe Secretary-General's gratitude to the Government of Cyprus and the Government of Greece for their voluntary contributions to the funding of UNFICYP, and his request for further voluntary contributions from other countries and organizations,

Welcoming and encouraging efforts by the United Nations to sensitize peacekeeping personnel in the prevention and control of HIV/AIDS and other communicable diseases in all its peacekeeping operations,

1. *Welcomes* the observation in the Secretary-General's report on progress since June , and in particular on developments since 8 July, and expresses appreciation for his personal efforts over the last 10 years, and those of his staff, aimed at achieving a comprehensive solution;

2. *Reaffirms* all its relevant resolutions on Cyprus, in particular resolution 1251 (1999) of 29 June 1999 and subsequent resolutions;

3. *Expresses* its full support for UNFICYP, including its mandate in the buffer zone, and decides to extend its mandate for a further period ending 15 June 2007;

4. *Calls on* the Turkish Cypriot side and Turkish forces to restore in Strovilia the military status quo which existed there prior to 30 June 2000;

5. *Expresses* full support for the process agreed by the leaders, *encourages* active participation in bicommunal discussions as described in Under-Secretary-General Gambari's letter of 15 November 2006, under the auspices of the SRSG, and *calls for* early completion of the preparatory phase so that a fully-fledged good offices process may resume as soon as possible;

6. *Requests* the Secretary-General to submit a report on implementation of this resolution by 1 June 2007;

7. *Welcomes* the efforts being undertaken by UNFICYP to implement the Secretary-General's zero tolerance policy on sexual exploitation and abuse and to ensure full compliance of its personnel with the United Nations code of conduct, request the Secretary-General to continue to take all necessary action in this regard and to keep the Security Council informed, and urges troop-contributing countries to take appropriate preventive action including the conduct of predeployment awareness training, and to take disciplinary

action and other action to ensure full accountability in cases of such conduct involving their personnel;

8. *Decides* to remain seized of the matter.

318. *Cyprus Mail,* online, July 9, 2006.

319. Ibid.

320. Ibid.

321. *Halkin Sesi,* online, July 11, 2006.

322. *Cyprus Mail,* July 16, 2006. U.S. Deputy Assistant Secretary of State Matthew Bryza meeting with Talat in his presidential office on July 18 caused Papadopoulos and Foreign Minister George Lillikas to refuse to receive him. American effort to prod the community leaders to commence twin-track talks laying the groundwork for negotiations towards a settlement was thwarted by Papadopoulos.

323. *Cyprus Mail,* online, April 27, 2007. See the Report of the Secretary-General on the United Nations Operation in Cyprus S/2007/328.

Resolution 1758 (2007)
Adopted by the Security Council at its 5696th meeting, on 15 June 2007
The Security Council,

Welcoming the report of the Secretary-General of 4 June 2007 (S/2007/328) on the United Nations operation in Cyprus,

Noting that the Government of Cyprus is agreed that in view of the prevailing conditions in the island it is necessary to keep UNFICYP beyond 15 June 2007,

Echoing the Secretary-General's firm belief that the responsibility of finding a solution lies first and foremost with the Cypriots themselves and noting the primary role of the United Nations in assisting the parties to bring the Cyprus conflict and division of the island to a comprehensive and durable settlement,

Taking note of the assessment of the Secretary-General that the security situation on the island and along the Green Line remains generally stable, but noting with concern the increase in the overall number of violations of the buffer zone, and urging both sides to avoid any action which could lead to an increase in tension,

Underlining that activity in the buffer zone should not be at the expense of stability and security, and noting the Secretary-General's firm belief that the situation in the buffer zone would be improved if both sides accepted the 1989 aidememoire used by the United Nations,

Welcoming the principles and decisions enshrined in the 8 July 2006 Agreement, stressing that a comprehensive settlement based on a bicommunal, bizonal federation and political equality, as set out in the relevant Security Council resolutions, is both desirable and possible and should not be further delayed,

Noting, with regret, the failure to date to implement the 8 July 2006 Agreement, and urging the leaders of both communities to act to start the process without delay in order to prepare the ground for fully-fledged negotiations leading to a comprehensive and durable settlement,

Regretting that demining activity in the buffer zone has stalled, welcoming the provision by the European Union of funds to support these activities, and urging the Turkish Forces and the Turkish Cypriot side to allow the resumption of demining activities,

Reiterating its call to the parties to assess and address the humanitarian issue of all missing persons with due urgency and seriousness, and welcoming in this regard the progress and continuation of the important activities of the Committee on Missing Persons; expressing the hope that this process will promote reconciliation between the communities,

Welcoming the continuing crossings of the Green Line by Cypriots and encouraging further progress on other confidence-building measures, such as the opening of additional crossing points including, but not limited to, at Ledra Street, taking into account the arrangements already in place at existing crossing points,

Welcoming all efforts to promote bicommunal contacts and events, including, inter alia, on the part of all United Nations bodies on the island urging the two sides to promote the active engagement of civil society and the encouragement of cooperation between economic and commercial bodies and to remove all obstacles to such contacts,

Expressing concern, in this respect, that opportunities for constructive public debate about the future of the island, within and between the communities, are becoming fewer, and that this atmosphere is hampering, in particular, efforts to foster bicommunal activities intended to benefit all Cypriots, and to promote reconciliation and build trust in order to facilitate a comprehensive settlement,

Reaffirming the importance of the Secretary-General continuing to keep the operations of UNFICYP under close review while continuing to take into account developments on the ground and the views of the parties, and reverting to the Council with recommendations as appropriate for further adjustments to UNFICYP's mandate, force levels and concept of operation as soon as warranted,

Noting the unacceptable accommodation conditions endured by many UNFICYP troops, and welcoming the recent commitment by the Republic of Cyprus to address this issue without delay,

Echoing the Secretary-General's gratitude to the Government of Cyprus and the Government of Greece for their voluntary contributions to the funding of UNFICYP, and his request for further voluntary contributions from other countries and organizations,

Welcoming and encouraging efforts by the United Nations to sensitize peacekeeping personnel in the prevention and control of HIV/AIDS and other communicable diseases in all its peacekeeping operations,

1. *Welcomes* the observations in the Secretary-General's report;
2. *Expresses* full support for the 8 July process, notes with concern the lack of progress, and calls upon all parties to immediately engage constructively with the United Nations efforts, as described in Under-Secretary-General Gambari's letter of 15 November 2006, to demonstrate measurable progress in order to allow fully fledged negotiations to begin, and to cease mutual recriminations;
3. *Reaffirms* all its relevant resolutions on Cyprus, in particular resolution 1251 (1999) of 29 June 1999 and subsequent resolutions;
4. *Reaffirms* that the status quo is unacceptable, that time is not on the side of a

settlement, and that negotiations on a final political solution to the Cyprus problem have been at an impasse for too long;

5. *Expresses* its full support for UNFICYP and decides to extend its mandate for a further period ending 15 December 2007;

6. *Calls on* both sides to engage, as a matter of urgency and while respecting UNFICYP's mandate, in consultations with UNFICYP on the demarcation of the buffer zone, in particular in relation to the Ledra Street crossing point, with a view to reaching agreement on the United Nations 1989 aide-memoire;

7. *Calls on* the Turkish Cypriot side and Turkish forces to restore in Strovilia the military status quo which existed there prior to 30 June 2000;

8. *Requests* the Secretary-General to submit a report on implementation of this resolution by 1 December 2007;

9. *Welcomes* the efforts being undertaken by UNFICYP to implement the Secretary-General's zero tolerance policy on sexual exploitation and abuse and to ensure full compliance of its personnel with the United Nations code of conduct, requests the Secretary-General to continue to take all necessary action in this regard and to keep the Security Council informed, and urges troop-contributing countries to take appropriate preventive action including the conduct of predeployment awareness training, and to take disciplinary action and other action to ensure full accountability in cases of such conduct involving their personnel;

10. *Decides* to remain seized of the matter.

324. On November 16, Turkey suspended all military ties with France. BBC News, online, November 16, 2006.

325. *Cyprus Mail*, online, October 18, 2006.

326. "Turkey: Troubles Ahead," *The Economist*, vol. 381, no. 1843, October 21, 2006, p. 59.

327. Turkey's founding father Mustafa Kemal Ataturk "argued passionately that the armed forces should never involve themselves in politics. . . . the military has violated Kemal's principle of noninvolvement in politics for forty years." Ian Bremmer, *The J Curve: A New Way to Understand Why Nations Rise and Fall* (New York: Simon and Schuster, 2006), p. 200. Under the constitution, the military is subordinate to the civilian government, but the Turkish military elite believes that it is the guardian of Kemalist ideology, but not its dictator. Since 1923, the military dismissed four civilian politicians. Ultra-nationalist generals and judges continue to steer Turkey from behind the scenes and have plotted three potential coup d'etat against the Justice and Development Party (AKP) government in 2003 and in 2004. A shadowy group dubbed *Ergenekon* of retired commanders were accused of plotting to overthrow the government in 2008 and prevent the implementation of Annan Plan for the reunification of Cyprus. *Today's Zaman*, online, July 10, 2008; *Sunday Mail*, online, July 13, 2008.

328. *Cyprus Mail*, online, November 21, 2006.

329. *Star*, online November 22, 2006.

330. Reuters, online, November 29, 2006.

331. BBC News, online, November 27, 2006.

332. *Cyprus Mail*, online, December 1, 2006.

333. BBC News, online, November 30, 2006.
334. *New York Times*, online, November 28, 2006. The pope presented an alternative course of action, but "whether Benedict really has overcome his personal doubts about Turkey's EU membership is open to question." "The Pope in Turkey: Tiptoeing Through a Spiritual Minefield," *The Economist*, vol. 381, no. 8506, December 2, 2006, p. 53.
335. *New York Times*, online, November 29, 2006.
336. Ibid.
337. BBC News, online, September 15, 2006; Tom Hundley, "Pope Proves Himself a Diplomat on Trip to Turkey," *Chicago Tribune*, online, December 2, 2006.
338. Reuters, online, *New York Times*, online, December 7, 8, 2006.
339. *Times*, online, *Cyprus Weekly*, online, *Washington Post*, online, *Cyprus Mail*, online, December 8, 2006.
340. *New York Times*, online, December 7, 2006.
341. Cyprus veto blocked Turkey's memberships in the European Defense Agency that forced Ankara to purchase F-35 planes from the United States rather than the Eurofighter's Typhoon plane for $10 billion. *Turkiye*, December 14, 2006.
342. *New York Times*, online, December 30, 2006.
343. *Cyprus Mail, Turkiye*, online, March 8, 2007.
344. BBC News, online, March 29, 2007.
345. *Halkin Sesi*, online, March 4, 2007.
346. *Cyprus Mail*, online, May 30, 2007.
347. *Kibris*, online, October 24, 2007; *Cyprus Mail*, online, *Kathimerine*, online, October 25, 2007.
348. *New York Times*, October 4, 2005. Despite the protest of Turkey, France, a major opponent of Turkish EU membership, signed a bilateral military agreement with Cyprus on February 28, 2007, that involved military training, joint maneuvers, and information sharing. *Cyprus Weekly*, online, March 2, 2007. The French military will have access to the Andreas Papandreou air base near Paphos built by Greece to provide air defense in case of war with Turkey. The military pact gives France a military foothold in the Levant and reaffirms the French foreign policy and military doctrine of an independence from U.S. decision-making. *Cyprus Mail*, online, March 2, 2007; *Washington Times*, March 5, 2007. The Turks contend that the agreement between Cyprus and France is contrary to the February 19, 1959, Treaty of Guarantee.
349. *Aksam*, online, March 28, 2007.
350. *International Herald Tribune*, online, May 24, 2007.
351. BBC News, online, November 17, 2007.
352. *New York Times*, online, January 8, 2008.
353. *New York Times*, online, April 3, 2009.
354. *Today's Zaman, New York Times*, June 9, 2009.
355. Niyazi Berkes, *Turk Dusununde Bati Sorunu (The Western Question in Turkish Thought)* (Ankara: Bilgi Yayinevi, 1975), p. 167.
356. *Cyprus Mail*, online, August 8, 2007.
357. *Milliyet*, online, August 14, 2007.
358. Ankara Anatolia News Agency, online, August 13, 2007; *Cyprus Mail*, August 15, 2007.

359. *Cyprus Mail*, online, August 17, 2007.

360. *Cyprus Mail*, online, November 23, 25, 2008.

361. *Today's Zaman*, online, November 25, 2008.

362. *Hurriyet*, online, August 17, 2007.

363. *Today's Zaman, Kibris*, online, May 29, 2009.

364. *Cyprus Mail, Today's Zaman*, online, May 30, 2009.

365. The Cyprus News Agency, online, June 18, 2009.

366. *Daily Star* (Lebanon), online, March 23, 2012; *Jerusalem Post*, online, April 30, 2012.

367. http://www.dw.de/dw/article/, online, March 27, 2012.

368. Nicos Rolandis, "Proven Right Over Gas, But Will We Get It Right?" *Cyprus Mail*, online, June 13, 2012.

369. Dogu Ergil, "NATO's Near Future," *Today's Zaman*, online, May 30, 2012.

370. *Today's Zaman*, online, July 17, 20, 2009.

371. http://www.aljazeera.com/news/europe/, September 20, 2011.

372. http://www.dw.de/dw/article, March 27, 2012.

373. http://news.yahoo.com/turkish-ship-begins-oil-exploration-off-Cyprus/, March 27, 2012.

374. http://www.huffingtonpost.com/Turkey-Cyprusdrilling/, September 27, 2011.

375. http://www.asianews.it/news-en/Turkey-Israel-Greece-and-Russia-mobilesing-over-Cyprus/, March 27, 2012.

376. The Cyprus News Agency, http://www.cyna.org.cy, May 4, 2012.

377. Ibid.

378. *Today's Zaman*, online, April 26, 2012.

379. *Cyprus Mail*, online, April 27, 2012.

380. *Cyprus Mail*, online, April 27, 2012.

381. *Cyprus Mail*, online, July 14, 2012.

382. In April 2007, General Yasar Buyukanit threatened a coup. "Turkey's Economy: A Cloud No Bigger Than a Hand," *The Economist*, vol. 385, no. 8559, December 15, 2007, p. 64.

383. *Turkish Daily News*, online, September 1, 2007.

384. *New York Times*, online, October 3, 2007.

385. *Middle East Times*, online, September 18, 2007.

386. *Daily Star* (Lebanon), *Cyprus Mail*, online, September 19, 2007.

387. The Cyprus New Agency, online, September 21, 2007.

388. Press Release: United Nations, September 30, 2007.

389. *Cyprus Weekly, Cyprus Mail*, The Cyprus News Agency, online, February 1, 2008.

390. *Kibris*, online, February 1, 2008.

391. *Cyprus Mail*, online, December 5, 2007. For the full text, see the Report of the Secretary-General on the United Nations operation in Cyprus S/2007/699, December 3, 2007, pp. 1–12.

392. **Resolution 1789 (2007)**
   Adopted by the Security Council at its 5803rd meeting, on 14 December 2007
   The Security Council,

   Welcoming the analysis on developments on the ground over the last six months in the report of the Secretary-General of 3 December 2007 (S/2007/699) on the

United Nations operation in Cyprus, in accordance with his mandate, *Noting* that the Government of Cyprus is agreed that in view of the prevailing conditions on the island it is necessary to keep UNFICYP beyond 15 December 2007,

Echoing the Secretary-General's firm belief that the responsibility of finding a solution lies first and foremost with the Cypriots themselves, that the upcoming year offers an important window of opportunity to make decisive progress, which must be grasped by all parties, in the search for a comprehensive solution, and noting the primary role of the United Nations in assisting the parties to bring the Cyprus conflict and division of the island to a comprehensive and durable settlement,

Taking note of the assessment of the Secretary-General that the security situation on the island and along the Green Line remains generally stable, welcoming the decrease in the overall number of incidents involving the two sides, and urging both sides to avoid any action which could lead to an increase in tension, *Underlining* that activity in the buffer zone, in particular proposals for large scale commercial projects, which are not compatible with returning to normal conditions as expressed in the UNFICYP mandate, should not be at the expense of stability and security; *reiterating* the Secretary-General's firm belief that the situation in the buffer zone would be improved if both sides accepted the 1989 aidememoire used by the United Nations,

Welcoming the principles and decisions enshrined in the 8 July 2006 Agreement, stressing that a comprehensive settlement based on a bicommunal, bizonal federation and political equality, as set out in the relevant Security Council resolutions, is both desirable and possible and should not be further delayed,

Deploring the continued failure to date to implement the 8 July 2006 Agreement, and urging the leaders of both communities to act to start the process without delay in order to prepare the ground for fully fledged negotiations leading to a comprehensive and durable settlement,

Welcoming the agreement to allow European Union funds to support demining activities; urging the rapid finalization of the protocol between the relevant parties governing the remaining demining activities in order to complete demining of the buffer zone,

Welcoming the progress and continuation of the important activities of the Committee on Missing Persons; expressing the hope that this process will promote reconciliation between the communities,

Welcoming the proposed confidence-building measures advanced by both sides, as a means of creating greater trust between the two communities and encouraging their early implementation; encouraging also progress on measures such as the opening of additional crossing points including, but not limited to, at Ledra Street, taking into account the arrangements already in place at existing crossing points, and reaffirming the importance of continued crossing of the Green Line by Cypriots,

Welcoming all efforts to promote bicommunal contacts and events, including, inter alia, on the part of all United Nations bodies on the island, urging the two sides to promote the active engagement of civil society and the encouragement of cooperation between economic and commercial bodies and to remove all obstacles to such contacts,

Agreeing that an active and flourishing civil society is essential to the political process and *expressing concern*, in this respect, that opportunities for constructive public debate about the future of the island, within and between the communities, are becoming fewer, and that this atmosphere is hampering, in particular, efforts to foster bicommunal activities intended to benefit all Cypriots, and to promote reconciliation and build trust in order to facilitate a comprehensive settlement,

Reaffirming the importance of the Secretary-General continuing to keep the operations of UNFICYP under close review while continuing to take into account developments on the ground and the views of the parties, and reverting to the Council with recommendations as appropriate for further adjustments to UNFICYP's mandate, force levels and concept of operation as soon as warranted,

Welcoming the steps taken by the Republic of Cyprus to address the living conditions of many UNFICYP troops,

Echoing the Secretary-General's gratitude to the Government of Cyprus and the Government of Greece for their voluntary contributions to the funding of UNFICYP, and his request for further voluntary contributions from other countries and organizations,

Welcoming and encouraging efforts by the United Nations to sensitize peacekeeping personnel in the prevention and control of HIV/AIDS and other communicable diseases in all its peacekeeping operations,

1. *Welcomes* the analysis on developments on the ground over the last six months in the Secretary-General's report, in accordance with his mandate;

2. *Reaffirms* that the status quo is unacceptable, that time is not on the side of a settlement, and that negotiations to reunify the island have been at an impasse for too long;

3. *Expresses* full support for the 8 July process, notes with deep concern the lack of any progress, and calls upon all parties immediately to engage constructively with the United Nations efforts, as described in Under-Secretary-General Gambari's letter of 15 November 2006 and to cease mutual recriminations; *urges* all parties to show flexibility and political will over the coming months to make measurable progress which will allow fully fledged negotiations to begin;

4. *Reaffirms* all its relevant resolutions on Cyprus, in particular resolution 1251 (1999) of 29 June 1999 and subsequent resolutions;

5. *Expresses* its full support for UNFICYP and decides to extend its mandate for a further period ending 15 June 2008;

6. *Calls on* both sides to continue to engage, as a matter of urgency and while respecting UNFICYP's mandate, in consultations with UNFICYP on the demarcation of the buffer zone, in particular in relation to the Ledra Street crossing point, and on the United Nations 1989 aide-memoire, with a view to reaching early agreement on outstanding issues;

7. *Calls on* the Turkish Cypriot side and Turkish forces to restore in Strovilia the military status quo which existed there prior to 30 June 2000;

8. *Requests* the Secretary-General to submit a report on implementation of this resolution by 1 June 2008;

9. *Welcomes* the efforts being undertaken by UNFICYP to implement the

Secretary-General's zero tolerance policy on sexual exploitation and abuse and to ensure full compliance of its personnel with the United Nations code of conduct, requests the Secretary-General to continue to take all necessary action in this regard and to keep the Security Council informed, and urges troop-contributing countries to take appropriate preventive action including the conduct of predeployment awareness training, and to take disciplinary action and other action to ensure full accountability in cases of such conduct involving their personnel;

10. *Decides* to remain seized of the matter.

393. *Cyprus Mail*, online September 6, 2007.

394. Ibid.

395. *Cyprus Mail*, 2008.

396. *Cyprus Mail*, BBC News, *Turkiye*, online, *Halkin Sesi*, online, January 23, 2008.

397. Dimitris Christofias has been an active member of the communist party AKEL (the Progressive Party of the Working People of Cyprus) since the age of fourteen. He studied at the Institute of Social Sciences and the Academy of Social Sciences in Moscow from 1969 to 1974 and graduated with a degree of doctor of philosophy. In April 1988, he was elected general secretary of the Central Committee of AKEL, and in January 2009, he was succeeded by Andros Kyprianou.

398. *Cyprus Mail*, online, February 8, 2008.

399. *Cyprus Mail*, online, February 18, 2008.

400. *Cyprus Mail*, online, February 21, 2008.

401. *Cyprus Mail*, online, February 25, 2008.

402. *Cyprus Weekly* online, February 25, 2008.

403. Ibid.

404. Ibid.

405. John Paul Lederach, *Preparing for Peace: Conflict Transformation Across Cultures* (New York: Syracuse University Press, 1995), p. 212.

406. Norbert Ropers, "From Resolution to Transformation: Assessing the Role and Impact of Dialogue Projects," in Andreas Wimmer, et al., (ed.), *Facing Ethnic Conflicts: Toward a New Realism*, op. cit., p. 181.

407. Turkish TV Channel NTV, March 26, 2008.

408. *Bayrak Television*, February 27, 2008.

409. Michael Moller was replaced on March 29, 2008, by Canadian, Elizabeth Spehar as the UN secretary-general's special representative in Cyprus on an interim basis. Moller served in Cyprus from 2006 to 2009, but failed to gain the Turkish trust. *Cyprus Mail*, online, March 27, 2008. Taye-Brook Zerihoun of Ethiopia replaced Elizabeth Spehar on May 8 as the special representative of the secretary-general in Cyprus and head of UNFICYP. *Today's Zaman*, online, May 12, 2008.

410. Georgios Kyriakou Iacovou served as foreign minister of Cyprus from September 1983 to 1988 and from 1988 to 1993 and for a third term from 2003 to June 2006. He served as the Greek Cypriot high commissioner to the United Kingdom from 2006 to 2008.

411. *Cyprus Mail*, BBC News, *Halkin Sesi*, online, March 21, 2008.

412. *Cyprus Mail*, *Cyprus Weekly*, online, May 3, 2008.

413. During the EOKA terrorism against the British colonialism in the 1950s, several British

soldiers were shot dead and Ledra Street earned the moniker "Murder Mile." Nikos Sampson, who participated in Athens-engineered coup against Makarios in 1974, and served as the eight-day president, as a twenty-five-year-old photojournalist, was suspected of killing three British soldiers on Murder Mile in 1956 and photographed their dead bodies for print in the Greek Cypriot newspapers.

414. *Cyprus Mail, Today's Zaman*, online, June 17, 2008.

415. Markos Kyprianou studied law at the University of Athens, Cambridge University, and Harvard Law School. He was elected to the House of Representatives for the Nicosia District in 1991, 1996, and 2001, and he is a member of the Democratic Party. He served as minister of Finance from March 1, 2003, to April 30, 2004. Kyprianou was a member of the European Commission from May 1, 2004, until his appointment as minister of foreign affairs in 2008 by President Dimitris Christofias. He is the younger son of Spyros Kyprianou, who was president of Cyprus from 1977 to 1988.

416. The Athens New Agency, online, April 22, 2008

417. *Cyprus Mail*, online, May 13, 2008.

418. Lynn M. Wagner, *Problem-Solving and Bargaining in International Negotiations* (Leiden, The Netherlands: Martinus Nijhoff publishers, 2008), p.3.

419. The Cyprus News Agency, htpp://www.cyna.org.cy; *Today's Zaman*, online, May 23, 2008; *Cyprus Mail*, online, May 24, 2008.

420. *Cyprus Mail*, online, May 25, 2008.

421. *Cyprus Mail, Today's Zaman*, online, June 7, 2008; *Halkin Sesi*, online, June 8, 2008.

422. **Resolution 1818 (2008)**
Adopted by the Security Council at its 5911th meeting, on 13 June 2008
The Security Council,

Welcoming the report of the Secretary-General of 2 June 2008 (S/2008/353) on the United Nations operation in Cyprus,

Noting that the Government of Cyprus is agreed that in view of the prevailing conditions on the island it is necessary to keep UNFICYP beyond 15 June 2008,

Echoing the Secretary-General's firm belief that the responsibility of finding a solution lies first and foremost with the Cypriots themselves, that there now exists an important window of opportunity to make decisive progress which must be fully utilized by all parties in the search for a comprehensive solution, and *noting* the primary role of the United Nations in assisting the parties to bring the Cyprus conflict and division of the island to a comprehensive and durable settlement,

Welcoming the agreement of 21 March and the Joint Statement of 23 May 2008 which, inter alia, have demonstrated a renewed political willingness to support and engage fully and in good faith with the United Nations efforts, reaffirmed the commitment of the leaders to a bicommunal, bizonal federation with political equality, as set out in the relevant Security Council resolutions, and to consider further civilian and military confidence-building measures,

Welcoming the opening of the Ledra Street crossing which has helped foster greater trust and interaction between the two communities; *reaffirming* the importance of continued crossings of the Green Line by Cypriots, and *encouraging* the opening of other crossing points,

Welcoming the intention of the Secretary-General to appoint a Special Adviser at the appropriate time and to keep the Council informed of further developments and progress,

Taking note of the assessment of the Secretary-General that the security situation on the island and along the Green Line remains generally stable, welcoming the decrease in the overall number of incidents involving the two sides, and urging both sides to avoid any action, including restrictions on UNFICYP's movements, which could lead to an increase in tension,

Welcoming the coordination arrangements agreed with the United Nations to address unauthorized construction within the buffer zone, including large-scale commercial projects, and *echoing* the Secretary-General's firm belief that the situation in the buffer zone would be improved if both sides accepted the 1989 aidememoire used by the United Nations,

Welcoming the agreement with the Turkish forces to proceed with demining activities, but *urging* that further guidelines be agreed to permit such activities to take place in all outstanding minefields; *noting with concern* that funding for the Mine Action Centre beyond 2008 has not yet been secured but that this work will need to continue beyond that period,

Welcoming the progress and continuation of the important activities of the Committee on Missing Persons; expressing the hope that this process will promote reconciliation between the communities,

Agreeing that an active and flourishing civil society is essential to the political process and *welcoming* all efforts to promote bicommunal contacts and events, including, inter alia, on the part of all United Nations bodies on the island, and *urging* the two sides to promote the active engagement of civil society and the encouragement of cooperation between economic and commercial bodies and to remove all obstacles to such contacts,

Reaffirming the importance of the Secretary-General continuing to keep the operations of UNFICYP under close review while continuing to take into account developments on the ground and the views of the parties, and reverting to the Council with recommendations as appropriate for further adjustments to UNFICYP's mandate, force levels and concept of operation as soon as warranted,

Welcoming the appointment of Tayé-Brook Zerihoun as the Secretary-General's new Special Representative to Cyprus, and *echoing* the Secretary-General's appreciation for the work of the previous Special Representative, Michael Moller,

Echoing also the Secretary-General's gratitude to the Government of Cyprus and the Government of Greece for their voluntary contributions to the funding of UNFICYP, and his request for further voluntary contributions from other countries and organizations,

Welcoming and encouraging efforts by the United Nations to sensitize peacekeeping personnel in the prevention and control of HIV/AIDS and other communicable diseases in all its peacekeeping operations,

1. *Welcomes* the analysis of developments on the ground over the last six months in the Secretary-General's report;

2. *Urges* the parties to build on the present momentum and continue their efforts to identify to the greatest possible extent areas of convergence and

disagreement, while preparing options where feasible on the more sensitive elements, and to work to ensure that fully fledged negotiations can begin expeditiously and smoothly, in line with the agreement of 21 March and the Joint Statement of 23 May;

3. *Reaffirms* all its relevant resolutions on Cyprus, in particular resolution 1251 (1999) of 29 June 1999 and subsequent resolutions;

4. *Expresses* its full support for UNFICYP and decides to extend its mandate for a further period ending 15 December 2008;

5. *Calls on* both sides to continue to engage, as a matter of urgency and while respecting UNFICYP's mandate, in consultations with UNFICYP on the demarcation of the buffer zone, and on the United Nations 1989 aide-memoire, with a view to reaching early agreement on outstanding issues;

6. *Calls on* the Turkish Cypriot side and Turkish forces to restore in Strovilia the military status quo which existed there prior to 30 June 2000;

7. *Requests* the Secretary-General to submit a report on implementation of this resolution by 1 December 2008 and to keep the Security Council updated on events as necessary;

8. *Welcomes* the efforts being undertaken by UNFICYP to implement the Secretary-General's zero tolerance policy on sexual exploitation and abuse and to ensure full compliance of its personnel with the United Nations code of conduct, requests the Secretary-General to continue to take all necessary action in this regard and to keep the Security Council informed, and urges troop-contributing countries to take appropriate preventive action including the conduct of pre-deployment awareness training, and to take disciplinary action and other action to ensure full accountability in cases of such conduct involving their personnel;

9. *Decides* to remain seized of the matter.

423. *Cyprus Mail*, online, June 15, 2008.
424. Ibid.
425. *Cyprus Mail, Kibris, Hurriyet,* online, June 18, 2007.
426. *Cyprus Weekly*, online, June 19, 2008.
427. *Cyprus Mail, Today's Zaman*, online, July 2, 2008.
428. *Kibris*, online, July 2, 2008; *Turkish Daily News*, online, July 7, 2008.
429. *Cyprus Mail, Kibris, Hurriyet, Cyprus Weekly, Volkan,* online, July 4, 2008.
430. *Cyprus Mail, Hurriyet*, online, July 19, 20, 2008.
431. *Turkiye,* online, July 21, 2008.
432. Ibid. *Turkish Daily News*, online, July 21, 2008.
433. *Cyprus Mail, Turkish Dailey News, Today's Zaman*, online, July 26, 2008.
434. *Cyprus Mail*, online, August 30, 2008.
435. *Cyprus Mail*, online August 21, 2008.
436. *Cyprus Mail*, online, December 25, 2009.
437. *Cyprus Weekly*, online, August 22, 2008.
438. The Cyprus News Agency, http://www.org.cy, August 26, 2008.
439. South Ossetia, comprising an area of about 2,418 square miles, wants to join ethnic Ossetians in North Ossetia, which has been under Russian control since 1767. In

---

1921, the Soviet Union created the South Ossetian Autonomous Oblast (district), but in 1990, the Georgian government abolished South Ossetia's autonomy. The military confrontation between Georgians and Ossetians stopped with the ceasefire agreement in 1992. Georgian offer of autonomy to South Ossetia was rejected, and in an unofficial referendum in 2006, it pursued independence. Georgian attempt to bring South Ossetia and Abkhazia under its control by resort to arms in 2008 provided Russia the opportunity to reassert its authority in the region and paved the way for annexation. Ossetia and Abkhazia signed a military, diplomatic, and economic cooperation treaties on September 17, 2008, with Russia, which commits Moscow to defend the two states from any Georgian attack. Only Nicaragua has followed Russia's lead in recognizing the two separatist regions from Georgia on August 26. *New York Times*, September 17, 2008.

440. *New York Times, Cyprus Mail, Cyprus Weekly*, online, September 4, 2008.

441. *Today's Zaman*, online, September 11, 12, 2008; BBC News, online, September 11, 2008.

442. *Hurriyet*, online, October 1, 2008; *Cyprus Mail*, online, October 2, 2008.

443. Ibid., TurkishPress.com, online, October 1, 2008.

444. The Athens News Agency, http://www.ana.gr, October 1, 2008.

445. *Cyprus Mail, Kibris, Hurriyet, Today's Zaman, Cyprus Weekly*, online, September 19, 2008.

446. *Kibris*, online October 6, 2008.

447. *Cyprus Mail*, online, October 3, 2008.

448. The Elders Group consisting of former Algerian foreign minister Lakhdar Brahimi and former Norwegian foreign minister Gro Brundtland visited Cyprus on September 9, 2009, to reiterate their support to ongoing Cyprus peace talks. They met separately with President Christofias and President Talat. The Elders Group also held meetings in Ankara and Athens. *Cyprus Mail*, online, September 11, 2009. The group of Elders, Tutu, Brahimi, and Carter returned to Cyprus for the third time on December 8–10, 2009, to support UN-backed peace talks. *Cyprus Mail,* online, December 9, 2009.

449. *Cyprus Mail, Today's Zaman*, online, October 15, 2008.

450. *Today's Zaman*, online, October 20, 2008.

451. *Today's Zaman*, online, December 7, 2008.

452. *Cyprus Weekly, Cyprus Mail*, online, October 31, 2008. According to a survey, 61 percent of Greek Cypriots had no hope of a Cyprus settlement. *Cyprus Mail*, online, December 20, 2009.

453. *Cyprus Mail, Cyprus Weekly*, online, February 21, 2009.

454. *Cyprus Mail*, online, February 20, 2009.

455. *Cyprus Mail*, online, November 15, 21, 2008.

456. **Resolution 1847 (2008)**
Adopted by the Security Council at its 6038th meeting, on 12 December 2008
The Security Council,

Welcoming the report of the Secretary-General of 28 November 2008 (S/2008/744) on the United Nations operation in Cyprus,

Noting that the Government of Cyprus is agreed that in view of the prevailing

———

conditions on the island it is necessary to keep the United Nations Peacekeeping force in Cyprus (UNFICYP) beyond 15 December 2008,

Echoing the Secretary-General's firm belief that the responsibility for finding a solution lies first and foremost with the Cypriots themselves, *stressing* that there now exists an unprecedented opportunity to make decisive progress, and *reaffirming* the primary role of the United Nations in assisting the parties to bring the Cyprus conflict and division of the island to a comprehensive and durable settlement,

Welcoming the launch of fully fledged negotiations on 3 September 2008, the progress made so far, and the leaders' joint statements,

Emphasizing the importance of all parties engaging fully, flexibly and constructively in those negotiations, in order to make decisive progress towards a comprehensive settlement based on a bicommunal, bizonal federation with political equality, as set out in the relevant Security Council resolutions,

Encouraging continued momentum in negotiations and the maintenance of goodwill and trust, *looking forward* to substantive progress and the full exploitation of the current opportunity, *commending* the Greek and Turkish Cypriot leaders for the political leadership they have shown so far, *and welcoming* the intention of the Secretary-General to keep the Council informed of further development and progress,

Welcoming the announcement of confidence building measures and the cancellation of military exercises, and *looking forward* to the implementation of these measures and agreement on and implementation of further steps to build trust between the communities,

Reaffirming the importance of continued crossings of the Green Line by Cypriots, *reiterating* its welcome for the opening of the Ledra Street crossing, *encouraging* the opening by mutual agreement of other crossing points, and *noting* in this context the commitment in the leaders' joint statements to pursue the opening of the Limnitis/**Yeşilirmak** crossing point,

Convinced of the many important benefits for all Cypriots that would flow from a comprehensive and durable Cyprus settlement, and *encouraging* both sides clearly to explain these benefits, as well as the need for flexibility in order to secure them, to both communities well in advance of any eventual referenda,

Highlighting the supportive role the international community will continue to play in helping the Greek and Turkish Cypriot leaders to exploit fully the current opportunity,

Taking note of the assessment of the Secretary-General that the security situation on the island and along the Green Line remains generally stable, *welcoming* the decrease in the overall number of incidents involving the two sides and *urging* both sides to avoid any action, including restrictions on UNFICYP's movements, which could lead to an increase in tension, undermine the good progress achieved so far, or damage the goodwill on the island,

Recalling the Secretary-General's firm belief that the situation in the buffer zone would be improved if both sides accepted the 1989 aide memoire used by the United Nations,

Welcoming the progress made in proceeding with demining activities, *echoing* the Secretary's General's call for the remaining minefields to be cleared, *and noting with*

concern that funding is urgently required by the Mine Action Centre beyond 2008 to allow this work to continue beyond that period,

Welcoming the progress and continuation of the important activities of the Committee on Missing Persons, and *trusting* that this process will promote reconciliation between the communities,

Agreeing that an active and flourishing civil society is essential to the political process, *welcoming* all efforts to promote bicommunal contacts and events including, inter alia, on the part of all United Nations bodies on the island, and *urging* the two sides to promote the active engagement of civil society and the encouragement of cooperation between economic and commercial bodies and to remove all obstacles to such contacts,

Reaffirming the importance of the Secretary-General continuing to keep the operations of UNFICYP under close review while continuing to take into account developments on the ground and the views of the parties, and reverting to the Council with recommendations as appropriate for further adjustments to UNFICYP's mandate, force levels and concept of operation as soon as warranted,

Welcoming the appointment of Alexander Downer as the Secretary-General's Special Advisor with a mandate to assist the parties in the conduct of fully-fledged negotiations aimed at reaching a comprehensive settlement,

Echoing also the Secretary-General's gratitude to the Government of Cyprus and the Government of Greece for their voluntary contributions to the funding of UNFICYP, and his request for further voluntary contributions from other countries and organizations,

Welcoming and encouraging efforts by the United Nations to sensitize peacekeeping personnel in the prevention and control of HIV/AIDS and other communicable diseases in all its peacekeeping operations,

1. *Welcomes* the analysis of developments on the ground over the last six months in the Secretary-General's report, in accordance with his mandate;

2. *Welcomes* also the launch of fully fledged negotiations on 3 September 2008, and the prospect of a comprehensive and durable settlement that this has created;

3. *Urges* full exploitation of this opportunity, including by intensifying the momentum of negotiations, preserving the current atmosphere of trust and goodwill, and engaging in the process in a constructive and open manner;

4. *Welcomes* the announcement on confidence-building measures and the cancellation of military exercises, and *looks forward* to these measures being fully implemented as well as to agreement on further such steps, including the possible opening of other crossing points, as mentioned in the leaders' joint statements;

5. *Reaffirms* all its relevant resolutions on Cyprus, in particular resolution 1251 (1999) of 29 June 1999 and subsequent resolutions;

6. *Expresses* its full support for UNFICYP and *decides* to extend its mandate for a further period ending 15 June 2009;

7. *Calls on* both sides to continue to engage, as a matter of urgency and while respecting UNFICYP's mandate, in consultations with UNFICYP on

the demarcation of the buffer zone, and on the United Nations 1989 aide-memoire, with a view to reaching early agreement on outstanding issues;

8. *Calls on* the Turkish Cypriot side and Turkish forces to restore in Strovilia the military status quo which existed there prior to 30 June 2000;

9. *Requests* the Secretary-General to submit a report on implementation of this resolution by 1 June 2009 and to keep the Security Council updated on events as necessary;

10. *Welcomes* the efforts being undertaken by UNFICYP to implement the Secretary-General's zero tolerance policy on sexual exploitation and abuse and to ensure full compliance of its personnel with the United Nations code of conduct, *requests* the Secretary-General to continue to take all necessary action in this regard and to keep the Security Council informed, and *urges* troop-contributing countries to take appropriate preventive action including the conduct of predeployment awareness training, and to take disciplinary action and other action to ensure full accountability in cases of such conduct involving their personnel;

11. *Decides* to remain seized of the matter.

457. *Cyprus Weekly*, online, February 13, 2009; *Cyprus Mail*, online, February 15, 2009.
458. *Wall Street Journal, Cyprus Mail, Hurriyet*, online, April 30, 2009.
459. Ankara Anatolia News Agency, online, May 15, 2009.
460. *Cyprus Mail*, online, March 6, 2010.
461. *Today's Zaman*, online, March 6, 2010.
462. Hermes Solomon, "A Sort of Closure: The Long Saga of a Greek Cypriot Refugee Who Sought Compensation from the Immovable Property Commission Is Finally Over," *Cyprus Mail*, online, June 24, 2012. *Kibris*, online, July 16, 2012. For an in-depth study of the property issue, see Murat Metin Hakki, "Property Wars in Cyprus: The Turkish Position According to the International Law," *Turkish Studies*, vol. 12, no. 1, 79–90, March 2011. 79–91 pp.
463. *Today's Zaman*, online, March 8, 2010.
464. The Cyprus News Agency, online, March 18, 2010.
465. *Cyprus Mail, Haberdar, Kibris*, online, July 12, 2012.
466. *Today's Zaman*, online, February 7, 2009.
467. *Bayrak Television*, February 8, 2009.
468. *Bayrak Television*, February 6, 2009.
469. *Cyprus Mail*, online, March 1, 2009.
470. Ibid.
471. Ibid.
472. *Hurriyet*, online, March 4, 2009.
473. *Cyprus mail*, online, March 1, 2009.
474. See the article by Mehmet Ali Talat, "Cyprus Should Not Miss What May Be the Last Chance for Unification and a Common Future," *Turkish Policy Quarterly*, vol. 7, no. 3, Fall 2008, pp. 11–17; see *Today's Zaman*, online, March 9, 2009; and *Cyprus Mail*, online, March 22, 2009.
475. *Cyprus Mail*, online, March 15, 2009.
476. *Today's Zaman, Cyprus Weekly, Hurriyet, Kibris*, online, July 13, 2009.

---

477. *Phileleftheros, Simerini,* July 15, 2009. According to Cypriot press reports, EU was ready to promote Taiwan-style state in the northern Cyprus incase the peace talks failed. The Cyprus News Agency, online, July 12, 2009.
478. *Hurriyet,* Ankara Anatolia News Agency, *Today's Zaman, Kibris,* online, April 28, 2010.
479. *Hurriyet,* online, April 21, 22, 2009; *Today's Zaman,* BBC News, online, April 19, 2009; *The Economist,* online, April 25, 2009; Dervis Eroglu—elections, "Divided Cyprus: A Hawkish Problem," *The Economist,* vol. 391, no. 8628, April 25, 2009, pp. 56–57.
480. *Cyprus Mail,* online, April 22, 2009.
481. *Hurriyet,* online, April 20, 2009.
482. *Today's Zaman, Hurriyet,* online, April 22, 2009.
483. *Today's Zaman,* online, April 19, 2009.
484. *Haberdar,* online, May 17, 2012.
485. *Cyprus Mail,* online, April 26, 2009.
486. *Cyprus Mail,* online, May 7, 2009.
487. Jasper Mortimer, "Where to Now for Turkey and the Talks?" *Cyprus Mail,* online, May 11, 2010. Turkey is funding a pipeline project and construction at a cost of $650 million to bring drinking water by underwater pipeline from Anamar Alakopru Dam in southern province of Turkey to northern Cyprus. The 80-kilometer (48-mile) pipeline will be suspended at a water depth of minimum 250M and will provide 75 million cubic meters of water per year and the project will be completed by March 7, 2014. Turkey's Alakopru Dam started in 2011 on the Dragon River in Anamur, and after its completion, it will have the capacity to store 130.5 million cubic meters of water. The water will be transferred by underwater pipeline to Gecitkoy Dam near Girne (Kyrenia) in TRNC. The Gecitkoy Dam, built after the 1974 crisis, will be expanded to increase the water capacity of the dam to 26 million cubic meters. *Hurriyet,* online, March 23, 31, 2012. The water will provide the arid island with enough water for both Cypriot communities. But the Greek Cypriots declared that they will only accept water if the island is reunited. During the 2008 drought, the Greek Cypriot government forked out 50 million euros to ship in water by tanker from Greece. The south for their drinking and irrigation water depends on a series of desalinization plants, which is expensive and environmentally destructive. The idea of a water pipeline idea dates back to 1986, the period of Prime Minister Turgut Ozal. The previous plans to float drinking water in containers holding 10,000 cubic meters from Turkey to northern Cyprus had to be abandoned after the balloon containers kept bursting.
488. **Resolution 1873 (2009)**

Adopted by the Security Council at its 6132nd meeting, on 29 May 2009

The Security Council,

Welcoming the report of the Secretary-General of 15 May 2009 (S/2009/248) on the United Nations operation in Cyprus,

Noting that the Government of Cyprus is agreed that in view of the prevailing conditions on the island it is necessary to keep the United Nations Peacekeeping force in Cyprus (UNFICYP) beyond 15 June 2009,

Echoing the Secretary-General's firm belief that the responsibility for finding a solution lies first and foremost with the Cypriots themselves, *stressing* that there now exists a rare opportunity to make decisive progress, and *reaffirming* the primary role of the United Nations in assisting the parties to bring the Cyprus conflict and division of the island to a comprehensive and durable settlement,

Commending the Greek Cypriot and Turkish Cypriot leaders for the political leadership they have shown, and warmly *welcoming* the progress made so far in the fully fledged negotiations, and the leaders' joint statements,

Strongly urging the leaders to increase the momentum in the negotiations to ensure the full exploitation of this opportunity to reach a comprehensive settlement based on a bicommunal, bizonal federation with political equality, as set out in the relevant Security Council resolutions,

Emphasizing the importance attached by the international community of all parties engaging fully, flexibly and constructively in the negotiations, and looking forward to decisive progress in those negotiations in the near future,

Welcoming the intention of the Secretary-General to keep the Council informed of further development and progress,

Welcoming also the implementation of some of the confidence-building measures announced by the leaders, and *calling for* a renewed effort to implement the remaining measures and for agreement on and implementation of further steps to build trust between the communities,

Reaffirming the importance of continued crossings of the Green Line by Cypriots, *encouraging* the opening by mutual agreement of other crossing points, *noting* the commitment in the leaders' joint statements to pursue the opening of the Limnitis/ Yesilirmak crossing point, *encouraging* implementation of the commitment to a second phase of the restoration of the Ledra Street crossing, and *urging* in this context the leaders to make every effort to implement those measures,

Convinced of the many important benefits for all Cypriots that would flow from a comprehensive and durable Cyprus settlement, and *encouraging* both sides clearly to explain these benefits, as well as the need for increased flexibility and compromise in order to secure them, to both communities well in advance of any eventual referenda,

Highlighting the supportive role the international community will continue to play in helping the Greek Cypriot and Turkish Cypriot leaders to exploit fully the current opportunity,

Taking note of the assessment of the Secretary-General that the security situation on the island and along the Green Line remains stable, *welcoming* the decrease in the overall number of incidents involving the two sides and *urging* all sides to avoid any action, including restrictions on UNFICYP's movements as noted in the Secretary-General's report (S/2009/248), which could lead to an increase in tension, undermine the good progress achieved so far, or damage the goodwill on the island,

Recalling the Secretary-General's firm belief that the situation in the buffer zone would be improved if both sides accepted the 1989 aide-memoire used by the United Nations,

Welcoming the progress made in proceeding with demining activities, and *looking forward* to the clearance of the remaining minefields,

Welcoming the progress and continuation of the important activities of the

Committee on Missing Persons, *echoing* the Secretary-General's call for every possible action to be taken to speed up the exhumation process, and *trusting* that this process will promote reconciliation between the communities,

Agreeing that active participation of civil society groups is essential to the political process and can contribute to making any future settlement sustainable,

Welcoming all efforts to promote bicommunal contacts and events including, inter alia, on the part of all United Nations bodies on the island, and *urging* the two sides to promote the active engagement of civil society and the encouragement of cooperation between economic and commercial bodies and to remove all obstacles to such contacts,

Stressing the need for the Council to pursue a rigorous, strategic approach to peacekeeping deployments,

Welcoming the intention of the Secretary-General to keep all peacekeeping operations, including those of UNFICYP, under close review and *noting* the importance of contingency planning in relation to the settlement, including recommendations as appropriate for further adjustments to UNFICYP's mandate, force levels and concept of operations, taking into account developments on the ground and the views of the parties,

Welcoming the continued efforts of Alexander Downer as the Secretary-General's Special Adviser with a mandate to assist the parties in the conduct of fully fledged negotiations aimed at reaching a comprehensive settlement,

Echoing also the Secretary-General's gratitude to the Government of Cyprus and the Government of Greece for their voluntary contributions to the funding of UNFICYP, and his request for further voluntary contributions from other countries and organizations,

Welcoming and encouraging efforts by the United Nations to sensitize peacekeeping personnel in the prevention and control of HIV/AIDS and other communicable diseases in all its peacekeeping operations,

1. *Welcomes* the analysis of developments on the ground over the last six months in the Secretary-General's report, in accordance with his mandate;

2. *Welcomes* also the progress made so far in the fully fledged negotiations, and the prospect of further progress in the near future towards a comprehensive and durable settlement that this has created;

3. *Urges* full exploitation of this opportunity, including by intensifying the momentum of negotiations, improving the current atmosphere of trust and goodwill, and engaging in the process in a constructive and open manner;

4. *Urges* also the implementation of confidence-building measures, and *looks forward* to agreement on and implementation of further such steps, including the opening of other crossing points;

5. *Reaffirms* all its relevant resolutions on Cyprus, in particular resolution 1251 (1999) of 29 June 1999 and subsequent resolutions;

6. *Expresses* its full support for UNFICYP and *decides* to extend its mandate for a further period ending 15 December 2009;

7. *Calls* on both sides to continue to engage, as a matter of urgency and while respecting UNFICYP's mandate, in consultations with UNFICYP on

the demarcation of the buffer zone, and on the United Nations 1989 aide-memoire, with a view to reaching early agreement on outstanding issues;

8. *Calls* on the Turkish Cypriot side and Turkish forces to restore in Strovilia the military status quo which existed there prior to 30 June 2000;

9. *Requests* the Secretary-General to submit a report on implementation of this resolution, including on contingency planning in relation to the settlement, by 1 December 2009 and to keep the Security Council updated on events as necessary;

10. *Welcomes* the efforts being undertaken by UNFICYP to implement the Secretary-General's zero tolerance policy on sexual exploitation and abuse and to ensure full compliance of its personnel with the United Nations code of conduct, *requests* the Secretary-General to continue to take all necessary action in this regard and to keep the Security Council informed, and *urges* troop-contributing countries to take appropriate preventive action including the conduct of predeployment awareness training, and to take disciplinary action and other action to ensure full accountability in cases of such conduct involving their personnel;

11. *Decides* to remain seized of the matter.

489. Ibid.

490. Ibid.

491. *Cyprus Mail*, online, June 13, 2009.

492. *Cyprus Mail, Cyprus Weekly, Today's Zaman*, online, June 26, 27, 2009.

493. The reunification talks scheduled for September 3, 2009, were postponed by Christofias because of a row of over 650 Greek Cypriot pilgrimage to the Church of Ayios Mamas in Morphou in the north. The Turkish Cypriot administration identity card checks at the Limnitis checkpoint caused delays and ultimately culminated in a decision by the Greek Cypriot passengers to return to the south in protest rather than comply with orders of the Turkish Cypriot police. The actual reason for the postponement was Turkish Foreign Minister Ahmet Davutoglu's warning to the Greek Cypriots during his visit to northern Cyprus on September 1 that Turkey will never allow the "assimilation" of the Turkish Cypriots by the Greek Cypriot administration and the status quo will not continue in the event of failure to reach a resolution to the Cyprus problem. *Cyprus Mail, Today's Zaman*, online, September 3, 2009.

494. Since 1974, the two ethnic groups in Cyprus have extended citizenship to people from abroad in order to boost their number demographically. The Greek Cypriot administration has permitted 40,000 Pontic Greeks from Russia and thousands of Greeks from Greece to settle in Cyprus. In addition, due to the Lebanese civil war in the 1980s, about 20,000 Lebanese have settled in the south. The Turkish Cypriot administration in the north allowed over 115,000 Turks from Anatolia to settle in the island. *Hurriyet*, online, August 3, 2009.

495. *Cyprus Mail*, online, September 19, 2009.

496. Ibid.

497. *Kibris*, online, January 7, 2010; *Havadis, Hurritet*, online, January 8, 2010.

498. *Hurriyet*, online, January 17, 2010.

499. *Cyprus Mail, New York Times*, online, February 1, 2010.

500. *Cyprus Mail*, online, February 3, 2010.
501. The Cyprus News Agency, online, July 19, 2009.
502. *Today's Zaman*, online, July 20, 2009.
503. *Today's Zaman*, online, July 19, 2009.
504. *Kibris*, online, July 17, 2009.
505. The European Court of Justice (ECJ) in April 2009 ruled that Meletis Apostolides could enforce the Greek Cypriot court ruling against the Orams (David and Linda Oram are British citizens) in the United Kingdom. *Cyprus Mail*, online, May 5, 2009. The British High Court of Appeal on January 19, 2010, ruled that the decision of the Greek Cypriot courts with regard to legal rights against individuals using their property in northern Cyprus could be enforced in the UK. The Orams, who had built a holiday villa on the Greek Cypriot property, were ordered to comply with the Cyprus court orders and return the land belonging to Meletis Apostolides, pay rent for the period they were using the land, demolish the villa, and pay the legal fees. The court ruling is a fatal blow to Talat's reelection bid in April 2010, but it boosted the campaign for the presidency of Eroglu who supports the two-state solution. *Cyprus Mail*, online, January 20, 2010. Cyprus problem will not be solved by resort to legal means but by a comprehensive political resolution.
506. *Hurriyet*, online, July 20, 2009.
507. For the full text of European Parliamen Resolution of 10 February 2010, on Turkey's progress report 2009, http://www.europerl.en/sides/getDoc. p. 5. See also *Today's Zaman, Cyprus Mail, Hurriyet*, online, February 11, 2010.
508. *Today's Zaman*, online, February 12, 2010.
509. Ibid.
510. *Hurriyet, Today's Zaman*, online, February 11, 2010.
511. *Cyprus Mail, Cyprus Weekly*, online, February 9, 2010.
512. *Cyprus Mail*, online, February 10, 2010.
513. *Cyprus Mail*, online, July 28, 2009.
514. FinancialTimes.com, online, December 19, 2009.
515. SETimes.com, online, December 9, 2009. "Cyprus, Turkey and the European Union: A Mediterranean Malestrom," *The Economist*, vol. 393, no. 8661, December 12–18, 2009, pp. 56–58.
516. *Cyprus Mail, Today's Zaman, Hurriyet*, online, November 27, 2009.
517. EurActiv.com, online, November 18, 2009.
518. *Hurriyet*, online, June 19, 2012; *Milliyet*, online, June 18, 2012; BBC News, online, March 23, 2012.
519. **Resolution 550 (1984)**
Adopted 11 May 1984
The Security Council,
   Having considered the situation in Cyprus at the request of the Government of the Republic of Cyprus,
   Having heard the statement made by the President of the Republic of Cyprus,
   Taking note of the report of the Secretary-General,
   Recalling its resolutions 365 (1974), 367 (1975), 541 (1983), and 544 (1983),

---

Deeply regretting the non-implementation of its resolutions, in particular resolution 541(1983),

Gravely concerned about the further secessionist acts in the occupied part of the Republic of Cyprus which are in violation of Resolution 541 (1983), namely, the purported exchange of ambassadors between Turkey and the legally invalid "Turkish Republic of Northern Cyprus" and the contemplated holding of a "constitutional referendum" and "elections," as well as by other actions or threats of actions aimed at further consolidating the purported independent State and the division of Cyprus,

Deeply concerned about recent threats for settlement of Varosha by people other than its inhabitants,

Reaffirming its continuing support for the United Nations Peace-keeping Force in Cyprus,

1. *Reaffirms* its resolution 541 (1983) and calls for its urgent and effective implementation;

2. *Condemns* all secessionist actions, including the purported exchange of ambassadors between Turkey and the Turkish Cypriot leadership, declares them illegal and invalid and calls for their immediate withdrawal;

3. *Reiterates* the call upon all States not to recognize the purported State of the "Turkish Republic of Northern Cyprus" set up by secessionist acts and calls upon them not to facilitate or in any way assist the aforesaid secessionist entity;

4. *Calls upon* all States to respect the sovereignty, independence, territorial integrity, unity and non-alignment of the Republic of Cyprus;

5. *Considers* attempts to settle any part of Varosha by people other than its inhabitants as inadmissible and calls for the transfer of that area to the administration of the United Nations;

6. *Considers* any attempts to interfere with the status of the deployment of the United Nations Peacekeeping Force in Cyprus as contrary to the resolutions of the United Nations;

7. *Requests* the Secretary-General to promote the urgent implementation of Security Council resolution 541 (1983);

8. *Reaffirms* the mandate of good offices given to the Secretary-General and requests him to undertake new efforts to attain an overall solution to the Cyprus problem in conformity with the principles of the Charter of the United Nations and the provisions for such a settlement laid down in the pertinent United Nations resolutions, including resolution 541 (1983) and the present resolution;

9. *Calls upon* all parties to co-operate with the Secretary-General in his mission of good offices;

10. *Decides* to remain seized of the situations with a view to taking urgent and appropriate measures, in the event of non-implementation of resolution 541 (1983) and the present resolution;

11. *Requests* the Secretary-General to promote the implementation of the present resolution and to report thereon to the Security Council as developments require.

520. *Cyprus Mail, Today's Zaman,* online, June 18, 2012; *Sabah,* online, June 13, 2012.
521. *Bayrak Television,* online, March 7, 2012.
522. **Resolution 1898 (2009)**

Adopted by the Security Council at its 6239th meeting, on 14 December 2009

The Security Council,

Welcoming the reports of the Secretary-General of 25 November 2009 (S/2009/609) on the United Nations operation in Cyprus and of 30 November 2009 (S/2009/610) on his mission of good offices in Cyprus,

Noting that the Government of Cyprus is agreed that in view of the prevailing conditions on the island it is necessary to keep the United Nations Peacekeeping force in Cyprus (UNFICYP) beyond 15 December 2009,

Echoing the Secretary-General's firm belief that the responsibility for finding a solution lies first and foremost with the Cypriots themselves, *stressing* that there now exists a rare opportunity to make decisive progress in a timely fashion, and *reaffirming* the primary role of the United Nations in assisting the parties to bring the Cyprus conflict and division of the island to a comprehensive and durable settlement,

Commending the Greek Cypriot and Turkish Cypriot leaders for the political leadership they have shown, and warmly *welcoming* the progress made so far in the fully-fledged negotiations, and the leaders' joint statements,

Strongly urging the leaders to increase the momentum in the negotiations to ensure the full exploitation of this opportunity to reach a comprehensive settlement based on a bicommunal, bizonal federation with political equality, as set out in the relevant Security Council resolutions,

Emphasizing the importance attached by the international community of all parties engaging fully, flexibly and constructively in the negotiations, and *looking forward* to decisive progress in those negotiations in the near future,

Welcoming the intention of the Secretary-General to keep the Council informed of further developments and progress,

Welcoming also the implementation of some of the confidence-building measures announced by the leaders, and *calling* for a renewed effort to implement the remaining measures and for agreement on and implementation of further steps to build trust between the communities,

Reaffirming the importance of continued crossings of the Green Line by Cypriots, *encouraging* the opening by mutual agreement of other crossing points, *welcoming* the leaders' agreement to open the Limnitis/Yesilirmak crossing point and the successful first trial crossing of ambulances from both sides, and *urging* implementation of the second phase of the restoration of the Ledra Street crossing,

Convinced of the many important benefits for all Cypriots that would flow from a comprehensive and durable Cyprus settlement, and *encouraging* both sides clearly to explain these benefits, as well as the need for increased flexibility and compromise in order to secure them, to both communities well in advance of any eventual referenda,

Highlighting the supportive role the international community will continue to play in helping the Greek Cypriot and Turkish Cypriot leaders to exploit fully the current opportunity,

Taking note of the assessment of the Secretary-General that the security situation on the island and along the Green Line remains stable, and *urging* all sides to avoid any action which could lead to an increase in tension, undermine the good progress achieved so far, or damage the goodwill on the island,

Recalling the Secretary-General's firm belief that the situation in the buffer zone would be improved if both sides accepted the 1989 aide-memoire used by the United Nations,

Welcoming the progress made in proceeding with demining activities, *looking forward* to the clearance of the remaining minefields, and *regretting* the tragic loss of life on 28 October of a civilian contractor working for the Mine Action Centre,

Welcoming the progress and continuation of the important activities of the Committee on Missing Persons, and *trusting* that this process will promote reconciliation between the communities,

Agreeing that active participation of civil society groups is essential to the political process and can contribute to making any future settlement sustainable, *welcoming* all efforts to promote bicommunal contacts and events including, inter alia, on the part of all United Nations bodies on the island, and *urging* the two sides to promote the active engagement of civil society and the encouragement of cooperation between economic and commercial bodies and to remove all obstacles to such contacts,

Stressing the need for the Council to pursue a rigorous, strategic approach to peacekeeping deployments,

Welcoming the intention of the Secretary-General to keep all peacekeeping operations, including those of UNFICYP, under close review and noting the importance of contingency planning in relation to the settlement, including recommendations as appropriate for further adjustments to UNFICYP's mandate, force levels and concept of operations, taking into account developments on the ground and the views of the parties,

Welcoming the continued efforts of Alexander Downer as the Secretary-General's Special Advisor with a mandate to assist the parties in the conduct of fully-fledged negotiations aimed at reaching a comprehensive settlement,

Echoing also the Secretary-General's gratitude to the Government of Cyprus and the Government of Greece for their voluntary contributions to the funding of UNFICYP, and his request for further voluntary contributions from other countries and organizations,

Welcoming and encouraging efforts by the United Nations to sensitize peacekeeping personnel in the prevention and control of HIV/AIDS and other communicable diseases in all its peacekeeping operations,

1. *Welcomes* the analysis of developments on the ground over the last six months in the Secretary-General's reports, in accordance with his mandate;

2. *Welcomes* also the progress made so far in the fully fledged negotiations, and the prospect of further progress in the near future towards a comprehensive and durable settlement that this has created;

3. *Urges* full exploitation of this opportunity, including by intensifying the momentum of negotiations, improving the current atmosphere of trust and goodwill, and engaging in the process in a constructive and open manner;

4. *Urges also* the implementation of confidence-building measures, and *looks forward* to agreement on and implementation of further such steps, including the opening of other crossing points;

5. *Reaffirms* all its relevant resolutions on Cyprus, in particular resolution 1251 (1999) of 29 June 1999 and subsequent resolutions;

6. *Expresses* its full support for UNFICYP and decides to extend its mandate for a further period ending 15 June 2010;

7. *Calls* on both sides to continue to engage, as a matter of urgency and while respecting UNFICYP's mandate, in consultations with UNFICYP on the demarcation of the buffer zone, and on the United Nations 1989 aide-memoire, with a view to reaching early agreement on outstanding issues;

8. *Calls* on the Turkish Cypriot side and Turkish forces to restore in Strovilia the military status quo which existed there prior to 30 June 2000;

9. *Requests* the Secretary-General to submit a report on implementation of this resolution, including on contingency planning in relation to the settlement, by 1 June 2010 and to keep the Security Council updated on events as necessary;

10. *Welcomes* the efforts being undertaken by UNFICYP to implement the Secretary-General's zero-tolerance policy on sexual exploitation and abuse and to ensure full compliance of its personnel with the United Nations code of conduct, requests the Secretary-General to continue to take all necessary action in this regard and to keep the Security Council informed, and urges troop-contributing countries to take appropriate preventive action including the conduct of predeployment awareness training, and to take disciplinary action and other action to ensure full accountability in cases of such conduct involving their personnel;

11. *Decides* to remain seized of the matter.

523. **Resolution 1930 (2010)**
Adopted by the Security Council at its 6339th meeting, on 15 June 2010
The Security Council,

Welcoming the reports of the Secretary-General of 28 May 2010 (S/2010/264) on the United Nations operation in Cyprus and of 11 May 2010 (S/2010/238) on his mission of good offices in Cyprus,

Noting that the Government of Cyprus is agreed that in view of the prevailing conditions on the island it is necessary to keep the United Nations Peacekeeping Force in Cyprus (UNFICYP) beyond 15 June 2010,

Echoing the Secretary-General's firm belief that the responsibility for finding a solution lies first and foremost with the Cypriots themselves, *stressing* that there now exists a unique opportunity to make decisive progress in a timely fashion, and *reaffirming* the primary role of the United Nations in assisting the parties to bring the Cyprus conflict and division of the island to a comprehensive and durable settlement,

Commending the political leadership shown by the Greek Cypriot and Turkish Cypriot leaders, and warmly *welcoming* the progress made so far in the fully fledged negotiations, and the leaders' joint statements including those of 23 May and 1 July 2008,

Strongly urging the leaders to increase the momentum in the negotiations to ensure the full exploitation of this opportunity to reach a comprehensive settlement based on a bicommunal, bizonal federation with political equality, as set out in the relevant Security Council resolutions,

Emphasizing the importance attached by the international community of all parties engaging fully, flexibly and constructively in the negotiations, echoing the Secretary-General's view that a solution is well within reach, and *looking forward* to decisive progress in the near future building on the progress made to date consistent with the hope expressed by the two sides on 21 December 2009 that, if possible, 2010 would be the year of solution,

Welcoming the intention of the Secretary General to keep the Council informed of further developments and progress, and *noting* the Secretary-General's intention to submit a report in November 2010 on the state of the process,

Welcoming also the implementation of some of the confidence-building measures announced by the leaders, and *calling for* a renewed effort to implement the remaining measures and for agreement on and implementation of further steps to build trust between the communities,

Reaffirming the importance of continued crossings of the Green Line by Cypriots, *encouraging* the opening by mutual agreement of other crossing points, *welcoming* the continuing construction work towards opening the Limnitis/Yesilirmak crossing point and *urging* implementation of the second phase of the restoration of the Ledra Street crossing,

Convinced of the many important benefits for all Cypriots that would flow from a comprehensive and durable Cyprus settlement, and *encouraging* both sides clearly to explain these benefits, as well as the need for increased flexibility and compromise in order to secure them, to both communities well in advance of any eventual referenda,

Highlighting the supportive role the international community will continue to play in helping the Greek Cypriot and Turkish Cypriot leaders to exploit fully the current opportunity,

Taking note of the assessment of the Secretary-General that the security situation on the island and along the Green Line remains stable, and *urging* all sides to avoid any action which could lead to an increase in tension, undermine the good progress achieved so far, or damage the goodwill on the island,

Recalling the Secretary-General's firm belief that the situation in the buffer zone would be improved if both sides accepted the 1989 aide memoire used by the United Nations,

Welcoming the progress made in proceeding with demining activities, and *looking forward* to the clearance of the remaining minefields, *Welcoming* the progress and continuation of the important activities of the Committee on Missing Persons, and *trusting* that this process will promote reconciliation between the communities,

Agreeing that active participation of civil society groups is essential to the political process and can contribute to making any future settlement sustainable, *welcoming* all efforts to promote bicommunal contacts and events including, inter alia, on the part of all United Nations bodies on the island, and *urging* the two sides to promote the active engagement of civil society and the encouragement of cooperation between economic and commercial bodies and to remove all obstacles to such contacts,

Stressing the need for the Council to pursue a rigorous, strategic approach to peacekeeping deployments,

Welcoming the intention of the Secretary-General to keep all peacekeeping operations, including those of UNFICYP, under close review and *noting* the importance of contingency planning in relation to the settlement, including recommendations as appropriate for further adjustments to UNFICYP's mandate, force levels and concept of operations, taking into account developments on the ground and the views of the parties,

Welcoming the continued efforts of Alexander Downer as the Secretary- General's Special Advisor with a mandate to assist the parties in the conduct of fully-fledged negotiations aimed at reaching a comprehensive settlement, *expressing* appreciation for the work of Tayé Brook Zerihoun as the Secretary-General's Special Representative, and *welcoming* the appointment of Lisa Buttenheim as the Secretary-General's new Special Representative,

Echoing also the Secretary-General's gratitude to the Government of Cyprus and the Government of Greece for their voluntary contributions to the funding of UNFICYP, and his request for further voluntary contributions from other countries and organizations,

Welcoming and encouraging efforts by the United Nations to sensitize peacekeeping personnel in the prevention and control of HIV/AIDS and other communicable diseases in all its peacekeeping operations,

1. *Welcomes* the analysis of developments on the ground over the last six months in the Secretary-General's reports, in accordance with his mandate;
2. *Welcomes also* the progress made so far in the fully fledged negotiations, and the prospect of further progress in the near future towards a comprehensive and durable settlement that this has created;
3. *Urges* full exploitation of this opportunity, including by intensifying the momentum of negotiations, preserving the current atmosphere of trust and goodwill, and engaging in the process in a constructive and open manner;
4. *Urges* also the implementation of confidence-building measures, and *looks forward* to agreement on and implementation of further such steps, including the opening of other crossing points;
5. *Reaffirms* all its relevant resolutions on Cyprus, in particular resolution 1251 (1999) of 29 June 1999 and subsequent resolutions;
6. *Expresses* its full support for UNFICYP and *decides* to extend its mandate for a further period ending 15 December 2010;
7. *Calls* on both sides to continue to engage, as a matter of urgency and while respecting UNFICYP's mandate, in consultations with UNFICYP on the demarcation of the buffer zone, and on the United Nations 1989 aide-memoire, with a view to reaching early agreement on outstanding issues;
8. *Calls* on the Turkish Cypriot side and Turkish forces to restore in Strovilia the military status quo which existed there prior to 30 June 2000;
9. *Requests* the Secretary-General to submit a report on implementation of this

resolution, including on contingency planning in relation to the settlement, by 1 December 2010 and to keep the Security Council updated on events as necessary;

10. *Welcomes* the efforts being undertaken by UNFICYP to implement the Secretary-General's zero tolerance policy on sexual exploitation and abuse and to ensure full compliance of its personnel with the United Nations code of conduct, *requests* the Secretary-General to continue to take all necessary action in this regard and to keep the Security Council informed, and *urges* troop-contributing countries to take appropriate preventive action including the conduct of pre-deployment awareness training, and to take disciplinary action and other action to ensure full accountability in cases of such conduct involving their personnel;

11. *Decides* to remain seized of the matter.

524. **Resolution 1953 (2010)**

Adopted by the Security Council at its 6445th meeting, on 14 December 2010

The Security Council,

Welcoming the reports of the Secretary-General of 29 November 2010 (S/2010/605) on the United Nations operation in Cyprus and of 24 November 2010 (S/2010/603) on his mission of good offices in Cyprus,

Noting that the Government of Cyprus is agreed that in view of the prevailing conditions on the island it is necessary to keep the United Nations Peacekeeping Force in Cyprus (UNFICYP) beyond 15 December 2010,

Echoing the Secretary-General's firm belief that the responsibility for finding a solution lies first and foremost with the Cypriots themselves, and *reaffirming* the primary role of the United Nations in assisting the parties to bring the Cyprus conflict and division of the island to a comprehensive and durable settlement,

Welcoming the progress made so far in the fully fledged negotiations, and the leaders' joint statements including those of 23 May and 1 July 2008,

Expressing concern at the slow pace of progress in recent months, *stressing* that the status quo is unsustainable and that there now exists a unique opportunity to make decisive progress in a timely fashion, and *strongly urging* the leaders to increase the momentum in the negotiations to ensure the full exploitation of this opportunity to reach an enduring, comprehensive and just settlement based on a bicommunal, bizonal federation with political equality, as set out in the relevant Security Council resolutions,

Emphasizing the importance attached by the international community of all parties engaging fully, flexibly and constructively in the negotiations, echoing the Secretary-General's view that a solution is well within reach, and *looking forward* to decisive progress in the near future building on the progress made to date,

Welcoming the efforts of the Secretary-General to stimulate progress during his meeting with the two leaders on 18 November 2010, his intention to meet with the two leaders in January 2011, and *noting* his intention to submit to the Security Council in February 2011 an updated assessment on the state of the process,

Welcoming also the implementation of some of the confidence-building measures announced by the leaders, and *calling for* a renewed effort to implement the remaining measures and for agreement on and implementation of further steps to build trust between the communities,

Reaffirming the importance of continued crossings of the Green Line by Cypriots, *welcoming* the opening of the Limnitis/Yesilirmak crossing point in October 2010, and *encouraging* the opening by mutual agreement of other crossing points,

Convinced of the many important benefits for all Cypriots that would flow from a comprehensive and durable Cyprus settlement, *urging* the two sides and their leaders to foster positive public rhetoric, and *encouraging* them clearly to explain the benefits of the settlement, as well as the need for increased flexibility and compromise in order to secure it, to both communities well in advance of any eventual referenda,

Considering that undermining the UN's credibility undermines the peace process itself,

Highlighting the supportive role the international community will continue to play in helping the Greek Cypriot and Turkish Cypriot leaders to exploit fully the current opportunity,

Taking note of the assessment of the Secretary-General that the security situation on the island and along the Green Line remains stable, and *urging* all sides to avoid any action which could lead to an increase in tension, undermine the progress achieved so far, or damage the goodwill on the island,

Recalling the Secretary-General's firm belief that the situation in the buffer zone would be improved if both sides accepted the 1989 aide memoire used by the United Nations,

Welcoming the progress made in proceeding with demining activities, *looking forward* to the clearance of the remaining minefields, and *urging* agreement on extension of demining operations to other remaining areas,

Welcoming also the progress and continuation of the important activities of the Committee on Missing Persons, and *trusting* that this process will promote reconciliation between the communities,

Agreeing that active participation of civil society groups is essential to the political process and can contribute to making any future settlement sustainable, *welcoming* all efforts to promote bicommunal contacts and events including, inter alia, on the part of all United Nations bodies on the island, and *urging* the two sides to promote the active engagement of civil society and the encouragement of cooperation between economic and commercial bodies and to remove all obstacles to such contacts,

Stressing the need for the Council to pursue a rigorous, strategic approach to peacekeeping deployments,

Welcoming the intention of the Secretary-General to keep all peacekeeping operations, including those of UNFICYP, under close review and *noting* the importance of contingency planning in relation to the settlement, including recommendations as appropriate for further adjustments to UNFICYP's mandate, force levels and concept of operations, taking into account developments on the ground and the views of the parties,

Welcoming also the continued efforts of Alexander Downer as the Secretary-General's Special Advisor with a mandate to assist the parties in the conduct of fully-fledged negotiations aimed at reaching a comprehensive settlement, and the efforts of Lisa Buttenheim as the Secretary-General's Special Representative,

Echoing the Secretary-General's gratitude to the Government of Cyprus and the Government of Greece for their voluntary contributions to the funding of UNFICYP, and his request for further voluntary contributions from other countries and organizations, and *expressing* appreciation to member states that contribute personnel to UNFICYP,

Welcoming and *encouraging* efforts by the United Nations to sensitize peacekeeping personnel in the prevention and control of HIV/AIDS and other communicable diseases in all its peacekeeping operations,

1. *Welcomes* the progress made so far in the fully fledged negotiations, and the prospect of further progress in the near future towards a comprehensive and durable settlement that this has created;

2. *Takes note* of the recommendations of the report of the Secretary-General (S/2010/603) and *calls upon* the two leaders to:

   a) intensify the momentum of negotiations, and engage in the process in a constructive and open manner, including by developing a practical plan for overcoming the major remaining points of disagreement in preparation for their meeting with the Secretary-General in January 2011;

   b) improve the public atmosphere in which the negotiations are proceeding, including by focussing public messages on convergences and the way ahead, and delivering more constructive and harmonised messages; and

   c) increase the participation of civil society in the process as appropriate;

3. *Urges* the implementation of confidence-building measures, and *looks forward* to agreement on and implementation of further such steps, including the opening of other crossing points;

4. *Reaffirms* all its relevant resolutions on Cyprus, in particular resolution 1251 (1999) of 29 June 1999 and subsequent resolutions;

5. *Expresses* its full support for UNFICYP and *decides* to extend its mandate for a further period ending 15 June 2011;

6. *Calls* on both sides to continue to engage, as a matter of urgency and while respecting UNFICYP's mandate, in consultations with UNFICYP on the demarcation of the buffer zone, and on the United Nations 1989 aide-memoire, with a view to reaching early agreement on outstanding issues;

7. *Calls* on the Turkish Cypriot side and Turkish forces to restore in Strovilia the military status quo which existed there prior to 30 June 2000;

8. *Requests* the Secretary-General to submit a report on implementation of this resolution, including on contingency planning in relation to the settlement, by 1 June 2011 and to keep the Security Council updated on events as necessary;

9. *Welcomes* the efforts being undertaken by UNFICYP to implement the Secretary-General's zero tolerance policy on sexual exploitation and abuse and to ensure full compliance of its personnel with the United Nations code

of conduct, *requests* the Secretary-General to continue to take all necessary action in this regard and to keep the Security Council informed, and *urges* troop-contributing countries to take appropriate preventive action including the conduct of pre-deployment awareness training, and to take disciplinary action and other action to ensure full accountability in cases of such conduct involving their personnel;

10. *Decides* to remain seized of the matter.

525. **Resolution 1986 (2011)**
Adopted by the Security Council at its 6554th meeting, on 13 June 2011
The Security Council,

Welcoming the reports of the Secretary-General of 31 May 2011 (S/2011/332) on the United Nations operation in Cyprus and of 4 March 2011 (S/2011/112) on his mission of good offices in Cyprus,

Noting that the Government of Cyprus is agreed that in view of the prevailing conditions on the island it is necessary to keep the United Nations Peacekeeping Force in Cyprus (UNFICYP) beyond 15 June 2011,

Echoing the Secretary-General's firm belief that the responsibility for finding a solution lies first and foremost with the Cypriots themselves, and *reaffirming* the primary role of the United Nations in assisting the parties to bring the Cyprus conflict and division of the island to a comprehensive and durable settlement,

Welcoming the progress made so far in the fully fledged negotiations, and the leaders' joint statements including those of 23 May and 1 July 2008,

Expressing concern at the continued slow pace of progress, *stressing* that the status quo is unsustainable and *strongly urging* the leaders to increase the momentum in the negotiations, particularly on the core issues, to reach an enduring, comprehensive and just settlement based on a bicommunal, bizonal federation with political equality, as set out in the relevant Security Council resolutions,

Emphasizing the importance attached by the international community of all parties engaging fully, flexibly and constructively in the negotiations, echoing the Secretary-General's view that a solution is well within reach, and *looking forward* to decisive progress in the near future, including leading up to the Secretary General's meeting with the leaders in July 2011, building on the progress made to date,

Welcoming the efforts of the Secretary-General to stimulate progress during his meeting with the two leaders on 26 January 2011, his intention to meet with the two leaders in July 2011, and *noting* his intention to submit to the Security Council in July 2011 an updated assessment on the state of the process,

Noting the need to advance the consideration of and discussions on military confidence building measures, *calling for* renewed efforts to implement all remaining confidence building measures, and for agreement on and implementation of further steps to build trust between the communities,

Reaffirming the importance of continued crossings of the Green Line by Cypriots, and encouraging the opening by mutual agreement of other crossing points,

Convinced of the many important benefits for all Cypriots that would flow from a comprehensive and durable Cyprus settlement, *urging* the two sides and their leaders to foster positive public rhetoric, and *encouraging* them clearly to explain the benefits

---

of the settlement, as well as the need for increased flexibility and compromise in order to secure it, to both communities well in advance of any eventual referenda,

Considering that undermining the United Nations credibility undermines the peace process itself,

Highlighting the supportive role the international community will continue to play in helping the Greek Cypriot and Turkish Cypriot leaders to exploit fully the current opportunity,

Taking note of the assessment of the Secretary-General that the security situation on the island and along the Green Line remains stable, and *urging* all sides to avoid any action which could lead to an increase in tension, undermine the progress achieved so far, or damage the goodwill on the island,

Recalling the Secretary-General's firm belief that the situation in the buffer zone would be improved if both sides accepted the 1989 aide memoire used by the United Nations,

Noting with regret that the sides are withholding access to the remaining minefields in the buffer zone, and that demining in Cyprus has ceased as a result, noting the continued danger posed by mines in Cyprus, and *urging* rapid agreement on facilitating the recommencement of demining operations and clearance of the remaining minefields,

Welcoming the progress and continuation of the important activities of the Committee on Missing Persons, and *trusting* that this process will promote reconciliation between the communities,

Agreeing that active participation of civil society groups is essential to the political process and can contribute to making any future settlement sustainable, *welcoming* all efforts to promote bicommunal contacts and events including, inter alia, on the part of all United Nations bodies on the island, and *urging* the two sides to promote the active engagement of civil society and the encouragement of cooperation between economic and commercial bodies and to remove all obstacles to such contacts,

Stressing the need for the Council to pursue a rigorous, strategic approach to peacekeeping deployments,

Welcoming the intention of the Secretary-General to keep all peacekeeping operations, including those of UNFICYP, under close review and *noting* the importance of contingency planning in relation to the settlement, including recommendations as appropriate for further adjustments to UNFICYP's mandate, force levels and concept of operations, taking into account developments on the ground and the views of the parties,

Welcoming also the continued efforts of Alexander Downer as the Secretary-General's Special Advisor with a mandate to assist the parties in the conduct of fully-fledged negotiations aimed at reaching a comprehensive settlement, and the efforts of Lisa Buttenheim as the Secretary-General's Special Representative,

Echoing the Secretary-General's gratitude to the Government of Cyprus and the Government of Greece for their voluntary contributions to the funding of UNFICYP, and his request for further voluntary contributions from other countries and organizations, and expressing appreciation to member states that contribute personnel to UNFICYP,

Welcoming and *encouraging* efforts by the United Nations to sensitize peacekeeping personnel in the prevention and control of HIV/AIDS and other communicable diseases in all its peacekeeping operations,

1. *Welcomes* the progress made so far in the fully fledged negotiations, and the prospect of further progress in the near future towards a comprehensive and durable settlement that this has created;

2. *Takes note* of the report of the Secretary-General (S/2011/112);

3. *Recalls* Security Council resolution 1953 (2010), and *calls upon* the two leaders to:

    a) intensify the momentum of negotiations, engage in the process in a constructive and open manner, and work on reaching convergences on the remaining core issues in preparation for their meeting with the Secretary-General in July 2011;

    b) improve the public atmosphere in which the negotiations are proceeding, including by focussing public messages on convergences and the way ahead, and delivering more constructive and harmonised messages; and

    c) increase the participation of civil society in the process as appropriate;

4. *Urges* the implementation of confidence-building measures, and *looks forward* to agreement on and implementation of further such steps, including military confidence building measures and the opening of other crossing points;

5. *Urges* all parties to be more forthcoming in accommodating the Committee for Missing Persons exhumation requirements throughout the island including in military areas in the north;

6. *Reaffirms* all its relevant resolutions on Cyprus, in particular resolution 1251 (1999) of 29 June 1999 and subsequent resolutions;

7. *Expresses* its full support for UNFICYP and *decides* to extend its mandate for a further period ending 15 December 2011;

8. *Calls* on both sides to continue to engage, as a matter of urgency and while respecting UNFICYP's mandate, in consultations with UNFICYP on the demarcation of the buffer zone, and on the United Nations 1989 aide-memoire, with a view to reaching early agreement on outstanding issues;

9. *Calls* on the Turkish Cypriot side and Turkish forces to restore in Strovilia the military status quo which existed there prior to 30 June 2000;

10. *Calls* on both sides to allow access to deminers and to facilitate the removal of the remaining mines in Cyprus within the buffer zone, and *urges* both sides to extend demining operations outside the buffer zone;

11. *Requests* the Secretary-General to submit a report on implementation of this resolution, including on contingency planning in relation to the settlement, by 1 December 2011 and to keep the Security Council updated on events as necessary;

12. *Welcomes* the efforts being undertaken by UNFICYP to implement the Secretary-General's zero tolerance policy on sexual exploitation and abuse and to ensure full compliance of its personnel with the United Nations code of conduct, *requests* the Secretary-General to continue to take all necessary

action in this regard and to keep the Security Council informed, and *urges* troop-contributing countries to take appropriate preventive action including the conduct of pre-deployment awareness training, and to take disciplinary action and other action to ensure full accountability in cases of such conduct involving their personnel;

13. *Decides* to remain seized of the matter.

526. **Resolution 2026 (2011)**
Adopted by the Security Council at its 6685th meeting, on 14 December 2011
The Security Council,

Welcoming the report of the Secretary-General of 30 November 2011 (S/2011/746) on the United Nations operation in Cyprus,

Noting that the Government of Cyprus is agreed that in view of the prevailing conditions on the island it is necessary to keep the United Nations Peacekeeping Force in Cyprus (UNFICYP) beyond 15 December 2011,

Echoing the Secretary-General's firm belief that the responsibility for finding a solution lies first and foremost with the Cypriots themselves, and *reaffirming* the primary role of the United Nations in assisting the parties to bring the Cyprus conflict and division of the island to a comprehensive and durable settlement,

Welcoming the progress made so far in the fully fledged negotiations, and the leaders' joint statements including those of 23 May and 1 July 2008,

Welcoming the move towards a more intensive phase of negotiations, *stressing* that the status quo is unsustainable and *strongly urging* the leaders to increase the momentum in the negotiations, particularly on the core issues, to reach an enduring, comprehensive and just settlement based on a bicommunal, bizonal federation with political equality, as set out in the relevant Security Council resolutions,

Emphasizing the importance attached by the international community of all parties engaging fully, flexibly and constructively in the negotiations, *echoing* the Secretary-General's view that a comprehensive settlement can be achieved, *looking forward* to decisive progress in the near future, leading up to the Secretary-General's meeting with the leaders in January 2012, and *echoing* the Secretary-General's expectation that "all internal aspects of a settlement will have been resolved by then so that we can move to a multilateral conference shortly thereafter" with the consent of the two sides,

Welcoming the efforts of the Secretary-General to stimulate progress during his meeting with the two leaders on 31 October 2011, his intention to meet with the two leaders in January 2012, and *noting* his intention to submit to the Security Council in January 2012 an updated assessment on the state of the process,

Noting the need to advance the consideration of and discussions on military confidence building measures, *calling for* renewed efforts to implement all remaining confidence building measures, and for agreement on and implementation of further steps to build trust between the communities,

Reaffirming the importance of continued crossings of the Green Line by Cypriots, and encouraging the opening by mutual agreement of other crossing points,

Convinced of the many important benefits for all Cypriots that would flow from a comprehensive and durable Cyprus settlement, *urging* the two sides and their leaders to foster positive public rhetoric, and *encouraging* them clearly to explain the benefits of the settlement, as well as the need for increased flexibility and compromise in order to secure it, to both communities well in advance of any eventual referenda,

Considering that undermining the UN's credibility undermines the peace process itself,

Highlighting the importance of the supporting role of the international community, and in particular that of the parties concerned in taking practical steps towards helping the Greek Cypriot and Turkish Cypriot leaders to exploit fully the current opportunity,

Taking note of the assessment of the Secretary-General that the security situation on the island and along the Green Line remains stable, and *urging* all sides to avoid any action which could lead to an increase in tension, undermine the progress achieved so far, or damage the goodwill on the island,

Recalling the Secretary-General's firm belief that the situation in the buffer zone would be improved if both sides accepted the 1989 aide memoire used by the United Nations,

Noting with regret that the sides are withholding access to the remaining minefields in the buffer zone, and that demining in Cyprus has ceased as a result, noting the continued danger posed by mines in Cyprus, and *urging* rapid agreement on facilitating the recommencement of demining operations and clearance of the remaining minefields,

Highlighting the importance of the activities of the Committee on Missing Persons, *urging* the opening up of access to all areas to allow the Committee to carry out their work, and *trusting* that this process will promote reconciliation between the communities,

Agreeing that active participation of civil society groups, including women's groups, is essential to the political process and can contribute to making any future settlement sustainable, *recalling* that women play an important role in peace processes, *welcoming* all efforts to promote bicommunal contacts and events including, inter alia, on the part of all United Nations bodies on the island, and *urging* the two sides to promote the active engagement of civil society and the encouragement of cooperation between economic and commercial bodies and to remove all obstacles to such contacts,

Stressing the need for the Council to pursue a rigorous, strategic approach to peacekeeping deployments,

Welcoming the intention of the Secretary-General to keep all peacekeeping operations, including those of UNFICYP, under close review and *noting* the importance of contingency planning in relation to the settlement, including recommendations as appropriate for further adjustments to UNFICYP's mandate, force levels and other resources and concept of operations, taking into account developments on the ground, and the views of the parties,

Welcoming also the continued efforts of Alexander Downer as the Secretary-General's Special Advisor with a mandate to assist the parties in the conduct of fully-fledged negotiations aimed at reaching a comprehensive settlement, and the efforts of Lisa Buttenheim as the Secretary-General's Special Representative,

Echoing the Secretary-General's gratitude to the Government of Cyprus and the Government of Greece for their voluntary contributions to the funding of UNFICYP, and his request for further voluntary contributions from other countries and organizations, and *expressing* appreciation to member states that contribute personnel to UNFICYP,

Welcoming and *encouraging* efforts by the United Nations to sensitize peacekeeping personnel in the prevention and control of HIV/AIDS and other communicable diseases in all its peacekeeping operations,

1. *Welcomes* the encouraging progress made so far in the fully fledged negotiations, and the prospect of further decisive progress in the coming months towards a comprehensive and durable settlement that this has created;

2. *Takes note of* the report of the Secretary-General (S/2011/498);

   a) *Recalls* Security Council resolution 1986 (2011), and *calls upon* the two leaders to:

   b) intensify the momentum of negotiations, engage in the process in a constructive and open manner, and work on reaching convergences on the remaining core issues in preparation for their meeting with the Secretary-General in January 2012, and for further work in the following months towards a settlement;

   c) improve the public atmosphere in which the negotiations are proceeding, including by focussing public messages on convergences and the way ahead, and delivering more constructive and harmonised messages; and

   d) increase the participation of civil society in the process as appropriate;

3. *Urges* the implementation of confidence-building measures, and *looks forward* to agreement on and implementation of further such steps, including military confidence building measures and the opening of other crossing points;

4. *Urges* all parties to be more forthcoming in accommodating the Committee for Missing Persons exhumation requirements throughout the island including in military areas in the north;

5. *Reaffirms* all its relevant resolutions on Cyprus, in particular resolution 1251 (1999) of 29 June 1999 and subsequent resolutions;

6. *Expresses* its full support for UNFICYP and *decides* to extend its mandate for a further period ending 19 July 2012;

7. *Calls* on both sides to continue to engage, as a matter of urgency and while respecting UNFICYP's mandate, in consultations with UNFICYP on the demarcation of the buffer zone, and on the United Nations 1989 aide-memoire, with a view to reaching early agreement on outstanding issues;

8. *Calls* on the Turkish Cypriot side and Turkish forces to restore in Strovilia the military status quo which existed there prior to 30 June 2000;

9. *Calls* on both sides to allow access to deminers and to facilitate the removal of the remaining mines in Cyprus within the buffer zone, and *urges* both sides to extend demining operations outside the buffer zone;

10. *Requests* the Secretary-General to submit a report on implementation of this resolution, including on contingency planning in relation to the settlement,

by 1 July 2012 and to keep the Security Council updated on events as necessary;

11. *Welcomes* the efforts being undertaken by UNFICYP to implement the Secretary-General's zero tolerance policy on sexual exploitation and abuse and to ensure full compliance of its personnel with the United Nations code of conduct, *requests* the Secretary-General to continue to take all necessary action in this regard and to keep the Security Council informed, and *urges* troop-contributing countries to take appropriate preventive action including the conduct of pre-deployment awareness training, and to take disciplinary action and other action to ensure full accountability in cases of such conduct involving their personnel;

12. *Decides* to remain seized of the matter.

527. UN Security Council, S/2012/149, March 12, 2012. "Assessment Report of the Secretary-General on the Status of the Negotiations in Cyprus," pp. 1–5.

528. *Cyprus Mail, Hurriyet*, online, June 30, 2012.

529. *Today's Zaman*, online, February 28, 2012.

530. *Havadis*, online, April 18, 2012.

531. *Cyprus Weekly*, online, April 25, 2012; *Today's Zaman*, online, April 29, 2012.

532. *Kibris*, online, May 1, 2012.

533. *Hurriyet*, online, June 30, 2012.

534. The Cyprus News Agency, http://www.cyna.org.cy, May 14, 2012; *Cyprus Mail*, online, May 15, 17, 2012.

535. **Resolution 2058 (2012)**
Adopted by the Security Council at its 6809th meeting, on 19 July 2012
The Security Council,

Welcoming the report of the Secretary-General of 29 June 2012 (S/2012/507) on the United Nations operation in Cyprus,

Noting that the Government of Cyprus is agreed that in view of the prevailing conditions on the island it is necessary to keep the United Nations Peacekeeping Force in Cyprus (UNFICYP) beyond 19 July 2012,

Echoing the Secretary-General's firm belief that the responsibility for finding a solution lies first and foremost with the Cypriots themselves, and *reaffirming* the primary role of the United Nations in assisting the parties to bring the Cyprus conflict and division of the island to a comprehensive and durable settlement,

Welcoming the progress made so far in the fully fledged negotiations, and the leaders' joint statements including those of 23 May and 1 July 2008,

Recalling the importance attached by the international community to all parties engaging fully, flexibly and constructively in the negotiations, and *noting* that the move towards a more intensive phase of negotiations has not yet resulted in an enduring, comprehensive and just settlement based on a bicommunal, bizonal federation with political equality, as set out in the relevant Security Council resolutions, *encouraging* the sides to proceed with the substantive negotiations on the core issues, and stressing that the status quo is unsustainable,

Welcoming the efforts of the Secretary-General to stimulate progress during his meeting with the two leaders on 31 October 2011 and 23 January 2012, and expressing continued support for his efforts,

Noting the need to advance the consideration of and discussions on military confidence building measures, *calling for* renewed efforts to implement all remaining confidence building measures, and for agreement on and implementation of further steps to build trust between the communities,

Reaffirming the importance of continued crossings of the Green Line by Cypriots, and *encouraging* the opening by mutual agreement of other crossing points,

Convinced of the many important benefits, including economic benefits, for all Cypriots that would flow from a comprehensive and durable Cyprus settlement, *urging* the two sides and their leaders to foster positive public rhetoric, and *encouraging* them clearly to explain the benefits of the settlement, as well as the need for increased flexibility and compromise in order to secure it, to both communities well in advance of any eventual referenda,

Considering that undermining the United Nations credibility undermines the peace process itself,

Highlighting the importance of the supporting role of the international community, and in particular that of the parties concerned in taking practical steps towards helping the Greek Cypriot and Turkish Cypriot leaders to exploit fully the current opportunity,

Taking note of the assessment of the Secretary-General that the security situation on the island and along the Green Line remains stable, and *urging* all sides to avoid any action which could lead to an increase in tension, undermine the progress achieved so far, or damage the goodwill on the island,

Recalling the Secretary-General's firm belief that the situation in the buffer zone would be improved if both sides accepted the 1989 aide-memoire used by the United Nations,

Noting with regret that the sides are withholding access to the remaining minefields in the buffer zone, and that demining in Cyprus must continue, noting the continued danger posed by mines in Cyprus, and *urging* rapid agreement on facilitating the recommencement of demining operations and clearance of the remaining minefields,

Highlighting the importance of the activities of the Committee on Missing Persons, *urging* the opening up of access to all areas to allow the Committee to carry out their work, and *trusting* that this process will promote reconciliation between the communities,

Agreeing that active participation of civil society groups, including women's groups, is essential to the political process and can contribute to making any future settlement sustainable, *recalling* that women play an important role in peace processes, *welcoming* all efforts to promote bicommunal contacts and events including, inter alia, on the part of all United Nations bodies on the island, and *urging* the two sides to promote the active engagement of civil society and the encouragement of cooperation between economic and commercial bodies and to remove all obstacles to such contacts,

Stressing the need for the Council to pursue a rigorous, strategic approach to peacekeeping deployments,

Welcoming the intention of the Secretary-General to keep all peacekeeping operations under close review to ensure efficiency and effectiveness, *including* a review of UNFICYP when appropriate, and *noting* the importance of contingency planning in relation to the settlement, including recommendations as appropriate for further adjustments to UNFICYP's mandate, force levels and other resources and concept of operations, taking into account developments on the ground and the views of the parties,

Welcoming also the continued efforts of Alexander Downer as the Secretary-General's Special Advisor with a mandate to assist the parties in the conduct of fully-fledged negotiations aimed at reaching a comprehensive settlement, and the efforts of Lisa Buttenheim as the Secretary-General's Special Representative, *Echoing* the Secretary-General's gratitude to the Government of Cyprus and the Government of Greece for their voluntary contributions to the funding of UNFICYP, and his request for further voluntary contributions from other countries and organizations, and *expressing* appreciation to member states that contribute personnel to UNFICYP,

Welcoming and encouraging efforts by the United Nations to sensitize peacekeeping personnel in the prevention and control of HIV/AIDS and other communicable diseases in all its peacekeeping operations,

1. *Acknowledges* the progress made so far in the fully fledged negotiations, but notes that this has not been sufficient and has not yet resulted in a comprehensive and durable settlement, and urges the sides to continue their discussions to reach decisive progress on the core issues;

2. *Takes note of* the report of the Secretary-General (S/2012/507);

3. *Recalls* Security Council resolution 2026 (2011), and *calls upon* the two leaders to:
   a) Put their efforts behind further work on reaching convergences on the core issues;
   b) Continue to work with the Technical Committees with the objective of improving the daily lives of the Cypriots;
   c) Improve the public atmosphere in which the negotiations are proceeding, including by focussing public messages on convergences and the way ahead, and delivering more constructive and harmonised messages; and
   d) Increase the participation of civil society in the process as appropriate;

4. *Urges* the implementation of confidence-building measures, and *looks forward* to agreement on and implementation of further such steps, including military confidence building measures and the opening of other crossing points;

5. *Urges* all parties to be more forthcoming in accommodating the Committee for Missing Persons exhumation requirements by providing unrestricted access throughout the island, including in military areas in the north;

6. *Reaffirms* all its relevant resolutions on Cyprus, in particular resolution 1251 (1999) of 29 June 1999 and subsequent resolutions;

7. *Expresses* its full support for UNFICYP and *decides* to extend its mandate for a further period ending 31 January 2013;

8. *Calls* on both sides to continue to engage, as a matter of urgency and while

---

respecting UNFICYP's mandate, in consultations with UNFICYP on the demarcation of the buffer zone, and on the United Nations 1989 aide-memoire, with a view to reaching early agreement on outstanding issues;

9. *Calls* on the Turkish Cypriot side and Turkish forces to restore in Strovilia the military status quo which existed there prior to 30 June 2000;

10. *Calls* on both sides to allow access to deminers and to facilitate the removal of the remaining mines in Cyprus within the buffer zone, and *urges* both sides to extend demining operations outside the buffer zone;

11. *Requests* the Secretary-General to submit a report on implementation of this resolution, including on contingency planning in relation to the settlement, by 10 January 2013 and to keep the Security Council updated on events as necessary;

12. *Welcomes* the efforts being undertaken by UNFICYP to implement the Secretary-General's zero tolerance policy on sexual exploitation and abuse and to ensure full compliance of its personnel with the United Nations code of conduct, *requests* the Secretary-General to continue to take all necessary action in this regard and to keep the Security Council informed, and *urges* troop-contributing countries to take appropriate preventive action including the conduct of pre-deployment awareness training, and to take disciplinary action and other action to ensure full accountability in cases of such conduct involving their personnel;

13. *Decides* to remain seized of the matter.

536. *Hurriyet, Cyprus Mail,* online, November 19, 20, 2009.
537. Charles W. Kegley Jr. and Gregory A. Raymond, *How Nations Make Peace* (New York: St. Martin's, 1999), p. 249.
538. UN doc. S/6253, March 6, 1965, *Report of the United Nations Mediator on Cyprus to the Secretary-General.*
539. Ibid., para. 163.
540. Ibid.
541. Michael A. Attalides, *Cyprus: Nationalism and International Politics* (New York: St. Martin's Press, 1979), p. 20.
542. United Nations. Security Council. *Resolution as Proposed by 5 Powers* (S5/557.) *Adopted Unanimously by the Security Council* on March 4, 1964. S/5575.
543. Ibid.
544. Leigh H. Bruce, "Cyprus: A Last Chance," *Foreign Policy* 58: Spring, 1985, p. 133. See also Mario Mondiano, "Reagan's Letter Generates Cyprus' Breakthrough," *Sunday Times* (London), December 16, 1984.
545. *New York Times,* June 14 and 18, 1988.
546. Tozun Bahcheli, *Greek-Turkish Relations Since 1955* (Boulder, Colorado: Westview Press, 1990), p. 13.
547. For the text of the UN Secretary-General's "Set of Ideas" cf. S/24472, August 21, 1992, annex, pp. 9–24, and appendix, pp. 25–26, and map, p. 26.
548. S/25912 of June 1993, p. 10, para. 45.
549. United Nations. Security Council. S/26777, November 22, 1993, p. 11.
550. S/26777 of November 22, 1993, pp. 12–13, paras. 44–45.

551. The Constitution of Switzerland, article 3, of which stipulates tht the cantons are sovereign insofar as their sovereignty is not limited by the Federal Constitution. United Nations. Security Council. *Report of the Secretary-General on his Mission of Good Offices in Cyprus* (S/2003/398), April 1, 2003, p. 16.

552. For the full text of the document, see Kofi Annan, (2004). *The Comprehensive Settlement of the Cyprus problem.* http://www.UN.org/Depts/dpa/annanplan/annanplan.pdf. For an in-depth study of UN peace proposals, see Michalis Stavrou Michael, *Resolving the Cyprus Conflict: Negotiating History* (London: Palgrave Macmillan, 2009).

553. *Cyprus Mail*, February 20, 2008.

554. *Cyprus Mail*, online, May 11, 2008.

555. For an in-depth study of these issues, see M. Abramoixty (ed.), *Turkey's Transformation and U.S. Policy* (New York: Century Foundation, 2000); and D. Keridis and D. Triantaphyllou (eds.), *Greek-Turkish Relations in the Era of Globalization* (London: Brassey's, 2001).

556. As quoted in Vamik Volkan and Norman Itskowitz, *Turks and Greeks: Neighbours in Conflict* (Cambridgeshire, England: Eothen Press, 1994), pp. 158–159.

557. Cited in FBIS-WE, June 5, 1988, p. 22.

558. Hans Kohn, in his book on nationalism, describes nationalism as "a state of mind." Hans Kohn, "Western and Eastern Nationalism," in John Hutchinson and Anthony D. Smith, eds. *Nationalism* (New York: Oxford University Press, 1994), p. 162.

559. For the full report of *The UN in Cyprus: An Inter-communal Survey of Public Opinion by UNFICYP*, April 24, 2007, 56 pp., go to www.unificyp.org.

560. *Kibris*, online, August 10, 2008.

561. *Cyprus Mail*, online, October 5, 2008.

562. See also *Hurriyet*, online, March 11, 2009.

563. Watts L., Ronald, *Comparing Federal Systems*, 2nd ed. (Montreal: McGill-Queen's University Press, 1999). p. 85.

564. Tim Potier, "Britain and Cyprus: From Referendum to Reunification?" in Hubert Faustmann and Nicos Peristianis (ed.), *Britain in Cyprus: Colonialism and Post-Colonialism 1878–2006* (Berlin: Mannheim and Mohnesee, 2006), p. 610.

565. Richard Patrick, *Political Geography and the Cyprus Conflict, 1963–1971* (Waterloo: University of Waterloo Press, 1976), p. 28. See also *Report of the Secretary General on his Missions of Good Offices in Cyprus.* United Nations, Security Council, S/2004/437, May 28, 2004, p. 27.

566. David Miller, *On Nationality* (Oxford: Clarendon Press, 1995), pp. 18–19.

567. Charles Howard McIlwain, *Growth of Political Thought in the West: From the Greeks to the End of the Middle Ages* (New York: Macmillan, 1932), p. 390.

568. Andrew Vincent, *Nationalism and Particularity* (Cambridge: Cambridge University Press, 2002), pp. 17, 24.

569. *The Independent*, online, December 3, 2007.

570. *Kibris, Hurriyet, Today's Zaman*, online, November 6, 2009.

571. *Yeni Duzen*, online, February 26, 2010.

572. George P. Fletcher and Jens David Ohlin, *Defending Humanity: When Force Is Justified and Why* (New York: Oxford University Press, 2008), pp. 138–140.

---

573. Peter Wallensteen, *Understanding Conflict Resolution: War, Peace and the Global System*, 2nd ed. (California: Sage Publications, 2007), pp. 185–187.

574. *New York Times*, online, October 30, 2009.

575. *Cyprus Mail*, online, November 3, 2009.

576. *Cyprus Mail*, online, February 15, 2008.

577. Ibid.

www.ingramcontent.com/pod-product-compliance
Lightning Source LLC
Chambersburg PA
CBHW030250290526
45785CB00001B/31